THE COMMUNICATION HANDBOOK
A DICTIONARY

THE
COMMUNICATION
HANDBOOK
A DICTIONARY

JOSEPH A. DEVITO
Hunter College of the City University of New York

HARPER & ROW, PUBLISHERS, New York
Cambridge, Philadelphia, San Francisco,
London, Mexico City, São Paulo, Singapore, Sydney

1817

Sponsoring Editor: Louise H. Waller
Project Editor: Eleanor Castellano
Text Design: Betty L. Sokol
Cover Design: Ron Kellum
Text Art: Repro Draw
Production: Delia Tedoff
Compositor: ComCom Division of Haddon Craftsmen, Inc.
Printer and Binder: R. R. Donnelley & Sons Company

Portions of this book have been published previously in other books by Dr. DeVito. Books are *The Interpersonal Communication Book, Human Communication,* and *The Elements of Public Speaking.*

The Communication Handbook: A Dictionary

Library of Congress Cataloging-in-Publication Data

DeVito, Joseph A., 1938–
    The communication handbook.

    Includes bibliographical references
    1. Communication—Dictionaries.   I. Title.
P87.5.D46 1986   001.51'0321   85-17547
ISBN 0-06-041638-6

85 86 87 88 9 8 7 6 5 4 3 2 1

PREFACE

The Communication Handbook: A Dictionary discusses central terms used in the broad field of communication. It is a guide to the further study of communication concepts and theories, and a handbook for using communication more effectively in a variety of situations and contexts. The principal criterion for inclusion of terms was usefulness for those interested in understanding the expanding field of communication.

Some terms are briefly defined, others are discussed at some length or in extended essays. In all cases, the objective was to make the terms understandable and useable and I, therefore, allowed the concept and its relevance to communication to dictate its treatment. In many cases references are provided to sources where the terms were originally presented, or where further information may be found.

Terms defined in brief essays are of two types: (1) explanations of theories central to the study of communication (for example, *Attraction, Attribution, Self-Disclosure*) and (2) discussions of practical communication situations (for example, speaking in public, leading a group, interviewing).

The Communication Handbook: A Dictionary is addressed to four major audiences: students, professionals, communication practitioners, and teachers and researchers.

Students will find definitions, explanations, and suggestions for in-depth study of the technical terms of the discipline used in classes and readings. This volume should prove a useful reference tool throughout their classroom and professional study of communication.

Second, it is addressed to professionals in a variety of fields that interface with communication: sociology, advertising, psychology, public relations, marketing, linguistics, publishing, computer science, and the like. It is also useful for those professionals in specialized areas within communication, such as film, speech pathology, and television. These professionals will find a ready reference to the terminology of a field now having a major impact on all other disciplines.

Third, it is addressed to the communication practitioner, the person who needs brief and practical presentations of the principles of effective communication for a wide variety of situations: preparing a public speech, leading a small discussion group, being interviewed, and a variety of other situations. This audience is served primarily through the essays with a decided practical orientation noted in the "Guide to Selected Essays."

Fourth, it is addressed to teachers and researchers in communication who will find both definitions of the basic vocabulary of communication and convenient references to the seminal articles or books in which the central concepts of the discipline are developed and explained in depth.

THE ENTRIES

A variety of terms from the broad area of communication are included—from literary and rhetorical criticism, television, speech and language, science, and various others. The essay entries focus more narrowly on "human communication" or "speech communication" areas. Many of the essay entries have a decided practical orientation, and are designed primarily to provide a ready reference guide to some of the more significant communication skills.

Many entries include references to articles or books in which these terms were first introduced or explained in considerable detail. Where that was not possible, a more general reference was included. These should provide suitable starting places for further exploration of the terms. Wherever possible, references relating the defined concept to communication and/or providing measurement procedures or scales are given priority.

The *q.v.* references direct readers to related entries that further clarify the definitions. *See also* references direct the reader to additional entries that will clarify the concept and, in some cases, to a significant reference. Both *q.v.* and *see also* references will prove useful for placing the concept in a broader framework, perspective, or system. Where applicable, I have indicated the term's opposite meaning with "opposed to XYZ (q.v.)" designations.

Although this handbook contains terms from related disciplines, it is not intended to substitute for the more specialized dictionaries that are available in these other areas. Moreover, it is not intended to provide definitions for the expert in any of the areas covered; rather, it is addressed specifically to the nonexpert— the person who knows something about communication but wants to know more. Experts in any area will surely find some definitions inadequate; for instance, Burkian scholars will feel that Burkian concepts are dealt with too briefly. This is inevitable in a book designed to survey the terminology of a multifaceted discipline and yet addressed to the nonexpert—a book intended for academic as well as practical purposes.

It is hoped that with this volume the student will have a handy reference guide, the practitioner a useful handbook of practical advice for increasing communication effectiveness in a wide variety of situations, and the teacher-researcher a guide to the increasingly complex maze of communication terminology.

The Communication Handbook: A Dictionary represents a first attempt to define the terms of a field that spans over 2000 years of scholarly activity. In such a process, errors, omissions, and assorted inadequacies are bound to have occurred. Reader comments, corrections, suggestions for inclusion, and the like would be most appreciated and will help improve a second edition, should one be warranted. Please address any such reactions to: Joseph DeVito, Department of Communications, Hunter College, 695 Park Avenue, New York, New York 10021.

Joseph A. DeVito

GUIDE TO SELECTED ESSAYS

The following guide to some of the essays and extended entries is designed to facilitate the use of *The Communication Handbook* for study of a specific area of communication. The essays are grouped into eight major topic areas:

INTERPERSONAL COMMUNICATION ESSAYS

(See also the essays under "Language and Nonverbal Communication Essays.")

Active Listening
Adult Ego State
Apprehension, Communication
Argumentativeness
Assertiveness
Attraction
Attribution
Cherishing Behaviors
Child Ego State
Communication Style
Complementary Transactions
Conflict Resolution
Conflict Strategies
Content and Relationship Communication
Crossed Transactions
Dialogue
Dogmatism
Double-Bind Messages
Ego States
Empathy
Equity Theory
Family Communication Patterns
Feedback Regulation
Feedforward
FIRO (Fundamental Interpersonal Relations Orientation)

Five Freedoms
Friendship
Interpersonal Communication Effectiveness
Johari Model (Window)
Life Positions
Listening
Love
Lying
Machiavellianism
Monologue
Noise
Parent Ego State
Power
Punctuation of Communication Events
Relational Deterioration
Relationship Development
Satisfaction
Self-Awareness
Self-Disclosure
Self-Fulfilling Prophecy
Self-Monitoring
Shyness
Social Exchange and Equity Theory
Social Penetration
Stroking
Ulterior Transactions

PERSUASION ESSAYS
(See also the essays under "Public Speaking Essays.")

Argumentativeness

Balance Theory

Credibility

Dogmatism

Machiavellianism

Motivated Sequence

Persuasion

Power

Propaganda Devices

Toulmin Model

PUBLIC SPEAKING ESSAYS
(See also the essays under "Persuasion Essays.")

Apprehension, Communication

Attention: Securing and Maintaining
  Audience Attention

Audiovisual Aids

Balance Theory

Credibility

Definition

Feedback Regulation

Feedforward

Information, Principles for
  Communicating

Listening

Motivated Sequence

Need Hierarchy

Oral Style

Propaganda Devices

Public Speaking

Self-Confidence as a Speaker

Sleeper Effect

SMCR Model of Communication

Toulmin Model

SMALL GROUP COMMUNICATION ESSAYS
*(See also essays under "Interpersonal Communication Essays" and "Organizational
Communication Essays.")*

Apprehension, Communication

Brainstorming

Group Communication: Analysis
  Guidelines

Group Communication: Leader
  Guidelines

Group Communication: Member
  Guidelines

Groupthink

Interaction Diagrams

Interaction Process Analysis

Interviewing

Problem-Solving Group

Quality Circles

Risky-Shift Phenomenon

THE
COMMUNICATION
HANDBOOK
A DICTIONARY

ABC (Audit Bureau of Circulation). Provides data on the circulation of newspapers and magazines; founded in 1914 by publishers and advertisers.

Abclution. The rejection of acculturation (q.v.).

Abduction. In Aristotelian logic, a syllogism whose minor premise is probable but whose major premise is certain.

Abort. To end a particular operation; to terminate the operation of a program.

Aboulia. See ABULIA.

Abreaction. In psychoanalysis, the process of expressing one's problems verbally and/or nonverbally and thus discharging tension; catharsis.

Abridge (Abridgement). To shorten. An abridged book is one that has been shortened by omitting designated parts or by condensing certain ideas, whereas an unabridged work is complete—one that has not been shortened.

Absolute Pitch. The position of a tone in reference to the whole range of pitch and independently determined by its rate of vibration; the relative highness or lowness of a sound as perceived by a listener.

Abstract. A synopsis of a longer communication, for example, a novel, article, play, or short story; the essential points of the complete work.

Abstraction. A general concept (for example, man, liberty, friendship) derived from a class of objects; a part representation of some whole.

Abstractionism. The illogical use of abstraction; the confusion between abstractions and reality; not adequately differentiating abstractions from reality.

Abstraction Process. The process by which a general concept is derived from specifics; the process by which some (never all) characteristics of an object, person, or event are perceived by the senses or included in some term, phrase, or sentence.

Abulia (Aboulia). The inability to reach a decision or to act; the lack of will power characteristic of some psychotic and neurotic conditions.

Academy. Generally refers to Plato's school of philosophy (Plato taught at the Academy).

Acalculia. A type of aphasia due to brain damage in which there is a loss of the ability to perform arithmetical operations.

Accent. The stress placed on a syllable; the particular pronunciation of a dialect (for example, a Boston accent). In literature and rhetoric, *accent* is often used to refer to the emphasis given a particular character, theme, or argument.

Access. In computer terminology, the process or act of extracting information from or putting information into a computer storage system.

Access Time. In computer terminology, the time it takes a computer to find or utilize information. In mass media, that prime-time period (one-half hour) during which the networks must relinquish usage to local stations. Network prime-time programming is three hours (from 8PM to 11PM EST), thus 7:30 to 8PM EST is access time. In video playback, the time that elapses between a request for information and its transmittal. In memory, the time it takes to recall the meaning of a term.

Accismus. The act or process of refusing some reward with the intention that it will be offered again more forcefully; a refusal that is insincere and that has a hidden meaning or motivation.

Acclamation. A voice vote indicating overwhelming approval.

Accommodation. A state of cold war conflict; a condition in which the parties, although still in conflict, agree not to battle; a state in which conflicting individu-

als have adjusted to each other's position allowing interpersonal communication to take place (although real cooperation is absent); a process of associating oneself with another by approximating or matching the speech style of the other person.
[H. Giles and P. F. Powesland, *Speech Style and Social Evaluation* (New York: Academic Press, 1975).]

Accountability. Legal term referring to liability, responsibility; the requirement that persons in decision-making roles be held accountable or responsible for their decisions.

Account Executive. A liaison or contact person who coordinates activities between their advertising agency and its clients.

Accounts. Statements that people use to justify their behaviors or to reduce their own responsibility for some action; excuses offered for one's behaviors. See also EXCUSE.
[M. B. Scott and S. M. Lyman, "Accounts," *American Sociological Review* 33 (1968):46–62; P. Schonbach, "A Category System for Account Phrases," *European Journal of Social Psychology* 10 (1980):195–200.]

Acculturation. The process by which an individual acquires socially acceptable patterns of behavior. In mass media, the process by which reporters or researchers take on the beliefs and attitudes of those with whom they interact extensively. See also ABCLUTION.
[Jin K. Kim, "Explaining Acculturation in a Communication Framework: An Empirical Test," *Communication Monographs* 47 (1980):155–179.]

Acknowledgement Page. That page in a book where the author gives credit to those who assisted in some way (research, writing, editing, etc.) in the preparation of the book.

Acoustic. Pertaining to sound.

Acoustics. The science of sound. Physiological acoustics is the study of the physiology of sound production and reception; psychological acoustics is the study of the psychological dimensions of speech (sound) perception.

Acoustic Filter. A device that filters out certain sound frequencies.

Acoustic Phonetics. The science of speech sounds as perceived by a listener. See also ARTICULATORY PHONETICS.

Acoustic Pressure. The force exerted on the eardrum.

Acoustic Spectrum. The range of sounds that the human ear is capable of hearing.

Acquired Drive. A learned, as opposed to an innate or organically based drive, for example, status. See also PRIMARY DRIVE.

Acronym. A word comprised of the initial letters or syllables of other words, usually the name of an organization, for example, CORE (Congress of Racial Equality).

Acrostic. A sequence of words in which particular letters (for example, initial letters or final letters) spell out some other message.

Act. In Kenneth Burke's system of rhetoric (q.v.), those events that took place, what the actors thought or did; answers the question, "What was done?" See also PENTAD.

Action Language. Movements of the body, for example, the way in which one walks, runs, or sits.

Action Research. Research that is directed toward practical rather than theoretical or academic ends.

Action Step. In the motivated sequence (q.v.), the action step is the fifth and final part of the public speech—here the speaker moves the audience toward some action, some behavioral response.

Active Listening. A process of sending back to the speaker what you as a listener think the speaker meant—both in terms of content and in terms of feelings. Active listening takes into consideration both verbal and nonverbal signals. Active listening is not a process of merely repeating back to the speaker the exact words, but rather one of putting together in some meaningful whole the listener's understanding of the speaker's total message—the verbal and the nonverbal, the content and the feelings.

Purposes of Active Listening

Active listening serves a number of important purposes. First, it enables the listener to check on the accuracy of his or her understanding of what the speaker said and, more important, what the speaker meant. By reflecting back to the speaker what the listener perceived to be the speaker's meaning, the speaker is given an opportunity to confirm or deny the listener's perceptions and to clarify whatever may need clarification. In this way, future messages will have a better chance of being relevant and purposeful.

Second, through the process of active listening the listener expresses acceptance of the speaker's feelings. The active listener who reflects back to the speaker what he or she thought was said gives the speaker acceptance. The speaker's feelings are not challenged; rather, they are echoed in a sympathetic and empathic manner.

Third, and perhaps most important, is that active listening stimulates the speaker to explore further his or her feelings and thoughts. Active listening helps create a climate that encourages the speaker to further explore and express thoughts and feelings. Active listening sets the stage for meaningful dialog—a dialog of mutual understanding rather than a dialog in which one person must defend his or her feelings. In stimulating this further exploration, active listening also encourages the speaker to solve his or her own problems by providing the opportunity to talk about them.

Techniques of Active Listening

Three simple techniques may prove useful in learning the process of active listening.

Paraphrase the Speaker's Thoughts

State in your own words what you think the speaker meant. This paraphrase will help to ensure understanding since the speaker will be able to correct or modify your restatement. It will also serve to show the speaker that you are interested in what is being said. The active listening response confirms this to the speaker. The paraphrase also provides the speaker with the opportunity to elaborate or extend what was originally said. In your paraphrase, be especially careful that you do not lead the speaker in the direction you *think* he or she should go or wants to go; paraphrases should be objective descriptions.

Express Understanding of the Speaker's Feelings

In addition to paraphrasing the content, echo the feelings you felt were expressed or implied. Just as the paraphrase enables you to check on the accuracy of your perception of the content, the expression of feelings will enable you to check on the accuracy of your perception of the speaker's feelings. This expression of feelings will also provide the speaker with the opportunity to see his or her feelings more objectively. This is particularly helpful when an individual is feeling angry, hurt, or depressed. We need that objectivity; we need to see our feelings from a somewhat less impassioned perspective if we are to deal with them effectively. Most of us hold back on our feelings until we are certain they will be accepted; when we feel they are accepted, we feel free to go into more detail, to elaborate. Active listening provides the speaker with this important opportunity. In echoing these feelings be careful that you do not maximize or minimize the speaker's emotions and feelings—just try to restate these feelings as accurately as you can.

Ask Questions

Ask questions to ensure your own understanding of the speaker's thoughts and feelings and to secure additional relevant information. The questions should be designed to provide just enough stimulation and support for the speaker to express the thoughts and feelings he or she wants to express, not to pry into areas that are not germane to the issue or to challenge the speaker in any way. [Carl R. Rogers and Richard E. Farson, "Active Listening," in Joseph A. DeVito, ed., *Communication: Concepts and Processes,* 3d ed. (Englewood Cliffs, N.J.: Prentice-Hall, 1981), pp. 137–147; Thomas Gordon, *P.E.T.: Parent Effectiveness Training* (New York: New American Library, 1975).]

Active Therapy. A form of therapy in which the therapist assumes an active, directive role as opposed to a passive, nondirective one.

Active Vocabulary. The words that an individual is capable of using in regular discourse as opposed to merely understanding or recognizing them when used by others (that is, passive vocabulary, q.v.).

Activity Meaning. A kind of connotative meaning (q.v.) that may be indexed in terms of such scales as fast-slow and active-passive. See also SEMANTIC DIFFERENTIAL.

Activity Principle. A principle holding that the primary concern of psychology is the activity of the person and that this activity is socially determined.

Aculalia. Unintelligible speech resulting from aphasia (q.v.).

Adage. A saying that is felt to embody some universal truth or, at least, an observation with which most persons would agree, for example, "An ounce of prevention is worth a pound of cure."

Adaptation. A change in behavior that increases the individual's ability to deal with his or her environment; a loss of sensitivity occurring as a result of prolonged stimulation. In literature and mass communication, *adaptation* refers to the structuring of a novel or biography to better fit another medium, for example, when a novel is adapted for television.

Adapted Child. See CHILD EGO STATE.

Adaptive Behavior. Behaviors that enable the individual to deal more effectively with the environment.

Adaptive Rule. Those rules, in contingency rules theory (q.v.), that connect persuasive action and goal-achievement. See also SELF-EVALUATIVE RULES.

Adaptors. Nonverbal behaviors that, when emitted in private, serve some kind of need and occur in their entirety, for example, scratching one's head until the itch is eliminated.

Ad Baculum, Argumentum. An argument that relies on fear appeals; an argument in which persuasion is attempted by threatening or appealing to the fears of the audience.

Addendum (*pl.* Addenda). Material that is added to a complete text.

Ad Diem. At the appointed day.

Address, Forms of. See FORMS OF ADDRESS.

Ad Hoc. "For this purpose"; for a specific purpose.

Ad Hoc Committee. A committee established for a specific purpose and usually disbanded after the purpose has been served.

Ad Hominem. A fallacious argument in which the person, rather than the issue, is attacked.

ADI. See AREAS OF DOMINANT INFLUENCE.

Ad Ignorantiam, Argumentum. An argument based on incorrect or inappropriate data but whose inadequacy is not recognized by one's audience; an argument that relies on the ignorance of the audience for effectiveness.

Ad Infinitum. To infinity; indefinitely.

Adjacencies. Those time periods between regular television programming that are available to local advertisers (about two minutes in length).

Adjourn. The act of ending a meeting.

Adjourn *Sine Die*. The closing of a meeting without any provision for reconvening the meeting.

Ad Judicium, Argumentum. A type of reasoning in which the speaker attempts to appeal to common sense—to the judgment of the people—in order to prove one's proposition.

Adjustment, Principle of. The principle of verbal interaction that claims that communication may take place only to the extent that the parties communicating share the same system of signals (language).

Ad Lib. To speak without prior planning, "off the cuff"; impromptu speaking (q.v.).

Ad Misericordiam, Argumentum. A fallacious argument in which the speaker appeals to such emotions as pity in order to persuade an audience; an argument based on the mercy of the listeners.

Adopter. A person who takes on, accepts, or uses an innovation. Distinctions among adopters are usually categorized as innovators, early adopters, the early majority, the late majority, and the laggards, in order of the timeliness of their adoption of the innovation. See also DIFFUSION OF INNOVATIONS.

Adoption. The act of using an innovation. See also ADOPTER.

Adoption Curve. A statistical curve representing the number of persons and the time it takes for the adoption of an innovation. See also DIFFUSION OF INNOVATIONS.

Ad Populum, Argumentum. A fallacious argument where the speaker appeals to the sentiments of the crowd.

Ad Rem, Argumentum. An argument that directly addresses the proposition as opposed to arguments that circumvent or avoid the proposition.

Adult Ego State. In the ego state (q.v.) of Adult, the individual is oriented to the world as it is, not as it is talked about. The Adult is logical rather than emotional, calm rather than excitable, inquiring rather than accusatory. The Adult is particularly oriented to accumulating and processing relevant information and to estimating the probabilities in any given situation. The Adult questions a great deal, asking "How?" "What?" "Why?" "When?" and "Where?" (rather like the good reporter: "What can we learn from this situation?" "What do the statistics say?" "What might we predict based on the probabilities?") Nonverbally the Adult's body communicates interest and attention. This individual stands straight (but not rigid) and engages the attention of others by maintaining appropriate eye contact and physiçal distance and by moving close to the speaker to hear and see better.

In considering the Adult state it is important to distinguish between "being in your Adult" and "having your Adult in control." Being in your adult is sometimes appropriate and sometimes inappropriate. When you are in your Adult, you act as an Adult, gathering information, being logical and so on. But in some instances these behaviors may not be appropriate. There is a time to laugh and a time to cry; there is a time to be a Child and a time to be a nurturing Parent, for example. If you are always in your Adult, these other ego state behaviors, however appropriate, will not be possible.

On the other hand, having your Adult in control is never inappropriate since the Adult is managing the rest of your behaviors. In this state the Adult evaluates the situation and the available information and decides, for example, that in this instance the Child should cry or play or the Parent should comfort the individual or criticize or praise the child.

In analyzing whether or not you are in your Adult, it is helpful to look at the language you are using. Language that is tentative, that differentiates one situation from another, that recognizes the inevitability of change, and that takes into account the fact that the world is infinitely complex and that the information you have is necessarily limited is most often uttered by the Adult. Another clue is to look at the behavior of the person with whom you are interacting. If that person is in the Adult state, it is likely that you are, too, since the Adult in one person seems to draw out the Adult in the other person. See also CHILD EGO STATE; PARENT EGO STATE.

[Eric Berne, *Games People Play* (New York: Grove Press, 1964); Gerald M. Goldhaber and Marylynn B. Goldhaber, *Transactional Analysis: Principles and Applications* (Boston: Allyn and Bacon, 1976).

Advance. In publishing, the money paid by a publisher or other agency before the completion of a contracted work and later deducted from the royalty (q.v.) payments due the author. In video and film, the number of frames of film that occur between the picture and its accompanying sound on a composite film print.

Advance Copy. An article written prior to the occurrence of an event, usually the article is distributed to the media with a release date (the day the article may be printed or broadcast).

Advance Sales. Commitments to purchase a work before its publication.

Ad Verecundiam, Argumentum. An argument in which the speaker appeals to some respected authority—a great person, institution, or custom—in an attempt to prove one's point or to persuade one to accept one's proposition.

Adversary Relationship. The relationship existing between people or institutions in conflict; often used to refer to the conflict between the media and the government concerning the public's access to certain information.

Advertising. Persuasive messages designed to sell a product or service. The media in the United States are sustained largely through the support of advertisers who pay enormous sums of money for brief periods of broadcast air time or relatively small spaces in newspapers or magazines. For example, in 1981, one page in color in the national edition of *TV Guide* cost approximately $70,000; in *Good Housekeeping* one page was approximately $45,000; and one page in *Playboy* was approximately $51,000. During the 1985 Superbowl, network television advertising was priced at $1 million per minute; $525,000 for 30 seconds.

Advertorial. An advertisement that has the appearance of an editorial but is paid for by the advertiser, usually such material is accompanied by the word *advertisement* so that readers will know it is a paid announcement.

Advocacy Journalism. Journalism focused not on reporting or describing but on persuading the reader to accept a particular point of view.

Advocate. One who argues for a particular proposition; a lawyer.

Aesthetic Distance. Objectivity, noninvolvement, detachment. Used with particular reference to the detachment an author has with his or her characters and a critic or reader has with critical judgments rendered or evaluations made; when there is aesthetic distance there is no personal involvement.

Aesthetics. That branch of philosophy that addresses beauty and the beautiful, especially in the arts, and deals with the critical standards used in judging the artistic work.

Affect. Emotion, feeling; to produce an effect; to give a false appearance.

Affectation. An artificial mode of behavior taken on in order to impress others.

Affect Blends. A combination of emotions communicated simultaneously by the face. Facial expressions do not always portray single or pure emotions but rather a combination of emotions; these expressions are called affect blends because the expressions are a blend of several emotions.

Affect Displays. Movements of the facial area that convey emotional meaning, for example, anger, fear, and surprise.

Affection. One of the three interpersonal needs in Schutz's Fundamental Interpersonal Relations Orientation (FIRO) theory; the need for close personal and emotional feelings between people ranging from love to hate. See FIRO.
[William C. Schutz, *FIRO: A Three-Dimensional Theory of Interpersonal Behavior* (New York: Holt, Rinehart and Winston, 1958).]

Affective Domain. That area of learning (behavior objectives, q.v.) concerned with emotional, attitudinal, or psychological issues, for example, feelings of love, affection, and passion. See also BEHAVIORAL OBJECTIVE.

Affective Fallacy. In literary or rhetorical criticism, the judging of a work on the basis of its emotional impact; the evaluation of a communication in terms of its effect on an audience rather than in terms of the message conveyed by the communication.
[W. K. Wimsatt, Jr. and Monroe C. Beardsley, "The Affective Fallacy," in W. K. Wimsatt, Jr., ed., *The Verbal Icon* (New York: The Noonday Press, 1962). For a defense of effect as a criterion for judging literature, see David Daiches, "The 'New Criticism': Some Qualifications," *Literary Essays* (Chicago: University of Chicago Press, 1956).]

Affective Logic. A chain of reasoning that appears to be based on logical laws and relationships but which actually has an emotional basis.

Affective Meaning. The emotional dimension of meaning; connotative meaning (q.v.); that aspect of meaning measured by the semantic differential (q.v.).

Affective State. An emotional state.

Affiliate. Local media station owned and/or operated by a major network that airs the same programs.

Affiliation. The process of achieving close interpersonal relationships. The need for affiliation is one of the basic needs and refers to the need for close, friendly, interpersonal relationships.

Affiliative Appeals. Appeals to one's desire to achieve or have close and intimate relationships with others.

Affiliative Drive. The drive to establish and maintain interpersonal relationships.

Affinity-Seeking Function of Communication. That function of communication by which people get others to like them and to feel positive about them.
[Robert A. Bell and John A. Daly, "The Affinity-Seeking Function of Communication," *Communication Monographs* 51 (1984):91–115.]

Affirmative Action. Positive actions taken by an organization to correct existing imbalances in their employment policies or in existing staff; used to refer to the steps necessary to incorporate a representative number of minority group members into an organization.

Affirmative Case. A collection of evidence and arguments for adopting a debated proposition. Generally, the affirmative case is built on three main elements: the need for a change, the specific plan to meet the aforementioned need, and the advantages of the plan.
[Austin J. Freeley, *Argumentation and Debate: Reasoned Decision Making,* 5th ed. (Belmont, Calif.: Wadsworth, 1981).]

Affix. An addition to a word that changes its grammatical function and/or meaning by using prefixes (additions prefacing the word such as *un-* or *non-*), suffixes (additions to the end of a word such as *-ing, -ed*), or infixes (additions within the word). English does not have true infixes although some linguists would count the plural morpheme (q.v.) used in such words as *man-men, woman-women* as infixes.

A Fortiori. "All the more reason." Used in reference to reinforcing a conclusion to something because an even more compelling reason is presented.

After-Dinner Speech. A special occasion speech, usually given after dinner, that may serve a number of specific purposes, for example, to motivate, to humor.

AFTRA (American Federation of Television and Radio Artists). A union for performers and creative specialists working in television, radio, and film.

Agape. Compassionate love; an egoless, self-giving love; a love that is nonrational and nondiscriminative. Agapic love is a spiritual love that seeks nothing in return; the agapic lover loves without even expecting that the love will be returned or reciprocated. Jesus, Buddha, and Gandhi practiced agapic love. See also LOVE.

Ageism. A discriminatory attitude against the aged in which they are viewed as incapable, senile, or lacking in the ability to learn and remember.

Agenda Control. Control over what happens and when it happens; control over the events or interactions that occur.

Agenda Theory (Agenda Setting). A theory in mass communication that attempts to explain the origin of the public's perception of the relative importance of various current issues. Basically, agenda theory holds that the public's perception of the importance of various issues can be explained by the way in which the media treat the issues; those items given great emphasis and exposure by the media are those that the public will perceive as important and those that the media does not emphasize will be perceived as of less importance.
[D. L. Shaw and M. E. McCombs, *The Emergence of American Political Issues: The Agenda-Setting Function of the Press* (St. Paul, Minn.: West, 1977).]

Agency. In Kenneth Burke's system of rhetoric (q.v.), the means through which the agent (q.v.) or actor accomplishes the act (q.v.); the strategies, means of communication, and instruments used to perform the act; answers the questions, "How?" or "Through what means was the act accomplished?" See also PENTAD.

Algorithm   **9**

Agent. In ethical theory, a person who acts and, therefore, one who may be judged as good or bad. It is assumed that the agent is free and possesses the maturity of a normal adult. In media, the person who represents an artist (actor, writer, director) for a fee, usually a percentage of the artist's earnings. In Kenneth Burke's system of rhetoric (q.v.), the actor or person who performs the act (q.v.); the actor's total being (personality, reputation, etc.); answers the question, "Who did it?" See also PENTAD.

Agglutinating (Agglutinative) Language. A language that combines various linguistic elements [for example, prefixes (q.v.) and suffixes (q.v.)] with a word to express grammatical categories or relationships, for example, Turkish.

Agglutination. The process by which an affix (q.v.) is added to a word in order to express grammatical categories or relationships.

Aggression. Behavior designed to advance one's own goals without concern or regard for any harm done to others. Distinctions are often made between habitual (or generalized) and occasional (or situational) aggressiveness, the former being generally characteristic of the individual and the later occurring only under certain circumstances. Aggression is distinguished from assertiveness (q.v.) because although the behavior is designed to achieve one's rights and to prevent one from being taken advantage of, it is exercised with concern and respect for others involved.

Agitative Rhetoric. Arguments or messages aimed at producing an extreme reversal of the status quo.
[Mary G. McEdwards, "Agitative Rhetoric: Its Nature and Effect," *Western Speech Communication Journal* 32 (1968):36–43.]

Agitolalia (Agitophasia). Rapid speech brought on by stress and characterized by the distortion and omission of sounds, syllables, or words.

Agitophasia. See AGITOLALIA.

Agnosia. The general term for the loss of the ability to perceive sensory impressions, usually created by brain damage. Individual types of agnosia are identified with and correspond to the various individual senses.

Agrammatism. A form of aphasia (q.v.) characterized by the loss of the ability to form grammatically correct sentences, usually due to brain damage.

Agraphia. A form of aphasia (q.v.) characterized by the loss of one's writing ability, usually brought on by brain damage.

Agreement. In grammar, the state or condition in which one term in a sentence corresponds to another, as, for example, a subject and verb agreeing in number (whether singular or plural).

Aided Recall. The remembrance of some prior knowledge stimulated by some sort of prompting or cue. This technique is used extensively in interviewing (referred to as aided recall interviewing) where information or media exposure is sought.

Alalia. The absence of meaningful speech due to an impairment in the peripheral speech organs, for example, the muscles or sense organs.

Alexia. A form of aphasia (q.v.) characterized by the loss of the ability to understand written communications; word blindness.

Algorithm. The procedure of following a set system of analysis that utilizes every possibility with the result that the solution will eventually be attained; a system of rules each of which is broken down into precisely defined steps that when followed will yield a specific output from a specific input. (The rules must be so specific that a computer can execute them.) For example, one could solve a scrambled word game by an algorithm by taking the various letters and arranging them into every possible combination—eventually the desired word would be found.

[Donald E. Knuth, "Algorithms," *Scientific American* 236 (1977):63–80.]

Alias. A name other than one's own by which someone is known.

Alibi Copy. A duplicate copy of a manuscript or film retained in case questions of legitimacy or complaints are made.

Alienation. The feeling or state of estrangement, of being apart and separate from other human beings, from oneself, from the environment, and from the society in general; the lack of friendly interpersonal relationships.

Allegory. A narrative form in which the characters and their actions represent historical or political persons or ideas and abstract concepts; an extended metaphor; a literary device in which a situation or character is used for something in addition to itself.

Alliteration. A figure of speech in which the same initial sound is repeated in two or more words as in "fifty favorite flavors."

Allness. The fallacious assumption that everything (all) can be known about anything—a given person, issue, object, or event.

The world is infinitely complex, and because of this we can never say all there is to know about anything—at least we cannot logically say all about anything. And this is particularly true in dealing with people. We may *think* we know all there is to know about individuals or about why they did what they did, yet clearly we do not know all. We can never know all the reasons we ourselves do something, and yet we often think that we know all the reasons why our parents or our friends or our enemies did something. And because we are so convinced that we know all the reasons, we are quick to judge and evaluate the actions of others with great confidence that our doing so is justified.

The parable of the six blind men and the elephant is an excellent example of an allness orientation and its attendant problems. You may recall from elementary school the poem by John Saxe that concerns six blind men of Indostan who came to examine an elephant, an animal they had only heard about. The first blind man touched the elephant's side and concluded that the elephant was like a wall. The second felt the tusk and said the elephant must be like a spear. The third held the trunk and concluded that the elephant was much like a snake. The fourth touched the knee and knew the elephant was like a tree. The fifth felt the ear and said the elephant was like a fan. And the sixth grabbed the tail and concluded that the elephant was like a rope. Each of these learned men reached his own conclusion regarding what this marvelous beast, the elephant, was really like. Each argued that he was correct and that the others were wrong. Each, of course, was correct; but at the same time, each was wrong. The point this poem illustrates is that we are all in the position of the six blind men: we never see all of something; we never experience anything fully; we see only part of an object, an event, a person—and on that limited basis conclude what the whole is like. This procedure is a relatively universal one; we have to do this since it is impossible to observe everything. And yet we must recognize that when we make judgments of the whole based only on a part, we are actually making inferences that can later be proven wrong. If we assume that we know all of anything, we fall into the pattern of misevaluation called *allness*.

Disraeli once said that "to be conscious that you are ignorant is a great step toward knowledge." That observation is an excellent example of a nonallness attitude. If we recognize that there is more to learn, more to see, more to hear, we will leave ourselves open to this additional information and will be better prepared to assimilate it into our existing structures.

In conflict situations, negative allness statements—especially those containing *always* and *never*—are particularly troublesome. Allness statements ("You *always* criticize me in front of your friends," "You *never* do what I want," "You're *always* nagging," "You *never* want to visit my family") encourage defensiveness and are more in the nature of attacks than attempts to bring problems to the surface and resolve them.

It would be just as easy and much more constructive to say, for example: "At Pat's party, you said how bad a cook I was. This really embarrassed me. I don't know if you realized it but I really felt hurt. If you want to criticize something I think it should be kept private and said when we're alone." Note that phrased in this way there is no attack, no encouragement of defensiveness. Instead there is a clear and descriptive statement of the problem and a proposed solution that can be discussed reasonably. See also ETC.

Allokine. An individual variant of a kineme (q.v.).

Allonym. The fictional name used by a writer or speaker as an alias (q.v.).

Allophone. An individual variant of a phoneme (q.v.).

All-or-None Principle. The principle referring specifically to the neuron firing or not firing, their being no inbetween or intermediate strengths; more generally, it refers to any digital or discrete system, for example, the verbal language system; opposed to a more-or-less or continuous system, for example, the nonverbal communication system.

Allusion. A usually casual or indirect reference to some situation or person that is assumed by the communicator to be familiar to the listener.

Alphabet. A set of linguistic elements (e.g., letters) with which larger units are constructed (e.g., words); written and oral languages are constructed from alphabets of letters and sounds.
[D. Diringer, *The Alphabet: A Key to the History of Mankind,* 3d ed., 2 vols. (London: Hutchinson, 1968).]

Alter Adaptors. Nonverbal movements learned in the manipulation of material things, for example, changing a tire. See also ADAPTORS.

Altercasting. The procedure whereby one person informs the other of the role he or she will be cast in and consequently the perspective to be assumed by that person when responding. For example, "As an advertising executive, what do you think of the practice of corrective advertising?" casts the person into the role of advertising executive and asks that he or she pursue the question from this particular perspective.
[Eugene A. Weinstein and Paul Deutschberger, "Some Dimensions of Altercasting," *Sociometry* 26 (1963):454–466.]

Alter Ego. Literally "another self," as in an extremely close friend; a friend who is so close that he or she is considered "a second self." See also EGO.

Altruism. A quality that leads one to do good for others rather than for any personal gain. In sociobiology, *altruism* refers to behaviors that benefit others who are not offspring.

AM (Amplitude Modulation). The situation in which the carrier wave height is varied when the information wave is superimposed upon it. In television, the video signal is AM. See also FM.

Ambient Light. The surrounding secondary light as opposed to the intentional light focused on the subject.

Ambient Noise. Surrounding noise as opposed to noise designed or produced for specific effects.

Ambiguity. In language, the situation where a linguistic unit (word, phrase, or sentence) may have more than one meaning. Generally, three types of language ambiguity are identified: (1) *lexical ambiguity* occurs when a word may have more than one meaning, for example: "He found a *bat* in the park" (a stick or a flying rodent?); (2) *surface structure ambiguity* occurs when a sentence may be given more than one meaning but where the ambiguity may be resolved by bracketing the sentence into its constituents, for example, "They are folding tables" where the sentence may be bracketed in two different ways to illustrate two meanings, "They (are folding) tables", or "They are (folding tables)"; (3) *deep structure ambiguity* occurs when a sentence may be given more than one meaning but where an analysis of its constituents cannot identify its different meanings, for example, "The boy read a letter to his mother." This sentence may mean that the boy read a letter aloud to his mother or that he read a letter addressed to his mother. One could not, however, distinguish these two meanings by analyzing the surface structure of the sentence.

Ambiguity Tolerance. A measure of the degree to which an individual is able to tolerate conflicts, unresolved problems, or complexities without experiencing excessive psychological stress.

Ambiversion. A personality orientation possessing equal amounts of introversion (q.v.) and extroversion (q.v.).

Ambivalence. The condition of having two contradictory attitudes such as the desire to be alone and the desire to socialize; the condition of changing one's attitudes toward another individual.

Ambiguous Figures. Figures (usually line diagrams or drawings) used in experiments that can be perceived in at least two different ways. These are often used in projective tests of personality.

American Research Bureau. See ARBITRON.

American Sign Language (ASL). A nonverbal communication system used by many deaf persons. In ASL each gesture or movement stands for a concept or an idea rather than for an individual letter as in finger spelling (q.v.). ASL was used by Alan and Beatrice Gardner to teach Washoe, the chimpanzee, to communicate and has been used in several other chimp projects (see TALKING CHIMPS). In the United States, ASL is the fourth most frequently used language, ranking behind English, Spanish, and Italian.

Ames Demonstration. Illusions developed by Adelbert Ames, Jr., and used widely in the study of visual perception. The most famous of these demonstrations is probably the distorted room which at first sight looks normal but when seen occupied by people or objects, they, and not the room, appear distorted.

Amoral. Without a sense of morals; neither moral nor immoral, neither right nor wrong; nonmoral. Some theorists consider rhetoric (q.v.) to be basically amoral; others hold that rhetoric is inextricably bound to certain moral principles.

Amorphous. Without shape or structure; an amorphous sentence is one without normal syntactic (q.v.) structure, a collection of words strung together without adherence to the rules of syntax.

Amphiboly (Amphibology). A type of ambiguity (q.v.) that arises from the syntactic structure of a sentence, as in, for example, "Lost, a black man's umbrella."

Amplification. Expansion of a statement or proposition through comparisons, illustrations, examples, audiovisual aids, and the like.

Amplitude. The intensity of a sound wave, measured in decibels, which determines the sound's volume and the perception of loudness.

Amusia. The loss of the ability to comprehend or to produce musical sounds.

Anachronism. A chronological error; the placement of something or someone out of its proper time period, for example, a digital clock in a Civil War film would be an anachronism.

Anaclitic Relationship. An intense but nonsexual relationship; the dependent kind of love relationship a child has with its mother.

Anacoluthon. A figure of speech involving the completion of a sentence that has a structure which violates the anticipated or expected structure; refers to a sudden and unexpected shift in subject matter in a speech or prose composition, usually designed to gain or regain an audience's attention or to achieve some other effect.

Anacusis. Total deafness.

Anadiplosis. A figure of speech in which the last word of one sentence is used as the first word in the immediately following sentence, for example, "The teacher advised the student to learn the value of communication. Communication is the most essential tool for surviving in contemporary society."

Anagram. A word formed by transposing the letters or sounds in another word, for instance, the name *Serutan,* a digestive aid, was formed (and used extensively in its advertising) from "Natures" spelled backwards.

Analogic Communication. Communication consisting of continuous rather than discrete signals. Nonverbal communication systems are, in most instances, analogic. See also DIGITAL COMMUNICATION.

Analogic System. A continuous, rather than a digital or discrete, system; a system that works on a more-or-less (analogic) rather than an all-or-none (digital) principle. A rheostat or dimmer is analogic whereas an on–off switch is digital. See also ANALOGIC COMMUNICATION.

Analogue. Something similar to or having certain parallels with something else. Related words from different languages are referred to as analogues, as are similar novels, television shows, and films, for example, the television series *Dallas* is an analogue of a soap opera.

Analogy. In argumentation, a form of comparison in which it is reasoned that since two cases are alike in certain known ways, that they are, therefore, also alike in unknown ways. In language, a process of comparison through which some words are created or pronunciations are established on the basis of other words or other existing patterns of pronunciation.

Analysis by Synthesis. A perceptual theory holding that stimuli are perceived by being first broken down into component parts (analysis) and then put into a meaningful whole (synthesized).
[K. N. Stevens, "Segments, Features, and Analysis by Synthesis," in J. F. Kavanagh and I. G. Mattingly, eds., *Language by Ear and Eye: The Relationships Between Speech and Reading* (Cambridge, Mass.: M.I.T. Press, 1972).]

Analytic Criticism. A form of criticism in which there is a thorough examination of the structure of a speech or literary work without any concern for evaluating the quality of the work. The concern here is with describing the style of the work, for example, the types of words and sentences used. See also CRITICISM.

Analytic Language. A language in which relationships are expressed primarily by word order, for example, whether a noun is the subject or the object in a sentence is expressed largely through its position in the sentence, that is, whether it is presented before or after the verb. English, for example, is an analytic language.

Analytic Sentence. A sentence that is necessarily true by virtue of its syntax and the meaning of its lexical elements or words, for example, "The bachelor is unmarried."

Anaphora. The repetition of a word or word group in successive sentences, for example, "Give them love when they succeed. Give them love when they fail."

Anastrophe. A figure of speech in which normal sentence order is reversed in some way, for example, "Through killing and looting, the soldiers gained control of the country" involves the reversal of normal word order. See also INVERSION.

Anchor. The main or principal talent or attraction; most often used to refer to the leading news reporter.

Anchor Attitude. One's existing attitude against which newly proposed attitudes are judged. See also SOCIAL JUDGMENT INVOLVEMENT THEORY.

Androgeny. The state of possessing the characteristics of both male and female. This state can refer to both physical and psychological characteristics.

Anecdotal Evidence. Unsystematic observations used to support a proposition, theory, or hypothesis; evidence used to support an argument that involves essentially specific events or examples. Such "evidence" is usually of high interest value but weak in its ability to support an argument logically. See also ANECDOTE.

Anecdote. A short story or brief account of a particular incident used to amplify a proposition in a speech or essay. See also ANECDOTAL EVIDENCE.

Anima. In Jungian psychology, the feminine side of a man's basic nature. See also ANIMUS.

Animal Communication. Communication from animal to animal (intraspecies) as well as communication between animal and human (interspecies). See also TALKING CHIMPS.

Animus. From the Latin meaning "spirit" or "soul," in Jungian psychology, the masculine side of a woman's basic nature. See also ANIMA.

Annotate. The act or process of writing notes to explain or comment on a more extensive communication. An annotated speech, for example, might contain notes explaining the rhetorical strategies used by the speaker or the speaker's references to places and people that may be unfamiliar to a reader.

Annotation. The note or notes that explain or augment a particular communication.

Anomalous Sentence. A sentence that deviates from the norm in meaning and/or structure.

Anomie. Normlessness; the state of an individual, group, or society in which normative standards of behavior are severely reduced or lost.

Anomia. A form of aphasia (q.v.) characterized by the loss of naming ability, the ability to recall the names of people and objects.

Antagonist. The main opponent in a conflict, usually considered the "villain." The antagonist's opponent is the protagonist, the "hero."

Anthology. A collection of articles, speeches, plays, poems, and literature presented in one book. The selected communications usually have a unifying theme, for example, all are speeches written by Lincoln or all are poems of the twentieth century.

Anthropocentrism. The tendency to see the human being as central to the entire universe, as the most important element in the entire universe.

Anthropomorphism. The process of attributing human characteristics to animals or even inanimate objects, for example, anthropomorphism is seen in ascribing lying behavior to a dog because it wags its tail in innocence after it has chewed up the rug.

Anticlimax. That part of a message that comes after the climax and is usually concerned with the incidental or less important aspects of the characters or plot; those final minutes in a film or drama when the audience's interest level drops off.

Anticlimax Order. A pattern of arranging the main ideas or the evidence in a communication so that the general conclusion is presented first and the specifics are presented later.

Antihero. A leading character or protagonist who does not possess the qualities normally attributed to a hero (for example, bravery, honesty, faithfulness).

Antiphrasis. A figure of speech in which a word is used to mean its literal opposite. Marc Antony's "Brutus is an honorable man" involves antiphrasis; Antony was calling attention to Brutus's dishonorable nature and behavior.

Antisocial Behavior. Behavior that is contrary to the accepted standards of society; behavior that is harmful or damaging to others.

Antithesis. A figure of speech in which contrary ideas are presented in parallel form. In philosophy, a statement or proposition that is in opposition or contrast to a given thesis.

Antonomasia. A figure of speech in which the common or normal name is substituted with another designation, for example, an epithet-type name or title as in "the dictator," "a real Doris Day," or "the computer."

Antonym. A word that means the opposite of another, for example, *up-down, above-below, black-white* are antonym pairs.

Antonymy. The opposite meaning relationship between two words.

Apathy. A lack of involvement or interest; indifference.

Aphasia. A loss of the ability to use language due to brain damage. Specific forms of aphasia are distinguished on the basis of the specific type of language loss such as anomia (q.v.), agraphia (q.v.), and agrammatism (q.v.). Distinctions are also made between expressive aphasia (q.v.) and receptive aphasia (q.v.) on the basis of whether the loss is to the expressive or receptive abilities.

Aphorism. A brief expression of some generally accepted principle or feeling, for example, "No man is an island."

Aphemia. The term originally used by Paul Broca to describe the language loss due to brain damage and now commonly referred to as aphasia (q.v.).

Aphonia. The absence of speech brought about through physical or psychological problems.

Aphrasia. The loss of the ability to comprehend or to speak in phrases.

Apocalyptic. A communication in which the future is predicted or revealed in some way. This term comes from the Apocalypse of Saint John in which the future is revealed.

Apocope. The process of word change in which the final sound or syllable of a word is dropped.

Apology. From the "Apology of Socrates," Plato's account of the speech given by Socrates at his trial in his own defense; the term used generally to refer to a speech in defense of someone.

Apophasis. A figure of speech in which the speaker or writer denies the intention of speaking on a subject but in the denial actually does speak of it, for example, "I'm not going to mention why I think you should vote for Schmedley—the contributions to the school board, the vast knowledge of local and national political issues, . . ."

A Posteriori. In logic, inductive reasoning—reasoning based on observations from which a conclusion is drawn; reasoning from the effect to the cause. In psychology, the information and data acquired through actual experience rather than innately. See also A PRIORI.

Apostrophe. The interruption of a speech in order to address some person who may be either physically present or absent from the audience.

Apothegm. A brief saying that is generally instructive or educational in some way.

Aporia. A figure of speech in which difficulty or doubt about alternatives is noted, for example, "Can we say that she loved too much or perhaps that she loved too little?"

Apparent Regression. That stage in language development when a child is learning the rules of the language and applies these rules to cases that are exceptions in the language therefore yielding an incorrect form. Thus, where a child once said *saw* and *mice*—on the basis of imitation—he or she now applies the rule for past tense and plural to yield the incorrect *seed* and *mouses*. When this happens it appears as if the child has regressed, but it is only apparent regression; in actuality, the child has advanced in language ability as demonstrated by the application of the new linguistic rule.

Appeal for a Suspension of Judgment. A type of disclaimer (q.v.) in which the speaker asks the listener to withhold judgment until the speaker has a chance to explain the situation in detail: "Before you walk out on me, let me explain the whole situation." See also DISCLAIMER.

Appellate-Type Debate. A debate structure that imitates or follows the legal debate pattern of the appellate courts: first affirmative, first negative, second affirmative, second negative, negative rebuttal, affirmative rebuttal. Debaters in this appellate-style structure prepare briefs that are exchanged prior to the actual debate. Judges question the debaters and determine the winning side in the debate.

Appendix. Material added to a book or other printed communication, for example, a glossary, a collection of relevant maps, a set of charts or tables. Appendixes are not integral parts of the book but add relevant information to it.

Apperception. A perceptual state in which the receiver's expectations are derived from past experiences.

Applied Communication. The application of research and theory to practical communication issues, usually concerning increasing effectiveness.

Applied Communication Research. Research in communication addressed to practical issues of increasing effectiveness.

Applied Research. Research that addresses practical real-life problems and seeks solutions that are immediately useful.

Apprehension, Communication. Cognitively, communication apprehension is a fear of engaging in communication transactions. That is, people develop negative feelings and predict negative results as a function of engaging in communication interactions. They feel that whatever gain would accrue from engaging in communication is clearly outweighed by the fear.

Behaviorally, communication apprehension is a decrease in the frequency, the strength, and the likelihood of engaging in communication transactions. That is, speakers avoid communication situations and, when forced to participate, participate as little as possible.

Trait and State Apprehension

The distinction between trait and state apprehension will further clarify apprehension. *Trait* apprehension refers to a fear of communication in general, regardless of the specific situation; it would appear in dyadic, small group, public speaking, and mass communication situations. *State apprehension,* on the other hand, is a fear that is specific to a given communication situation. For example, a speaker may fear public speaking but have no difficulty with dyadic communication, or may fear job interviews but have no fear of public speaking, and so on. State apprehension is extremely common; it is experienced by most persons in some situations.

Differences in Degree

Speaker apprehension exists on a continuum. Persons are not either apprehensive or not apprehensive; we all experience some degree of apprehension. Some people are extremely apprehensive and become incapacitated in a communication situation. They suffer a great deal in a society oriented, as ours is, around communication and in which success depends on one's ability to communicate effectively. Others are so mildly apprehensive that they appear to experience no fear at all when confronted by communication situations; they actively seek out communication experiences and rarely experience even the slightest apprehension. Most people lie between these two extremes.

Measuring Communication Apprehension

The following Questionnaire, developed by James McCroskey, is composed of 24 statements concerning your feelings about communication with other people. Please indicate in the space provided the degree to which each statement applies to you by marking whether you (1) Strongly Agree, (2) Agree, (3) Are Undecided, (4) Disagree, or (5) Strongly Disagree with each statement. There are no right or wrong answers. Many of the statements are similar to other statements. Do not be concerned about this. Work quickly, just record your first impression.

Questionnaire

_____ 1. I dislike participating in group discussions.

_____ 2. Generally, I am comfortable while participating in group discussions.

_____ 3. I am tense and nervous while participating in group discussions.

_____ 4. I like to get involved in group discussions.

_____ 5. Engaging in a group discussion with new people makes me tense and nervous.

_____ 6. I am calm and relaxed while participating in group discussions.

_____ 7. Generally, I am nervous when I have to participate in a meeting.

_____ 8. Usually, I am calm and relaxed while participating in meetings.

_____ 9. I am very calm and relaxed when I am called upon to express an opinion at a meeting.

_____ 10. I am afraid to express myself at meetings.

_____ 11. Communicating at meetings usually makes me uncomfortable.

_____ 12. I am very relaxed when answering questions at a meeting.

_____ 13. While participating in a conversation with a new acquaintance, I feel very nervous.

_____ 14. I have no fear of speaking up in conversations.

_____ 15. Ordinarily I am very tense and nervous in conversations.

_____ 16. Ordinarily I am very calm and relaxed in conversations.

_____ 17. While conversing with a new acquaintance, I feel very relaxed.

Questionnaire (*Continued*)

_____ 18. I'm afraid to speak up in conversations.
_____ 19. I have no fear of giving a speech.
_____ 20. Certain parts of my body feel very tense and rigid while giving a speech.
_____ 21. I feel relaxed while giving a speech.
_____ 22. My thoughts become confused and jumbled when I am giving a speech.
_____ 23. I face the prospect of giving a speech with confidence.
_____ 24. While giving a speech I get so nervous I forget facts I really know.

Scoring

To obtain your apprehension score, follow these instructions provided by McCroskey.

This test permits computation of one total score and four subscores. The subscores relate to communication apprehension in each of four common communication contexts: group discussions, meetings, interpersonal conversations, and public speaking. To compute your scores merely add or subtract your scores for each item as indicated below.

Subscore Desired	Scoring Formula
Group discussions	18 + scores for items 2, 4, and 6; − scores for items 1, 3, and 5.
Meetings	18 + scores for items 8, 9, and 12; − scores for items 7, 10, and 11.
Interpersonal conversations	18 + scores for items 14, 16, and 17; − scores for items 13, 15, and 18.
Public speaking	18 + scores for items 19, 21, and 23; − scores for items 20, 22, and 24.

To obtain your total score, simply add your four subscores together.

Each subscore should range from 6 to 30; the higher the score the greater the apprehension. "Any score above 18," according to McCroskey, "indicates some degree of apprehension." Most people score above 18 for the public speaking context, so if you scored relatively high in this subdivision, you are among the vast majority of people. Most people also score higher on public speaking than on any of the other subdivisions.

[James McCroskey, *An Introduction to Rhetorical Communication,* 4th ed. (Englewood Cliffs, N.J.: Prentice-Hall, 1982).]

Some Causes of Apprehension

James McCroskey, the leading researcher in apprehension, has identified a number of major causes of apprehension.

1. *Lack of communication skills and experience.*
2. *Degree of evaluation.* The more we perceive the situation as one in which we will be evaluated, the greater will be our apprehension.
3. *Degree of conspicuousness.* The more conspicuous we are, the more we are likely to feel apprehensive.
4. *Degree of unpredictability.* The more unpredictable the situation, the greater will be the apprehension.
5. Prior successes and failures. Prior success generally (though not always) reduces apprehension whereas prior failure generally (though not always) increases apprehension.

Managing Communication Apprehension

It is probably impossible to eliminate communication apprehension altogether. We can, however, effectively manage apprehension so that it does not debilitate us or prevent us from achieving our communication goals. The following guidelines will help manage apprehension.

1. *Acquire communication skills and experience.*
2. *Prepare and practice.* The more preparation and practice you put into something, the more comfortable you are going to feel with it and consequently the less apprehension you will feel.
3. *Focus on success.* Think positively. Put negative thoughts and thoughts of failure out of your mind.
4. *Familiarize yourself with the situation.* The more you familiarize yourself with the situation the better. This will reduce the ambiguity and the perceived newness of the situation.
5. *Physical relaxation helps.* Apprehension is reduced when you are physically relaxed. Breathing deeply and engaging in some kind of physical activity (for example, walking or writing on a chalkboard) will help reduce the tension and lessen the apprehension and anxiety you feel.
6. *Put communication apprehension in perspective.* Remember that others are not able to perceive your apprehension in the same way you do. You feel the drying in your throat and the rapid heart beat, but others do not.

See also RETICENCE, SHYNESS, UNWILLINGNESS TO COMMUNICATE, LISTENING APPREHENSION, WRITING APPREHENSION.

[James C. McCroskey, "Oral Communication Apprehension: A Summary of Recent Theory and Research," *Human Communication Research* 4 (Fall 1977):78–96.]

Approach-Approach Conflict. A conflict where there are two desirable alternatives, only one of which can be chosen.

Approach-Avoidance Conflict. A conflict where a goal has both positive characteristics (which lead the individual to approach) and negative characteristics (which lead the individual to avoid it).

Approach Gradient. The gain in the perceived attractiveness of a goal as it is more closely approached.

Appropriateness. One of the qualities of style referring to the suitability of language to the specific communication act; the suitability of communication strategies, techniques, and behaviors to all the other elements in the communication act.

Apraxia. The inability to execute purposeful movements although there is no motor or sensory impairment.

A Priori. In logic, deductive reasoning in which a general proposition accepted without the need for empirical verification is used to deduce various specifics; reasoning from the cause to the effect. In psychology, information and data acquired innately, as part of one's natural native endowment. See also A POSTERIORI.

Arbitration. A method of conflict resolution that involves resolving the conflict through the intercession of a third party who attempts to determine a settlement that is fair to all parties. In binding arbitration, the decision of the arbitrator or third party must be adopted.

Arbitrariness. The feature of human language that refers to the fact that there is no real or inherent relationship between the form of a word and its meaning. If we do not know anything of a particular language, we could not examine the form of a word and thereby discover its meaning because form and meaning are arbitrarily related.

ARBITRON (American Research Bureau). A research organization that divides the country into areas of dominant influence (ADIs, q.v.) defined and ranked according to the number of televisions and radios in its households. This information is then used as a basis for advertising rates and as a guide to advertisers who wish to appeal to specific markets.

Archaism. A language form from an earlier period of history that is seldom used today.

Archaic. A word that was once frequently used but is no longer; a word from a past time in history.

Archetype. In Jungian psychology, the content of the collective unconscious that serves as a kind of frame of reference through which one perceives and experiences the world; an inherited universal image or concept—for example, hero, self, shadow, anima (q.v.), animus (q.v.)—that is derived from evolutionary development and on which personality is based. In literary criticism, an abstract idea that represents the essential elements of a class; a particularly clear-cut and precisely defined type of person, for example, Don Juan as the ardent lover. [Carl G. Jung, *Memories, Dreams, Reflections* (New York: Random House, 1961).]

Areas of Dominant Influence (ADIs). Particular areas of the country defined by the number of television and radio households as established by the American Research Bureau (ARBITRON, q.v.) for sales and rating purposes.

Argot. A kind of sublanguage (q.v.); the cant (q.v.) and jargon (q.v.) of a particular class—generally an underworld or criminal class—which is difficult and sometimes impossible for outsiders to understand.

Arguing in a Circle. A form of argument in which two unsupported propositions are used to prove the truth or validity of each other.

Argument. The presentation of evidence together with the conclusion which the evidence supports. In popular usage, a disagreement or dispute. In linguistics, the element or elements that complete the action of the verb; those elements that, together with the verb, make up a proposition (q.v.).

Argument, Types of. See AD BACULUM, ARGUMENTUM; AD IGNORANTIAM, ARGUMENTUM; AD JUDICIUM, ARGUMENTUM; AD MISERICORDIAM, ARGUMENTUM; AD POPULUM, ARGUMENTUM; AD REM, ARGUMENTUM; AD VERECUNDIAM, ARGUMENTUM.

Argumentativeness. A personality trait that leads a person to approach or avoid arguments and argumentative situations; a disposition to recognize controversial issues, to defend relevant positions, and to refute the positions of others. The following scale measures argumentativeness.

THE ARGUMENTATIVENESS SCALE

Instructions

This questionnaire contains statements about arguing controversial issues. Indicate how often each statement is true for you personally by placing the appropriate number in the blank to the left of the statement. If the statement is Almost Never True for you, place a 1 in the blank. If the statement is Rarely True for you, place a 2 in the blank. If the statement is Occasionally True for you, place a 3 in the blank. If the statement is Often True for you, place 4 in the blank. If the statement is Almost Always True for you, place a 5 in the blank.

_____ 1. While in an argument, I worry that the person I am arguing with will form a negative impression of me.

THE ARGUMENTATIVENESS SCALE (*Continued*)

_____ 2. Arguing over controversial issues improves my intelligence.
_____ 3. I enjoy avoiding arguments.
_____ 4. I am energetic and enthusiastic when I argue.
_____ 5. Once I finish an argument I promise myself that I will not get into another.
_____ 6. Arguing with a person creates more problems for me than it solves.
_____ 7. I have a pleasant, good feeling when I win a point in an argument.
_____ 8. When I finish arguing with someone I feel nervous and upset.
_____ 9. I enjoy a good argument over a controversial issue.
_____ 10. I get an unpleasant feeling when I realize I am about to get into an argument.
_____ 11. I enjoy defending my point of view on an issue.
_____ 12. I am happy when I keep an argument from happening.
_____ 13. I do not like to miss the opportunity to argue a controversial issue.
_____ 14. I prefer being with people who rarely disagree with me.
_____ 15. I consider an argument an exciting intellectual challenge.
_____ 16. I find myself unable to think of effective points during an argument.
_____ 17. I feel refreshed and satisfied after an argument on a controversial issue.
_____ 18. I have the ability to do well in an argument.
_____ 19. I try to avoid getting into arguments.
_____ 20. I feel excitement when I expect that a conversation I am in is leading to an argument.

Scoring Instructions

Tendency to approach argumentative situations: add scores on items 2, 4, 7, 9, 11, 13, 15, 17, 18, 20.

Tendency to avoid argumentative situations: add scores on items 1, 3, 5, 6, 8, 10, 12, 14, 16, 19.

Argumentativeness trait: subtract the total of the 10 tendency to avoid items from the total of the 10 tendency to approach items.

Dominick A. Infante and Andrew S. Rancer, "A Conceptualization and Measurement of Argumentativeness," *Journal of Personality Assessment* 46 (1982):72–80.

Aristotelian(ism). An approach using the methodology, theories, or perspective of Aristotle (384–322 B.C.), the Greek philosopher.

Articulation. The process of enunciating or producing speech.

Articulators. The anatomical structures (tongue, teeth, lips, larynx, vocal cords, velum) that are manipulated to produce speech.

Articulatory Phonetics. The science of speech sounds from the point of view of their production by a speaker. See also ACOUSTIC PHONETICS.

Artifact. Any object that serves to nonverbally communicate a message, for example, jewelry, sunglasses, jeans, sneakers, and the like; objects used to adorn or modify the appearance or perception of a person.

Artifactual Communication. Communication through the manipulation of artifacts (q.v.).

Artistic Proofs. In Aristotelian rhetoric (q.v.), those proofs constructed by the speaker: ethos (q.v.)—the proof derived from the character of the speaker; pathos (q.v.)—emotional appeals; and logos (q.v.)—logical argument.

ASCAP (American Society of Composers, Authors, and Publishers). A professional union of media personnel.

Ascriptor. In Charles Morris's (1901–   ) system, an ascriptor is similar to a proposition or statement; identifies something and says something about this identified thing, for example, the sentence, "The linguist is sick" is an ascriptor in which the linguist is the something identified and sickness is the something said (or signified) about the linguist. Morris distinguished among several types of ascriptors: *designative ascriptors*— those that identify or describe, for example, "He is a linguist"; *appraisive ascriptors*—those that are evaluative, for example, "He is a brilliant linguist"; and *prescriptive ascriptors*—those that request specific behaviors from the listener, for example, "Strangle the linguist."

[Charles Morris, *Signs, Language and Behavior* (New York: George Braziller, 1946).]

Asianism. In classical rhetorical theory, a type of style characterized as flowery and ornate; contrasted with atticism (q.v.).

Aside. A line or series of lines uttered by a character in a play or novel that reveals his or her inner thoughts and although other characters may be present when the aside is made, for purposes of the drama, they do not hear it.

Assembly. The members of a group transacting business.

Assertiveness. A willingness, a readiness, to stand up for one's rights, to not allow others to usurp what rightfully belongs to one. The assumption made by numerous researchers and theorists is that we have been taught to be unassertive and to allow others to take advantage of us and, as a result, we need to be retrained to become more assertive.

Assertiveness is largely an interpersonal communication characteristic. It is mainly in interpersonal situations (though also in small groups and at times in large group situations) that the occasion and the need to assert ourselves arises.

Nonassertiveness, Aggressiveness, and Assertiveness

There are two kinds of nonassertiveness. First, there is *situational nonassertiveness.* This is the nonassertiveness that is only displayed in certain situations, for example, situations that create a great deal of anxiety—perhaps because of the person one is interacting with or because of the topic being considered.

Generalized nonassertiveness is, as the term implies, behavior that is normally or typically nonassertive. People who exhibit these behaviors are timid and reserved, and regardless of the specifics of the situation, they are unable to assert their rights. These people do what others tell them to do—parents, employers, and the like—without questioning and without concern for what is best for them. When these persons' rights are infringed upon, they do nothing about it and even at times accuse themselves of being nonaccepting. Generalized nonassertive persons often ask permission from others to do what is their perfect right. Social situations create anxiety for these individuals, and they find, more often than not, that their self-esteem is generally low. In the extreme, a generalized nonassertive person would be characterized as inhibited and emotionally unresponsive with feelings of personal inadequacy.

Aggressiveness may also be considered as being of two types: situational and generalized. *Situationally aggressive* people are aggressive only under certain conditions or in certain situations. The important characteristic is that these people are usually not aggressive; only in certain situations do they behave aggressively. *Generally aggressive* people, on the other hand, meet most situations with aggressive behavior.

Assertive behavior is the desired alternative to both types of aggression and has been characterized in various ways. Basically, assertive individuals are willing to assert their own rights, but unlike their aggressive counterparts they do not hurt others in the process. Assertive individuals speak their minds and welcome others doing likewise.

In an exploration of assertiveness as a communication variable, Robert Norton and Barbara Warnick found that four characteristics may be identified as describing and defining assertiveness in interpersonal communication. Assertive individuals are, first, open persons. They engage in frank and open expression of their feelings to people in general as well as to those for whom there may be some sexual interest. Second, assertive individuals are not anxious; they readily volunteer opinions and beliefs, deal directly with interpersonal communication situations that may be stressful, and question others without fear. Their communications are dominant, frequent, and of high intensity. They have a positive view of their own communication performance and this view seems to be shared by those with whom they communicate. Third, assertive interpersonal communicators are contentious; they stand up and argue for their rights, even if this entails a certain degree of unpleasantness with relatives or close friends. Fourth, assertive persons are not intimidated and are not easily persuaded.

Principles for Increasing Assertiveness

The general assumption made by most assertiveness trainers is that the majority of people are situationally nonassertive. Most people are able to modify their behavior, with a resultant increase in general interpersonal effectiveness and in self-esteem. Those who are generally nonassertive, however, probably need training with a therapist. Those who are only moderately nonassertive and who wish to understand their assertiveness—and perhaps to behave differently in certain situations—should find the following principles of value. The rationale and the specific principles derive from the behavior modification techniques of B. F. Skinner and the systematic desensitization techniques of Joseph Wolpe and others. In formulating these five principles, the techniques of these theorists, as well as specific assertiveness training manuals were most helpful.

Analyze the Assertive Behavior of Others

The first step in increasing our assertiveness is to understand the nature of these behaviors. On an intellectual level this understanding should already have been achieved. What is necessary and more important than an intellectual understanding, however, is to understand actual assertive behavior, and the best way to start is to observe and analyze the behaviors of others. We should become able to distinguish the differences among assertive, aggressive, and nonassertive behaviors. Focus on what makes one behavior assertive and another behavior shy, or aggressive, or nonassertive. Listen to what is said and how it is said. Recall the nonverbal behaviors and try to categorize nonverbal behaviors as assertive, aggressive, or nonassertive.

Analyze Your Own Behaviors

It is generally easier to analyze the behaviors of others than our own. We find it difficult to be objective with ourselves, but after we have acquired some skills in observing the behaviors of others, we can turn our analysis to ourselves. We should be able to analyze those situations in which we are normally assertive, nonassertive, and aggressive. What characterizes these situations? What do the situations in which you are normally aggressive have in common? How do these situations differ from the situations in which you are normally nonassertive? What do the situations in which you are normally shy have in common?

Record Your Behaviors

A simple three-part form with space for recording assertive, aggressive, and nonaggressive behaviors will suffice. Be as specific as possible in recording your behaviors, and give as many details of the actual situation as seem reasonable.

Rehearse Assertive Behaviors

A number of different systems have been proposed for effective rehearsal of assertive behaviors. One of the most popular is to select a situation in which you are normally nonassertive and build a hierarchy that begins with a relatively nonthreatening behavior and ends with the desired behavior.

Be Assertive

You can only increase assertiveness when you act out these behaviors; you cannot become assertive by acting nonassertively. Again, do this in small steps. After performing the behavior, get feedback from others. Start with people who are generally supportive. They should provide you with the social reinforcement helpful in learning new behavior patterns.

In applying these principles, be careful that you do not go beyond what you and others can handle—physically and emotionally. Do not, for example, assert yourself out of a job. It is best to be careful in changing any behavior but especially, it seems, with assertiveness.

[Robert E. Alberti and Michael L. Emmons, *Your Perfect Right: A Guide to Assertive Behavior* (San Luis Obispo, Calif.: Impact, 1970), and *Stand Up, Speak Out, Talk Back: The Key to Self-Assertive Behavior* (New York: Pocket Books, 1970); Ronald B. Adler, *Confidence in Communication: A Guide to Assertive and Social Skills* (New York: Holt, Rinehart and Winston, 1977); Robert Norton and Barbara Warnick, "Assertiveness as a Communication Construct," *Human Communication Research* 3 (Fall 1976):62–66.]

Assimilation. A process whereby new experiences and concepts are incorporated into existing cognitive structures and are used in a meaningful way. In phonetics (q.v.), an articulatory change of one sound to more closely conform to the articulation of a neighboring sound; one of the most common sources of sound change. In serial communication (q.v.), a process of message distortion in which the message is influenced by the special interests, needs, and motives of the receiver. See also LEVELING; SHARPENING.

Assimilation Effect. In the social judgment involvement theory (q.v.) of attitude change, the tendency of an individual to minimize the degree of difference between one's initial or anchor attitudes (q.v.) and the attitudes of others that are seen to be similar. See also CONTRAST EFFECT.

Associative Meaning. An approach to meaning that focuses on how the meaning of one word stimulates thoughts of related terms. In some views the meaning of a term consists of all the word associations that a subject makes to it, hence associative meaning.

Assonance. The repetition of vowel sounds in words that are arranged near each other, as in "twinkle, twinkle little star."

Assumption. A proposition assumed to be true for the sake of deducing inferences from it so that these inferences or consequences may be examined more carefully.

Asyndeton. A figure of speech in which grammatical connectives (such as conjunctions and articles) are omitted in a series, for example, "The doctor ran like a thief, cried like a baby, fled like a cat."

Ataxic Writing. Impaired writing usually due to brain damage and characterized by muscular coordination disturbances.

Attention. The process by which one perceives selectively.

Attention Decrement Hypothesis. An hypothesis designed to explain primacy (q.v.) proposing that people pay more attention to what is presented early and less to what is conveyed late in a message or sequence of messages. As attention decreases so does the perceived importance and truth value.
[Norman H. Anderson, "Primacy Effects in Personality Impression Formation Using a Generalized Order Effect Paradigm," *Journal of Personality and Social Psychology* 2 (1965):1–9.]

Attention Level. A measure of the clarity with which one perceives a stimulus.

Attention: Securing and Maintaining Audience Attention. Especially in the introduction but throughout any speech, it is essential that a speaker secure and maintain the attention of the audience. If their minds wander for any significant amount of time, it will be impossible to achieve your purpose. There are numerous and varied devices to help you maintain audience attention. Here are just 10 of them.

1. *Ask a question.* Questions are effective because they are a change from the normal statements but also because they directly involve the audience; they tell the audience that you are talking directly to them and that you care about their responses.
2. *Make reference to the audience members themselves.* This generally makes all members perk up and pay attention because of the possibility that they too will be involved directly. But this is a useful technique also because it demonstrates that you are speaking to this specific audience and that you know them.
3. *Introduce change.* Change seems a universal attention-getter. Changes from a flood of statistics to a personal illustration or from a series of examples to a quotation are most effective attention devices.
4. *Make reference to recent happenings.* Referring to a previous speech, a recent event, or to some prominent person currently making news will help to secure attention because the audience is familiar with this and will attend to see how you are going to approach it.
5. *Be humorous.* A clever (and appropriate) joke or anecdote is always useful in holding attention. But, unless you are a good joke teller and unless the joke is a good one, avoid this method. Nothing is worse than a joke that no one laughs at or a joke that is so stale that audience members finish the joke for you.
6. *Tell a dramatic story.* Much as we are drawn to television soap operas and dramas, so are we drawn to illustrations and stories about people. Perhaps this is true because we can identify with these people or because we would like to be like them or because it makes us feel our condition is not so bad in comparison with the fate of these others. For whatever reason, we seem anxious to listen to dramatic stories.
7. *Use audiovisual aids.* The use of audio and visual materials is particularly valuable because it is new and different and we are universally attracted

to the new and different. In using these aids, be sure that they are used effectively.

8. *Vary the intensity of your delivery.* Your voice and bodily action are among the most effective attention-getters you have available. An increase or decrease in loudness, rate, or bodily movement will gain attention, again because it is a change from what the audience has been hearing and seeing.

9. *Relate your supporting material directly to the audience.* In addition to telling them that the rate of unemployment is going to increase (probably too general to relate to), tell them that this means that 4 out of a class of 30 will be out of work for at least one year after graduation and that 6 of them will have at least one parent out of a job by the end of the year. In addition to telling them that budget cuts will hurt education in the state (again, too general to relate to), tell them that this means that their college courses will be increased from 30 to 50 students, that laboratory courses will be cut in half, and that tuition will be increased 40 percent. In short, tell the audience what the facts and figures will mean to them as individuals.

10. *Tell the audience to pay attention.* Statements such as "now hear this" or "listen to this most frightening statistic" or "focus your attention on this argument" are found to be most effective in securing audience attention. As you might guess, you cannot use these more than a few times in a speech; yet, they are most helpful if placed strategically and are phrased with some subtlety and novelty.

Attention Step. In the motivated sequence (q.v.), the first step in a public speech. In the attention step the speaker must gain the favorable attention of the audience and relate it and focus it on the major ideas to be developed in the speech.

Attentiveness. A process that signals message reception; behaviors communicating that one is attending to the message.
[Robert W. Norton and Lloyd S. Pettegrew, "Attentiveness as a Style of Communication: A Structural Analysis," *Communication Monographs* 46 (1979):13–26.]

Attic Orators. Ten orators from ancient Greece whom critics have established as standards or models of excellence. The Attic orators greatly influenced the speeches of others through the use of their speeches as models; many of the Attic 10 were professional speech writers and teachers of oratory. The Attic orators, originally identified as such by Caecilius of Calacte, included Antiphon, Isocrates, Lysias, Andocides, Deinarchus, Isaeus, Lycurgus, Hyperides, Aeschines, and Demosthenes.
[R. C. Jebb, *The Attic Orators* (London, 1893).]

Atticism. In classical rhetorical theory, a type of style characterized by restraint and the absence of stylistic extravagances; a view of style that established the Attic orators (q.v.) as models to be followed; contrasted with asianism (q.v.).

Attitude. A predisposition to respond for or against an object, person, or position.

Attitude Functions. Daniel Katz has identified four major functions that attitudes may serve: (1) the *instrumental* or *utilitarian function* enables one to maximize rewards; (2) the *ego-defensive function* enables one to protect one's ego from threats; (3) the *value-expressive function* enables one to give expression to important values; (4) the *knowledge function* enables one to give meaning to an otherwise unorganized world.
[Daniel Katz, "The Functional Approach to the Study of Attitudes," *Public Opinion Quarterly* 24 (1960):163–204.]

Attitude Test. An instrument designed to measure the attitudes of an individual or group of individuals toward issues, groups of people, or anything about which one could have an attitude.

Attitude Scale. A device by which attitudes may be quantitatively measured. Semantic differential (q.v.) type scales are among the most popular means of measuring attitude strength.

Attraction. A positiveness or liking for another person. Most people are interpersonally attracted to others on the basis of five major variables: attractiveness (physical and personality), proximity, reinforcement, similarity, and complementarity.

Attractiveness (Physical and Personality)

Attractiveness comes in at least two forms. When we say, "I find that person attractive," we probably mean either (1) that we find that person physically attractive or (2) that we find that person's personality or ways of behaving attractive. For the most part we tend to like physically attractive people rather than physically ugly people, and we tend to like people who possess a pleasant personality rather than an unpleasant personality. Few would find fault with these two generalizations. The difficulty arises when we try to define *attractive.* The same difficulty besets us when we attempt to define *pleasant personality.* To some people this means an aggressive, competitive, forceful individual, whereas to others it might mean an unassuming, shy, and bashful individual.

Although attractiveness (both physical and personality) is difficult, if not impossible, to define universally, it is possible to define it for any one individual for specific situations. Thus if a person were interested in dating someone, he or she would choose someone who possessed certain characteristics that are considered "attractive." And in all probability, this same person in another, similar situation, would again look for someone who possessed these same characteristics. That is, we seem relatively consistent in the characteristics we find "attractive."

Forming Impressions

Generally, we attribute positive characteristics to people we find attractive and negative characteristics to people we find unattractive. If people were asked to predict which qualities a given individual possessed, they would probably predict the possession of positive qualities if they thought the person attractive and negative characteristics if they thought the person unattractive. Numerous studies have supported this commonsense observation.

Even children have prejudices and are the object of attractiveness bias. For example, children between the ages of 4 and 6 believed that aggressive, antisocial behavior was more characteristic of unattractive than of attractive children. And female students, given a written description of some delinquent act and a photograph of the person who supposedly committed the act, judged the unattractive child as having more antisocial impulses and as being more likely to misbehave in the future. Attractive female college students received more favorable evaluations from fellow male students on essays they supposedly wrote and higher overall gradepoint averages in college than did unattractive females.

It seems clear from hundreds of studies that attractiveness is an asset for both men and women but is especially important for women. It also seems clear that this is a cultural phenomenon; we have been conditioned throughout our lives to look at women in terms of attractiveness and at men in terms of ability. This difference is well illustrated in one study in which men and women were asked to rate the qualities they find most important in the opposite sex. The results are presented in the accompanying table.

QUALITIES JUDGED MOST IMPORTANT IN A POTENTIAL PARTNER

For Men	For Women
1. achievement	1. physical attractiveness
2. leadership	2. erotic ability
3. occupational ability	3. affectional ability
4. economic ability	4. social ability
5. entertaining ability	5. domestic ability
6. intellectual ability	6. sartorial ability
7. observational ability	7. interpersonal understanding
8. common sense	8. art appreciation
9. athletic ability	9. moral and spiritual understanding
10. theoretical ability	10. art and creative ability

From R. Centers, "The Completion Hypothesis and the Compensatory Dynamic in Intersexual Attraction and Love," *Journal of Psychology* 82 (1972):111–126.

Proximity

Proximity refers to the physical closeness between people and is one of the most important variables determining attractiveness. Here we examine briefly how proximity works and why proximity works.

How Proximity Works

If we look around at the people we find attractive, we would probably find that they are the people who live or work close to us. This is perhaps the one finding that emerges most frequently from the research on interpersonal attraction. In college dormitories and in city housing projects with a number of floors, most friendships develop between people living on the same floor; few develop between people on different floors. In fact, proximity influences not only who become friends but also how close the friendships come to be: the closer the living quarters, the closer the friendships. The vast majority of marriages are between people who have lived very close to each other. Cadets at the Training Academy of the Maryland State Police who were asked to name their friends named persons who sat in class and roomed in close proximity with them, and with whom they, therefore, had more frequent interaction.

The importance of physical distance varies with the type of situation one is in. For example, in anxiety-producing situations we seem to have more need for company and hence are more easily attracted to others than when we are in situations with low or no anxiety. It is also comforting to be with people who have gone through (or who will go through) the same experiences as we. We seem especially attracted to these people in times of stress. We are also more attracted to someone else if we have previously been deprived of such interaction. If, for example, we were in a hospital or prison without any contact with other people, we would probably be attracted to just about anyone. Anyone seems a great deal better than no one. We are also most attracted to people when we are feeling down or when self-esteem is particularly low.

Why Proximity Works

When we attempt to discover the reasons for the influence that physical closeness has on interpersonal attraction, we can think of many. We seem to have positive expectations of people and consequently fulfill these by liking or being attracted to those we find ourselves near. Proximity also allows us the opportunity to get to know the other person—to gain some information about him or her. We come to like people we know because we can better predict their behavior, and perhaps because of this they seem less frightening to us than complete strangers.

Still another approach argues that mere exposure (q.v.) to others leads us to develop positive feelings for them. In one study women were supposedly participating in a taste experiment and throughout the course of the experiment were exposed to other people. The subjects were exposed to some people 10 times, to others 5 times, to others 2 times, to others 1 time, and to others not at all. The subjects did not talk with these other people and had never seen them before this experiment. The subjects were then asked to rate the other people in terms of how much they liked them. The results showed that they rated highest those persons they had seen 10 times, next highest those they had seen 5 times, and so on down the line. How can we account for these results except by mere exposure?

Of course, if our initial interaction with a person is unpleasant, then repeated exposure may not increase attraction. Mere exposure seems to work when the initial interaction is favorable or even neutral; in these cases exposure increases attraction. When the initial interaction is negative, however, mere exposure may actually decrease attraction.

Connected to this "mere exposure" concept is the finding that the greater the contact between people, the less they are prejudiced against each other. For example, whites and blacks living in housing developments became less prejudiced against each other as a result of living and interacting together.

Reinforcement

We tend to like those who reward or reinforce us. The reward or reinforcement may be social, as in the form of compliments or praise of one sort or another or it may be material, as in the case of the suitor whose gifts eventually win the hand of the beloved. But reward can backfire. When overdone, reward loses its effectiveness and may even lead to negative responses. The people who reward us constantly soon become too sweet to take, and in a short period we come to discount whatever they say. Also, if the reward is to work, it must be perceived as genuine and not motivated by selfish concerns.

The order in which reinforcement occurs and whether or not it is coupled with negative evaluations also affects its influence. Researchers investigated this issue by having subjects "overhear" conversations by others about themselves. Four conditions were established, each consisting of overhearing seven conversations. In the positive condition, all seven conversations the subjects overheard were positive; in the negative condition, all conversations were negative. In the negative-positive condition, the first three conversations were negative and the last four were positive. In the positive-negative condition, the first three conversations were positive and the last four were negative. After overhearing these conversations, the subjects were asked to indicate the extent to which they liked the "gossiping" individual on a scale ranging from -10 to $+10$. The most-liked persons were the ones who first spoke negatively and then spoke positively; that is, the negative-positive condition produced the greatest amount of attraction $(+7.67)$. The next most-liked persons were those in the positive condition $(+6.42)$. The third most-liked were the persons in the negative condition $(+2.52)$. The least liked were the persons who first spoke positively and then spoke negatively, that is, the positive-negative condition $(+0.87)$.

Gain-Loss Theory

Elliot Aronson has proposed that a *gain-loss theory* (q.v.) can account for such findings as these. Basically, the theory states that increases in rewards have greater impact than constant invariant rewards. We like a person more if that person's liking (rewards) for us increases over time than if that person constantly rewards us indiscriminately. This holds true even if the number of rewards given by the person who always likes us are greater than those given by the person whose liking for us increases over time. Conversely, decreases in rewards have a greater impact than constant punishments; we dislike the person whose rewards decrease over time more than the person who always punishes us or who never has anything good to say about us.

Rewarding Others

We also become attracted to persons we reward. We come to like people for whom we do favors. Although our initial reaction might be to say that we give rewards to people because we like them—and this is certainly true—it also works in reverse. Giving others rewards increases our liking for them as well. It seems we justify going out of our way by convincing ourselves that the person is worth the effort and is a likeable person.

Similarity

If people could construct their mates they would look, act, and think very much like themselves. By being attracted to people like ourselves we are in effect validating ourselves, saying to ourselves that we are worthy of being liked, that we are attractive. Although there are exceptions, we generally like people who are similar to ourselves in color, race, ability, physical characteristics, intelligence, and so on. We are often attracted to mirror images of ourselves.

The Matching Hypothesis

If you were to ask a group of friends, "To whom are you attracted?," they would probably name very attractive people; in fact, they would probably name the most attractive people they know. But if we were to observe these friends, we would find that they go out with and establish relationships with people who are quite similar to themselves in terms of physical attractiveness. The *matching hypothesis* (q.v.) is useful in this connection and states that although we may be attracted to the most physically attractive people, we date and mate people who are similar to ourselves in physical attractiveness. Intuitively this, too, seems satisfying. In some cases, however, we notice discrepancies; we notice an old man dating an attractive younger partner or an unattractive woman with a handsome partner. In these cases, we will probably find that the less attractive partner possesses some quality that compensates for his or her lack of physical attractiveness. Prestige, money, intelligence, power, and various personality characteristics are obvious examples of qualities that may compensate for being less physically attractive.

Attitude Similarity

Similarity is especially important when it comes to attitudes. We are particularly attracted to people who have attitudes similar to our own, who like what we like, and who dislike what we dislike. The more salient or significant the attitude, the more important is the similarity. For example, it would not make much difference if the attitudes of two people toward food or furniture differed (though even these can at times be significant), but it would be of great signifi-

cance if their attitudes toward children or religion or politics were very dispa-
rate. Marriages between people with great and salient dissimilarities are more
likely to end in divorce than are marriages between people who are very much
alike.

Generally we maintain balance with ourselves by liking people who are similar to us and who like what we like. It is psychologically uncomfortable to like
people who do not like what we like or to dislike people who like what we like.
And so our attraction for similarity enables us to achieve psychological balance
or comfort. Agreement with ourselves is reinforcing. Another reason we are
attracted to similarly minded people is that we can predict that since they think
like us, they will like us as well. And so we like them because we think they like
us.

Complementarity

Although many people would argue that "birds of a feather flock together,"
others would argue that "opposites attract." This latter concept is the principle
of complementarity.

Take, for example, the individual who is extremely dogmatic. The similarity
principle predicts that this person will be attracted to those who are like him or
her (that is, high in dogmatism), while the complementarity principle predicts
that this person will be attracted to those who are unlike him or her (that is, low
in dogmatism).

It may be found that people are attracted to others who are dissimilar only in
certain situations. For example, the submissive student may get along especially
well with an aggressive teacher rather than a submissive one but may not get
along with an aggressive spouse. The dominant wife may get along with a
submissive husband but may not relate well to submissive colleagues.

Theodore Reik in *A Psychologist Looks at Love* argues that we fall in love with
people who possess characteristics that we do not possess and that we actually
envy. The introvert, for example, if displeased with being shy, might be attracted
to an extrovert.

There seems intuitive support for both complementarity and similarity and
certainly neither can be ruled out in terms of exerting significant influence on
interpersonal attraction. The experimental evidence, however, seems to favor
similarity.

[Ellen Berscheid and Elaine Hatfield Walster, *Interpersonal Attraction,* 2nd ed. (Reading,
Mass.: Addison-Wesley, 1978); S. Duck and R. Gilmour, *Personal Relationships,* 5 vols.
(London: Academic Press, 1981–1984).]

Attraction, Law of. Formulated by psychologist Donn Byrne, an hypothesis holding that attraction increases when positive reinforcement (q.v.) is greater than
negative reinforcement (q.v.).

[Donn Byrne, *The Attraction Paradigm* (New York: Academic Press, 1971).]

Attribution. The process by which we identify the motives for the behaviors of
others and ourselves; the process of assigning behaviors to various motivations.

Developed largely by E. E. Jones and K. E. Davis, and expanded and clarified
greatly by H. H. Kelley, attribution is a process through which we attempt to
understand the behaviors of others (as well as our own), particularly the reasons
or motivations for these behaviors. Most of our inferences about a person's
motivations—a person's reasons for behaving in various ways—come from our
observations of the person's behaviors.

If our eventual aim is to discover the causes of another's behavior, then our
first step is to determine if the individual is responsible for the behavior or if

some outside factor is responsible. Internal and external are the two kinds of causality with which attribution theory is concerned, so we first have to determine if the cause of the behavior is internal (for example, if the behavior is due to the person's personality or to some such enduring trait) or if the cause of the behavior is external (for example, if the behavior is due to some situational factor).

Three Principles of Attribution

The three principles we use in making causal judgments in interpersonal perception are: (1) consensus, (2) consistency, and (3) distinctiveness. We use each of these principles every day in making judgments about people though we talk about them using a different jargon.

Consensus

When we focus on the principle of consensus, we ask essentially, "Do other people react or behave in the same way as the person on whom we are focusing?," that is, are they acting in accordance with the general consensus? If the answer is "no," then we are more likely to attribute the behavior to some internal cause. When only one person acts contrary to the norm, we are more likely to attribute that person's behavior to some internal motivation.

Consistency

When we focus on the principle of consistency, we ask if this person repeatedly behaves the same way in similar situations. If the answer is "yes," there is high consistency, and we are likely to attribute the behavior to the person— to some internal motivation.

Distinctiveness

When we focus on the principle of distinctiveness, we ask if this person reacts in similar ways in different situations. If the answer is "yes," there is low distinctiveness and we are likely to conclude that there is an internal cause. A low distinctiveness indicates that the situation is not distinctive and that this person reacts in similar ways in different situations.

Low consensus, high consistency, and low distinctiveness lead us to attribute a person's behavior to internal causes. High consensus, low consistency, and high distinctiveness lead us to attribute a person's behavior to external causes. A summary with a specific example is presented in the accompanying table.

A SUMMARY OF CONSENSUS, CONSISTENCY, AND DISTINCTIVENESS IN CAUSAL ATTRIBUTION

Situation: A student is observed complaining about a grade received in a philosophy course. On what basis will we conclude whether this behavior is internally or externally caused?

Internal If:	External If:
1. No one else complained. (low consensus)	1. Many others have complained. (high consensus)
2. Student has complained in the past. (high consistency)	2. Student has never complained in the past. (low consistency)
3. Student has complained to other teachers in other courses. (low distinctiveness)	3. Student has never complained to other teachers. (high distinctiveness)

Revealing and Unrevealing Behaviors

Not all behaviors are equally revealing of internal motivations. Some behaviors tell us a great deal about an individual while other behaviors fail to separate this person from thousands of others. First, behaviors that are produced by one motivation are more revealing than are behaviors produced by various and numerous motivations. Consider attempting to account for the reason why a friend took a position with Hulk Industries. The job is a boring one, the work required is physically demanding and unpleasant, but it pays well. Further, our friend has turned down easier and more exciting jobs that did not pay well. From this we would likely conclude that this individual was motivated by money (assuming we had all the facts). This behavior is therefore more revealing of motivation than would taking a position with Wonder, Inc. where the job was interesting, the work was easy and pleasant, and the money was good. Here we would not be able to make a strong inference concerning which motive operated to produce the given behavior. Second, behaviors that are uncommon or are drastically different from those produced by others are more revealing than are behaviors common to everyone. Likewise, uncommon behaviors are more revealing than common behaviors. Consider the mother who buys her children new clothes, sees that they go to bed on time, and supervises their homework. These are the functions of many mothers and hence would not be particularly revealing; they would not enable us to separate this mother from thousands of other mothers. However, take the mother who beats her child for hanging her new dress on a wire hanger—as the book and film *Mommie Dearest* depicted. This behavior is uncommon enough for us to find it revealing; it tells us something about this particular individual and enables us to distinguish her from thousands of other mothers.

Self-Attribution

In self-attribution—the attempt to account for our own behaviors—we follow the same general patterns with two main differences. First, there is a general tendency to see the behaviors of others as internally caused but our own behaviors as externally caused. In part this seems due to the fact that in accounting for our own behaviors, we have a great deal more information than we do when accounting for the behaviors of others. For example, we know that we have acted differently in other situations and therefore can more easily attribute this specific behavior to this specific situation. Also, since we cannot focus directly on our own behaviors and see them as objectively as we see the behaviors of others, we focus most of our attention on the environment or situation. Both of these tendencies, then, lead us to attribute the majority of the causes of our own behaviors to situational factors.

The second major difference in self-attribution involves what has been called the *self-serving bias*. Generally, this self-serving bias leads us to take credit for the positive and to deny responsibility for the negative. Thus, when attempting to account for our negative behaviors, we would be more apt to attribute them to situational or environmental factors, and when accounting for our positive behaviors, we are likely to attribute them to internal factors.

[H. H. Kelley, *Personal Relationships: Their Structures and Processes* (Hillsdale, N.J.: Erlbaum, 1979); E. E. Jones and K. E. Davis, "From Acts to Dispositions: The Attribution Process in Person Perception," in *Advances in Experimental Social Psychology,* vol. 2, L. Berkowitz, ed. (New York: Academic Press, 1965), pp. 219–266; S. T. Fiske and S. E. Taylor, *Social Cognition* (Reading, Mass.: Addison-Wesley, 1983); J. H. Harvey and G. Weary, *Perspectives on Attributional Processes* (Dubuque, Iowa: Brown, 1981).]

Attribution Therapy. A therapeutic approach that teaches people to attribute or reattribute problems (for example, insomnia) to external rather than internal forces.

[M. Storms and R. E. Nisbett, "Insomnia and the Attribution Process," *Journal of Personality and Social Psychology* 16 (1970):319–328.]

Audience. A group of people united by a common purpose or exposed to the same message. In public speaking, the individuals are physically together whereas in mass communication situations, such as television, the individuals may be alone. Audiences may be described in terms of such variables as their willingness-unwillingness to listen, their favorableness-unfavorableness to the speaker or purpose, their passivity-activity, their cohesiveness-noncohesiveness, their knowledge or lack of it, and their homogeneity-heterogeneity.

Audience Adaptation. The process of fitting a message to a specific audience.

Audience Analysis. The process of securing information about the nature of one's audience, for example, their ages, economic status, attitudes, beliefs, and the like; one of the essential steps in any effective communication and preliminary to effective audience adaptation.

Audience Composition. The demographic characteristics (age, income, sex, area of residence) of an audience.

Audience Duplication. A measure of the number of listeners/readers reached by more than one message sponsored by the same advertiser.

Audience Flow. The change in the audience during a particular television program or between programs. The number of people who switch from one station to another or from tuning in or off the airwaves.

Audience Profile. The demographic description of those homes or individuals exposed to a message.

Audience Turnover. The changing of the audience during a program or a series of programs.

Audience Variable. The speaker's verbal behavior that is influenced by or under the control of the audience, for example, the people with whom one is interacting. The audience influences both the form and the content of verbal behavior; one speaks differently and about different things to different people.

[B. F. Skinner, *Verbal Behavior* (New York: Appleton-Century-Crofts, 1957).]

Audile. An individual who has an acute ability to perceive imagery stimulated by sound; an individual who comprehends largely in auditory terms.

Audimeter. An electronic device attached to a television set that records its usage. Developed and used by the A. C. Nielsen Company and used now by ARBITRON (q.v.).

Audiogenic. Having its origin in sound; caused by sound.

Audiogram. A record of one's hearing ability.

Audiometer. A device for measuring one's hearing ability.

Audiovisual Aids. Audiovisual aids are one of the most powerful means of amplifying a speech. To aid comprehension and to make ideas vivid and easier to remember, few forms of amplifying material serve as well as the audiovisual aid. A few of the more popular and useful aids are identified here.

Types of Aids

The Actual Object

If you are speaking on the care and feeding of elephants, it would be difficult to bring the actual thing to the audience. On the other hand, if you were talking about the workings of a computer or a lie detector or certain kinds of tropical fish, it might be quite possible to use these as visual aids. As a general rule (to which there are probably many exceptions), the best audiovisual aid is the object itself; bring it to your speech if you possibly can.

Models
Models—replicas of the actual object—are particularly useful when attempting to explain complex structures such as the hearing mechanism, the vocal apparatus, the brain, and the like. These models help to clarify for the audience the size of the various structures, their position, and how they interface with each other.

The Chalkboard
The chalkboard is particularly useful because of its ease of use and general availability. The chalkboard may be effectively used to record key terms or important definitions or even to outline the main structure of the speech.

Transparent and Opaque Projections
Serving a purpose similar to the chalkboard are transparent and opaque projections. A transparency is made from any carbon imprint (pencil, Xerox, or typing done with a carbon ribbon) and then projected onto the wall or a screen, making a relatively small image large enough to be seen from all parts of the room. This is most useful for outlines that are complex and for which you do not wish to take up a great deal of time writing on the board. Another advantage is that you can write on the transparencies while you are speaking—circle important items, underline key terms, and draw important connections among terms. Opaque projections serve a similar function but use the actual page or photograph rather than a specially made transparency. Perhaps the greatest advantage of such projections is that they can be presented to the audience and then removed from sight by just flicking the light switch.

Handouts
Handouts are helpful in explaining complex material and providing audience members with a permanent record of what went on during the lecture. Handouts are also useful for presenting complex information that you want your audience to refer to throughout your speech. Handouts have the disadvantage that if they are extremely interesting or contain information not yet conveyed in your speech, the audience members may peruse them when you would rather they devoted their attention to what you are saying.

Charts, Graphs, and Diagrams
"Graphics" are most useful in conveying a variety of types of information. Organizational charts show clearly how an organization is structured and the relationships among the individuals. Flow charts are excellent for illustrating various processes such as the production of a widget from solid disc to completed, polished, and packaged widget. Bar graphs and line graphs are most useful for showing differences among elements over time.

Maps
Maps are useful for showing not only the obvious geographical elements but for showing changes throughout history, population density, immigration patterns, economic conditions, the location of various resources, and hundreds of other issues you may wish to develop in your speeches.

People
People can function quite effectively as "audiovisual aids." To demonstrate the muscles of the body, for example, a well-built weight lifter is an ideal visual aid. Also, to demonstrate different voice patterns, skin complexions, or hairstyles, people are most appropriate. Aside from the obvious assistance they will provide in demonstrating their muscles or voice qualities, they almost invariably help you to secure and maintain the attention and interest of the audience.

Slides
Slides are useful for showing various scenes or graphics that you simply cannot describe in words. The great advantages of slides are their visual appeal (and hence their attention-getting value) and their ease of preparation and use.

Films, Filmstrips, and Videotapes
Films are especially useful because they enable you to regulate timing more closely. Thus, if during a lecture there are a number of questions, you can easily stop the film to address these issues.

Pictures
Assuming that you do not have films or slides, the next best visual aid is a picture. If the picture is large enough for all members of the audience to see clearly (say, poster size), if it clearly illustrates what you want to illustrate, and if it is mounted on cardboard, then use it. Otherwise, do not.

Records and Tapes
To deliver a speech about music and not provide the audience with samples would seem strange and very likely the audience's attention would be diverted from what you are saying to why you have not provided the actual music. But records and tapes can be useful for many other types of speeches as well. A speech on advertising would be greatly helped, for example, by having actual samples of advertisements as played on radio or television. A tape of such examples would go a long way to help clarify what you are talking about and would also serve to break up the oral presentation most effectively.

Testing Audiovisual Aids as Support
In using audiovisual aids ask yourself the following questions.
1. *Is the aid relevant?* It may be attractive, well-designed, easy to read, and possess all the features one could hope for in an audiovisual aid, but if it is not relevant to the topic, it would be better left at home.
2. *Does the aid reinforce the message?* All messages being sent to the listeners should reinforce each other. The same is true of audiovisual aids. They must reinforce both verbal and nonverbal messages. Audiovisual aids are not something apart from the speech; they are an integral part of the speech as a whole.
3. *Is the message conveyed by the aid evident?* If it is not clear, it will significantly detract from the effect of the speech since the listeners will devote attention to trying to decipher what the aid conveys and lose part of what you are saying in the speech. Two guidelines should govern clarity: First, it should be legible; it should be easy to read. Second, it should be simple enough to comprehend without great difficulty.
4. *Is the aid appealing?* Audiovisual aids, like people, work best when they are appealing. Sloppy, poorly designed, and dirty visual aids will detract from the purpose they are intended to serve. Visual aids should be attractive enough to

engage the attention of the audience, being careful, however, not to make the aid so attractive that it engages the attention of the audience to the point of distraction. The well-developed almost nude body may be effective in selling underwear, but such gimmicks probably detract if your object is to explain the profit-and-loss statement of Exxon.

Using Audiovisual Aids Effectively

In using audiovisual aids keep the following points in mind. First, use the aid only when it is relevant. Show it when you want the audience to concentrate on it and then remove it. If you are using the chalkboard, write the terms or draw the diagrams when you want the audience to see them and then erase them. If you do not remove the visual, the audience's attention may remain focused on the board when you want to go on to something else.

Second, when you are using a number of audiovisual aids, be familiar with their order and subject matter.

Third, when using visual aids, test them prior to the speech. Be certain that they can be easily seen from all parts of the room. Ask someone to react to them so that you can get a fresh and unbiased perspective. If you are using a phonograph, make sure the electricity works for your equipment. If using films, make sure the shades can be pulled down and that the room can be made dark enough for projection.

Fourth, decide exactly how and when you want to use the aids. Rehearse the speech with the audiovisual aids incorporated into the presentation. Practice the actual motions. If you are going to use a chart, how will you use it? Will it stand by itself? Will you tape it to the board? Will you ask someone to hold it? Will you hold it yourself?

Fifth, and most important, do not talk to your visual aid. Talk with your audience at all times. Know your aids so well that you can point to what you want to point to, without breaking eye contact with your audience.

Audit Bureau of Circulation (ABC). An organization that collects and distributes information concerning the circulation of newspapers and magazines.

Audition. The sense or process of hearing. In theatre or film, a trial hearing to test for effectiveness.

Auditory Acuity. The sensitivity of one's hearing ability.

Auditory Aphasia. See RECEPTIVE APHASIA.

Auditory Discrimination. The ability to distinguish one sound from another based on differences in intensity, quality, or pitch.

Auditory Feedback. Feedback of sound; the reception of one's own speech.

Auditory Memory. The memory one has for sound stimuli.

Auditory Threshold. The minimal level necessary for auditory stimulation or hearing.

Auditory Training. Training procedures used to improve a hearing-impaired individual's ability to deal with auditory stimuli, for example, training to use more effectively the hearing ability that remains.

Authoritarian Leader. A group leader who controls the group processes and directs the group toward the goals she or he has selected. See also LAISSEZ-FAIRE LEADER; DEMOCRATIC LEADER.

Authoritarian Personality. A collection of qualities or characteristics which together are regarded as defining a specific personality type characterized by an intolerance for ambiguity, prejudice against minorities, a desire for rigidly struc-

tured interpersonal relationships, a ready submission to authority, and a rejection of those who deviate from the norms of the group.
[Theodor W. Adorno, Else Frenkel-Brunswik, Daniel J. Levinson, and R. Nevitt Sanford, *The Authoritarian Personality* (New York: Harper & Row, 1950).]

Authority, Argument from. An argument based on the opinion of some noted or qualified authority.

Autism. A psychosis affecting children in which they withdraw from society and become unresponsive to social stimuli. The major symptoms of autism are withdrawal, echolalia (q.v.), perseveration (q.v.), and the lack of verbal communication.

Autocompetition. Competition with oneself in an effort to surpass one's previous performance.

Automatic Processing. Processing that is accomplished without conscious guidance and monitoring—it is accomplished smoothly and without effort.

Automatic Speaking. Speech emitted without conscious control. Automatic speech is often seen in adult aphasics who verbalize the months of the year or numbers without any reference to the demands of the communication context.

Automatic Writing. Writing produced without conscious control; refers to the process of writing where the individual concentrates on the content rather than on the physical act of writing.

Autophilia. The love of self. See also NARCISSISM.

Auxesis. A figure of speech in which an extreme term is used to describe an individual or some behavior, for example, "She was Venus come to life."

Auxiliary Channel. An informal interpersonal communication channel built around personal friendships.

Available Audience. That audience theoretically available as receivers for a particular program, usually measured in terms of the number of households.

Avant-Garde. A style of writing or film production, for example, that is experimental in nature and which is innovative in substance and/or style.

Average Audience (AA). As used by Nielsen, the number of households receiving a program during an average television minute.

Avoidance-Avoidance Conflict. A conflict between two alternatives, both of which are negative but one of which must be chosen.

Avoidance Behavior. Behavior designed to avoid negative stimuli.

Avoidance Gradient. The loss in perceived attractiveness as one removes oneself from a negative stimulus. See also APPROACH GRADIENT.

Axiology. A theory of values; a theory of what is good or desired.

Axiom. A universally or nearly universally accepted truth; a proposition that is accepted as true without actual proof, for example, it is axiomatic that communication is complex and that communication is inevitable, although actual proof for the truth of these assumptions has not been produced.

Aye. A yes vote at a meeting.

B

Babble-Luck Theory. A theory of language origin developed by experimental psychologist Edward L. Thorndike proposing that the vocalizations primitives made when they worked or played would, at a later time when repeated, recall that work or play experience. These sounds and sound combinations enabled primitives to more easily remember and recall various situations and soon came to serve as names for these experiences.

Babbling. An early stage of speech development in the child in which vocalizations become syllabic in nature and most include repetitions of various sound combinations.

Babel, Tower of. The famed tower of biblical times constructed in an attempt to reach heaven, but the task was foiled when God made the tower builders speak different languages as their punishment. This reflects the divine origin theory of language differences (from Genesis 11:1–9):

> *The whole earth used the same language and the same speech. While men were migrating eastward, they discovered a valley in the land of Sennaar and settled there. They said to one another, "Come let us make bricks and bake them." They used bricks for stone and bitumen for mortar. They said, "Let us build ourselves a city and a tower with its top in the heavens; let us make a name for ourselves lest we be scattered all over the earth." The Lord came down to see the city and the tower which men had built. And the Lord said, "Truly they are one people and they all have the same language. This is the beginning of what they will do. Hereafter they will not be restrained from anything which they determine to do. Let us go down, and there confuse their language so that they will not understand one another's speech." So the Lord scattered them from that place all over the earth; and they stopped building the city. For this reason it was called Babel, because there the Lord confused the speech of all the earth. From there the Lord scattered them all over the earth.*

Baby Talk. The language used by the adult community in talking to babies or young children and is characterized by the use of a simplified vocabulary and an alteration of the sounds of certain words, for example, "wawa" instead of "water"; the speech of babies.

Backlist. A list of books previously published but still in print more than a year after the date of publication.

Backup Copy. A duplicate copy of a program or text kept in case the original copy is damaged or destroyed.

Balance. A state of psychological comfort in which all the attitude objects in our minds are related as we want them to be or as we psychologically expect them to be; consonance (q.v.); opposed to imbalance (q.v.) or dissonance (q.v.).

Balance Theory. General term denoting those attitude change theories that claim that imbalance motivates attitude changes in the direction of balance restoration; denotes that theory of attitude change developed by Fritz Heider.

The assumptions of balance theory, also referred to as consistency and homeostasis, are simple. The general assumption of all balance theories (and there are numerous variations) is that there is a universal human tendency to maintain balance. *Balance* is a state of psychological comfort in which your attitudes and the objects and persons about which you have attitudes are related as you would want them to be or as you would psychologically expect them to be. The alternative, *imbalance,* is a state of psychological discomfort in which the attitudes and attitude objects are related in ways that are undesirable and psychologically unexpected.

Let me make these two states more specific. If you love someone, you expect that person to love you in return. If that love is returned, you are in a state of balance. But if that love is not returned, you are in a state of imbalance or psychological discomfort. Another example: You expect your best friend to dislike your worst enemy. If this is the case, you are in a state of psychological comfort, of balance. If, on the other hand, your friend likes your enemy, you are in a state of psychological discomfort or imbalance.

Balanced and Unbalanced States

The following three situations are representative of the balanced states:

1. Well-liked Professor Schmedley favors positively evaluated marijuana reform laws $(P + P)$.
2. Disliked Senator Millstone favors negatively evaluated capital punishment $(N + N)$.
3. Well-liked M. M. Birdfood dislikes disliked W. W. Bigtoe $(P - N)$ and vice versa $(N - P)$.

In (1), two positively evaluated objects (denoted by P) relate positively ("favors," denoted by $+$). You expect two positively evaluated objects to be positively connected. You expect two of your friends, for example, to like each other: $P + P$. In (2), two negatively evaluated objects are connected positively ("favors"). You expect two negatively evaluated objects to go together, to like each other. You expect two of your enemies to like each other: $N + N$. In (3), a positively evaluated object relates negatively ("dislikes") to a negatively evaluated object. You expect a positively and a negatively evaluated object to be disconnected (or negatively related). You expect your friend to dislike your enemy: $P - N$.

The following three situations represent states of imbalance or psychological discomfort. In such cases, individuals will be motivated to change their attitudes in order to restore balance.

1. Well-liked Professor Schmedley argues against positively evaluated marijuana reform laws $(P - P)$.
2. Disliked Senator Millstone argues against negatively evaluated capital punishment $(N - N)$.
3. Well-liked M. M. Birdfood likes disliked W. W. Bigtoe $(P + N)$ and vice versa $(N + P)$.

In (1), two positives are negatively related. Since you expect two positives to be positively related (as in the case of two friends liking each other), you are psychologically uncomfortable in this situation. In (2), two negatives are negatively related. Since you expect two negatives to be positively related (as in the case of your two enemies liking each other), you are in a state of psychological discomfort. In (3), a positive and a negative are positively related. Since you expect a positive and a negative to be negatively related (as in the case of expecting your friend to dislike your enemy), you are in a state of imbalance.

The Motivation to Restore Balance

When we are in a state of imbalance, we are motivated to change our attitudes in an effort to restore balance. Consider the three imbalanced situations. In the first, you might restore balance by changing your attitudes toward Professor Schmedley or toward marijuana reform laws. Or you might even change your perception of the connection between the two positively evaluated objects and say, for example, that the good professor objects publicly but privately favors such laws. Any one of these changes would produce balance states.

Note, however, that two changes would only produce another imbalanced state. For example, if you changed your attitude toward both the professor and the reform laws, you would have two negatives negatively connected, $N - N$, another imbalanced state.

In the second example, you might change your negative evaluation of the senator to a positive one or your negative attitude toward capital punishment to a positive one. Or you might perceive the negative connection between the two as somehow not being accurate and come to believe that there is really a positive connection between these two negative objects.

In the third example, you can change your evaluation of either one of the elements (either toward Birdfood or toward Bigtoe) or, as in the previous examples, question the connection between the two attitude objects.

[Fritz Heider, *The Psychology of Interpersonal Relations* (New York: Wiley, 1958).]

Bandwagon Technique. A persuasive technique that urges the audience to accept a certain position or engage in a particular behavior because "everyone is doing it." The appeal is to "jump on the bandwagon" with everyone else; one of the propaganda techniques identified during the Second World War by the Institute for Propaganda Analysis.

[Alfred McClung Lee and Elizabeth Briant Lee, *The Fine Art of Propaganda* [1939], (San Francisco, Calif.: International Society for General Semantics, 1979).]

Barbarisms. Words based on Greek or Latin terms or roots but not formed in strict accordance with the rules of these languages.

Bard–Cannon Theory. See CANNON–BARD THEORY.

Bargaining. A conflict resolution procedure in which the relevant parties attempt to reach agreement through a process of give and take.

[Linda L. Putnam and Tricia S. Jones, "The Role of Communication in Bargaining," *Human Communication Research* 8 (1982):262–280.]

BASIC (Beginner's All-Purpose Symbolic Instruction Code). An easy-to-learn and widely applicable computer language.

Basic English. A "language" developed by C. K. Ogden consisting of 850 English words that could be used to express almost every idea or concept. It was originally designed as a teaching aid to teach the most essential words first, and it became a candidate for a universal language at one time.

The Words of Basic English

a able about account acid across act addition adjustment advertisement after again against agreement air all almost among amount amusement and angle angry animal answer ant any apparatus apple approval arch argument arm army art as at attack attempt attention attraction authority automatic awake

baby back bad bag balance ball band base basin basket bath be beautiful because bed bee before behavior belief bell bent berry between bird birth bit bite bitter black blade blood blow blue board boat body boiling bone book boot bottle box boy brain brake branch brass bread breath brick bridge bright broken brother brown brush bucket building bulb burn burst business but butter button by cake camera canvas card care carriage cart cat cause certain chain chalk chance change cheap cheese chemical chest chief chin church circle clean clear clock cloth cloud coal coat cold collar color comb come comfort committee common company comparison competition complete complex condition connection conscious control cook copper copy cord cork cotton cough country cover cow crack credit crime cruel crush cry cup current curtain curve cushion cut

damage danger dark daughter day dead dear death debt decision deep degree delicate dependent design desire destruction detail development different digestion direction dirty discovery discussion disease disgust distance distribution division do dog door doubt down drain drawer dress drink driving drop dry dust

ear early earth east edge education effect egg elastic electric end engine enough equal error even event ever every example exchange existence expansion experience expert eye

face fact fall false family far farm fat father fear feather feeble feeling female fertile fiction field fight finger fire first fish fixed flag flame flat flight floor flower fly fold food foolish foot for force fork form forward fowl frame free frequent friend from front fruit full future

garden general get girl give glass glove go goat gold good government grain grass gray great green grip group growth guide gun

hair hammer hand hanging happy harbor hard harmony hat hate have he (it, they, etc.) head healthy hearing heart heat help here high history hole hollow hook hope horn horse hospital hour house how humor

I (us, our, etc.) ice idea if ill important impulse increase industry ink insect instrument insurance interest invention iron island

jelly jewel join journey judge jump

keep kettle key kick kind kiss knee knife knot knowledge

land language last late laugh law lead leaf learning leather left leg let letter level library lift light like limit line linen lip liquid list little living lock long look loose loss loud love low

machine make male man manager map mark market married mass match material may (might) meal measure meat medical meeting memory metal middle military milk mind mine minute mist mixed money monkey month moon morning mother motion mountain mouth move much (more, etc.) music muscle

nail name narrow nation natural near necessary neck need needle nerve net new news night no noise normal north nose not note now number nut observation of off offer office oil old on only open operation opinion opposite or orange order organization ornament other out oven over owner

page pain paint paper parallel parcel part past paste payment peace pen pencil person physical picture pig pin pipe place plane plant plate play please pleasure plow pocket point poison polish political poor porter position possible pot potato powder power present price print prison private probable process produce profit property prose protest public pull pump punishment purpose push put

quality question quick quiet quite

rail rain range rat rate ray reaction reading ready reason receipt record red regret regular relation religion representative request respect responsible rest reward rhythm rice right ring river road rod roll roof room root rough round rub rule run

sad safe sail salt same sand say scale school science scissors screw sea seat second secret secretary see seed seem selection self send sense separate serious servant sex shade shake shame sharp sheep shelf ship shirt shock shoe short shut side sign silk silver simple sister size skin skirt sky sleep slip slope slow small smash smell smile smoke smooth snake sneeze snow so soap society sock soft solid some son song sort sound soup south space spade special sponge spoon spring square stage stamp star start statement station steam steel stem step stick sticky stiff still stitch stocking stomach stone stop store story straight strange street stretch strong structure substance such sudden sugar suggestion summer sun support surprise sweet swim system

table tail take talk tall taste tax teaching tendency test than that the then theory there thick thin thing this though thought thread throat through thumb thunder ticket tight till time tin tired to toe together tomorrow tongue tooth top touch town trade train transport tray tree trick trouble trousers true turn twist

umbrella under unit up use

value verse very vessel view violent voice

waiting walk wall war warm wash waste watch water wave wax way weather week weight well west wet wheel when where while whip whistle white who (what, which, etc.) why wide will (would) wind window wine wing winter wire wise with woman wood wool word work worm wound writing wrong

year yellow yes yesterday you (your) young

[C. K. Ogden, *The ABC of Basic English* (1932), *The Basic Words* (1932), and *The Basic Dictionary* (1932).]

Basic Occupational Literacy Test (BOLT). A test used to access the literacy level of persons with mental and/or educational deficiencies.

Bathos. An unintentional descent in significance where the writer or speaker tries to deliver an impassioned pathetic plea but goes to an undesirable extreme and descends to the trivial; a term derived from Alexander Pope's essay, "On Bathos, or of the Art of Sinking in Poetry," in which he parodied Longinus's *On the Sublime.*

Batons. Bodily movements that accent or emphasize a specific word or phrase.

Becoming. In Gordon Allport's (1897–1967) view, a developmental process whereby an individual moves in the direction of self-actualization.
[Gordon Allport, *Becoming: Basic Considerations for a Psychology of Personality* (New Haven, Conn.: Yale University Press, 1955).]

Baud Rate. A measure of the speed with which computers transfer data from one medium to another (measured in bits per second).

Begging the Question. A reasoning fallacy in which the individual avoids the question asked and answers a seemingly similar but actually quite different question.

Behavioral Engineering. The set of principles for the control of behavior based on the work of behavioral psychologists, most notably B. F. Skinner.

Behavioral Objective. A goal or some desired behavior stated in objective, overt terms; behaviors specified without reference to mentalistic concepts. Generally, three major types of objectives are identified: cognitive (q.v.), affective (q.v.), and psychomotor (q.v.).
[Robert J. Kibler, Larry L. Barker, and David T. Miles, *Behavioral Objectives and Instruction* (Boston: Allyn and Bacon, 1970).]

Behavioral Synchrony. A situation in which two people behave in the same way. This synchrony may be a result of one person imitating the nonverbal behavior of the other or it may be simply that the two people behave "spontaneously" in the same way. Although we normally think of behavioral synchrony in connection with general body movements and hand gestures, nonverbal synchrony is also evidenced in posture, (one's way of standing, sitting, or crossing the legs) and verbal synchrony in voice patterns (one's rate of speaking, loudness, or pausing). Generally, behavioral synchrony is taken as an index of mutual liking.

Behaviorism. A school of thought that contended that psychology was the science of behavior and should make no appeals to mentalistic concepts; psychology concerned with stimuli and responses, developed in the United States by such psychologists as John Watson (1878–1958) and B. F. Skinner (1904–   ). Behaviorism has come under considerable attack from the generative grammarians who claim that language cannot be analyzed in terms of stimuli and responses.
[John B. Watson, *Behaviorism* (New York: Norton, 1925); B. F. Skinner, *The Behavior of Organisms* (New York: Appleton-Century-Crofts, 1938).]

Belief. Confidence in the existence or truth of something; a conviction.

Belles-Lettres. From the French meaning "fine letters," light writings, especially on the aesthetics of literature.

Beltlining. An unproductive conflict strategy in which one hits one's opponent below the belt, below the level of tolerance.
[George R. Bach and Peter Wyden, *The Intimate Enemy* (New York: Avon, 1968).]

Bestseller Lists. Lists of best-selling books, compiled from the sales reported by a selected sample of bookstores. Among the most popular bestseller lists are those appearing in the *New York Times Book Review* and in *Publishers Weekly.*

Better Business Bureau. Organization concerned with monitoring unfair business practices.

Bibliography. A list of books and/or articles used in the writing of a book and generally presented either at the end of each chapter or at the end of the book.

Big Lie Technique. Propoganda tactic in which a big lie (a statement that deviates greatly from the truth) is presented repeatedly in the belief that it will be believed more than will a less extreme lie.

Bilingual. Person who has facility in more than one language or sublanguage; sometimes applied to persons who speak two or more dialects of a language or styles of speech. See also COMPOUND BILINGUAL; COORDINATE BILINGUAL.

Binaural. Relating to both ears.

Biofeedback. The self-generated process of "feeding back" to a person information on his or her physiological processes with the goal of enabling that person to more effectively control bodily processes; a technique or procedure by which an individual may control the normally involuntary activity of the body organs and functions.

Biorhythms. Biological rhythms or cycles that are thought to influence the way in which we feel and behave. Three major cycles are usually identified: the *physical* cycle which lasts 23 days, the *sensitivity* cycle which last 28 days, and the *intellectual* cycle which lasts 33 days. The cycles are seen to go through an up period (during which it is thought that one is at one's best) and a down period (during which one is thought to be at one's worst). Also, there are critical days during which the cycles change from up to down or from down to up; during these days the individual is most likely to function at a reduced capacity. The three cycles repeat themselves throughout one's lifetime; exactly where one is at any point in time may be calculated from the time of birth; each cycle begins at birth. [Gay Gaer Luce, *Body Time: Physiological Rhythms and Social Stress* (New York: Pantheon Books, 1971).]

Bit. A shortened form for "binary digit," a measure of information; the amount of information needed to reduce the number of possible alternatives in half.

Black English. An American dialect used by some black speakers. Previous to the 1960s, black English was viewed as a substandard form of English with inconsistent and inadequate rules of grammar. Linguists and sociolinguists, however, demonstrated that black English was not substandard but instead was a dialect of English, with roots in African languages, and with a consistent set of rules of syntax (q.v.), semantics (q.v.), and phonology (q.v.). [Joseph Dillard, *Black English* (New York: Random House, 1972); *Lexicon of Black English* (New York: Seabury, 1977).]

Blacklisting. The technique of censure whereby a person is excluded from getting a job or publishing an article or book. During the 1940s and into the 1950s, many actors, directors, and other film industry people who were at one time members of communist party organizations—or thought to be—were prevented from working by having their name put on a "blacklist" that producers as a group had drawn up.

Blend. A word made from the parts of two other words, for example, *brunch* is a blend formed from *breakfast* and *lunch;* portmaneau word (q.v.); a type of speech error in which two words, similar in meaning, are combined to form a nonexistent "word," for example, the creation of the nonexistent "grastly" from the blending of *grizzly* and *ghastly.*

Blindering. A misevaluation in which a label prevents us from seeing as much of the object as we might see, leaving us "blind"; a process of concentrating on the verbal level while neglecting the nonverbal level; a form of intensional orientation (q.v.). [William V. Haney, *Communication and Organizational Behavior: Text and Cases,* 3d ed. (Homewood, Ill.: Richard D. Irwin, 1973).]

Blind Self. In the Johari model (q.v.), the self that is known to others but not to oneself.

Block Booking. A procedure in which an entire group of programs or films is purchased or leased. These usually include both popular and unpopular programs and the stations or theatre owner is forced to take the unpopular with the popular.

Body Contact Needs. The need to touch others and be touched by others.

Body Language. A form of nonverbal communication (q.v.) in which messages are communicated by gesture, posture, spatial relations, and so forth; a popular term covering all aspects of nonverbal communication but more correctly limited to those messages communicated by movements and changes in the body.

Body-Mind Problem. See MIND-BODY PROBLEM.

Body Satisfaction. The degree to which one is satisfied or dissatisfied with one's own body.

[E. Berscheid, E. Walster, and G. Bohrnstedt, "The Happy American Body: A Survey Report," *Psychology Today* 7 (1973):119–123, 126, 128–129.]

Body Type. The major characteristics of body type or physique in males, and to a lesser extent in females, can be described under three general headings: (1) endomorphy, the fatty dimension; (2) mesomorphy, the muscular dimension; and (3) ectomorphy, the skinny dimension. We might then attempt to classify any given body in terms of the degree to which it possessed each of these three dimensions. Each body would be described by a three-digit number, with each digit a number from 1 to 7. The first number would describe the endomorphic dimension, the second the mesomorphic dimension, and the third the ectomorphic dimension. An extremely fat individual, for example, the fat man or woman of the circus, would be described as 7-1-1 indicating that he or she is high on endomorphy but low on the other two dimensions. Mr. America, Hercules, and Atlas would be described as 1-7-1—all muscle. The thin man or woman of the circus would be 1-1-7—just skin and bones. Of course few people are at these extremes. We might attempt to illustrate this by estimating the body types of persons who most of us have seen. Johnny Carson, for example, might be described as 2-5-4, whereas Merv Griffin might be described as 3-4-2. Joe Namath might be described as 3-6-1 and Mick Jagger as 1-3-6. These, of course, are simply estimates that illustrate the concept; they are not accurate measurements. These three-digit numbers, then, represent one's *somatotype,* or the degree to which a person is fat, muscular, and skinny. Male examples are used here because these body types were formulated on the basis of studies of the male body.

Try to picture the following individuals as they are described; try to see their physical characteristics or, better still, attempt to draw them.

Person 1. This man is dominant, confident, impetuous, domineering, enterprising, adventurous, competitive, determined, and hot-tempered.

Person 2. This man is dependent, contented, sluggish, placid, affable, tolerant, forgiving, sociable, generous, soft-hearted.

Person 3. This man is tense, anxious, withdrawn, cautious, serious, introspective, suspicious, cool, precise.

If your responses were consistent with those of others to whom similar tests were given, you probably pictured Person 1 as high on mesomorphy, as having a rather muscular build. Person 2 was probably pictured as high in endomorphy, as rather short and fat. Person 3 was probably pictured as high in ectomorphy, as relatively tall and thin.

There is considerable debate over the relationship between personality characteristics, such as those listed above, and somatotype. Some research does seem to indicate a rather strong relationship between body build and personality. A further question is "To what can this relationship be ascribed?" Is it genetic? Are people born with tall skinny bodies also born with certain personality traits, such as tenseness, withdrawnness, and so on? Is the relationship cultural? Are heavy people expected to be affable, sluggish, tolerant, forgiving, and so on, and do they therefore take on these characteristics, which everyone seems to think they possess anyway? This question has not been settled. What is clear is that people have certain reactions to different body types; the body types communicate something to us. We expect the heavy person to be sociable, generous, and affable. We expect the muscular individual to be dominant, confident, impetuous, and hot-tempered. We expect the thin person to be tense, precise, cool, and suspicious. At least in general we seem to have these expectations. Whether or not our judgments are well founded, we do seem to make inferences about people's personality from merely looking at their body build. And just as we have expectations of others based on their body build, they will have expectations of us based on our body build. Further, if these stereotypes are strong enough—and in many cases they seem to be—we will have expectations about ourselves based on our body build. The fact that these characteristics, these stereotypes, are so common across large sections of the population attests to the importance of body build in nonverbal communication.

It should also be noted that because of these different perceptions, we will also have different perceptions of the same actions when they are performed by persons of a different body build. For example, if a man at a dance sits in the corner with his head down and his arms clasped in front of him, we would probably read different things into this depending on whether he were heavy, muscular, or thin.

See also SOMATOTYPE.

Bonding. The process whereby people are joined together into a cohesive unit; an intimate or close connection between two or more people; an intense affiliation; a stage in the development of a close interpersonal relationship.
[Arthur P. Bochner, "The Functions of Human Communication in Interpersonal Bonding," in *Handbook of Rhetorical and Communication Theory,* Carroll C. Arnold and John Waite Bowers, eds. (Boston: Allyn and Bacon, 1984), pp. 544–621.]

Bone Deafness. Hearing loss caused by damage to the bones of the middle ear.

Bon Mot. From the French meaning "good word," a clever or witty expression.

Boomerang Effect. The effect of a message that is opposite to that intended by the source or persuader; repeated or prolonged exposure to messages that are consistent with one's attitudes but at times lead to a lessening of commitment to these attitudes—the messages have a boomerang effect.
[David L. Paletz, Judith Koon, Elizabeth Whitehead, and Richard B. Hagens, "Selective Exposure: The Potential Boomerang Effect," *Journal of Communication* 22 (1972):48–53.]

Bound Morpheme. A morpheme (q.v.) that cannot stand alone, for example, the adverbial *-ly* or the prefix *non-* or *un-*. See also FREE MORPHEME.

Bowdlerize. Derived from the Reverend Thomas Bowdler (1754–1825) who eliminated passages from Shakespeare he felt were unfit for mixed company. The term now refers to the procedures of expurgating certain passages, which might be considered "unfit," from literary works.

Braille. A system of writing invented by Louis Braille (1809–1852) consisting of raised-dot letters in various configurations that enable the blind to "read" through their sense of touch.

Brainstorming. A technique for literally bombarding a problem and generating as many ideas as possible. In this system group members meet in two periods: the first is the brainstorming period proper and the second is the evaluation period. The procedure is relatively simple. A problem is selected that is amenable to many possible solutions or ideas. Group members are informed of the problem to be brainstormed before the actual session so that some prior thinking on the topic is done. When the group meets, each person contributes as many ideas as he or she can think of. Ideas should be recorded either in writing or on tape. During this idea-generating session four general rules are followed.

1. *No negative criticism is allowed.* All ideas are treated in exactly the same way; they are written down by a secretary. They are not evaluated in this phase, nor are they even discussed. Any negative criticism—whether verbal or nonverbal—is itself criticized by either the leader or the members.

2. *Quantity is desired.* The assumption made here is that the more ideas the better; somewhere in a large pile of ideas will be one or two good ones that may be used. The more ideas generated, the more effective the brainstorming session.

3. *Combinations and extensions are desired.* While we may not criticize a particular idea, we may extend it or combine it in some way. The value of a particular idea, it should be noted, may well be in the way it stimulates another member to combine or extend it.

4. *Freewheeling is wanted.* By "freewheeling" is meant that the wilder the idea the better. Here the assumption is that it is easier and generally more profitable to tone an idea down than to spice it up. A wild idea can easily be tempered, but it is not as easy to elaborate on a simple or conservative idea.

After all the ideas are generated—a period that takes no longer than 15 or 20 minutes—the entire list of ideas is evaluated, and the ones that are unworkable are thrown out while the ones that show promise are retained and evaluated. Here, of course, negative criticism is allowed.

[Alex F. Osborn, *Applied Imagination* (New York: Scribners, 1957).]

Brainwashing. A technique of psychological manipulation intended to gain the total attitudinal conversion of an individual. Made especially popular during the Korean War, reports were widely circulated that the North Koreans and the Chinese were able to totally change the loyalties of those they captured by "brainwashing" them. These reports, however, were greatly exaggerated.

Brand Name Author. An author who has a reputation as a best-selling writer.

Breadth. The number of topics about which individuals in a relationship communicate. As relationships become more and more intimate, the breadth gets wider. See also SOCIAL PENETRATION.

Breakdown in Communication. The failure to communicate intended meaning or message, usually applied to situations in which there is a gross or total lack of communication.

Breathiness. Vocal quality characterized by excessive breath being used in speaking with the result that the speech sounds whispered. Breathiness is caused by the vocal folds not being brought together and thereby allowing excessive air to escape while speaking.

Brief. In law, a statement of a case in which the central issues are defined and arguments are developed.

Broca's Area. Named after surgeon Paul Broca (1824–1880), that area of the brain that controls the expressive language function. Damage to this area results in expressive aphasia (q.v.), the inability of an individual to express himself or herself.

Buffer. A temporary storage area used to hold data in its passage from one system to another.

Burden of Proof. In any debate or argument, the responsibility of proving a point, for example, the one who would argue to change the status quo assumes the burden of proof and must demonstrate that the status quo should be changed. The concept was developed by Richard Whately (1787–1863) in his *Rhetoric* (1828). See also PRESUMPTION.

Burnout. Psychological (but sometimes accompanied by physical) exhaustion brought on by job-related stress.
[Herbert J. Freudenberger with Geraldine Richelson, *Burn Out* (New York: Bantam, 1980).]

Buzz Groups. A small group communication technique in which a large group is broken down into small groups in which each discusses one or more issues and reports back to the entire group the results of their deliberations. These results are then pooled.

Buzz Words. The terminology adopted by an "ingroup" and used to facilitate ingroup communication; "the language of leadership: words, phrases or zingo-lingo used by an ingroup, a cult, or the cognoscenti for rapid communication within the group, i.e., sport model language stripped down to get more speed with less horsepower."
[Robert Kirk Mueller, *Buzzwords: A Guide to the Language of Leadership* (New York: Van Nostrand Reinhold, 1974).]

Bylaws. The rules by which a group or organization operates and conducts its business.

Byline. The author's name appearing with the published article.

By-Passing. A misevaluation caused by the same word being used but with the speaker and listener giving it a different meaning.
[William V. Haney, *Communication and Organizational Behavior: Text and Cases,* 3d ed. (Homewood, Ill.: Irwin, 1973).]

Bystander Effect. The situation in which observers fail to aid strangers in distress. Generally, the more observers, the less likely will anyone intervene to offer aid; also referred to as bystander apathy. See also DIFFUSION OF RESPONSIBILITY.
[B. Latane and J. M. Darley, *The Unresponsive Bystander: Why Doesn't He Help?* (New York: Appleton-Century-Crofts, 1970).]

Byte. Eight bits of information; the combination of bits that represent a character (a number or a letter).

Cable Penetration. The percentage of homes subscribing to cable TV compared to the total number of homes with television.

Cable TV. A television system whereby signals are sent and may be received through wires, for example, telephone cables. The central source may transmit signals picked up from satellites or may send original programming; reception of such programming is by subscription for which a fee is charged.

Cacophony. Unpleasant, unharmonious sounds; opposed to euphony (q.v.).

California Test of Personality. Widely used questionnaire-type test for all age levels, designed to measure total adjustment, personal worth, self-reliance, be-longingness, and various social skills.

Calligraphy. Beautiful, script penmanship; fancy, ornate lettering.

Call System. Communication system used by some animals for intraspecies communication.

Canalization. Articulated by Gardner Murphy, the psychological process through which motivational energy is channeled into behavior. In mass media, the tendency of the media to channel general behavior patterns into specific behaviors, for example, given a pattern to buy expensive jeans, the media functions to channel or canalize this behavior into buying specific name brands. See also CANALIZE.
[Gardner Murphy, *Personality: A Biosocial Approach to Origins and Structures* (New York: Harper & Row, 1947).]

Canalize. The process of channeling (or canalizing) an attitude or behavior pattern in a particular direction once a desired effect has been established; a type of persuasive function served by the media. See also CANALIZATION; MASS COMMUNICATION FUNCTIONS.

Cannon–Bard Theory. A theory of emotion holding that environmental stimuli trigger hypothalamic responses which in turn send impulses to the brain (resulting in awareness or cognitive recognition) and to the autonomic nervous system; a theory of emotions holding that feelings (for example, smiling or crying) are experienced before cognitive recognition (for example, happiness or sadness); opposed to the James–Lange theory (q.v.).

Canon 35. Guideline of the American Bar Association prohibiting the use of television/recording equipment in court during trials.

Canons of Rhetoric. The major areas with which rhetoric (q.v.) is concerned. In classical rhetoric, there were five canons: invention (finding the issues and arguments), disposition (the arrangement of ideas or organization and organizational strategies), elocution (style and language), memoria (memory), and disposition (delivery).

Cant. A kind of sublanguage (q.v.); the conversational language of a special group, usually a lower social-class group, generally understood only by members of the subculture.

Caption. Text that accompanies a photograph or drawing and that explains its content and connection with the text in which it appears. Also referred to as a "cutline."

Card Stacking. A persuasive technique whereby the advocate includes only that information which will make his or her case as effective as possible. As a propaganda tactic, card stacking refers to the situation in which a speaker advises the audience against listening to any argument or information which may be counter to the position being advocated.

Caretaker Speech. The speech of those who take care of babies that generally uses a simplified vocabulary, exaggerates the intonation patterns, and uses short simple sentences. Also known as "baby talk" (q.v.).
[Breyne Arlene Moskowitz, "The Acquisition of Language," *Scientific American* 239 (1978):92–108.]

Carrier Wave. High frequency wave; the information wave is superimposed on this carrier wave so that the information wave may travel through the air. See also INFORMATION WAVE.

Case Grammar. An approach to grammar that focuses on the semantic roles that words play in a sentence (that is, their "cases" such as agent or instrument) and derives the surface structure (q.v.) of a sentence from these underlying cases.
[Charles Fillmore, "The Case for Case," in *Universals in Linguistic Theory*, Emmon Bach and R. T. Harms, eds. (New York: Holt, Rinehart and Winston, 1968), pp. 1–90.]

Case Study. A research technique in which usually one individual or entity is studied. The assumption usually made here is that this one subject, this sole case, is representative of some larger group.

Casual Group. A temporary (usually short-lived) group of individuals who did not know each other before a given encounter and will not likely meet again, for example, people waiting on line for a movie or people in a restaurant.

Catalogia. The process of repeating meaningless words, phrases, and sentences; also known as verbigeration.

Catch Words. Striking, easily identifiable terms used to gain (catch) attention; also known as vogue words (q.v.) or buzz words (q.v.). In books (especially dictionaries), the words used at the top of the page to identify the page's contents.

Categorical Perception. The perceptual phenomenon that refers to our ability to perceive differences between categories but not within categories, for example, we can readily distinguish differences between the phonemes (q.v.) /p/ and /b/ but not the differences within the phoneme /p/ or /b/.
[Michael Studdert-Kennedy, "The Perception of Speech," in *Current Trends in Linguistics XII*, T. A. Sebeok, ed. (The Hague: Mouton, 1974), pp. 2349–2385 and David Pisoni, "Speech Perception," in *Handbook of Learning and Cognitive Processes*, vol. 6, W. K. Estes, ed. (Hillsdale, N.J.: Erlbaum, 1978), pp. 167–234.]

Catharsis. In media, the reduction of the tendency toward violent behaviors by viewing violent acts in the media. In psychoanalytic theory, the reduction of tension produced by "reliving" or retelling traumatic experiences.

Cause, Argument from. A form of argument in which one reasons from a known cause to some unknown but predicted effect, for example, in the familiar smoking and cancer connection, one reasons from the cause (smoking) to conclude that the effect will be cancer.

Censor. In psychoanalytic theory, that aspect of the personality that determines what thoughts or feelings enter consciousness and which are prevented from reaching consciousness because they may be too emotional or too threatening. In media, the person or organization that determines which messages may be made public and which should not be allowed public presentation.

Censorship. The act of preventing certain messages from being received by all or some particular portion of the population.

Central Deafness. Loss of hearing ability due to damage to the auditory nerve, the hearing centers in the brain, or the nerve pathways.

Central Processing Unit (CPU). The "brain" of the computer consisting of two parts: the ALU or the arithmetic-logic unit (the unit that performs arithmetical and logical functions), and the CS or control section (the unit that converts machine language instructions into the signals needed to effect the desired instructions).

Cerebral Dominance. The phenomenon whereby one-half of the brain assumes primary control of some processes.

Cerebral Palsy. Paralysis or lack of ability to coordinate muscular movements caused by intracranial damage and often affecting speech processes.

Cerebrotonia. A temperament type of the ectomorphic personality as developed by William Sheldon; characterized by tenseness and withdrawal from others.
[William Sheldon and S. S. Stevens, *The Varieties of Temperament* (New York: Harper & Row, 1942).]

Certainty. An attitude of closed-mindedness that creates a defensiveness (q.v.) among communication participants; opposed to provisionalism (q.v.).

Chain. A group of magazines or newspapers owned by one company, for example, Time, Inc. owns *Time, Life, Fortune, Sports Illustrated, People,* and *Money;* the Hearst Corporation owns *Good Housekeeping, Cosmopolitan, Harper's Bazaar, Popular Mechanics,* and *House Beautiful;* the Johnson Publishing Corporation owns *Ebony, Jet,* and *Tan.* Also used to refer to a communication network (q.v.) in which messages are sent from one person to another along a chainlike sequence.

Chained Responses. A series of responses that are frequently emitted together (as in typewriting, opening a lock, or tieing one's shoes) and become as links in a chain where one response serves as a stimulus for the next response, and so on.

Chair. A person who presides at a meeting; a nonsexist term that seems to be replacing the masculine *chairman* and the awkward *chairperson.*

Channel. The vehicle or medium through which signals are sent.

Channel Capacity. The maximum amount of signals or information that a communication channel can handle at any given time. Also used to refer to the number of channels available (currently or potentially) to a cable television system's subscriber.

Character. One of the qualities of credibility (q.v.); the honesty, basic nature, and morals of an individual speaker as perceived by the audience.

Characterization. The creation and depiction of persons in works of fiction.

Charisma. The power of an individual (by virtue of his or her personality and mannerisms) to influence others and to evoke strong positive responses.

Charismatic Term. See ULTIMATE TERMS.

Charlatan. From the Italian *ciarlare* meaning "to chatter," a fast, smooth talker who only pretends to have knowledge or skill.

Chemistry-Binders. A class of life characterized by the ability to combine chemicals in order to grow and survive; plants are chemistry-binders. See also SPACE-BINDERS; TIME-BINDERS.

Cherishing Behaviors. Positive behaviors that a person enjoys receiving. Four characteristics of cherishing behaviors are identified by William Lederer: the behaviors must be (1) specific and positive; (2) apart from any that you have quarreled over in the past; (3) those that can be done every day; and (4) minor or relatively easy to do. Examples are: Complimenting how you look in the morning, telling a neighbor you love me, smiling when you come home.
[William J. Lederer, *Creating a Good Relationship* (New York: Norton, 1984).]

Chiasmus. A figure of speech in which the terms used in one clause are presented in reverse order in the following clause, for example, "Let yourself love others, let others love you."

Child Ego State. In Transactional Analysis (q.v.), the ego state (q.v.) of Child is actually a three-part state. The Child may be the Natural Child, the Adapted Child, or the Little Professor.

The Natural Child is spontaneous, creative, intuitive, and rebellious. This Child does what he or she wants to do—and that is to have fun, play games, have sex, and otherwise please one's various appetites. This Child wants to explore new things and go to new places. The Natural Child will frequently use such expressions as "can't," "don't want to," "Is this O.K.?" "Let's play," "You don't love me," "Doesn't everybody love me?" "This is mine," "Don't hit me." Nonverbally, the Natural Child cries and screams and maintains an uninhibited posture regardless of the social situation. This Child bites his or her nails and picks his or her nose whenever the urge presents itself. If a person is denied something, he or she is apt to go into the Natural Child state and perhaps scream and yell (sometimes literally and sometimes figuratively) or otherwise demand what is wanted right now.

The Adapted Child is the Child socialized by the various Parent messages he or she has heard. This Child obeys the directives of the parents, modifies his or her behaviors on the basis of the commands of the parents, and otherwise does what the parents want and perhaps even becomes what the parents want (a teacher, a doctor, an alcoholic) when he or she gets older. In all of the responses of this Child we see the influence of the parents; in fact, we often see the parents themselves in miniature. This Child may also adapt to the parents by withdrawing, crying, or having a temper tantrum.

The Little Professor is the Adult but on a smaller scale. The Little Professor grows from the Child who is learning about the world outside and the world inside his or her own skin. The Little Professor gets even stronger as the individual grows older and becomes able to feel, taste, and smell everything in the environment. Frequently the Little Professor behaves as an Adult would—for example, gathering information and analyzing alternative modes of action. The difference between the two is that Little Professors do what they do with emotion, because they want to do it, because they are deriving enjoyment and reinforcement from their behaviors. See also ADULT EGO STATE; PARENT EGO STATE.

Chip. An electronic component that performs the functions of computing, for example, taking the information input on the keyboard and sending it to the CRT (q.v.) or to a disk; integrated circuit.

Chirology. A system of hand gestures used for communicating one's feelings and thoughts, and used extensively in elocutionary training and for communicating with the deaf.

Chreia. An elementary rhetorical exercise used in Greco-Roman education to teach the student to amplify a topic, its contemporary counterpart being the exercise to develop a theme around a thesis or topic sentence; a short exposition of something said or done.
[Donald Lemen Clark, *Rhetoric in Greco-Roman Education* (New York: Columbia University Press, 1957).]

Chronemics. The use of time as a form of nonverbal communication.

Chunking. The process by which remembered material is mentally reorganized into larger units, or chunks, thus increasing the amount of information that short-term memory can retain.

Cinemascope. Wide-screen motion picture system; trademark for a film system that compresses wide-angle images into regular-sized film for processing but which, during projection, allows the image to be expanded to fill a wide screen with minimal or no distortion.

Cinema Vérité. From the French meaning "film truth," a form of filmaking characterized by the filming of people as they really are, often with hidden cameras, real sounds, and little or no rehearsal or editing.

Circular Reasoning. Arguing in a circle *(circulus in probando)*; a fallacious argument in which the conclusion is inserted into the premise, for example, arguing that this car is a real bargain simply because the car dealer said it is, with no proof being given for the car being a bargain other than the dealer's saying it is so.

Circumlocution. Speech or writing that goes all around an issue rather than focusing on it directly and immediately; speech characteristic of certain aphasias (q.v.).

Civil Inattention. Polite ignoring of another so as not to invade his or her privacy. [Erving Goffman, *Interaction Ritual: Essays on Face-to-Face Behavior* (Garden City, N.Y.: Anchor, 1967).]

Claim. In Toulmin's system of argument (q.v.), the conclusion that the advocate wishes the receiver to agree with. Claims may concern policies, values, or facts.

Clang. A word that sounds like another word; a clang associate is a word given in response to a stimulus word it sounds like, for example, *moon, tune, soon.*

Classical Conditioning. A form of conditioning in which an originally neutral stimulus (the conditioned stimulus, CS) is repeatedly paired with an unconditioned stimulus (UCS) and through these repeated pairings comes to elicit a response (a conditioned response, CR) similar to the response emitted by the unconditioned stimulus. In Ivan Pavlov's (1849–1936) experiment, ringing the bell (CS) was repeatedly paired with the meat powder (UCS), with the result that after such pairings the bell came to elicit a response similar to the responses elicited by the meat powder, that is, salivation. Also referred to as "Pavlovian conditioning." See also OPERANT CONDITIONING.

Classical Rhetoric. A view of rhetoric (q.v.) that designates invention (q.v.) as the central canon of rhetoric (q.v.); a view of rhetoric based on the doctrines of Cicero.

Classification. A methodology used to identify the semantic features of words and to obtain measures of the degree of similarity or difference between words.

In classification a group of words are selected and are given to subjects to group into various classes. If a list of twelve words is given, each subject groups together the words that seem similar, forming two, three, four, five, or however many word groups seem necessary. After all the subjects have done this, a matrix similar to that presented in the following illustration is drawn, and the number of people who have put each word pair in the same group is entered in the appropriate box. In this way the similarity in meaning among various words can be measured. Those words that are put in similar groups by many people are judged as being more closely related in meaning than those words that are put in similar groups by only a few people.

	Dog	Metal	Hate	Gold	Lion	Flower	Glass	Wisdom	Love	Doctor
Dog		0	1	9	20	12	0	6	11	16
Metal			4	20	2	5	20	0	1	2
Hate				2	4	0	2	14	18	4
Gold					2	5	20	2	6	5
Lion						14	0	4	4	12
Flower							1	2	7	6
Glass								2	0	1
Wisdom									11	9
Love										10
Doctor										

Classification matrix.

[George A. Miller, "Empirical Methods in the Study of Semantics," *Semantics: An Interdisciplinary Reader in Philosophy, Linguistics and Psychology* (London: Cambridge University Press, 1971), pp. 569–585.]

Classifying Abstracting. A form or type of abstracting (q.v.) in which one places an object, person, or event in a particular class. See also EVALUATIVE ABSTRACTING; OBJECTIVE ABSTRACTING; RELATIONAL ABSTRACTING.

Clause. A series of words containing a subject and predicate. An independent clause is a complete sentence and may stand alone; a dependent clause is incomplete and must be combined with an independent clause to make a grammatically acceptable sentence.

Clever Hans. A horse that was once thought able to understand and use language; used frequently as a warning against anthropomorphism (q.v.).
[Oskar Pfungst, *Clever Hans: The Horse of Mr. Von Osten,* C. L. Rahn, trans., Robert Rosenthal, ed. (New York: Holt, Rinehart and Winston, 1965).]

Cliché. Derives from the French word for the printing plate used to print the same image over and over again. In language, an expression that is used so often that it calls attention to itself and whose meaning is either lost or considerably reduced because of its overuse.

Click Studies. A series of studies on sentence processing (how sentences are analyzed and understood) using clicks (click sounds superimposed on speech) whose locations had to be identified by subjects, and which were taken as signs of syntactic boundaries and the psychological reality of various linguistic units.
[Jerry A. Fodor, Thomas G. Bever, and M. F. Garrett, *The Psychology of Language* (New York: McGraw-Hill, 1974).]

Client-Centered Therapy. Developed largely by Carl Rogers (1902–   ) (who felt that psychoanalysis was "therapist centered"), a form of psychotherapy characterized by nondirective counseling where the therapist builds a permissive environment and offers encouragement rather than specific directions. The assumption here is that the person best equipped to deal with the client's problems is the actual client.
[Carl R. Rogers, *Client-Centered Therapy: Its Current Practice, Implications, and Theory* (Boston, Mass.: Houghton Mifflin, 1951).]

Climax. A figure of speech in which the individual phrases or sentences are arranged in ascending order of forcefulness, for example, "As a child he lied, as a youth he stole, as a man he killed."

Climax Order. A pattern of arranging the main ideas or the evidence in a communication in which the specifics are presented first and the general conclusion is presented last (as the climax).

Closed Marriage. A marriage arrangement where the parties agree that there will be no extramarital entanglements; opposed to open marriage (q.v.) where such extramarital arrangements are permissible and may even be sought actively.

Closed-mindedness. An unwillingness to receive certain communication messages; unwillingness to consider opposing points of view. See also DOGMATISM.

Closed Question. A question that asks for a short specific answer; a question that allows the respondent little freedom to elaborate or qualify; opposed to an open-ended question (q.v.).

Closed System. A system that cannot be altered; a system to which new elements and relationships cannot be added.

Closure. In perception, the tendency to fill in and complete an otherwise incomplete figure or statement.

Cloze Procedure. A technique, based on the Gestalt motion of closure (q.v.), used to measure the difficulty of written messages. In cloze, a message is mutilated by deleting every n^{th} word (usually every fifth word); the extent to which receivers can fill in the omitted words is the cloze score and a measure of the difficulty of the passage.

[Wilson Taylor, "Cloze Procedure: A New Tool for Measuring Readability," *Journalism Quarterly* 30 (1953):415–433.]

Cluttering. Jumbled speech that is difficult (at times impossible) to understand; speech in which words are run together, syllables interchanged, and words slurred.

Coaction. Two (or more) individuals working individually on the same problem or task in the same area.

Coarticulation. The phenomenon in which articulatory movements of the mouth and tongue made for one sound overlap with the movements made for the next or subsequent neighboring sounds.

COBOL (Common Business Oriented Language). A computer language designed for and especially applicable to business concerns.

Cochlea. A snail-shaped structure of the internal ear which contains the basilar membrane containing the hair cells of the eighth cranial nerve; the auditory mechanism of the internal ear.

Cocktail Party Effect. The process of listening to messages from one source even though there are many people communicating at the same time; localizing one message source and attending to it while not attending to other competing sources.

[Irwin Pollock and J. M. Pickett, "The Cocktail Party Effect," *Journal of the Acoustical Society of America* 19 (1957):1262.]

Cocktail Party Talk. The meaningless talk that goes on at cocktail parties; gossip and talk about other people that is kept on an extremely superficial level.

Code. A set of symbols used to translate a message from one form to another.

Code Mixing. The process of speaking in basically one language while inserting words, phrases, or larger units from another language. See also CODE SWITCHING.

[Mats Thelander, "Code-Switching or Code-Mixing?" *Linguistics* 183 (1976):103–124.]

Code Switching. The process of changing from using one linguistic code or dialect to another. In some languages different formalized dialects are used for, say, a formal lecture and an informal question-and-answer session; in English, code switching would involve the change from a formal and polite form to a more informal "street" style of speaking.

[John Gumperz, "The Sociolinguistic Significance of Conversational Code-switching," *RELC Journal* 8 (1977):1–34.]

Codifiability. The way in which a concept is expressed in a language. High codifiability refers to a short linguistic expression for a concept whereas low codifiability refers to a long linguistic expression.

Coding. In memory, putting information to be remembered into a code or system that can be more easily remembered and retrieved.

Coercion. The act of forcing another's compliance by means other than those of persuasion.

Coercive Power. The ability to punish individuals for noncompliance with one's directives. Punishment may take the form of removing or withholding a positive stimulus (for example, food, money, social approval) or the presentation of a negative stimulus (for example, physical punishment, prison confinement, social disapproval).

[William T. McGuire, "The Nature of Attitudes and Attitude Change," in *The Handbook of Social Psychology,* 2d ed., vol. 3, Gardner Lindsey and Eliot Aronson, eds. (Reading, Mass.: Addison-Wesley, 1969).]

Cognate. A word that is related to another through having the same origin.

Cognition. A general term denoting the variety of ways of "knowing," for example, memory, perception, judgment, comprehension, reason.

Cognitive Behavior Modification. A therapeutic procedure designed to identify maladaptive thought patterns and replace these with more appropriate ones. Also known as "cognitive restructuring." See also RATIONAL-EMOTIVE THERAPY.

Cognitive Complexity. The quality whereby an individual has a great number of concepts with which to address an issue, say, describing people, and which allows the cognitively complex individual to make finer differentiations than those possessing a fewer number of concepts; the degree of differentiation in a person's construction system (the sum total of a person's constructions); the degree to which a person has different and distinct categories for judgment. It is generally assumed that persons who have a high degree of cognitive complexity are more competent communicators.
[Daniel J. O'Keefe and Howard E. Sypher, "Cognitive Complexity Measures and the Relationship of Cognitive Complexity to Communication," *Human Communication Research* 8 (1981):72–92.]

Cognitive Disclaimer. A type of disclaimer (q.v.) in which the speaker confirms his or her own cognitive capacity: "I know you'll think I'm crazy but I'm as lucid as anyone." See also DISCLAIMER.

Cognitive Dissonance. A state of discomfort created by two cognitions (two items of knowledge) that are psychologically inconsistent, for example, the knowledge that one smokes and the knowledge that smoking is harmful will create cognitive dissonance since the two cognitions are inconsistent.
[Leon Festinger, *A Theory of Cognitive Dissonance* (Stanford, Calif.: Stanford University Press, 1957).]

Cognitive Dissonance Theory. A balance theory (q.v.) of attitude change that holds that an individual will be motivated to change attitudes when in a state of cognitive dissonance (q.v.), a condition of psychological discomfort brought about when two elements are related in such a way that the obverse of one element follows from the other. The attitude change predicted is in the direction of reducing the amount of dissonance and restoring consonance. See also DISSONANCE.

Cognitive Domain. That area of learning (behavioral objectives, q.v.) concerned with intellectual or cerebral issues, for example, the acquisition of information or new knowledge. See also BEHAVIORAL OBJECTIVE.

Cognitive Overload. See INFORMATION OVERLOAD.

Cognitive Processes. The variety of psychological processes through which one deals with information including, for example, perception, comprehension, and memory.

Cognitive Restructuring. See COGNITIVE BEHAVIOR MODIFICATION.

Cognitive Theory. Any theory that postulates the operation of intervening (mental) variables in an attempt to explain behavior, learning, memory, and so on. Cognitive theory is in contrast to behavior theory (q.v.) or stimulus-response theories which do not make use of such intervening variables.

Coherence. The comprehensibility of the connections between the various parts of the speech or essay; the unity of a conversation or discourse; the relevance of one utterance to adjacent utterances and to the discourse as a whole.

[Margaret L. McLaughlin, *Conversation: How Talk Is Organized* (Beverly Hills, Calif.: Sage, 1984).]

Cohesiveness. The property of togetherness. As applied to group communication situations, it refers to the mutual attractiveness among members; a measure of the extent to which individual members of a group work together as a group.

COIK. Acronym for "clear only if known," referring to messages that are unintelligible for anyone who does not already know what the messages refer to.

[Edgar Dale, "Clear Only If Known," *The News Letter* (School of Education, Ohio State University), 31 (April 1966):1–4.]

Collaboration. An interpersonal relationship that includes cooperation and sensitivity to the needs of the other; a joint venture.

[Harry Stack Sullivan, *The Interpersonal Theory of Psychiatry* (New York: Norton, 1953).]

Collapsing the Communication Float. Reducing the time it takes to send and respond to messages.

[John Naisbitt, *Megatrends* (New York: Avon, 1984).]

Colloquial. A level of language usage characteristic of informal speech.

Colloquialism. Language characteristic of informal speech; an informal expression.

Colloquy. A form of small group communication in which a panel of experts discuss a topic and audience members ask questions and comment on the panel's observations during the discussion. An amateur panel may also be used to question the experts, and the discussion may be followed by additional questions and comments from the audience.

Colophon. Originally, a symbol placed at the end of a handwritten manuscript or book to identify the author, but now more commonly used to refer to the publisher's symbol or emblem. Also known as a "tailpiece."

Color Communication. When we are in debt we speak of being "in the red"; when we make a profit we are "in the black." When we are sad we are "blue," when we are healthy we are "in the pink," when we are jealous we are "green with envy," and when we are happy we are "tickled pink." To be a coward is to be "yellow" and to be inexperienced is to be "green." When we talk a great deal we talk "a blue streak," and when we talk to no avail we talk until we are "blue in the face." When we go out on the town we "paint it red," and when we are angry we "see red." Our language, especially as revealed through these time-worn cliches, abounds in color symbolism.

The Meanings of Color

Henry Dreyfuss, in his *Symbol Sourcebook*, reminds us of some of the positive and negative meanings associated with various colors. Some of these are presented in the table of positive and negative messages of colors. Dreyfuss also notes some cultural comparisons for some of these colors. For example, red in China is a color for joyous and festive occasions, whereas in Japan it is used to signify anger and danger. Blue for the Cherokee Indian signifies defeat, but for the Egyptian it signifies virtue and truth. In the Japanese theater blue is the color for villains. Yellow signifies happiness and prosperity in Egypt, but in tenth-century France yellow colored the doors of criminals. Green communicates femininity to certain American Indians, fertility and strength to Egyptians, and youth and energy to Japanese. Purple signifies virtue and faith in Egypt, but grace and nobility in Japan.

POSITIVE AND NEGATIVE MESSAGES OF COLORS

Color	Positive Messages	Negative Messages
red	warmth	death
	passion	war
	life	revolution
	liberty	devil
	patriotism	danger
blue	religious feeling	doubt
	devotion	discouragement
	truth	
	justice	
yellow	intuition	cowardice
	wisdom	malevolence
	divinity	impure love
green	nature	envy
	hope	jealousy
	freshness	opposition
	prosperity	disgrace
purple	power	mourning
	royalty	regret
	love of truth	penitence
	nostalgia	resignation

Adapted from Henry Dreyfuss, *Symbol Sourcebook* (New York: McGraw-Hill, 1971).

In English our connotative meanings for colors vary considerably. In the table of evaluation, potency, and activity ratings, five color terms are presented with their average ratings on evaluation (for example, the good-bad, positive-negative dimension of language), potency (for example, the strong-weak, large-small dimension of language), and activity (for example, the active-passive, fast-slow dimension of language). The numbers are based on a 7-point scale ranging from +3 for the good, strong, and active sides of the scales through 0, which is the neutral position, to −3 for the bad, weak, and passive sides of the scale. As can be seen, red and blue are the most positive in terms of evaluation, and gray is the most negative. Red is the most potent and gray is the least potent. Red is the most active and gray the least active.

EVALUATION, POTENCY, AND ACTIVITY RATINGS
FOR FIVE COLOR TERMS

	Evaluation	Potency	Activity
yellow	.544	.212	−.637
red	1.256	1.012	−.050
green	.969	.706	−.619
gray	−.200	−.394	−1.362
blue	1.255	.812	−.375

Adapted from James Snider and Charles E. Osgood, eds. "Semantic Atlas for 550 Concepts," in *Semantic Differential Technique: A Sourcebook* (Chicago: Aldine, 1969), pp. 625–636.

There is also some scientific evidence that colors affect us physiologically. For example, respiratory movements increase with red light and decrease with blue light. Similarly, the frequency of eye blinks increases when eyes are exposed to red light and decreases when exposed to blue light. This seems consistent with our intuitive feelings about blue being more soothing and red being more active and also with the ratings noted in the evaluation table.

Colors and Personality

Perhaps the most talked about (but least documented) communicative function of color is its supposed reflection of personality. Faber Birren argues that if you like red, your life is directed outward and you are impulsive, active, aggressive, vigorous, sympathetic, quick to judge people, impatient, optimistic, and strongly driven by sex. If, on the other hand, you dislike red, you also dislike the qualities in those people who like red, such as aggressiveness, optimism, and the like. You feel that others have gotten the better deal in life and you never feel really secure. Sexually, you are unsatisfied.

If you like blue you are probably conservative, introspective, and deliberate. You are sensitive to yourself and to others and have your passions under control. In your own communications you are cautious, your opinions and beliefs seldom change, and you question just about everything you do not understand. If you dislike blue you resent the success of others, and in fact enjoy their failures. You feel that your emotional and your intellectual lives are not fulfilled. You get irritated and are somewhat erratic in your own behavior.

This analysis was drawn from the many comments of Faber Birren in *Color in Your World.* Analyses of your personality based on your likes and dislikes of 11 colors as well as on conflicts (liking one color and disliking another color) are readily supplied by Birren and by various other writers, though there seems to be no hard evidence for these claims. The idea of analyzing someone's personality on the basis of color preferences seems intriguing, and yet the validity of such analyses is uninvestigated.

The messages that colors communicate about a culture are easily determined, while the personality traits that colors supposedly reveal are quite difficult and perhaps impossible to determine. As is true of so many aspects of nonverbal communication, we should be particularly cautious in drawing conclusions about people on the basis of their preferences for different colors.

Command Message. That part of a message that refers to the relationship between the communicants. See also CONTENT AND RELATIONSHIP COMMUNICATION.

Committee of the Whole. A committee consisting of the entire membership of a group.

Common Fate. One of the principles in Gestalt psychology that attempts to account for how sensory stimuli are organized. Stimuli possessing common fate, for example, appear to be moving in the same direction and are perceived as a part of a unit.

Common Ground. The similarities existing between speaker and audience. Usually, the establishment of common ground helps the speaker to persuade more effectively.

Commonplaces. A general topic, argument, or description that could be used in a wide variety of situations. Speakers used to memorize selected commonplaces so that should they be called upon to speak, they would appear well prepared and knowledgeable.

Commonplaces, Book of. A collection of useful sayings, brief poems, and prose selections serving as a source of ideas for speakers and writers.

Communication. The process or act of transmitting a message from a sender to a receiver, through a channel and with the interference of noise (q.v.); the actual message or messages sent and received; the study of the processes involved in the sending and receiving of messages (also referred to as communicology, q.v.).

Communication Act. The total of all the elements and processes involved in the sending and receiving of messages.

Communication Adaptability. A dimension of communication competence (q.v.); the ability to adapt one's interpersonal communication goals and behaviors on the basis of the relationships between and among the communicants.
[Robert L. Duran, "Communication Adaptability: A Measure of Social Communicative Competence," *Communication Quarterly* 31 (1983):320–326.]

Communication Apprehension. See APPREHENSION, COMMUNICATION.]

Communication Audit. An analysis of communication systems, usually within an organization, with the purpose of making recommendations for improved efficiency and effectiveness.
[Gerald M. Goldhaber and D. P. Rogers, *Auditing Organizational Communication Systems: The ICA Communication Audit* (Dubuque, Iowa: Kendell/Hunt, 1979).]

Communication Competence. Used by most communication researchers to refer to the ability to interact interpersonally in ways that ensure the achievement of one's goals and the satisfaction of both interactants. Researchers have identified a number of specific behaviors that go into communication competence: other orientation (q.v.), immediacy (q.v.), interaction management (q.v.), expressiveness (q.v.), confidence (q.v.), empathy (q.v.), and supportiveness (q.v.).
[John M. Wiemann, "Explication and Test of a Model of Communication Competence," *Human Communication Research* 3 (1977): 195–213; Brian H. Spitzberg and William R. Cupach, *Interpersonal Communication Competence* (Beverly Hills, Calif.: Sage, 1984).]

Communication Gap. The inability to communicate on a meaningful level because of some difference between the parties, for example, age, sex, political orientation, or religion.

Communication, Index of. As developed by Joseph Greenberg, a measure of the likelihood that any two persons, from any specified society or area, selected at random, will be able to communicate with each other.
[Joseph Greenberg, "The Measurement of Linguistic Diversity," *Language* 32 (1956):109–115; Stanley Lieberson, "An Extension of Greenberg's Linguistic Diversity Measures," *Language* 40 (1964):526–531.]

Communication Models. Usually visual, but also verbal, descriptions of the elements and processes involved in the communication act.

Communication Networks. Communication networks are the channels messages pass through from one person to another. These networks may be viewed from two perspectives. First, small groups left to their own resources will develop communication patterns resembling the several network structures in the accompanying illustration. These networks, then, represent some of the most commonly employed systems of communication channels groups use to send messages from one person to another. Second, these networks may also be viewed as formalized structures, established by an organization, for communication within the company. With either perspective, these networks represent general types of group communication patterns whose counterparts, often in some modified form, can be found in most groups and in most organizations. Five major networks are examined briefly first in terms of structure and second in terms of their actual operation within an organization.

The Network Structures

The five patterns are presented in the illustration. Each contains five individuals (circles), although they may be enlarged to incorporate more or reduced to deal with fewer than five. The arrows indicate the direction the messages may take.

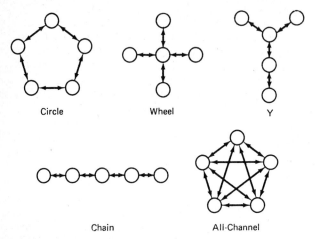

Circle   Wheel   Y

Chain   All-Channel

Five network structures.

The Wheel

The wheel is characterized by the centralized position in the center. In this type of communication pattern, there is a clear leader who is the only one who can send messages to all members and the only one who can receive messages from all members. All others are restricted to sending and receiving messages from only one other person (namely, the leader).

The Y

The Y pattern is somewhat less centralized than the wheel, but more centralized than some of the other patterns. Here there is also a clear leader (the third person from the bottom). But there is one other member who is in a kind of secondary leadership role (the second person from the bottom). This member can send and receive messages from two others, whereas the other three are restricted to communicating with only one other.

The Circle

The circle has no central leader; here there is total equality. Each member of the circle has exactly the same authority or power to influence the group; each of the members may communicate with the two members on either side.

The Chain

The chain is essentially the same as the circle except that the end members may communicate with only one person each. There is some centrality here; the middle position is more leaderlike than any of the other positions.

The All-Channel

The all-channel or star pattern is like the circle in that all members are equal and all have exactly the same amount of power to influence others, except that each member in this pattern may communicate with any other member. This pattern allows for the greatest member participation. Note another characteristic of the all-channel group: It can be restructured into any of the other four patterns, but the other four patterns have no such flexibility. (The one exception is that the circle can be restructured into the chain.) Thus, for example, the all-channel pattern may, if conditions warrant, be changed to the wheel to gain the advantage of a central leader.

Communication through these networks is often but not always face-to-face. Messages may be written in informal memos or in formal letters and reports. Messages may be sent and responded to by computer. Groups may also communicate in a teleconference where several members are simultaneously connected by telephone or in a video teleconference where each member can both see and hear each other member although they each may be in separate offices, buildings, or even cities.

The Networks in Operation

These networks are not good or bad in themselves; they are better viewed as useful-useless for a specific task. For example, the highly centralized patterns—the wheel and the Y—are the most efficient for dealing with relatively simple and repetitive tasks, such as those in which information must be collected in one place and disseminated to others. Information overload is most likely to occur in the highly centralized groups since it is all coming to one person. These central individuals also become gatekeepers and often prevent information from getting to the various members. Sometimes this may be due simply to information overload; at other times it may be due to the leader's evaluating the information as useless or harmful to the workings of the group.

Those in the central positions seem to have relatively high morale; they do a lot of work, have the most power, and are the most satisfied. The others in these centralized groups, however, develop relatively low morale since they do little and have little or no influence on the functioning of the group. Members of an all-channel group, in contrast, usually have high morale.

All highly centralized groups depend on the effectiveness of that one person in the central position. If that person is an effective leader-communicator, the success of the group as a whole is almost assured; conversely, if that person is ineffective, the entire group will suffer. In the all-channel pattern, however, the effectiveness of any one individual will not make or break the group; in fact, the contributions of any one individual in the all-channel are relatively unimportant.

But even the relationship between morale and participation or power may be oversimplified. Although, for example, it has been found that morale is high when participation is high, as in the all-channel group, this group is inefficient in dealing with relatively simple and repetitive tasks. This inefficiency may well lead to a decline in morale since few people want to be associated with an inefficient organization. Here, by the way, is a good example of the value of the systems view: all elements (here morale and efficiency) interact; they are not separate and distinct parts, but rather interrelated aspects of the same whole. Organizations are frequently faced with a conflict between morale and efficiency. Do they sacrifice worker satisfaction to increase productivity (and thus perhaps pave the way for mass resignations), or do they sacrifice production for satisfaction (and thus perhaps risk financial ruin)?

The structure of a network (and, more important, of an organization) will greatly influence the functioning of that network. For example, the wheel, once established, will greatly influence how individuals function; the central position will become the leader, and the spokes will function as followers because they do not have the information for selecting and evaluating various options.

Some groups seem to adapt well to change, whereas others do not. Groups in the wheel pattern, for example, seem to have difficulty adapting to changing tasks and changing conditions. But when the pattern is the circle, where everyone is equal, the group seems to adapt well. It accepts new ideas much more readily. Yet its inefficiency in terms of time—it takes a great deal longer to accomplish simple tasks in the circle than it does in the wheel—makes it a poor choice for dealing with simple, repetitive tasks.

The three approaches to organizations may also be viewed in terms of these networks. The scientific management (q.v.) school would prefer the wheel or the Y, where there is a strong leader who directs the activities of the group. The ideas and inputs of individual members are of little consequence. Likewise, communications between workers, as in the informal social groups, are also of little importance. What is important is the communications from leaders to workers—orders, instructions, and the like. The human relations (q.v.) school would favor the all-channel pattern, where each member has an equal say in the task to be accomplished and interpersonal interaction among workers is fostered. The all-channel pattern is a good example of "participatory management." The systems approach (q.v.) would view all these patterns, as well as various others, as useful and important, depending on the task. The wheel might be appropriate for simple tasks; the circle might be more appropriate for rapidly changing tasks; and the all-channel pattern might be more appropriate when there is no one strong leader or when the task requires creativity.

[John E. Baird, Jr., *The Dynamics of Organizational Communication* (New York: Harper & Row, 1977); A. Bavelas, "Communication Patterns in Task-Orientated Groups," *Journal of the Acoustical Society of America* 22 (1950):725–730; Gerald M. Goldhaber, *Organizational Communication,* 3d ed. (Dubuque, Iowa: Brown, 1983).]

Communication Rules. Prescriptive statements concerning communication behavior in specific contexts. Susan Shimanoff identifies four major characteristics of communication rules: rules are followable, concerned with behavior (rather than cognitive processes), prescriptive (rather than descriptive), and contextual (rules vary on the basis of the specifics of the situation).

[Susan B. Shimanoff, *Communication Rules: Theory and Research* (Beverly Hills, Calif.: Sage, 1980).]

Communication Style. The general pattern of communication that an individual uses frequently. Virginia Satir, for example, identifies four communication styles that are destructive of relationships: (1) *placating*—trying to please everyone at all times in order to retain their love, often makes others feel guilt or pity; (2) *blaming*—tries to force people into obeying, blames others for everything, makes others feel fearful and helpless; (3) *super reasonable*—emphasizes logic and ideas to demonstrate how smart he or she is, expresses no feelings, makes others feel inferior and stupid; (4) *irrelevant*—secures attention through any means available, makes others feel off balance. All four styles prevent real human contact and are damaging to one's self-esteem. In all four styles, the individual believes he or she is unlovable.

[Virginia Satir, *Making Contact* (Berkeley, Calif.: Celestial Arts, 1976).]

Communication Theory. Theory concerned with the analysis and explanation of communication (q.v.).

Communicativity, Index of. The potential of a given language to serve as the means of communication for the society. The index can be extended to be used as a measure of the likelihood of a specific language being used as the means of communication in a multilingual context.
[Eddie C. Y. Kuo, "Measuring Communicativity in Multilingual Societies: The Case of Singapore and West Malaysia," *Anthropological Linguistics* 21 (1979):328–340.]

Communicator Style. The habitual style (q.v.) of a communicator which, in some views, reveals a great deal about the speaker, for example, who the speaker is, who the speaker would like to be, who the speaker pretends to be, and so on.
[Robert Norton, *Communicator Style: Theory, Applications, and Measure* (Beverly Hills, Calif.: Sage, 1983).]

Communicology. The study of the processes involved in the sending and receiving of messages; the study of speech and language disorders and therapy.

Companionate Love. Love based on friendship rather than romance.

Comparative Method. In language study, a method by which languages are compared and contrasted and the forms from which they developed are reconstructed.
[H. Hoenigswald, *Language Change and Linguistic Reconstruction* (Chicago, Ill.: University of Chicago Press, 1960).

Compensation Theory. A theory or hypothesis holding that in the development of a relationship, one person will attempt to compensate for some perceived inadequacy (most often, relative unattractiveness) by being especially agreeable or considerate. Compensation is seen when, for example, the less attractive partner brings to the relationship some other asset, for example, wealth, education, or status. In psychoanalytic theory, compensation refers to the tendency to strengthen one asset or the ability to offset or compensate for some perceived inadequacy.

Competence. One of the characteristics or qualities of credibility; the intelligence and knowledge that a speaker is perceived to possess. See also COMMUNICATION COMPETENCE; LANGUAGE COMPETENCE.

Competition. An interpersonal process in which a person strives to attain something ahead of or in excess of someone else and at the same time to prevent others from attaining it.

Complementarity. One of the determinants of interpersonal attraction in which one is attracted to persons who possess qualities lacking in oneself—qualities that complement or complete the self.

Complementary Relationship. An interpersonal relationship in which the two individuals engage in different behaviors, with the behavior of one serving as the stimulus for the complementary behavior of the other. It is necessary in a complementary relationship for both parties to occupy different positions, one being the superior and one being the inferior, one being passive and one being active, one being strong and one being weak. At times such relationships are established by the culture, as, for example, the complementary relationship between teacher and student or between employer and employee. See also SYMMETRICAL RELATIONSHIP.

Complementary Transactions. Transactions involving messages that are sent and received by the same ego state (q.v.) for each of the participants. That is, A's messages are sent by the same ego state that B is addressing, and B's messages are sent by the same ego state that A is addressing. When A intends to address a particular ego state of B and does so successfully, and when B intends to address a particular ego state of A and does so successfully, the transaction is a complementary one. In all there are nine possible types of complementary transactions: P-P, P-A, P-C, A-P, A-A, A-C, C-P, C-A, and C-C.

Type I complementary transactions have the same ego states communicating with each other. This may be diagramed as follows:

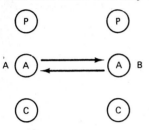

A dialogue representative of this kind of Adult-to-Adult communication transaction might go something like this:

SPOUSE A: This is great furniture; too bad we can't afford it.
SPOUSE B: Yes, let's go downstairs; they're having a sale on floor samples and we might be able to get some good buys.

In Type II complementary transactions each person is in a different ego state but each addresses his or her messages to the other's appropriate ego state. One such pattern is diagrammed as follows:

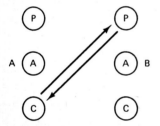

In this example, A's Child is addressing B's Parent, and B's Parent is addressing A's Child. This type of transaction might be identified from a dialogue such as the following:

SPOUSE A: Let's go out on the town and get drunk.
SPOUSE B: Now, you know you get sick when you drink. There's more to life than just having fun.

Here A is in the Child state and wants to have fun and play. B assumes the Parent state and restrains the Child. With transactions involving the Child ego state, we have to take into consideration the three types of the Child: Natural, Adapted, and Little Professor. For a transaction to be complementary, it is necessary that the appropriate Child be addressed and successfully reached. For example, messages addressed to the Natural Child but received by the Little Professor would not be complementary (see CHILD EGO STATE).

In complementary transactions communication may continue indefinitely. In the Type I example, as long as the couple remains as two Adults, communication will continue with little chance of breaking down. In the Type II example the same holds true. As long as A remains in the Child state and B in the Parent state, no barriers will be established, and communication will continue. This does not mean that the communications will necessarily be successful or effective. Many complementary interactions continue as if forever, but may be totally devoid of dialogue that is meaningful and productive.

See also CROSSED TRANSACTIONS; ULTERIOR TRANSACTIONS.

Complex Question. A question that on the surface asks for a "yes" or "no" answer but is actually more complex, for example, "Did you stop being such a loudmouth?"

Complex Sentence. A sentence with one independent and at least one dependent clause (q.v.).

Compliance. The act of yielding to the desires of others; conforming to the dictates of others; changing behavior as a response to group pressure without a corresponding attitude change; a process of opinion change occurring when an individual accepts influence because of his or her expectation of receiving rewards or avoiding punishments from the persuaders.

[Herbert C. Kelman, "Processes of Opinion Change," *Public Opinion Quarterly* 25 (1961): 57–78.]

Compliance-Gaining Behaviors. Those behaviors (techniques or strategies) that are used in interpersonal encounters to gain compliance (q.v.) and include, for example, threats or promises.

[G. Marwell and D. R. Schmitt, "Dimensions of Compliance-Gaining Behavior: An Empirical Analysis," *Sociometry* 39 (1967):350–364.]

Compliment. Expressed praise. Knapp, Hopper, and Bell, for example, found that compliments focus on selected content areas, the most important being: performance, attire, appearance, personality, possessions, and helping/service (compliments referring to the individual's attempts to help others).

[Mark L. Knapp, Robert Hopper, and Robert A. Bell, "Compliments: A Descriptive Taxonomy," *Journal of Communication* 34 (Autumn 1984):12–31.]

Componential Analysis. A method of analysis by which an expression is divided into its semantic parts or components; an ethnographic methodology for the analysis of a semantic field (for example, kinship terminology) that reduces (analyzes) all the terms into their semantic or meaningful components (for example, male-female, abstract-concrete).

[Ward H. Goodenough, "Componential Analysis and the Study of Meaning," *Language* 32 (1956):195–216.]

Componential Definition of Communication. An approach to the definition of communication that seeks to identify its parts or components, for example, "Communication is the process by which a source sends verbal and nonverbal signals to a receiver."

Compound Bilingual. A bilingual (q.v.) person whose two languages have the same meaning system, for example, when *casa* and *house* have the exact same referent for the speaker. Usually this situation is produced when the two languages are learned in the same context. See also COORDINATE BILINGUAL.

Compound Sentence. A sentence with two independent clauses.

Computerese. The communication jargon of computer programers, designers, and users.

Computer Simulation. A procedure whereby certain variables and instructions are programmed into a computer and the computer "acts out" (identifies) the behaviors that would result. In this way, variables may be more easily isolated and their interactions and effects more easily studied.

Comstockery. Coined from Anthony Comstock (1844–1915) who attempted to censor literature he considered immoral or obscene, and now used to refer to the zealous censorship or suppression of any communication considered obscene.

Conceit. An especially creative or elaborate figure of speech (most often found in poetry), it is usually designed to surprise the reader or hearer by its ingenuity.

Consensual Validation. A therapeutic procedure in which a patient compares his or her thoughts and behaviors with those of others in an attempt to demonstrate that these thoughts and behaviors are not abnormal.

Concord. See AGREEMENT.

Concrete Operational Period. In Jean Piaget's (1896–1980) theory of child development, the concrete operational period occurs around the ages from 6 or 7 to about 11 when the child is limited to dealing with only concrete events and cannot conceptualize and work with certain abstractions of substance and number.

Conditioned Reflex. See CONDITIONED RESPONSE.

Conditioned Response (CR). A response elicited by an originally neutral stimulus (conditioned stimulus) which, through frequent pairing and association with an unconditioned stimulus, has acquired some of the latter's properties, namely the ability to elicit the conditioned response. In the classic Pavlov's dog case, the unconditioned stimulus is the food powder which elicits the unconditioned response of salivation. When the bell (the conditioned stimulus) is repeatedly paired with the food powder, it acquires the power to elicit a response similar to the unconditioned response, namely salivation. Technically, the conditioned response and the unconditioned response are similar but not identical. See also UNCONDITIONED RESPONSE.

Conditioned Stimulus (CS). A stimulus that acquires the ability to elicit a response because it is frequently paired with an unconditioned stimulus. See also UNCONDITIONED STIMULUS.

Conduction Deafness. A form of deafness resulting from interference with the conduction of sound to the neural mechanism of the inner ear; a hearing impairment due to damage of the ear canal, the ossicular chain of the middle ear, or the drum membrane.

Confederate. Someone who acts as if he or she is a subject in an experiment but is actually working with the experimenter.

Confidence. As a quality of communication competence (q.v.), confidence refers to vocal and postural flexibility, appropriateness, an at-ease quality, and the absence of, for example, rigidity, shakiness, and self- and other adaptors (q.v.).

Confirmatio. In classical rhetoric (q.v.), the fourth and major part of the speech in which the orator advances an argument to prove a case. See also PARTS OF THE SPEECH.

Conflict. An extreme form of competition in which a person attempts to bring his or her rival to surrender; a situation in which one person's behaviors are directed at preventing, interferring with, or harming another individual; interpersonal disagreement. See also CONFLICT RESOLUTION; CONFLICT STRATEGIES.
[Joseph P. Folger and Marshall Scott Poole, *Working Through Conflict: A Communication Perspective* (Glenview, Ill.: Scott, Foresman, 1984).]

Conflict Approach. An approach to personality, developed largely by Sigmund Freud (1856–1939), that holds that within each individual there are opposing forces that conflict with one another.

Conflict Grid. An approach to conflict and problem solving, developed by Robert Blake and Jane Mouton, that analyzes conflict styles on a 9-point scale in terms of one's concern for people and one's concern for results.
[Robert Blake and Jane Mouton, *The New Managerial Grid* (Houston, Texas: Gulf Publish-

ing, 1978), and "The Fifth Achievement," *Journal of Applied Behavioral Science* 6 (1970): 413–426.]

Conflict Resolution. Any conflict situation may be approached as would a problem requiring a decision. The methods suggested for dealing with conflict are similar to the methods of reflective thinking long taught as educational techniques and in small group communication. Here are distinguished five principal stages in conflict resolution. A diagram of these essential stages is presented in the accompanying illustration. This diagram and the discussion that follows should not be taken to imply that all conflicts may be resolved in this way or in any other prescribed way. Some conflicts may not be amenable to solution; some differences may be irreconcilable. Communication can help us to understand and to resolve many conflicts but not all.

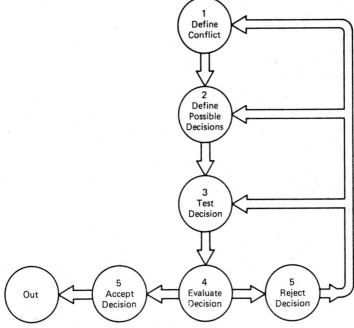

The five principle stages in conflict resolution.

Define the Conflict

Defining the conflict is perhaps the most essential step of conflict resolution, and yet many omit this stage entirely. We need to ask ourselves what the specific nature of the conflict is and why this conflict exists. It is at this stage that we should collect as much relevant data and as many opinions as we possibly can. Special care should be taken to ensure that we collect data and opinions that may disagree with our positions as well as the more supportive data and opinions.

In defining the conflict "operationalize" it to make it as concrete as possible. Conflict defined in the abstract is difficult to deal with and resolve. Deal with conflicts in behavioral terms if possible. It is one thing for a husband to say that his wife is "cold and unfeeling" and quite another to say she does not call him at the office or kiss him when he comes home or hold his hand when they are at a party. These behaviors can be dealt with, whereas the abstract "cold and unfeeling" will be most difficult to handle. Further, it is useful to operationalize conflicts because it forces us to be specific and to spell out exactly what we are fighting about.

Define Possible Decisions

For any conflict there are a number of possible decisions that can be made. In some instances any one of three or four possible decisions will resolve the conflict; in other cases only one possible decision will work. But in all cases we need first to analyze all possible alternatives.

In analyzing the possible decisions to resolve the conflict attempt to predict the consequences of each of them. This is impossible to do with complete accuracy, yet some attempt should be made in this direction. Guard against any tendency to dismiss possible decisions before giving them a fair hearing. Many excellent decisions are never put into operation because they at first seem strange, incorrect, or too difficult to implement.

Test the Decision

The true test of any decision can only be made when the decision is put into operation. Play the odds—select the decision that seems the most logical and try it out. Although each decision put into operation should be given a fair chance, recognize that if a particular decision does not work, another decision should be put to the test. It is self-destructive to put a decision into operation with the idea that if it does not work, then conflict resolution is impossible.

Evaluate the Decision

When the decision is in operation we need to evaluate it, examining the ways in which it helps to resolve (or aggravate) the conflict. Does it feel right? Does it make for improved interpersonal communication? Does it significantly lessen the conflict?

Accept or Reject the Decision

As a result of our evaluation we move to accept or reject the decision. If we accept the decision we move to the "Out" position and we are ready to put the decision into operation or perhaps to move on to consider other conflict situations and problems. If we move to reject the decision there are three alternatives: First, we might attempt to test another decision. Perhaps the decision we ranked as number two will prove more satisfactory, and again we try it out. A second possibility is to redefine the various decisions and then test one of them. The third course of action is to go back and reanalyze and redefine the conflict itself. That is, we can reenter the conflict resolution process at any of the first three stages. In any case, another decision must eventually be put into operation, which it is hoped will work better than the previous one. And perhaps we will have learned something from the last decision-making process that will prove useful in subsequent conflict resolution attempts.

Conflict Strategies. In dealing with conflict, keep in mind the following law of conflict: Any conflict is easier to create than to resolve. This law is simple enough (advanced as a tribute to Murphy's original law, "If anything can go wrong, it will"), but there are some rather spiteful corollaries. For example, the time it takes to create a conflict is always shorter than the time it takes to resolve the conflict. Alternatively, the energy expenditure needed to create a conflict is often minor, but to resolve that conflict the energy expenditure is major. Both unproductive and productive strategies are noted here.

Unproductive Conflict Strategies

Avoidance or Redefinition

Avoidance may take the form of actual physical flight (whereby the individual leaves the scene of the conflict), falling asleep, or just mentally withdrawing. Or it may take the form of emotional or intellectual avoidance, whereby the individual leaves the conflict psychologically by not dealing with any of the arguments or problems raised.

Avoidance often takes the form of changing the subject, or by talking about the problem so abstractly or in such incomprehensible language that mutual understanding is impossible. A similar method is to redefine the conflict so that it becomes no conflict at all or so that it becomes irrelevant to the individuals and hence unnecessary to deal with.

Force

Perhaps the most common picture of a pseudomethod of conflict resolution is that involving physical force. When confronted with a conflict, many prefer not to deal with the issues but rather simply to force his or her decision or way of thinking or behaving on the other by physically overpowering the individual, or at least by the threat of such physical force. At other times the force used is more emotional than physical. In either case, however, the issues are avoided and the individual who "wins" is the individual who exerts the most force. This, of course, is the technique of warring nations and spouses.

Minimization

Sometimes we deal with conflict by making light of it, by saying and perhaps believing that the conflict, its causes, and its consequences are really not important. We might argue that if left alone, time will resolve it. But time does absolutely nothing; over time *we* may do something, but time itself never acts in one way or the other.

Sometimes we minimize the conflict with humor (especially sarcasm and ridicule) and may literally laugh at it. Sometimes it is obvious, however, that our laughter is prompted by fear, embarrassment, or personal inadequacy in dealing with the conflict situation. But in many instances the humor seems logical enough; it eases the tension and, at least for a time, makes for more effective interpersonal relations. The problem is that the laughter does nothing to get at the root of the problem, and when the laughter dies the conflict is still very much alive.

Blame

Sometimes conflict is caused by the actions of one individual; sometimes it is caused by clearly identifiable outside forces. Most of the time, however, it is caused by such a wide variety of factors that any attempt to single out one or two factors is doomed to failure. And yet a frequently employed fight strategy is to avoid dealing with the conflict by blaming someone for it. In some instances we blame ourselves. This may be the result of a realistic appraisal of the situation, or it may be an attempt to evoke sympathy or to gain pity from the other individual. More often, however, we blame the other person. If a couple has a conflict over a child's getting into trouble with the police, for example, the parents may start blaming each other for the child's troubles instead of dealing with the conflict itself. As can easily be appreciated (at least when we are not parties to the conflict), blaming solves nothing other than temporarily relieving a degree of intrapersonal guilt.

Silencers

One of the most unfair but one of the most popular fight strategies is the use of silencers—a wide variety of fighting techniques that literally silence the other individual. One frequently used silencer is crying. When confronted by a conflict and unable to deal with it or when winning seems unlikely, the individual cries and thus silences the other person.

Gunnysacking

Gunnysacking refers to the practice of storing up grievances—as if in a gunnysack—and holding them in readiness to dump on the person when you are in conflict. Instead of dealing with and resolving conflicts as they come along, the gunnysacker saves them up for future use. When a conflict occurs, the sack is unloaded—"You always forget our dates. Remember last year, it was my birthday; you forgot completely. And what about my parents' anniversary. You forgot that too. You always forget my parents. But you always have time for your friends." And on and on it goes, always going further and further into the past and always getting further and further away from the source of the present conflict. Gunnysacking opens old wounds, avoids coming to grips with the immediate conflict, and never seems to result in resolving differences and disagreements.

Beltlining

Each of us has a "beltline" that separates what we can from what we cannot effectively tolerate. In an interpersonal relationship, we know where that beltline is because we know the other person so well. The task, of course, is not to go below that line in conflict encounters. When we do hit below the belt—and focus on the other's baldness, impotence, previous failures, low salary, history of mental illness, alcoholic parent—we aggravate the conflict and move further away from any resolution. Beltlining is played by persons who want to win the fight and destroy the opponent—a strategy that also quickly and effectively damages the interpersonal relationship.

Productive Conflict Strategies

Productive conflict strategies may be drawn from a variety of sources. Here, we reexamine the qualities of interpersonal communication effectiveness (q.v.) for suggestions for dealing productively with conflict. The five qualities of interpersonal communication effectiveness are: openness, empathy, supportiveness, positiveness, and equality.

Openness

1. State your position, your feelings, your thoughts openly, directly, and honestly without attempting to hide or disguise the real object of your disagreement. Only by bringing the conflict out into the open will an eventual and meaningful resolution be possible.

2. React openly to the messages of your combattant, even though this will be difficult—especially if the messages are hostile or personally insulting. It is

particularly important that each person listens to and reacts appropriately and honestly to the messages of the other.

3. Own your thoughts and feelings. Don't attribute your negative statements about your combattant to others ("Everybody thinks you're cheap; even your mother says you're stingy."). Take responsibility for what you feel and for what you say. Use I-messages: "I feel . . ., I want . . .."

4. Address the real issues that are causing the difficulties, at least insofar as you can identify and describe them. Don't focus your conflict on the burnt toast when the real source of anger is that you don't want your in-laws to vacation with you. Center your attention on the here and now; don't dredge up the past or gunnysack (q.v.) by recalling all your past hurts and your partners past indiscretions. If there is a specific source of conflict, address it as squarely and as directly as you can.

Empathy

5. Demonstrate empathic understanding. Try to feel what your intimate is feeling even though this may be drastically different from what you feel. Try to see the situation from the other person's point of view as clearly and as honestly as you can.

6. Once you have empathically understood your opponents feelings, validate those feelings where appropriate. If your partner is hurt or angry—and you feel that such feelings are legitimate and justified (from the other person's point of view), then say so: "You have a right to be angry; I shouldn't have called your mother a slob. I'm sorry. But I still don't want to go on vacation with her." Note that in expressing validation you are not necessarily expressing agreement on the issue in conflict but merely stating that your partner has feelings that are legitimate and that you recognize them as such.

Supportiveness

7. Concentrate on describing the behaviors with which you have difficulty (for example, the drinking, the joke telling, the lateness for appointments) rather than jumping quickly to evaluation. Make sure that you are both dealing with the same behaviors before you make any attempt to pin a label on them.

8. Express your feelings with spontaneity rather than with strategy. Remember that there is no need in interpersonal conflict situations to plan a strategy to win a war. The objective is not to win a war but to increase mutual understanding and to reach a decision that both parties can accept.

9. State your positions tentatively, provisionally. Demonstrate flexibility and a willingness to change your opinion or position should appropriate reasons be given. There will be little hope of reaching agreement and there is a good chance that the conflict will escalate if you approach it with the idea that things must be seen your way and only your way.

Positiveness

10. In any conflict situation there are areas and issues of agreement. Capitalize on these agreements and perhaps use them as a basis to gradually approach disagreements and impasses. Little is accomplished by emphasizing disagreement and minimizing agreement. This is not an invitation to avoid differences and disagreements; it is, rather, a suggestion to be sure that you do not overlook the real and important similarities and areas of agreement which may often help pave the way for greater understanding.

11. View the conflict experience, at least in part, in positive terms. Try not to see the conflict as an attempt to hurt one another or to get back at your partner for having hurt you. Rather, recall the positive values of conflict and especially the ultimate aim of the conflict, namely the achievement of greater understanding.

12. Express positive feelings for the other person and for the relationship between the two of you. Throughout any conflict there probably will be many harsh words exchanged; many of which you will be sorry for later. These cannot be unsaid or uncommunicated. Yet, they can be offset, partially, by the expression of positive statements. If you are engaged in combat with someone you love, then remember that you are fighting with a loved one and express that feeling. "I love you very much but I still don't want your mother on vacation with us. I want to be alone with you."

Equality

13. Regardless of how right you feel you are and how wrong you think your partner is, remember the principle of equality; even in combat situations, treat the other person as an equal. The other has feelings that have to be dealt with and understood and these must be treated with the same respect that you want shown your feelings.

14. Involve yourself on both sides of the communication exchange. Be an active participant as a speaker and as a listener; voice your own feelings and listen carefully to the voicing of your opponent's feelings. This is not to say that periodic moratoriums are hot helpful. Sometimes they are. Rather, this suggestion is noted to emphasize that we need to be willing to communicate as sender and receiver—to say what is on our minds and to listen to what the other person is saying.

Analyzing Conflict Behaviors

Every fight can be analyzed in terms of the extent to which the parties involved followed or did not follow these five characteristics of effective interpersonal interaction and the fourteen specific points noted here. In the accompanying Analysis Form, specific conflict behaviors are noted, in abbreviated form, on the left. In the center there is a place for indicating a score for each of the parties (P_1 and P_2). As noted on the analysis form, a simple 5-point scoring system is indicated. For each of the fourteen conflict behaviors, each of the combattants should be scored somewhere from a high of $+2$ (indicating a clear demonstration of the effective communication behaviors) to a low of -2 (indicating a clear demonstration of the ineffective communication behaviors). On the right there is space for recording your evidence and reasoning, that is, what did the combattants communicate (verbally or nonverbally) that led you to score them as you did.

CONFLICT ANALYSIS FORM

Conflict Behaviors	Score*		Evidence and Reasoning
	P_1	P_2	
Openness			
1. states one's position openly and without disguise			
2. reacts openly to incoming messages			

CONFLICT ANALYSIS FORM (*Continued*)

Conflict	Score*		Evidence and Reasoning
	P₁	P₂	
3. owns one's own thoughts and feelings			
4. addresses real, here-and-now issues			
Empathy			
5. demonstrates empathic understanding			
6. expresses validation			
Supportiveness			
7. describes other's behavior			
8. expresses feelings spontaneously			
9. states position provisionally			
Positiveness			
10. emphasizes agreement			
11. views conflict positively			
12. expresses positive feelings for other			
Equality			
13. treats other as equal combattant			
14. is involved as both speaker and listener			
Total Score			
Overall Evaluation			

*Point Scoring System
  +2 = definitely demonstrates this characteristic
  +1 = demonstrates this characteristic
   0 = not clear or doubtful on the basis of the evidence
  −1 = does not demonstrate this characteristic
  −2 = definitely does not demonstrate this characteristic

[George R. Bach and Peter Wyden, *The Intimate Enemy* (New York: Avon, 1968).]

Confutatio. In classical rhetoric, the fifth major part of the oration in which the speaker refuted the arguments of the opponent. See also PARTS OF THE SPEECH.

Congruence. In Carl Rogers's system, a condition in which an individual has a high degree of self-awareness, is in touch with his or her own feelings and emotions, and does not attempt to hide them from himself or herself; a state of harmony between one's self-concept and one's experiences; a condition in which one's words, bodily actions, facial expressions, and general behaviors accurately reflect one's feelings; an ideal state of psychological health, leading to

positive growth; opposed to incongruence (q.v.). A person's feelings are "accurately symbolized" and are a part of his or her self-concept.
[Carl Rogers, *On Becoming a Person* (Boston: Houghton Mifflin, 1961).]

Congruity Theory. A model of attitude change that proposes that incongruity—an inconsistency among attitudes—automatically produces attitude change in the direction of congruity restoration. This theory provides precise predictions concerning both the direction and the amount of attitude change.
[Charles E. Osgood and Percy H. Tannenbaum, "The Principle of Congruity in the Prediction of Attitude Change," *Psychological Review* 62 (1955):42–55.]

Conjoint Therapy. Family therapy in which both relationship partners (and even the children) interact with the therapist.
[Virginia Satir, *Conjoint Family Therapy* (Palo Alto, Calif.: Science and Behavior Books, 1967).]

Connotation. The feeling or emotional aspects of a word's meaning, generally viewed as consisting of the subjective and evaluative (for example, the good-bad, strong-weak, fast-slow dimensions); the associations of a term. See also DENOTATION.

Consciousness of Projection. An awareness that what is observed or perceived in any way is a function of both the objective reality and the observer.

Consciousness of Projection Terms. Terms indicative of consciousness of projection (q.v.) such as *seems to me, appears,* or *as I see it.*

Consensual Validation. A procedure whereby one checks and compares one's own perceptions of one's thoughts and feelings with those of others in an attempt to recognize what is real and what is distorted; a therapeutic procedure introduced by Harry Stack Sullivan (1892–1949) to help patients modify their distorted views of themselves.
[Harry Stack Sullivan, *The Interpersonal Theory of Psychiatry* (New York: Norton, 1953).]

Consensus. A method of decision making in which all members involved in the decision come to unanimous agreement. A jury in a criminal case must reach its decision by consensus.

Conservation. The ability to tell that some quantity is the same even though it has changed in, say, size or shape, for example, the ability to tell that a pint of liquid in a short wide container is the same amount even though it has been changed to a tall, thin container.

Consistency. See BALANCE.

Constative. A statement that asserts something but whose utterance performs no further function; opposed to performative (q.v.).

Constituent. A unit in linguistic structure varying from an individual morpheme to an entire sentence. For example, in the following constituent analysis box, each line represents a different level of constituents. In line 1 the constituent is the sentence (S); in line 2 the constituents are a noun phrase (NP) and verb phrase (VP); in 3 the constituents are two noun phrases and verb (V); in 4 the constituents are words (determiners (det.) or articles, nouns, verbs); in 5 the constituents are morphemes (q.v.).

Constituent Analysis. A linguistic procedure by which a sentence is broken down and categorized into its component parts, or constituents (q.v.).

Constitutional Perspective. A theoretical point of view in which biological factors are emphasized as determinants of behavior.

Constitutionalist. One who emphasizes the role of nature or innate factors in development and behavior.

1.	S					
	The boys ran the race					
2.	NP			VP		
	The boys			ran the race		
3.	NP		V		NP	
	The boys		ran		the race	
4.	det	N	V		det	N
	The	boys	ran		the	race
5.	det	N	pl	V	past tense	det	N
	The	boy	s	run		the	race

Constituent analysis box.

Constitutive Rule. In speech act theory (q.v.), a rule that states how an act should be defined.

Constructivism. A theoretical approach that is currently applied to communication and is based on the notion that people approach the world through interpretation processes which then channel their behaviors in various ways.
[Jesse G. Delia, Barbara J. O'Keefe, and Daniel J. O'Keefe, "The Constructivist Approach to Communication," in *Human Communication Theory,* Frank E. X. Dance, ed. (New York: Harper & Row, 1982), pp. 147–191.]

Consubstantiality. A sharing; a process of making common; to Kenneth Burke, a process that is essential to and defining of meaningful communication.
[Kenneth Burke, *A Rhetoric of Motives* (Englewood Cliffs, N.J.: Prentice-Hall, 1950).]

Contagion. In communication, the rapid spread of some emotion or behavior throughout the members of a group or crowd.

Content Analysis. A research methodology for analyzing the substance or content of any communication.
[B. Berelson, *Content Analysis in Communication Research* (New York: Free Press, 1952); John Waite Bowers, "Content Analysis," in *Methods of Research in Communication,* Philip Emmert and William D. Brooks, eds. (Boston: Houghton Mifflin, 1970), pp. 291–314.]

Content and Relationship Communication. Communications, to a certain extent at least, refer to the real world, to something external to both speaker and listener. At the same time, however, communications also refer to the relationship between the parties. For example, a teacher may say to a student, "See me after class." This simple message has a content aspect that refers to the behavioral responses expected—namely, that the student see the teacher after class—and a relationship aspect that tells us how the communication is to be dealt with. Even the use of the simple command states that there is a status difference between the two parties that allows the teacher to command the student. This is perhaps seen most clearly when we visualize this command being made by the student to the teacher. It appears awkward and out of place simply because it violates the normal relationship between teacher and student.

In any communication the content dimension may be the same but the relationship aspect different, or the relationship aspect may be the same and the content dimension different. For example, the teacher could say to the student, "You had better see me after class" or "May I please see you after class?" In each case the content is essentially the same; that is, the message being communicated about the behavioral responses expected is the same in both cases. But the relationship dimension is very different. In the first it signifies a very definite superior-inferior relationship and even a put-down of the student, but in the second a more equal relationship is signaled and a respect for the student is shown. Similarly, at times the content may be different but the relationship essentially the same. For example, a son might say to his parents, "May I go away this weekend?" or "May I use the car tonight?" The content is clearly very different in each case, and yet the relationship dimension is essentially the same. It is clearly a superior-inferior relationship in which permission to do certain things must be secured.

Relational Conflicts

Problems between people are often caused by the failure to recognize the distinction between the content and the relationship levels of communication. For example, consider the engaged couple arguing over the fact that the woman made plans to study during the weekend with her friends without first asking her fiancé if that would be all right. Probably both would have agreed that to study over the weekend was the right choice to make; thus the argument is not primarily concerned with the content level. The argument centers on the relationship level; the man expected to be consulted about plans for the weekend; the woman, in not doing this, rejected this definition of their relationship.

Arguments over the content dimension are relatively easy to resolve. Generally, we may look something up in a book or ask someone what actually took place or perhaps see the movie again. It is relatively easy to verify facts that are disputed. Arguments on the relationship level, however, are much more difficult to resolve, in part because we seldom recognize that the argument is in fact a relationship one. One of the clearest examples of the confusion between the content and the relationship aspects was reported in a letter to Ann Landers. A woman and her husband were playing bridge with her sister and her husband. The writer notes that her husband had a habit of overbidding his hand and on this particular evening made a "reckless bid of six spades." The writer reports that all she said was "either you are crazy or I'm blind." The husband then said, "Why don't you just keep your mouth shut and play the hand." "The dumb remark of yours," he later continued, "cost us the game. I don't want to play cards with you ever again." On one level this argument concerns content—the bridge game, proper bidding, winning strategies, and the like. On another level, however, the argument concerns the relationship between the husband and wife. We might venture to postulate that the relationship level involved such issues as the husband's feeling that his wife should be supportive regardless of what he does, the appropriateness of the wife's public criticism of her husband and of the husband's criticism of his wife, who was really the offended party, and probably many more. As long as the husband and wife assume that their conflict is totally content oriented, they are probably never going to resolve it. A resolution can only come about, it seems, if the relational aspect is understood and confronted. [Paul Watzlawick, Janet Helmick Beavin, and Don D. Jackson, *Pragmatics of Human Communication: A Study of Interactional Patterns, Pathologies, and Paradoxes* (New York: Norton, 1967).]

Content-Free Speech. Speech in which the content is absent or held constant, for example, reciting the alphabet while expressing a variety of emotions.
[Joel R. Davitz and Lois Jean Davitz, "The Communication of Feelings by Content-Free Speech," *Journal of Communication* 9 (1959):6–13.]

Content Word. A word that has some reference to subject matter rather than solely to linguistic structure, generally, a noun, verb, adjective, or adverb; opposed to function word (q.v.).

Context of Communication. The physical, social-psychological, and temporal environment in which communication takes place and which exert influence on the form and content of communication.

Contiguity Disorder. A type of aphasia (q.v.) described by Roman Jakobson resulting in a loss of the ability to combine linguistic units into intelligible sequences. See also SIMILARITY DISORDER.
[Roman Jakobson, "The Cardinal Dichotomy in Language," in *Language: An Enquiry into Its Meaning and Function*, Ruth Nanda Anshen, ed. (New York: Harper & Row, 1957), pp. 155–173, and *Child Language, Aphasia, and Phonological Universals*, Allan R. Keiler, trans. (The Hague: Mouton, 1968).]

Contingency. A dependency relationship between two variables such that the occurrence or nonoccurrence of one is dependent on the occurrence or nonoccurrence of the other.

Contingency Rules Theory. A theory of persuasion that attempts to account for persuasive behaviors by contending that they are purposive and are governed or controlled by their consequences as anticipated by the persuader. The theory attempts to develop behavioral contingency rules that state the expected or anticipated consequence in a specific context and the persuasive strategy or behavior in the form of "if . . . , then" rules, for example, "If A is the anticipated effect in context B, then persuasive behavior C is undertaken."
[Mary John Smith, "Contingency Rules Theory, Context, and Compliance Behaviors," *Human Communication Research* 10 (1984):489–512.]

Contract. A verbal or written agreement between or among people stating what behaviors will and will not be engaged in by each party. The contract system explicitly states what will be defined as acceptable-desirable and unacceptable-undesirable behaviors and what consequences (rewards and punishments) these behaviors will produce.

Contrast Effect. In the social judgment involvement theory (q.v.) of attitude change, the tendency of an individual to maximize the degree of difference between one's initial or anchor attitudes (q.v.) and the attitudes of others that are seen to be different. See also ASSIMILATION EFFECT.

Control. One of the three interpersonal needs in Schutz's Fundamental Interpersonal Relations Orientation theory (FIRO), the need to control or be controlled by others.
[William C. Schutz, *FIRO: A Three-Dimensional Theory of Interpersonal Behavior* (New York: Holt, Rinehart and Winston, 1958).]

Controversia. One of the two types of exercises in declamation (q.v.) (the other being, suasoria, q.v.) in which the student debates some fictional legal case involving, for example, rape, disinheritance, and tyranny.

Conundrum. A riddle or puzzle whose answer involves a pun (q.v.).

Convenience Relationship. One of four cohabitation patterns common among students and identified by C. A. Ridley and colleagues; a relationship of short duration in which the individuals experience regular sexual outlets without any of the responsibilities normally found in a committed relationship; opposed to Linus blanket (q.v.), emancipation (q.v.), and testing (q.v.) relationships.

[C. A. Ridley, D. J. Peterman, and A. W. Avery, "Cohabitation: Does It Make for a Better Marriage?" *The Family Coordinator* 27 (April 1978):129–137).]

Conventions. Procedural rules that specify what may and may not be done in given situations. In communication, conventions generally refer to the rules governing the interaction in an interpersonal relationship that may be established by the culture or social group (in which case, it is synonymous with *norms*) or by the individuals themselves.

Conversation. Informal talk; a type of interpersonal (q.v.) or small group interaction.

Conversational Deviance. A deviance from or violation of some commonly employed rule or norm in interpersonal communication.
[Kathleen Kelley Reardon, "Conversational Deviance: A Structural Model," *Human Communication Research* 9 (1982):59–74.]

Conversational Implicature. An utterance that implies something relevant to the conversation but does not state it explicitly, for example, responding to the statement "It's cold in here" with "That window should be replaced" implies that the cold is coming in through the window and that the window is somehow not functioning correctly.
[H. P. Grice, "Logic and Conversation," in *Syntax and Semantics, Vol. 3: Speech Acts*, P. Cole and J. L. Morgan, eds. (New York: Seminar Press, 1975), pp. 41–58.]

Conversational Maxims. Precepts that speakers follow in adhering to the cooperation principle (q.v.). Four such maxims have been identified by H. P. Grice: (1) *the maxim of quantity* states that speakers cooperate by being as informative as necessary, giving neither too much nor too little information; (2) *the maxim of quality* states that speakers cooperate by speaking what they understand to be true; (3) *the maxim of relation* states that speakers cooperate by saying what is relevant to the conversation; (4) *the maxim of manner* states that speakers cooperate by being clear and avoiding ambiguous or obscure language.
[H. P. Grice, "Logic and Conversation," in *Syntax and Semantics, Vol 3: Speech Acts*, P. Cole and J. L. Morgan, eds. (New York: Seminar Press, 1975), pp. 41–58.]

Conversation Plan. A goal plus a series of utterances that can lead to the goal's achievement.
[Margaret L. McLaughlin, *Conversation: How Talk is Organized* (Beverly Hills, Calif.: Sage, 1984).]

Conversational Repair. Conversational "corrections" addressed to real or imagined violations of some linguistic, communication, or social rule; used during the interaction process, after the perceived violation has occurred, in an attempt to "realign" the talk.
[E. A. Schegloff, G. Jefferson, and H. Sacks, "The Preference for Self-Correction in the Organization of Repair in Conversation," *Language* 53 (1977):361–382; Christopher J. Zahn, "A Reexamination of Conversational Repair," *Communication Monographs* 51 (1984):56–66.]

Conversion. The effect or outcome of persuasion whereby a person's initial belief is totally changed or reversed as in, for example, religious conversion where a person changes religions as a result of some persuasive effort. The media are generally viewed not as agents of conversion but rather of reinforcement where media persuasion is seen to result in a weakening or strengthening of existing beliefs rather than in a complete change as is characteristic of conversion.

Cool Medium. According to Marshall McLuhan (1911–1980), a communication medium that has low definition and is contrasted with a hot medium which has high definition. *Definition* refers to the amount of data or information transmitted by the communication medium. A cartoon is cool, having low definition whereas a photograph is hot, having high definition. Other cool media are the telephone, speech, and television. Cool media, because they contain less information than hot media, necessitate involvement from the receiver of the message. The receiver, for example, has to supply the omitted information in say a telephone conversation. Hot media, in contrast, provide all the necessary data and the receiver does not have to play such an active role in deciphering the message.

[Marshall McLuhan, *Understanding Media* (New York: McGraw-Hall, 1964).]

Cooperation. The act of combining resources, skills, and abilities with another to achieve some commonly desired end.

Cooperative Principle. The principle, articulated by H. P. Grice, stating that speaker and listener cooperate with each other in communicating and will employ specific conversational maxims (q.v.) in order to achieve this cooperation. See also CONVERSATIONAL MAXIMS.

Coordinate Bilingual. Bilingual (q.v.) whose two languages have different meaning systems, for example, *casa* and *house* have different referents for the speaker. Usually a coordinate bilingual is produced when the two languages are learned in different contexts, for example, one language is learned at home and one at school. See also COMPOUND BILINGUAL.

Coordinated Management of Meaning. A theory of communication dealing with the processes through which individuals, each beginning with individually established rules for interaction and interpreting meaning, eventually blend and mesh their individual systems into an interpersonal system in which the interactions and meanings are coordinated.

[Vernon E. Cronen, W. Barnett Pearce, and Linda M. Harris, "The Coordinated Management of Meaning: A Theory of Communication," in *Human Communication Theory*, Frank E. X. Dance, ed. (New York: Harper & Row, 1982), pp. 61–89.]

Coorientation. A condition in which two persons have an orientation (q.v.) to or focus on the same person or object at the same time.

Copy. The script that is to be read or recited by the actor or announcer.

Copybook. A manual for teaching handwriting that contains models of penmanship that the student was to emulate and eventually master.

Copyright. The legal tenent reserving the right to govern a written, filmed, or taped work's reproduction, distribution, and performance.

Corrective Advertising. Advertising designed to correct previous misleading advertisements. The FCC (q.v.) has forced many advertisers to alot a certain portion of their advertising time to publicize these corrections.

Correspondent Inferences. Inferences, or hypotheses, concerning the causes of another's behavior based on behaviors that have only one motivation and which are uncommon and about which we have considerable confidence.

Cost-Benefit Analysis. Originally developed for the analysis of economic systems and now used in the behavioral sciences, it is an approach to interpersonal relationships that focuses on the analysis of costs (effort, problems, punishments, anxiety, and all the negative effects of a relationship) and benefits (rewards, joy, pleasure, satisfaction, financial advantage, and all the positive effects of a relationship). (See also SOCIAL EXCHANGE THEORY.) In linguistics (q.v.) and sociolinguistics (q.v.), a method where the consequences between two alternatives in language planning are analyzed in terms of costs and benefits, advantages and disadvantages.

[Thomas Thorburn, "Cost-Benefit Analysis in Language Planning," in Joshua Fishman, ed., *Advances in the Sociology of Language,* Vol. 2 (The Hague: Mouton, 1972), pp. 511–519.]

Counterattitudinal Advocacy. Arguing for a position that is against a presently held attitude. Considerable evidence exists to show that arguing against one's own attitudes will lead one to change those attitudes in the direction of the advocacy.

Counterconditioning. A therapeutic procedure designed to reverse or extinguish a previously learned (conditioned) response. Normally, the procedure involves conditioning a new response to the old stimulus.

Counterdisqualification. A possible response to *disconfirmation;* the process or act of disqualifying or disconfirming one who disconfirms us. Also referred to as "counterdisconfirmation."

[Carlos E. Sluzki, Janet Helmick Beavin, Alejandro Tarnopolsky, and Eliseo Veron, "Transactional Disqualification," *Archives of General Psychiatry* 16 (April 1967):494–504.]

Courtesy Stigma. A stigma (q.v.) attached to a person because of his or her association with, or being related to, a stigmatized individual.

[Erving Goffman, *Stigma: Notes on the Management of Spoiled Identity* (Englewood Cliffs, N.J.: Prentice-Hall, 1963).]

Courtship. A communication exchange designed to open the channels of communication; phatic communion (q.v.); communication designed to encourage the growth and development of a romantic relationship.

[Kenneth Burke, *A Rhetoric of Motives* (Englewood Cliffs, N.J.: Prentice-Hall, 1950).]

Courtship Behavior. Behavior designed to entice another member to interact romantically and/or sexually. See also QUASICOURTSHIP BEHAVIORS.

Covering Law Perspective. An approach to communication that attempts to discover laws that cover the specific communication behavior under consideration.

[Charles R. Berger, "The Covering Law Perspective as a Theoretical Basis for the Study of Human Communication," *Communication Quarterly* 25 (1977):7–18.]

Covert Rehearsal. Repeating behavior in one's mind in an attempt to fix it more firmly in actual overt performance; internal rehearsal.

Cowboy Syndrome. Term used to describe the closed and unexpressive male, personified here as the John Wayne-type hero—a man who is strong but silent, who needs no one but himself, and who never expresses any of the "softer" emotions.

[J. O. Balswick and C. Peck, "The Inexpressive Male: A Tragedy of American Society?" *The Family Coordinator* 20 (1971):363–368.]

CP/M. Control program for microcomputers, a popular operating system that controls the operation of the computer.

Crash. A stoppage in computer functioning that results in a loss of work or data that is in progress or not yet saved on a disk.

Creativity. A quality of originality. In language, creativity refers to the characteristic of newness or novelty of each sentence; with a finite set of rules, we can create an infinite number of sentences, an ability referred to as creativity, novelty, or productivity.

Credentialling. A type of disclaimer (q.v.) in which one separates oneself from the negative utterances about to be made, for example, "Although I would have voted against it, the board passed the new regulation." (See also DISCLAIMER.) Also used to refer to the practice of awarding promotions or occupational positions on the basis of one's credentials.

[R. P. Dore, *The Diploma Disease* (London: Allen & Unwin, 1976).]

Credibility. The quality of believability. This section explains what constitutes credibility, how we form credibility impressions, and, most importantly, how we can increase our own credibility in all situations. The discussion here, however, uses the public speaking situation for illustration and example.

Credibility is that quality of persuasiveness that depends on the audience's *perception* of the moral character of the speaker. Credibility is something that a listener or receiver perceives a speaker to have; it is not something that the speaker has or does not have in any objective sense. In reality the speaker may be a stupid immoral person, but if perceived by the audience as intelligent and moral then that speaker is said to have high credibility and will, research tells us, be believable.

Writing some 2300 years ago Aristotle said in his *Rhetoric:* "There are three things which inspire confidence in the orator's own character—the three, namely, that induce us to believe a thing apart from any proof of it: good sense, good moral character, and good will."

Much contemporary research has been directed at the question of what makes a person believable. As can be appreciated, it is a question of vital concern to many. Advertisers are interested because it relates directly to the effectiveness or ineffectiveness of their ad campaigns. Is James Garner an effective spokesperson for Polaroid? Is Bill Cosby an effective spokesperson for Jello? For Coca-Cola? Credibility is important to the politician because it determines in great part how people vote. It influences education since the students' perception of teacher credibility will determine the degree of influence the teacher has on a class. There are probably few communication encounters that will not be influenced by considerations of credibility.

Forming Credibility Impressions

We form a credibility impression of a speaker on the basis of (1) the reputation of the speaker (as perceived in our minds), and (2) how that reputation is confirmed or refuted by what the speaker says and does during the public speaking situation. Most of us would find it difficult to operate with the philosophy of Henry Ford who observed, "It is all one to me if a man comes from Sing Sing or Harvard. We hire a man, not his history." Most of us—and the results of numerous experimental investigations clearly support this observation—do consider a person's history, weighing it very heavily in the total evaluation, and do combine that information from history with the more immediate information derived from present interactions. Information from these two sources—from history and from present encounters—interact and the audience forms some collective final assessment of your credibility.

There are, then, three types of credibility that should be considered: *initial credibility, derived credibility,* and *terminal credibility.*

Initial Credibility

Initial credibility is based on the speaker's reputation and on what we know of the speaker's history. It is the credibility that we perceive a speaker to have *before* she or he begins to speak.

Derived Credibility

Derived credibility is the credibility that a listener perceives based on what takes place during the speaking encounter. During any speech we naturally talk about ourselves, whether explicitly or implicitly. The topics we talk about, the vocal emphasis we give them, our facial expression as we talk about them, the degree of conviction we express, and so on, all say something about us. All communication is self-reflexive; all communications says something about the speaker or source. Consequently, all communications relate, directly or indirectly, to the speaker's credibility. Inevitably, in our speech we convey impressions of our competence, our character, or our charisma.

Terminal Credibility

Terminal credibility is the final assessment of credibility that results from the interaction between the initial and the derived credibility. On the basis of your reputation and what transpires during the speech, the audience forms some impression of your terminal credibility. Based on the initial credibility and the derived credibility, a terminal credibility image is formed. At times this is higher than the initial credibility, and at times it is lower. But it is always a product of the interaction of the before (or initial) and the during (or derived) credibility evaluations. The following formula, reflecting how we form credibility impressions, illustrates this interaction.

| Reputation [initial or extrinsic credibility] | $\times$ | During-the-Speech Activities [derived or intrinsic credibility] | $=$ | Final Assessment [terminal credibility] |

Increasing Credibility

Pooling the results of numerous research efforts, three major characteristics or components of credibility can be identified: *competence*—the knowledge and expertise the speaker is seen to possess; *character*—the intentions and concern of the speaker for the audience; and *charisma*—the personality and dynamism of the speaker. Each of these three characteristics and the ways in which a speaker may more effectively demonstrate them will be considered in depth.

As a speaker part of your task is to make your audience see you as a credible, believable, spokesperson. Here are some of the ways in which you may attempt to convey a favorable impression of your competence, your character, and your charisma.

Competence

Competence refers to the knowledge and expertise that a speaker is thought to possess. The more knowledge and expertise the audience perceives the speaker as possessing, the more likely that the speaker will be believed. For example, a writer is thought credible to the extent that she or he is perceived as an expert on the material and has the ability to communicate it in written form.

When you are in a public speaking role, your main task will be to demonstrate your competence to your audience, to make them aware of your knowledge and expertise. There are a number of methods that can be used.

1. *Tell the audience of your special experience or training that qualify you to speak on your specific topic.* If you are speaking on communal living and you have lived on a commune yourself, then include this in your speech. Tell the audience of your unique and personal experiences when these contribute to your credibility.

2. *Cite a variety of research sources.* Make it clear to your audience that you have thoroughly researched the topic by citing some of the books you have read,

the persons you have interviewed, the articles consulted, and so on. Spread these throughout the speech rather than bunching them together at one time.

3. *Stress the particular competencies of your sources if your audience is not aware of them.* Thus, for example, instead of saying simply, "Senator Smith thinks . . . ," also establish the Senator's credibility by saying "Senator Smith, who headed the finance committee for three years and who was formerly a professor of economics at MIT, thinks . . .." In this way it becomes clear to the audience that you have chosen your sources carefully and with a view toward providing the most authoritative sources possible.

4. *Demonstrate confidence with your materials and with the speech situation generally.* Rehearse the speech and familiarize yourself with the unique context in which you will deliver your speech. You should then be able to communicate the resulting confidence—the feeling of being comfortable and at ease—to the audience. If, for example, you are using visual aids, then become so familiar with them that you know exactly what order they are in and exactly at what point you will use each.

5. *Demonstrate your command of the language.* Your use of language and your voice will greatly influence the audience's perception of your credibility. Be especially careful to learn the correct pronunciations of terms or names about which you may be in doubt, and make certain that any potential grammatical errors have been eliminated.

6. *Do not needlessly call attention to your inadequacies as a spokesperson or to any gaps in your knowledge.* No one can know everything and your audience does not expect you to be the exception. But it is not necessary to remind them—stress your competencies, not your inadequacies.

Character

We will perceive a speaker as credible if we perceive that speaker as having what Aristotle referred to as a high moral character. Here we would be concerned with the individual's honesty and basic nature. We would want to know if we could trust that person. A speaker who can be trusted is apt to be believed.

As a speaker, demonstrate those qualities of character that will increase your credibility. A few suggestions may be added to those noted for demonstrating competence.

7. *Stress your fairness.* If delivering a persuasive speech, stress that you have examined both sides of the issue (if, indeed, you have). If you are presenting both sides, then make it clear that your presentation is an accurate and fair one. Be particularly careful not to omit any argument the audience may have already thought of—this is a sure sign that your presentation is not a fair and balanced one. Make it clear to the audience that you would not advocate a position if it were not the conclusion derived from an honest and fair evaluation of the various alternatives.

8. *Stress your concern for enduring values.* Speakers who appear to be concerned with small and insignificant issues are generally seen as less credible than are speakers who demonstrate a concern and a commitment to lasting truths and general principles. Thus, in your speech make it clear to the audience that your position—your thesis—is related to higher order values and, of course, show them exactly how this is true.

9. *Stress your similarity with the audience, particularly your beliefs, attitudes, values, and goals.* Generally, we perceive as believable people who are like

ourselves, especially in basic values. The more similar people are to our own attitudes and beliefs, goals and ambitions, the more likely it is that they will be perceived as credible. Closely related to this is the issue of "common ground." When people align themselves with what we align ourselves, they establish common ground with us and are generally perceived as more believable than people who do not establish this common ground.

10. *Demonstrate your long-term consistency.* Generally, we feel more comfortable putting our trust in someone who has been consistent over time. We become leery of persons who flit from one issue to another or from one team to another. If you have been in favor of XYZ for the last three years, then tell the audience this somewhere in your speech.

11. *Demonstrate a respect and a courtesy for the audience members.* To talk down to them or to insult their intelligence or ability to comprehend will only result in your own credibility suffering. Audiences generally look up to people who treat them with respect.

12. *Make it clear to the audience that you are interested in their welfare rather than simply seeking self-gain.* If the audience feels that you are "out for yourself," they will justifiably downgrade your credibility. Make it clear that the audience's interests are foremost in your mind.

Charisma

Charisma is best viewed as a composite of the speaker's personality and dynamism as seen by the audience. Generally, we perceive as credible or believable speakers we like rather than speakers we do not like; speakers who have what we commonly call a "pleasing personality"; speakers who are friendly and pleasant rather than aloof and reserved. Similarly, we seem to favor the dynamic over the hesitant, nonassertive speaker; the shy, introverted, soft-spoken individual is perceived as less credible than the extroverted and forceful individual.

13. *Demonstrate a positive orientation to the public speaking situation and to the entire speaker-audience encounter.* We seem to like listening to positive rather than negative people and so it will help if you accentuate the positive and eliminate the negative, as the old song goes. Positive and forward-looking people are seen as more credible than negative and backward-looking people.

14. *Demonstrate assertiveness.* Show the audience that you are a person who will stand up for your rights and will not back off simply because the odds may be against you or because you are outnumbered.

15. *Be enthusiastic.* The lethargic speaker, the speaker who somehow plods through the speech is the very opposite of the charismatic speaker. Try viewing a film of Martin Luther King or Billy Graham speaking; they are totally absorbed with the speech and with the audience. They are excellent examples of the enthusiasm that makes speakers charismatic.

16. *Be emphatic.* Use language that is emphatic rather than colorless and indecisive. Use gestures that are clear and decisive rather than random and hesitant. An emphatic speaker demonstrates commitment to the position advocated and the audience will be much more likely to agree with a speaker who is convinced of the proposition being presented.

General Guidelines

In addition to these specific suggestions for projecting competence, character, and charisma, here are four general guidelines that will assist you in putting these suggestions into operation most effectively.

17. *Develop or strengthen these characteristics as a person as well as as a speaker.* Enhance your competence, character, and charisma. I know that this is easy to say but may be extremely difficult to put into practice. Nevertheless, it is important to have these as goals because their actual development is the best insurance that they will function to make you credible in public speaking situations as well as in your everyday interactions.

18. *Demonstrate your possession of these three components of credibility, especially in your introduction.* Whether you introduce your own speech or whether someone else does it, it is important to legitimize yourself to the audience. If you have a broad knowledge of the topic or, say, firsthand experience, tell the audience of this knowledge and experience as early as possible. If there is some sort of formal introduction to your speech, you may have some important references integrated into this introduction to help establish your credibility. Thus, for example, if you are to speak on living under wartime conditions, the audience should know that you have in fact lived under these conditions, and you should supply the person introducing you with the pertinent data.

19. *Exercise moderation.* Be careful that you do not emphasize your competence so much that the audience concludes that you therefore must be incompetent. It is rather like people who keep telling us that they are telling the truth. They say it so often and forcefully that we conclude that they must be lying. "Doubt the man," advises Louise Colet, "who swears to his devotion." So, while you should stress your credibility, do so modestly and always truthfully.

20. *Use a variety of methods to establish your credibility.* Do not rely on the same few methods to build your credibility. Use a number of different methods and be sure to give consideration to all three components of credibility: competence, character, and charisma.

[Stephen W. Littlejohn, "A Bibliography of Studies Related to Variables of Source Credibility," *Bibliographic Annual in Speech Communication* 2 (1971):1–40; James C. McCroskey, *An Introduction to Rhetorical Communication,* 4th ed. (Englewood Cliffs, N.J.: Prentice-Hall, 1982).]

Credibility Gap. First used in the 1960s to describe public distrust and disbelief in political promises and the difference between what was promised and what was delivered, the term is now used more generally to refer to a tendency between or among people to disbelieve each other and to doubt the honesty and integrity of each other; the difference between the image a person tries to project (highly positive) and the image a receiver perceives (usually less positive), which is often taken as a measure of the extent to which the public image is disbelieved.

Creole. A language derived from a pidgin (q.v.) language and which is a native language to some speakers; a pidgin language that developed into the primary language of a particular speech community. Creole French spoken in Haiti is perhaps the most well-known example of a Creole language.

[Dell Hymes, ed. *Pidginization and Creolization of Languages* (Cambridge: Cambridge University Press, 1971).]

Criterion Group. A group whose performance on a test is used to establish the validity of the test; a group known, on the basis of other information, to possess a certain characteristic (for example, assertiveness) and which is tested on that characteristic (an assertiveness test) in order to measure the validity of the test. If these highly assertive people score high on this test, it is taken as an indication that the test is valid.

Critical Period. The time in the development of an animal or human during which the learning of a particular behavior is especially easy or possible. Language is currently assumed to have a critical period for acquisition and is thought to be from birth until around the age of puberty.

Criticism. The process of evaluation. Criticism, noted Hugh Blair in his *Lectures on Rhetoric and Belles Lettres,* teaches us "to admire and to blame with judgment, and not to follow the crowd blindly." Numerous types of criticism have been identified: (1) *impressionistic criticism* focuses on the critic's personal preferences and impressions of the work; (2) *analytic criticism* focuses on identifying and cataloging the elements in the work; (3) *synthetic criticism* focuses on reconstructing the entire situation in which the speech or literary work was constructed but does not interpret these reconstructions; (4) *judicial criticism* focuses on the elements of the work (as in analytic criticism) and the reconstruction of the situation (as in synthetic criticism) and on judging and evaluating the work. See also NEW CRITICISM; PRACTICAL CRITICISM; THEORETICAL CRITICISM; TEXTUAL CRITICISM.

[Herbert A. Wichelns, "The Literary Criticism of Oratory," in *Studies in Rhetoric and Public Speaking in Honor of James A. Winans* (New York: Century Co., 1925), pp. 181–216; Lester Thonssen, A. Craig Baird, and Waldo W. Braden, *Speech Criticism* (Melbourne, Fla.: Kreiger Publishing, 1981); Hendrie Weisinger and Norman M. Lobenz, *Nobody's Perfect (How to Give Criticism and Get Results)* (New York: Warner Books, 1981).]

Criticism, Conformity to the Principles of the Art as a Standard of. The standard, in criticism, by which a work is judged according to the degree to which it conformed or did not conform to the principles of the art. A communication would be judged positively if it conformed to the principles of effective communication and negatively if it did not conform.

Cross-Cultural Communication. See INTERCULTURAL COMMUNICATION.

Crossed Transactions. In transactional analysis (q.v.), a transaction involving a message sent to one ego state (q.v.) but responded to by another ego state. In all there are 72 possible crossed transactions all of which may be reduced to two general types. In Type I the communication—to use the most common pattern—begins as Adult to Adult. That is, A as Adult says to B, also as Adult, "This is great furniture; too bad we can't afford it." But B does not respond as an Adult, nor does B address the message to A's Adult. Rather, B responds as a Child to a Parent and says, for example, "Let's buy it anyway. I want it. Buy it for me." This transaction might be diagramed as follows:

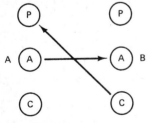

In Type II the transaction again begins with an Adult addressing an Adult, saying "This is great furniture; too bad we can't afford it." Here, however, B responds as a Parent to a Child, saying, "Now you know you can't afford it, so why waste your time and mine looking at it?" This dialogue can be diagramed as follows:

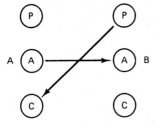

It is with crossed transactions that problems in interpersonal communication arise. For example, in Type I-crossed, A (as Adult) may try to reason with B (as Child), but success will be almost impossible since A's arguments presuppose that B is in the Adult state, which B is not. Or A might switch to the Parent state and answer B as a parent would: "I told you we can't afford it and that finishes that." This may end the conversation, but it does not clear up the communication breakdown. In Type II-crossed, A is again presented with a serious breakdown. A could attempt to reason with B and say something to the effect that he or she was just looking and realized that they could not afford it. But this kind of approach would only have an effect on someone in the Adult ego state.

We may generalize from these situations and note that communication has broken down largely because messages were addressed to inappropriate ego states. See also ADULT EGO STATE; CHILD EGO STATE; PARENT EGO STATE; COMPLEMENTARY TRANSACTIONS; ULTERIOR TRANSACTIONS.

[Eric Berne, *Games People Play* (New York: Grove Press, 1964).]

CRT. Cathode ray tube; the videodisplay portion of the computer system.

Cryptogram. Any message in secret writing or code.

Cryptograph. A system of secret writing or writing in code.

Cryptography. The study or science of secret writing.

[Fletcher Pratt, *Secret and Urgent: The Study of Codes and Ciphers* (Indianapolis: Bobbs-Merrill, 1939).]

Cue Deletion Hypothesis. A psycholinguistic hypothesis holding that the deletion of cue words (for example, *that, who, which*) increases the complexity of sentence processing.

[Jerry A. Fodor and M. F. Garrett, "Some Syntactic Determinants of Sentential Complexity," *Perception and Psychophysics* 2 (1967):289–296.]

Cued Recall. Recall aided by the presentation of cues or hints.

Cultural Script. See SCRIPT.

Culture Lag. The time delay between the development of a particular technology and the society's development of the means to control it.

Culture Shock. The shock (surprise, disorientation, inability to cope) one feels upon entering a strange culture, a culture with different mores, norms, values, and the like.

Cumulative Nature of Communication. A principle of communication that refers to the effects of communication being a composite of the effects of all of our experiences, especially previous communications. Message effects are not compartmentalized but instead are combined with everything else in our memories.

Cuneiform. Syllabic, wedge-shaped writing developed by the Sumerians around 4000 B.C. This system was used by the Sumerians and their neighbors (for example, the Hittites and the Akkadians) for almost 4000 years and then passed out of existence until cuneiform texts were discovered in the nineteenth century.

Cursive Writing. Simplified form of writing used for daily communication as distinguished from writing used for public or display purposes as was Egyptian hieroglyphics (q.v.) or contemporary calligraphy (q.v.).

Cybernetics. Coined by mathematician Norbert Wiener (1894–1964), the science of control and communication in information systems, both mechanical and human.
[Norbert Wiener, *Cybernetics* (Cambridge, Mass.: M.I.T. Press, 1948).]

Damping Effect. A lessening of the amplitude of vibrations due to the surrounding medium's absorbing part of the energy, for example, the dampers in a piano keep the strings from sounding brassy.

Data (*sing.* Datum). Information obtained from some kind of research or analysis. Usually refers to the results derived from scientific studies and may be, for example, behaviors observed, the number of particular messages recorded, or the scores or ratings derived from tests or scales.

Data Bank. All the data available for access by a computer; a data file usually containing information on some specific topic, for example, diseases, tax records, or marriage and divorce statistics.

Data Base. A collection of data stored in memory that can be accessed with relative ease.

Data Base Management. The procedure for storing data, organizing it in a variety of ways, and retrieving it.

Date. An extensional device (q.v.) used to emphasize the notion of constant change and symbolized by a subscript, for example, John Smith $_{1986}$ is not John Smith $_{1980}$.

Dead Metaphor. A figure of speech in which one item is compared with another (metaphor, q.v.) that is used so often that its metaphorical quality or origin goes unnoticed, for example, "the arm of the chair" or "the leg of the table" are dead metaphors.

Deaf. Congenital loss of useable hearing.

Deafened. Loss of hearing caused by accident or disease rather than by some congenital disorder.

Deaf-Mute. One who is both unable to hear or speak.

Debate. A relatively formal procedure whereby two sides of an issue are argued. Generally, a proposition is stated, for example, "The electoral system should be abolished" or "Federal aid should be granted to parochial schools" and the arguments in favor and those against the proposition are expressed in a series of speeches and questions and answers.
[Douglas Ehninger and Wayne Brockriede, *Decision by Debate,* 2d ed. (New York: Harper & Row, 1978).]

Decay. A theoretical process referring to the loss of information in memory due to the fading of impressions left in the brain by the previously learned material.

Deception Cues. Verbal or nonverbal behaviors that communicate that the source is lying but does not reveal what is the truth. See also LEAKAGE.

Decibel. A measure of sound intensity.

Declamation (Declamatio). An exercise used extensively by the ancients and revived periodically throughout history to train the student orator. This method soon degenerated into an unrealistic, sterile exercise in style and delivery, where the form and appearance of the speech was more important than its substance. A major part of Roman rhetorical education was devoted to instruction in elaborately styling and delivering these speeches, often on ficticious legal cases. Controversia (q.v.) and suasoria (q.v.) were the two popular forms of declamation. [D.L. Clark, *Rhetoric in Greco-Roman Education* (New York: Columbia University Press, 1957).]

Decoder. Something that takes a message in one form (for example, sound waves) and translates it into another form (for example, nerve impulses), from which meaning can be formulated (for example, in vocal-auditory communication). In human communication the decoder is the auditory mechanism; in electronic communication the decoder is, for example, the telephone earpiece. See also ENCODER.

Decoding. The process of extracting a message by changing it from one form to another; for example, translating speech sounds into nerve impulses. See also ENCODING.

Deduction. Reasoning that progresses from a general proposition or generally accepted truth to a specific instance.

Deep Structure. A sentence's underlying elements and their relationships to each other that closely represent its meaning; the representation of a sentence generated by the phrase structure (q.v.) rules in a generative grammar (q.v.).

Default. A value assigned by the computer program when another value is not supplied by the user.

Defense Mechanism. In psychoanalytic theory, those unconscious reactions designed to lessen anxiety, for example, rationalization (q.v.), projection (q.v.), displacement (q.v.).

Defensiveness. An attitude of an individual or an atmosphere in a group characterized by threats, fear, and domination; messages evidencing evaluation (q.v.), control (q.v.), strategy (q.v.), neutrality (q.v.), superiority (q.v.), and certainty (q.v.) are assumed to lead to defensiveness; opposed to supportiveness (q.v.). [Jack Gibb, "Defensive Communication," *Journal of Communication* 11 (1961):141–148.]

Definition. The explanation of the meaning of a word or phrase. Usually, definitions center on denotative or referential meaning (q.v.) but may at times also include connotative meaning (q.v.). Hugh Walpole, in his classic *Semantics: The Nature of Words and Their Meanings,* considers 25 ways in which a concept may be defined: by behavior ("a scientist is one who . . ."), by sex ("A rooster is the male of the domestic fowl"), by part relations ("A hand is part of the arm"), and so on. Noted here are some of the modes of definition.

Definition by Etymology

One is to define a term by its etymology. For example, in attempting to define the word *communication,* you might note that it comes from the Latin *communis* meaning "common": in "communicating" you seek to establish a commonness, a sameness, a similarity with another individual. And *woman* comes from the Anglo-Saxon *wifman,* which meant literally a "wife man," where the word *man* was applied to both sexes. Through phonetic change *wifman* became *woman.* Most of the larger dictionaries and, of course, etymological dictionaries will help you determine etymological definitions.

Definition by Authority

You may also define a term by authority. You might, for example, define *lateral thinking* by authority and say that Edward deBono, who developed lateral thinking in 1966, has noted that "Lateral thinking involves moving sideways to look at things in a different way. Instead of fixing on one particular approach and then working forward from that the lateral thinker tries to find other approaches." Or you might use the authority of cynic and satirist Ambrose Bierce and define *love* as nothing but "a temporary insanity curable by marriage" and *friendship* as "a ship big enough to carry two in fair weather, but only one in foul."

Definition by Operations

Operational definition is perhaps the most important means of definition. Here you define a concept by indicating the operations one would go through in constructing the object. Thus, for example, to operationally define a chocolate cake, you would provide the recipe. The operational definition of stuttering would include an account of how the act of stuttering is performed and by what procedures stuttering might be observed.

Definition by Negation

You might also define a term by noting what that term is not—that is, defining by negation. A *wife,* you might say, "is not a cook, a cleaning person, a baby sitter, a seamstress, a sex partner. A *wife* is . . ."

Definition by Direct Symbolization

You might also define a term by direct symbolization—that is, by showing the actual thing or, if that is not possible, a picture or model of it.

Deictic Element/Term. A gesture or word that points to the participants of an interaction or to the places talked about.

Deictic Movement. Bodily movements that point to an object, place, or event.

Delayed Auditory Feedback. A process of delaying the sound that is normally fed back to the speaker immediately for a specified amount of time, usually around two-tenths of a second, with the result that speech becomes disfluent and the speaker confused and disoriented. Used experimentally in stuttering research; analogous to delayed visual feedback (q.v.).

Delayed Reaction. Response that is consciously delayed while the situation is analyzed; opposed to signal reaction (q.v.).

Delayed Speech. Speech that has not developed to the level expected for the child's chronological age.

Delayed Visual Feedback. An experimental procedure in which, by means of videotaped recordings, visual presentation of a person's own behavior is delayed, creating a variety of problems for the subject; analogous to delayed auditory feedback (q.v.).

Deliberative Rhetoric. One of the three major types of rhetoric (q.v.) identified by Aristotle; rhetoric concerned with political oratory, with persuading an audience to act or not to act on the basis of expediency-inexpediency. See also EPIDEICTIC RHETORIC, FORENSIC RHETORIC.

Deliberative Speeches. Political speeches; speeches concerned with exhortation and dehortation, with expediency and inexpediency.

Delphi Method. Developed by the RAND Corporation, the Delphi method was used to help forecast new developments on a variety of subjects. In this method, a pool of experts is established, and there is no personal interaction. Unlike the nominal group, where all members sit around a table, the members of a Delphi group may be scattered throughout the world. A Delphi questionnaire is distributed to all members asking them to respond to what they feel are, for example, the communication problems the organization will have to face in the next

25 years. Members record their predictions, and the questionnaires are sent back anonymously.

Responses are tabulated, recorded, and distributed to the experts, who then revise their predictions in light of the composite list. They then submit these revised predictions (again anonymously). These are again tabulated, recorded, and returned. The process continues for a number of rounds, or until the responses seem not to change significantly. The composite or final list represents the predictions or forecast of this group of experts.

Note that with this approach, personality conflicts are eliminated; status differences that might inhibit open and honest responses are also eliminated. Although it takes a great deal of time to construct the questionnaire and to tabulate the responses, the process uses very little of the experts' time. Physical distance, which is such an important barrier to effective communication with most methods, is no problem here; the post office does the work.

[Richard E. Tersine and Walter E. Riggs, "The Delphi Technique: A Long-Range Planning Tool," *Business Horizons* 19 (April 1976):51–56.]

Demand Ticket. An utterance that demands or coerces the listener to return the conversation to the initial speaker, for example, "You know what?" or "Guess what happened last night?" or "Hey, Alice." See also TICKET.

[Robert E. Nofsinger, Jr., "The Demand Ticket: A Conversational Device for Getting the Floor," *Communication Monographs* 42 (1975):1–9.]

Demassification. The process of dividing up the audience of mass communication into smaller, more clearly defined and homogeneous groups so that programming and advertising may be more focused.

Democratic Leader. A leader who allows the group members to make their own decision but helps guide the decision-making process without attempting to direct the group to accept his or her point of view. See also AUTHORITARIAN LEADER; LAISSEZ-FAIRE LEADER.

Demographic Analysis. The analysis of certain population variables such as sex, age, occupational status, religion, and geographical distribution.

Demographics. Statistical data on audiences.

Denasality. Vocal quality characterized by a lack of nasal resonance when no air is emitted through the nose. See also NASALITY.

Denial. A defense mechanism (q.v.) whereby the individual blocks out threatening stimuli in an attempt to protect himself or herself.

Denotation. Referential meaning; the objective or descriptive meaning of a word. See also CONNOTATION.

Dependent Clause. See CLAUSE.

Depth. The degree to which the inner personality—the inner core of an individual—is penetrated in interpersonal interaction. As relationships become more intense, depth increases. See also SOCIAL PENETRATION.

Depth Hypothesis. A model of grammar or sentence production based on a constituent analysis (q.v.) framework and a basic linear, left-to-right sentence production analysis.

[Victor H. Yngve, "A Model and an Hypothesis for Language Structure," *Proceedings of the American Philosophical Society* 104 (1960):444–466.]

Deregulation. The elimination of government monitoring of business and industry.

Derivational Theory of Complexity (DTC). A psycholinguistic theory holding that psychological complexity varies proportionately with linguistic complexity, for example, according to the DTC, the more transformations (q.v.) a sentence has, the more difficult its comprehension or recall will be; understanding of a sentence—according to the DTC—involves essentially detransforming it or retracing the stages through which it was derived.

[J. A. Fodor and M. Garrett, "Some Syntactic Determinants of Sentential Complexity," *Perception and Psychophysics* 2 (1967):289–296.]

Derived Credibility. See INTRINSIC CREDIBILITY.

Descriptive Adequacy of a Grammar. The criterion of a grammar by which it must provide an analysis of the sentences of the language that represent the native speakers intuitive knowledge of the language. For example, a descriptively adequate grammar would have to represent paraphrases (which speakers know to have the same meaning) as similar and an ambiguous sentence as having at least two meanings. See also OBSERVATIONAL ADEQUACY OF A GRAMMAR.

[Noam Chomsky, *Current Issues in Linguistic Theory* (The Hague: Mouton, 1964).]

Descriptive Grammar. A grammar that describes the rules that speakers of a language use when they speak and understand sentences; opposed to prescriptive grammar (q.v.). No evaluative judgments are contained in descriptive grammar.

Desensitization. A form of conditioning (actually, counterconditioning) developed by Joseph Wolpe in which an individual develops a hierarchy of behaviors and gradually desensitizes himself or herself to the least threatening ones and eventually works up to the desired behaviors. See also FLOODING.

[Joseph Wolpe, *Psychotherapy by Reciprocal Inhibition* (Stanford, Calif.: Stanford University Press, 1958).]

Destigmatization. The removal or reduction in the effect of social stigma (q.v.).

Determinism. The assumption that behavior does not occur freely or randomly but instead results from the operation of other events.

Determinism, Principle of. The principle of verbal interaction that holds that all verbalizations are to some extent purposeful, that there is a reason for every verbalization.

[Robert E. Pittenger, Charles F. Hocket, and John J. Danehy, *The First Five Minutes: A Sample of Microscopic Interview Analysis* (Ithaca, N.Y.: Paul Martineau, 1960).]

Developmental Psycholinguistics. The study of first language acquisition in the child.

Deviant. One whose thinking or behaving differs significantly from the norm of the group or society.

Devil's Advocate. One who takes the opposing position in an attempt to have the arguments being presented examined in depth.

Devil Terms. See ULTIMATE TERMS.

Dewey's Reflective Thinking Steps. A way of thinking, systematized by educational theorist and philosopher John Dewey (1859–1952), which included the following steps: (1) the perception of a problem or difficulty; (2) the definition of the problem; (3) the formulation of possible solutions; (4) the analysis of the consequences of such solutions; and (5) the testing of the solution(s).

[John Dewey, *How We Think* (Boston: Heath, 1910).]

Diachronic. Historical. Diachronic linguistics deals with the development of languages over time. See also SYNCHRONIC.

Diacritics. Distinguishing marks on letters providing guides for pronunciation, including accent marks (é); dieresis (ä), used above the second of two adjacent vowels to indicate a separate pronunciation; and cedilla (ç), used under a consonant, for example in French, to indicate that it is to be pronounced differently.

Dialect. A social or regional variation of a language. Dialects, unlike other languages, are mutually intelligible. Dialectal variations occur at all levels of language—phonological, semantic, and syntactic. Over long periods of time dialects may develop into separate languages, for instance French, Italian, Spanish, and other languages were originally dialects of Latin.

Dialect Atlas. A collection of maps detailing the areas in which dialect variations are spoken.

Dialect Geography. See DIALECTOLOGY.

Dialectic. A method of reasoning, teaching, and analysis that proceeds through a series of questions and answers; the art of debating a proposition through question and answer, most clearly illustrated in Plato's dialogues where Socrates attempts to discover and teach truth through questions and answers. To Aristotle, rhetoric (q.v.) was the counterpart of dialectic; after the truth was discovered by using dialectic, it was necessary to persuade others of this truth through rhetoric.

Dialectology. The study of dialects (q.v.) and dialect patterns; also referred to as linguistic geography or area linguistics.

Dialogue. A form of communication in which there is two-way interaction—each person is both speaker and listener, both sender and receiver; opposed to monologue (q.v.). The term *dialogic communication* is an extension of this basic meaning and refers to a communication whose objective is mutual understanding and empathy. In dialogic communication there is a respect for the other person not because of what this person can do for you, but simply because this person is a human being and therefore deserves to be treated with honesty, caring, and sincerity.
[Martin Buber, *Between Man and Man,* Ronald G. Smith, trans. (New York: Macmillan, 1965), and *I and Thou,* 2d ed. (New York: Scribners, 1958); T. Dean Thomlison, *Toward Interpersonal Dialogue* (New York: Longman, 1982); Richard L. Johannesen, "The Emerging Concept of Communication as Dialogue," *Quarterly Journal of Speech* 62 (1971):373–382; Reuel L. Howe, *The Miracle of Dialogue* (New York: Seabury Press, 1963).]

Diary. A record of one's thoughts, feelings, and experiences. See also JOURNAL.

Diatribe. Derived from the Greek and originally meaning scholarly discourse, the term now refers to violent and abusive denunciation.

Dichotic Listening. An experimental procedure in which different messages are received by each ear while the subject is directed to listen to one of them.

Diction. In style, the proper use of words. In speech, the particular pronunciation or articulation of sounds and words.

Dictionary. The word list of a language with, for example, definitions, pronunciations, and part-of-speech identifications; in generative grammar (q.v.), a part of the semantic component of the grammar that provides the meanings of each lexical item of the language.

Differential Probability Hypothesis. An hypothesis holding that high frequency behaviors may be used to reinforce low frequency behaviors. Also known as the "Premack principle," after psychologist David Premack.
[David Premack, "Toward Empirical Behavioral Laws: I. Positive Reinforcement," *Psychological Review* 66 (1959).]

Differential Psycholinguistics. The study of differences in speech and language that have some relationship to cognitive and/or behavioral differences. See also PSYCHOLINGUISTICS.
[Joseph A. DeVito, *The Psychology of Speech and Language: An Introduction to Psycholinguistics* (New York: Random House, 1970; Washington, D.C.: University Press of America, 1981).]

Diffusion of Information. The passage of information throughout society.

Diffusion of Innovations. Diffusion refers to the new information, the innovation, or the new process as it passes through the society at large or through the relevant social system. The innovation may be of any type—for example, contact lenses, calculators, electric typewriters, food processors, behavioral objectives in teaching, experiential learning, multimedia instruction. Adoption refers to individuals' positive reactions to the innovation and its incorporation into their habitual behavior patterns.

Obviously all people do not choose to adopt or reject the innovation at the same time. Researchers in the area of information diffusion generally distinguish five types of adopters.

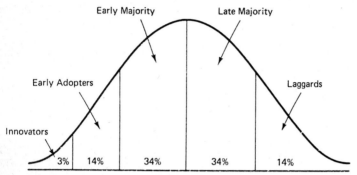

The five types of adopters as represented in the population.

1. Innovators. These are the first to adopt the innovation and constitute less than 3 percent of the total population. The innovators are not necessarily the originators of the new idea; rather, they are the ones who introduce the idea on a reasonably broad scale.
2. Early Adopters. These people adopt the innovation next and make up about 14 percent of the total population. Sometimes called "the influentials," these people legitimize the idea and make it acceptable to people in general.
3. Early Majority. These adopt the innovation next and constitute about 34 percent. This group follows the influentials and further legitimize the innovation.
4. Late Majority. This group also constitutes about 34 percent of the total population and are next-to-last in adopting the innovation. People in this group may follow either the influentials or the early majority.
5. Laggards. This group is the last to adopt the innovation and constitutes about 14 percent of the total population. People in this group may take the lead from people in any of the previous three groups.

These five groups constitute almost 100 percent of the population. The remaining portion are referred to as "diehards," and these are people who never adopt the innovation. These are the cooks who never use the blender or the food processor, the teachers who refuse to use audiovisual materials in their teaching, the doctors who refuse to use newly discovered medication, and so on. There are some instances in which there are no diehards. For example, teachers may wish to continue using a particular textbook, but when it goes out of print, they are forced to change and join the group of laggards.

It has been found that early as opposed to late adopters—the innovators as compared with the laggards—generally are younger, are of a higher socioeconomic status, have more specialized occupations, are more empathic, are less dogmatic, are most oriented toward change, make more use of available information, are closer to the actual agents of change, have a more cosmopolitan orientation, and are generally opinion leaders.

[Everett M. Rogers, *Diffusion of Innovations,* 3rd ed. (Riverside, N.J.: Free Press, 1983).]

Diffusion of Responsibility. The situation in which the responsibility to help a victim is spread over all the bystanders or observers; the responsibility is diffused throughout the crowd of observers. Often in large crowds no one offers to help a victim. See also BYSTANDER EFFECT.

[J. M. Darley and B. Latane, "Bystander Intervenion in Emergencies: Diffusion of Responsibility," *Journal of Personality and Social Psychology* 8 (1968):377–383.]

Digital Communication. Communication signals that are discrete—that may be analyzed as belonging to one of a fixed number of categories (for example, received or not received, yes or no, on or off)—rather than continuous; opposed to analogic communication (q.v.).

Digital System. A system that consists of discrete (rather than continuous) elements and works on an all-or-none principle. Verbal communication systems are generally considered to be basically digital. See also ANALOGIC SYSTEM.

Diglossia. A special form of bilingualism where one language is used for formal purposes and the other for informal or home purposes.

[Charles Ferguson, "Diglossia," *Word* 15 (1959):325–340.]

Dilatory Motion. A motion designed to accomplish an illegal delay in the conduct of business.

Dilemma. An argument in which the listener or opponent is offered two alternatives, both of which are undesirable; an argument that presents a kind of avoidance-avoidance conflict (q.v.); a type of refutation that involves demonstrating that the opponent's position can result in only two possibilities neither of which is desirable, and these two alternatives are the horns of a dilemma.

Ding-Dong Theory. Also referred to as the theory of phonetic types, a theory developed by linguist Max Muller to account for the origin of language, which holds that everything responds with some kind of sound when it is struck and that these sounds fall into basic phonetic types that became the roots for the words of the language.

Dingleberries. Message items that are thrown around during a speech but which are not really related to the main proposition, the central purpose, or the theme of the speech.

Directive Function of Communication. Communication intended to persuade; communication that serves to direct the receiver's thoughts or behaviors.

Disclaimer. Terms or phrases that attempt to deny responsibility for or interest in some person, object, or event. Disclaimers weaken the strength of a statement as in, for example, "I may be wrong about this but . . ."

[J. P. Hewitt and R. Stokes, "Disclaimers," *American Sociological Review* 40 (1975):1–11; Margaret L. McLaughlin, *Conversation: How Talk Is Organized* (Beverly Hills, Calif.: Sage, 1984).]

Disclosure. See SELF-DISCLOSURE.

Disconfirmation. The process by which one ignores or denies the right of the individual to define himself or herself. See also COUNTERDISQUALIFICATION.

Discordance. Messages containing two mutually incompatible meanings (for example, two conflicting emotions or feelings).

[Ernst Beier, "How We Send Emotional Messages," *Psychology Today* 8 (1974):53–56.]

Discounting Hypothesis. An hypothesis holding that inconsistent information, or information that is inconsistent with existing information, will be discounted or thought to be untrue; supports primacy (q.v.) over recency (q.v.).
[Norman H. Anderson and Ann Jacobson, "Effects of Stimulus Inconsistency and Discounting Impression Formation," *Journal of Personality and Social Psychology* 2 (1965):531–539.]

Discourse. The expression of thought in an extended stretch of speech, usually consisting of at least several sentences.

Discourse Analysis. The analysis of an extended stretch of speech as opposed to the analysis of linguistic units within the boundaries of a sentence.
[Zellig Harris, *Discourse Analysis Reprints* (The Hague: Mouton, 1963).]

Discrimination. In social psychology, the act of making distinctions among groups (for example, religious, ethnic, racial) and attributing negative characteristics to various groups; often a synonym for prejudice. In hearing, the act of perceiving differences among sounds.

Disengagement. The process of severing a relationship temporarily or permanently; the process or act by which one withdraws from a relationship.

Dish. An antenna shaped like a dish and used to receive signals from satellites.

Disk Drive. That part of a computer system that receives and records data on a disk.

Displaced Speech. Speech used to refer to that which is not present or in the immediate perceptual field.

Displacement. In language, the characteristic which makes possible the ability to communicate about things that are remote in both time and space. In psychoanalytic theory, a defense mechanism (q.v.) by which an individual gratifies otherwise thwarted impulses by focusing them on a substitute object, for example, an employee who is given a hard time by the boss and who cannot show aggression and hostility toward the boss (for fear of being fired) may redirect the aggressive impulses to his or her children or spouse.

Display Rules. Rules governing the appropriateness or inappropriateness of displaying various emotions. Display rules vary from one culture to another.

Disposition. In rhetorical theory, the arrangement of the parts of the speech and the strategies guiding such arrangements. In contemporary communication, this area is referred to as "organization."

Disqualification. The process of sending messages that invalidate one's other messages; the process of communicating contradictory, ambiguous, or self-contradictory messages.
[Janet Beavin Bavelas and Beverly J. Smith, "A Method for Scaling Verbal Disqualification," *Human Communication Research* 8 (1982):214–227.]

Dissimile. A figure of speech in which two things are contrasted, for example, "He was a tiger in business but a pussycat in love."

Distinctive Feature. A feature of the sound system of a language that distinguishes one phoneme (q.v.) from another, for example, /t/ and /d/ are identical except that /t/ is produced without a vibration of the vocal cords and /d/ is produced with such a vibration. This feature of voicing is therefore a distinctive feature since it distinguishes one phoneme from another.
[Noam Chomsky and Morris Halle, *The Sound Pattern of English* (New York: Harper & Row, 1968).]

Distress-Relief Quotient. Developed by John Dollard and O. Hobart Mowrer, the ratio of distress expression phrases to the sum of these plus relief expressing phrases: $D/D + R$.

[John Dollard and O. Hobart Mowrer, "A Method of Measuring Tension in Written Documents," *Journal of Abnormal and Social Psychology* 42 (1947):3–32.]

Divine Origin Theory. A theory attributing the origin of all things, including language, to God.

Documentary Film. A form of film making in which factual materials are presented for educational and/or persuasive purposes. Robert Flaherty's *Nanook of the North* (1922) is one of the most famous documentaries and has served as a model for many later ones.

Dogmatism. Closed-mindedness; an unwillingness or inability to consider opposing points of view or ideas contrary to existing attitudes.

This concept of dogmatism, or closed-mindedness, is significant in communication primarily because dogmatic people treat communications very differently. Closed-minded people are heavily dependent upon reinforcement for their reactions to information. They will evaluate information on the basis of the rewards and the punishments they receive. We all do this to some extent; the closed-minded person, however, does this to a greater degree than do most people. The open-minded person is better able to resist the reinforcements of other people and outside situations.

All communications are to an extent ego reflexive, that is, all say something about the speaker as well as about taxes, crime, pollution, or whatever. In dealing with this inevitable message duality, the closed-minded person has difficulty separating the information about the source or speaker from the information about the world. The open-minded person, on the other hand, can accept or reject the information about the world and either accept or reject the information about the speaker independently of each other.

Assume that a conservative wishes to obtain information about liberalism or for some reason has a need to obtain such information. If this individual is closed-minded, it is likely that this information will come from conservative sources writing or speaking about liberalism. Closed-minded people will rarely put themselves into the position of obtaining information from sources that will contradict their existing belief system. Thus when closed-minded individuals seek information relevant to their belief systems, that information will more likely be secondhand and particularly from the hand of a source sharing their belief systems. Whereas closed-minded people will fear obtaining information from firsthand sources which might contradict their own belief systems, open-minded people will not have this fear and will consult the best available sources whether they be in or out of sympathy with their own belief systems.

Closed-minded people see the world as generally threatening. Because of this perceived threat, they become anxious and unable to deal with the relevant information independent of the source (as already noted). Consequently, they come to rely very heavily on authority. They do not evaluate information themselves, but allow the authority to evaluate it for them. Then all there is to do is accept the authority's conclusions. Open-minded people, on the other hand, see the world as nonthreatening, even friendly. They are not anxious and hence may evaluate information calmly and rationally. Although they do not ignore authority they do not accept what an authority says uncritically.

In terms of interpersonal relationships, closed-minded people will evaluate others according to the similarity-dissimilarity of others' belief systems with their own. They evaluate positively those people who have similar belief systems and negatively those people who have dissimilar belief systems. Closed-minded people become friends with people who are of the same religion, same race, and same political persuasion. Open-minded individuals do not use similarity of belief systems or homophily as the measure of interpersonal relationships.

These two types are extremes. Few people are completely closed and few people are completely open. The vast majority of people exist somewhere in between these two extremes. The important issue to see is that we are all to some extent closed-minded and to the extent that we are we prevent meaningful interpersonal interaction.

[Milton Rokeach, *The Open and Closed Mind* (New York: Basic Books, 1960); Franklyn Haiman, "A Revised Scale for the Measurement of Open Mindedness," *Communication Monographs* 31 (June 1964):97–102.]

Dominant Hemisphere. That hemisphere of the brain that controls the higher functions, including speaking and comprehending verbal messages.

Door-in-the Face. A persuasive technique in which one begins with a large request and when this is rejected (i.e., when the door is slammed in one's face), makes a much smaller request that is then accepted. See also FOOT-IN-THE-DOOR.

[Robert B. Cialdini, J. E. Vincent, S. K. Lewis, J. Catalan, D. Wheeler, and B. L. Darby, "Reciprocal Concessions Procedure for Inducing Compliance: The Door-in-the-Face Technique," *Journal of Personality and Social Psychology* 31 (1975):206–215; Robert B. Cialdini, *Influence: How and Why People Agree to Things* (New York: William Morrow, 1984).]

Doppler Effect. The change in sound or light waves as the source of the stimulus changes distances from the receiver.

Double-Bind Messages. A particular type of contradictory message. Consider the following interpersonal interaction:

PAT: *Love me.*
CHRIS: *(Makes advances of a loving nature.)*
PAT: *(Nonverbal tenseness, failure to maintain eye contact and, in general, nonverbal messages that say, "Don't love me.")*
CHRIS: *(Withdraws.)*
PAT: *See, you don't love me.*

Five elements must be involved for an interaction to constitute a double-bind message.

1. The two persons interacting must share a relatively intense relationship where the messages and demands of one and the responses of the other are important. Clearly with lovers we have this first element or condition. If the relationship is not intense, then the various demands and counterdemands will have little effect. Examples of such intense relationships are many and include relationships between various family members, between husband and wife, and in some instances between employer and employee.

2. There must be two messages that demand different and incompatible responses. That is, the messages must be such that both cannot logically be verbalized. Usually, the positive message is communicated verbally, for example, "love me." The accompanying message, usually communicated nonverbally, contradicts the first message, for example, the withdrawal and general tenseness which communicates "stay away," "don't love me." Both parties in a double-bind relationship are likely to engage in sending such messages, either both in the same conversation, or separately on different occasions.

3. At least one or both of the individuals in a double-bind situation must be unable to escape from the contradictory messages. The individual or individuals lack the opportunities to meet their needs elsewhere or have been in their roles or positions so long that alternatives no longer seem available. People in double-bind situations feel trapped. Preventing an individual's escape from the contradictory message may be a legal commitment (like a marriage license) or, in the case of lovers, an understood but unwritten agreement that implies that each loves the other and cares about meeting mutual needs. No matter what response is made, the person receiving the message is failing to comply with at least one of the demands. If, for example, Chris makes loving advances, then the nonverbal injunction "Don't love me" is violated. If Chris does not make any loving advances, then the verbal injunction "Love me" is violated.

4. There must be a threat of punishment of some sort for the failure of the message receiver to comply with the sender's verbal or nonverbal demands. In our example, there is an implied threat of punishment for the failure to make loving advances but also for the failure to comply with the demand not to love. Regardless of how the lover responds—whether by making loving advances or not making such advances—some form of punishment will follow. This is one reason why the relationship between the people must be relatively intense, otherwise, the threat of punishment would not be significant.

5. For double-binding to be a serious communication problem, there must be frequent occurrences of it. Such frequent exposure has the effect of setting up a response pattern in the individual such that he or she comes to anticipate that whatever is done will be incorrect; that there is no escape from these confused and confusing communications; and that punishment will follow noncompliance (and since noncompliance is inevitable, punishment is inevitable).

Double-bind messages are particularly significant to children because they can neither escape from such situations nor can they communicate about the communications. They cannot talk about the lack of correspondence between the verbal and the nonverbal. They cannot ask their parents why they do not hold them or hug them when they say they love them.

Ernst Beier has argued that these double-bind messages—which he refers to as "discordance" (q.v.)—are the result of the desire of the individual to communicate two different emotions or feelings. For example, we may like a person and want to communicate this positive feeling but we may also dislike this person and want to communicate this negative feeling as well. The result is that we communicate both feelings, one verbally and one nonverbally.
[Gregory Bateson, "Double Bind," *Steps to an Ecology of Mind* (New York: Ballantine Books, 1972), pp. 271–278.]

Double Entendre. From the French meaning "double meaning," a word or phrase with a double meaning, one of which is usually sexually oriented.

Doubletalk. Evasive language used to avoid coming to grips with a question or to avoid taking a specific stand. Also referred to as "doublespeak."
[William Lambdin, *Doublespeak Dictionary* (Los Angeles: Pinnacle Books, 1979).]

Down. In computer terminology, out of order, not working.

Downlink. A station receiving satellite signals.

Downward Communication. Messages sent from the higher levels of the hierarchy to the lower levels—for example, messages sent by managers to workers, from deans to faculty members. Perhaps the most obvious example of downward communication is the giving of orders: type this in duplicate, send these crates out by noon, design and write the advertisement, and so on. Along with these order-giving messages are the accompanying explanations of procedures, goals, and the like. Managers are also responsible for giving appraisals of workers and for motivating them, all in the name of productivity and for the good of the organization as a whole.

There are a variety of problems that can be noted with regard to how downward communication affects the work environment. One obvious barrier is the faulty assumption that management makes—namely, that the goals of the workers and of the organization are the same, or that the workers agree with the goals of the company. Some managers feel that if there are no obvious signs of dissatisfaction, the workers find the policies of management acceptable. Obviously this is false because not all disagreements are voiced. It is essential for management to look for problems "voiced" in more subtle ways, for example in the nonverbal cues of workers. Management and labor often speak different languages, and many managers simply do not know how to make their messages understandable to laborers. Most managers, for example, have more education and a greater command of the technical language of the business; these differences can create communication problems. Today we also see a large number of workers in factories, auto plants, and the like who speak English very poorly or not at all. Many managers cannot speak the native language of the workers and so communication becomes nearly impossible.

In both upward and downward communication, management is in control of the communication system. The managers are the ones who have the time, the expertise, and the facilities to improve the communication that takes place in an organization. And it seems logical to assign the responsibility for an effective communication system to management. This is not to say that the workers or lower levels are absolved of their responsibility; effective communication is a two-way process. Nevertheless, management bears the larger responsibility for establishing and maintaining an effective and efficient internal communication system.
[Bruce Harriman, "Up and Down the Communication Ladder," *Harvard Business Review* 52 (September–October, 1974):143–151.]

Dramatistic Analysis. A type of message analysis based on the work of Kenneth Burke which utilizes Burke's pentad (q.v.) consisting of act (q.v.), agent (q.v.), agency (q.v.), scene (q.v.), and purpose (q.v.).
[Kenneth Burke, *A Grammar of Motives* (Englewood Cliffs, N.J.: Prentice-Hall, 1945), and *A Rhetoric of Motives* (Englewood Cliffs, N.J.: Prentice-Hall, 1950).]

Drive Theory. A biologically based theory which suggests that the most important human needs are physical, for example, food or water.

Dual Coding Hypothesis. A theory of memory holding that verbal and visual information are held separately in different areas of long-term memory (the verbal system and the imaginal system).
[A. Paivio, *Imagery and Verbal Processes* (New York: Holt, Rinehart and Winston, 1971).]

Dumb Terminal. A terminal that cannot be programmed to perform any additional functions; a terminal designed exclusively for inputting and outputting computer data; opposed to a smart terminal (q.v.).

Dyad. A two-person unit.

Dyadic Communication. Communication between two persons; frequently considered synonymous with interpersonal communication.

Dyadic Consciousness. An awareness of an interpersonal relationship or pairing of two individuals, as distinguished from situations in which two individuals are together but do not perceive themselves as being a unit or twosome.

Dysarthria. An articulation disorder generally considered to be caused by damage to the central nervous system and may be characterized by slurring or the omission of individual sounds.

Dyslalia. An articulation disorder attributed to improper learning or to some abnormality in the external speech organs rather than to any central nervous system disorder.

Dyslexia. An impairment in the ability to read.

Dyslogia. Speech impairment associated with a mental deficit.

Dysphemism. From the Greek meaning "bad speech," the use of an offensive term in place of an inoffensive one; the opposite of euphemism (q.v.).

Dysrhythmia. An abnormality in the characteristic of speech rhythm.

Echoic Word. A word that echos the sound it represents, for example, *snap* or *babble.* See also ONOMATOPOEIA.

Echoic Response. A verbal operant (q.v.) under the control of previously heard speech and which echoes previously heard speech in whole or in part, for example, when one person uses a specific word or phrase that is then used ("echoed") by others.
[B. F. Skinner, *Verbal Behavior* (New York: Appleton-Century-Crofts, 1957).]

Echoic Theory. See BOW-WOW THEORY.

Echolalia. Speech characterized by the repetition of words or phrases that have recently been heard; the echoing of previously heard speech; a normal stage in the child's acquisition of language; in adults, a pathology if excessive.

Echolocation. A process of locating the position of objects by analyzing the direction of the echo and the time it takes for a directed sound to echo off of the object. Dolphins and bats rely heavily on echolocation.

Ecology. The study of the relationships between people and their environment.

Ectomorphy. The skinny dimension of body build. See also SOMATOTYPE.

Educatorese. The jargon of the professional educator.

Effect, Law of. Developed by E. L. Thorndike (1874–1949), this law states that the connection between a stimulus and a response (S-R) is strengthened when accompanied by some positive effect or reward. This law also holds, although incorrectly, that punishment weakens the S-R connections, where in actuality, the punishment functions to suppress the response learned. See also EXERCISE, LAW OF.
[E. L. Thorndike, *The Fundamentals of Learning* (New York: Teachers College, 1932).]

Egalitarianism. A democratic attitude and point of view characterized by tolerance for opposing points of view and an emphasis on free expression; opposed to the authoritarian personality (q.v.).

Ego. The self; the "I." In Freudian theory, the *ego* represents the conscious awareness of the self and mediates between the unconscious pleasure oriented drives of the *id* and the restrictions of the conscience or *superego;* that part of one's personality that is most in touch with "reality."

Egocentric Speech. An early stage in the development of language in the child (up to around 7 or 8 years of age) which is essentially monologic, that is, there is an inability to, for example, describe objects from another's point of view—the child can only describe it from his or her perspective.
[Jean Piaget, *The Language and Thought of the Child,* trans. Majorie Gabain (New York: Humanities Press, 1959).]

Egocentrism. The attitude or belief of an individual that everything revolves (or should revolve) around the individual himself or herself; self-centeredness.

Ego-Involved Attitude. An attitude, highly resistant to change, that is closely related to an individual's view of self.
[Muzafer Sherif and Hadley Cantril, *The Psychology of Ego-Involvements* (New York: Wiley, 1947).]

Ego States. In transactional analysis (q.v.) (TA), distinctions are made among three ego states, which are defined as relatively consistent patterns of feelings that are or can be related to a corresponding consistent pattern of behavior. The three ego states are used in TA to describe the behaviors of people as they interact with each other. At any given time, individuals exhibit the behaviors characteristic of one of these ego states, although they may (and often do) shift from one ego state to another. The three ego states identified in TA are Parent, Adult, and Child. These ego states bear no relationship to the chronological age of the individual—a child may act as an Adult and an adult as a Child. See also ADULT EGO STATE; CHILD EGO STATE; PARENT EGO STATE.

Eidic Memory. A relatively rare type of memory where an individual remembers scenes in detail and can recount them as if they were present now; vivid imagery.

Either-Or Fallacy. See POLARIZATION.

Elaborated Code. The code or dialect of the middle class; a dialect containing many alternative expressions; opposed to restricted code (q.v.). The choices that its speakers make are drawn from a relatively large supply, hence the language is more difficult to predict. Also, the speaker's intentions are more often made explicit.
[Basil Bernstein, "Language and Social Class," *British Journal of Sociology* 11 (1960): 271–276.]

Electronic Mail. Messages sent via computer or satellite instead of the traditional letter carrier.

Elementalism. The process of dividing verbally what cannot be divided nonverbally, for example, speaking of body and mind as separate and distinct entities. See also HYPHEN.

Elision. The omission of a vowel or syllable in speech.

Ellipsis. The omission of a section of a document or speech but which does not impair understanding.

Elocution. In classical rhetoric (q.v.), *elocution* referred to language style but later, in the seventeenth, eighteenth, and nineteenth centuries, came to refer to delivery, especially vocal delivery.

Elocutionary Movement. A rhetorical movement that originally developed as an emphasis on style as one part of the five canons of rhetoric (q.v.) during the eighteenth century in England but eventually became associated with delivery as a goal in itself. Among the leading elocutionists were Thomas Sheridan (1719–

1788), John Walker (1732–1807), and Gilbert Austin (*fl.* 1800). All developed elaborate and detailed systems of gesture and voice for communicating the various emotions.

Eloquence. Speech or writing characterized by style, force, persuasiveness; a speech style that characterizes the great speeches and writings and distinguishes them from ordinary mundane discourse.

Emancipation Relationship. One of four cohabitation patterns common among students and identified by C. A. Ridley and colleagues, a relationship in which one or both partners have recently been "emancipated," for example, freed from parental supervision; opposed to convenience (q.v.), Linus blanket (q.v.), and testing (q.v.) relationships.
[C. A. Ridley, D. J. Peterman, and A. W. Avery, "Cohabitation: Does It Make for a Better Marriage?" *The Family Coordinator* 27 (April 1978):129–137.]

Embedding. The linguistic process by which a sentence is inserted into another sentence.

Emblematic Movements. Nonverbal behaviors used to illustrate a verbal statement, either repeating or substituting for a word or phrase. See also EMBLEMS.

Emblems. Nonverbal behaviors that directly translate words or phrases, for example, the signs for "O.K." and "peace."

Emic. Those elements, for example, of language, that are not universal but relative—the meaning of such elements can only be interpreted within the framework of a specific culture.
[Kenneth L. Pike, *Language in Relation to a Unified Theory of Human Behavior*, 2d ed. (The Hague: Mouton, 1967).]

Emotional Proof. See PATHOS.

Emotive Function of Communication. Communication that tells us something about the speaker as opposed to the external world, or serves some personal need of the speaker.

Empathic Listening. Listening characterized by the listener's feeling what the speaker is feeling, listening focusing on understanding what the speaker means and feels rather than on evaluating what is said.
[Charles M. Kelly, "Empathic Listening," in *Small Group Communication: A Reader*, 3d ed., Robert S. Cathcart and Larry A. Samovar, eds. (Dubuque, Iowa: Wm. C. Brown, 1979), pp. 350–357.]

Empathy. Empathy comes from the German word *einfühling*, meaning "to feel with." To empathize with someone is to feel as that person does. To sympathize, on the other hand, is to feel *for* the individual—to be sorry for the person, for example. To empathize is to feel *as* the individual feels, to be in the same shoes, to feel the same feelings in the same way.

If we are able to empathize with people, we are in a better position to understand, for example, their motivations and past experiences, their present feelings and attitudes, their hopes and expectations for the future. Empathy enables one to understand (emotionally and intellectually) what the other person is experiencing. This empathic understanding in turn enables the individual to better adjust his or her communications—what is said, how it is said, what is to be avoided, if and when silence is to be preferred, if self-disclosures should be made, and so on.

More difficult than defining *empathy* is describing or advancing ways to increase our empathic abilities. Perhaps the first step is to avoid evaluating the

other person's behaviors. If we evaluate them as right or wrong, good or bad, we will see these behaviors through these labels and will fail to see a great deal that might not be consistent with these labels. First, focus on understanding. Second, the more we know about a person—her or his desires, experiences, abilities, fears, and so on—the more we will be able to see what that person sees and feel as that person feels. We need to try to understand the reasons and the motivations that contribute to making the person feel as she or he does. Even if these reasons and motivations may appear illogical or self-destructive to you, they need to be understood if you are to achieve a meaningful degree of empathy with the other person. Third, try to experience what the other person is feeling from his or her point of view. Playing the role of the other person in our minds (or even out loud) should help us to see the world a little more as he or she does.
[Robert L. Katz, *Empathy* (New York: Free Press, 1963; William S. Howell, *The Empathic Communicator* (Belmont, Calif.: Wadsworth, 1982).]

Emphasis. A principle of communication referring to the need to give special attention—a sharper focus—to what is important.

Empirical Evidence. Scientific observations of phenomena.

Empirical Questions. Questions whose answers are capable of being verified (at least theoretically) through observation even if we do not yet have the means to make such observations now.

Encoder. Something that takes a message in one form (for example, nerve impulses) and translates it into another form (for example, sound waves). In human communication, the encoder is the speaking mechanism. In electronic communication, the encoder is, for example, the telephone mouthpiece. See also DECODER.

Encoding. The process of putting a message into a code, for example, translating nerve impulses into speech sounds. See also DECODING; ENCODER.

Encoding Specificity. The assumption (finding) that a cue facilitates the retrieval of a stimulus if the cue was processed at the same time as the stimulus.
[D. M. Thomson and E. Tulving, "Associative Encoding and Retrieval: Weak and Strong Cues," *Journal of Experimental Psychology* 86 (1970):255–262.]

Encomium (*pl.* Encomiums, Encomia). The praise of a person or thing; a speech of praise.

Encounter Group. Small groups that have as their goal the increased awareness of its members. Personal growth, rather than the learning of specific content or the solving of particular problems, is paramount.

Endomorphy. The fatty dimension of body build types. See also SOMATOTYPE.

Enthymeme. A rhetorical syllogism in which the conclusion is implied rather than stated, the idea being that the audience will "fill in" the conclusion themselves; at times viewed as a syllogism that has persuasion as its goal.
[Thomas M. Conley, "The Enthymeme in Perspective," *Quarterly Journal of Speech* 70 (1984):168–187.]

Entropy. A measure of the extent of disorganization or randomness in a system. Entropy is a measure of the degree of uncertainty that a receiver has about the messages to be communicated by a source. Entropy is high if the number of possible messages is high and low if the number of possible messages is low. In Jungian psychology, the principle referring to the tendency for energy to be distributed evenly throughout the psyche (the individual's entire personality).

Environmentalist. One who emphasizes the role of nature or learning of the environmental factors affecting development and behavior.

Epic. A long poem focusing on some heroic theme.

Epicureanism. A philosophy articulated by the Greek Epicurus (341–270 B.C.) emphasizing the pleasures of the mind rather than materialism. Pleasure was a temporary experience and could not be sustained for long periods of time; pleasure was to be pursued in moderation. Epicureans were generally hostile to rhetoric (q.v.) and rhetorical instruction; they viewed negatively the emphasis on style, and elegance, and political involvement.

Epideictic Rhetoric. One of the three major types of rhetoric (q.v.) identified by Aristotle; rhetoric concerned with ceremonial oratory, with praise and censure. See also DELIBERATIVE RHETORIC, FORENSIC RHETORIC.

Epideictic Speeches. Ceremonial speeches; speeches concerned with praise and censure, with honor and dishonor.

Epigram. A witty and wise saying; an inscription, for example, on a statue.

Epigrapher. One engaged in the study of ancient writings called "epigraphy" (q.v.).

Epigraphy. The science of ancient writing, particularly those inscriptions cut with a sharp tool on stone, metal, wood, or clay. See also PALEOGRAPHY.

Epilogue. The final words or section of a play or book.

Episode. Used by some researchers to designate a unit of discourse that contains a starting and an ending point.
[W. Barnett Pearce, *An Overview of Communication and Interpersonal Relationships* (Chicago: Science Research Associates, 1976).]

Episodic Memory. Memory for one's experiences in the context in which they occurred; opposed to semantic memory (q.v.).

Epistrophe. A figure of speech in which the same word or phrase is used to end a series of sentences, for example. "As a teacher he was unprepared. As a father he was unprepared. As a lover he was unprepared."

Eponym. The person for whom something is named or supposedly named; a name-giver. For example, *Aristotelian* and *McLuhanesque* denote ways of thinking developed by Aristotle and McLuhan and hence bear their names; in these cases Aristotle and McLuhan would be eponyms.

E-Prime (E′). A form of the language that omits the verb *to be* except when used as an auxiliary or in statements of existence. Designed to eliminate the tendency toward projection (q.v.) or the assumption that the characteristics that one attributes to a person—for example, "Pat is brave"—are actually in that person instead of in the observer's perception of that person.
[D. David Bourland, Jr., "A Linguistic Note: Writing in E-Prime," *General Semantics Bulletin* 32–33 (1965–1966).]

Equality. An attitude that recognizes that each individual in a communication interaction is equal, that no one is superior to any other; encourages supportiveness (q.v.); opposed to superiority (q.v.).

Equal Time Rule. Requirement that if a station allows a political candidate access to its facilities, then it must allow equal access to all other qualified candidates. This does not apply, however, to cable TV.

Equifinality. The capacity of a system to reach a similar end or final state through a variety of different means. Interpersonal relationships, for example, can achieve contentment, happiness, or love through a number of different means.

Equilibrium. See HOMEOSTASIS.

Equipotentiality. A principle articulated by Karl S. Lashley (1890–1958) referring to the ability of one part of the brain to assume the functions normally served by another, damaged portion.

[Karl S. Lashley, *Brain Mechanisms and Intelligence* (Chicago: University of Chicago Press, 1929).]

Equity Theory. A general theory of human behavior based on the following assumptions: (1) people seek pleasure and avoid pain; (2) people are selfish and in order to survive must compromise, must give if they are to receive; (3) people in a relationship feel comfortable when they receive what they feel they deserve and uncomfortable when there is inequity—when they are getting less or more than they feel they deserve; (4) people in an inequitable relationship attempt to restore equity through a redistribution of the costs and rewards. See also SOCIAL EXCHANGE AND EQUITY THEORY.

[Elaine Walster and G. William Walster, *Equity: Theory and Research* (Boston: Allyn and Bacon, 1978), and *A New Look at Love* (Reading, Mass.: Addison-Wesley, 1978).]

Equivocate. The use of ambiguous language for the purpose of avoiding commitment to a particular position; the use of evasive statements.

Equivocation. A reasoning fallacy where the same word is used in two or more senses; evasiveness; the use of ambiguous language so as not to reveal one's true feelings or position.

Erhard Seminar Training (EST). Training procedures developed by Werner Erhard (1935–   ) for increasing intrapersonal awareness and interpersonal sensitivity and effectiveness.

Eristic. The practice of disputation; argumentation that is designed to confuse one's opponent and to win an argument rather than arrive at the truth; opposed to dialectic (q.v.).

[James Benjamin, "Eristic, Dialectic, and Rhetoric," *Communication Quarterly* 31 (1983): 21–26.]

Erogenous Zones. Areas of the body which are especially sexually sensitive, for example, the genitals, mouth, and breasts; areas especially sensitive to tactile communication and about which society has the most restrictive rules prohibiting touch.

Eros. An ego-centered love, a love that is given to someone in anticipation of it being returned. Eros is a utilitarian, rational love because it expects some return. It is a sensual love that focuses on the physical qualities of the individual; in eros physical attraction is paramount. See also LOVE.

Erotographomania. The compulsion to write erotic messages.

Erotolalia. Sexually explicit speech.

Errata. Errors in written material; a compilation sheet of the errors in a text.

Esperanto. A proposed universal language developed by Polish physician Ludwik Zamenhof (1859–1917) and built on a number of existing languages. Zamenhof's pseudonym, Dr. Esperanto, meant literally "one who hopes."

EST. See ERHARD SEMINAR TRAINING.

Etc. An extensional device (q.v.) used to emphasize the notion of infinite complexity; "and so on." Since one can never know all about anything, any statement about the world or an event must end with an explicit or implicit "etc."

Ethical Proof. See ETHOS.

Ethicize. See MASS COMMUNICATION FUNCTIONS.

Ethics. The branch of philosophy that deals with the rightness or wrongness of actions; the study of moral values.

Ethnography. The descriptive study of cultures, for example, their institutions, histories, and relationships.

Ethnolinguistics. The science that studies the relationships between language, on the one hand, and culture, customs, and social institutions on the other.
[Dell Hymes, *Foundations in Sociolinguistics: An Ethnographic Approach* (Philadelphia: University of Pennsylvania Press, 1974).]

Etic. Those elements that are universal; opposed to emic (q.v.).
[Kenneth L. Pike, *Language in Relation to a Unified Theory of Human Behavior,* 2d ed. (The Hague: Mouton, 1967).]

Ethos. The aspect of persuasiveness that depends on the audience's perception of the character of the speaker. To Aristotle ethos, or ethical proof, depended upon the speaker's perceived goodwill, knowledge, and moral character. More commonly referred to as speaker credibility (q.v.).

Etiology. The study of the causes of some condition, either physical or mental.

Etymological Fallacy. Reasoning that the present meaning of a word must be based on its etymology, historical development, or linguistic derivation.

Etymology. The study of word origins and their development.

Eulogy. A speech designed to praise a dead person.

Euphemism. A polite, more pleasant expression used instead of some socially unacceptable form, for example, "pass away" and "rest room" are euphemisms for "die" and "toilet." See also TABOO.
[D. J. Enright, *Fair of Speech: The Uses of Euphemism* (London: Oxford University Press, 1985); Hugh Rawson, *A Dictionary of Euphemisms and Other Doubletalk* (New York: Crown, 1981).]

Euphony. Pleasant sound; opposed to cacophony (q.v.).

Euphuism. Artificial prose; overly embellished and styled prose.

Evaluation. A process whereby a value is placed on some person, object, or event.

Evaluative Abstracting. A form or type of abstracting (q.v.) by which is formed an evaluative judgment, for example, good-bad, positive-negative, pleasant-unpleasant. See also CLASSIFYING ABSTRACTING; OBJECTIVE ABSTRACTING; RELATIONAL ABSTRACTING.

Evaluative Assertion Analysis. A form of content analysis used to analyze attitudinal evaluation and the relationships existing among attitudes and attitude objects.
[Charles E. Osgood, Sol Saporta, and Jum Nunnally, "Evaluative Assertion Analysis," *Litera* 3 (1956):47–102.]

Evaluative Meaning. A dimension of connotative meaning (q.v.) which may be indexed in terms of such scales as good-bad, positive-negative. See also SEMANTIC DIFFERENTIAL.

Evidence. Information used to support the truth or probability of a proposition.

Example. A form of amplification consisting of a relatively brief specific instance. See also ILLUSTRATION.

Example, Argument from. A form of argument or reasoning in which a number of examples are used to support the truth or probability of a general proposition, for example, reasoning from the failure of students to learn reading (example one), the failure of students to learn arithmetic (example two) . . . , the failure of students to learn history (example *n*), to the general proposition that our educational system is not doing its job.

Exchange Theory. A theory of interpersonal interaction based on costs and rewards or profits and losses. See also SOCIAL EXCHANGE AND EQUITY THEORY.

Excuse. An explanation, gesture, or action designed to reduce the negative implications of an individual's verbal or nonverbal actions. An excuse is designed primarily to maintain a positive image to others as well as to oneself.
[C. R. Snyder, Raymond L. Higgins, and Rita J. Stucky, *Excuses: Masquerades in Search of Grace* (New York: Wiley-Interscience, 1983).]

Exercise, Law of. Developed by psychologist E. L. Thorndike (1874–1949), this law states that frequency or the exercise of a stimulus-response connection strengthens it. See also EFFECT, LAW OF.

Exegesis. Critical interpretation of a text; explanation or analysis of a message.

Existentialism. A philosophical position and literary movement concerned with an individual's attempt to make meaningful his or her existence; the belief that philosophy and literature should be concerned with the human being's existence, with the freedom to select and pursue personal goals and the general meaning of life. Soren Kierkegaard, Martin Heidegger, and Friedrich Nietzsche in philosophy and Jean-Paul Sartre, Albert Camus, and Simon de Beauvoir in literature laid the foundations for this movement that influenced research and theory in psychology and communication.

Exordium. An oration's introduction; an introduction to any discourse. In classical rhetoric (q.v.), the introduction or opening of the speech in which the orator was to gain the attention of the audience and put them into a receptive frame of mind. See also PARTS OF THE SPEECH.

Expectation, Law of. Developed by psychologist George Kelly (1905–1966), the law holding that our behaviors will be determined in large part by our expectations or how we think an event will turn out; the law stating that our expectations (both positive and negative) will influence our behavior in the direction of making these expectations come true.
[George A. Kelly, *The Psychology of Personal Constructs* (New York: Norton, 1955).]

Experiential Limitation. The limit of an individual's ability to communicate, as set by the nature and extent of his or her experiences.

Experimental Group. The group in an experiment that is manipulated. The experimental group is compared with the control group (which is not manipulated) so that the effects of the manipulation may be observed and measured.

Experimental Method. A scientific approach to studying the operation of certain variables. The basic procedure is to manipulate the independent variable(s) and observe the changes in the dependent variable(s).

Experimental Phonetics. The science of the description, analysis, and measurement of speech sounds.

Expiration. The process of expelling air from the lungs.

Expletive. A word or expression that adds nothing to the meaning of a sentence. *It* and *there* are the expletives of English when they occur at the beginning of a clause but have no real referent, for example, "*It* is stormy" and "*There* is a monster at the door."

Exposition. The act or art of communicating information; the act of explaining. See also NARRATION.

Expressive Speech. Speech that is concerned with communicating one's inner feelings; speech that reveals one psychological state.

Expressive and Instrumental Communication. In expressive communication one communicates to express one's feelings and thoughts, to get things off one's chest, whereas in instrumental communication, one communicates to influence others, to persuade.

Expressiveness. As a quality of communication competence (q.v.), expressiveness refers to the involvement and animation of the interactants in a conversation or interpersonal interaction.

Extemporaneous Method of Delivery. A method of delivering the public speech in which there is thorough preparation, a commitment to memory of the main ideas and the order in which they will appear, and perhaps a commitment to memory of the first few and the last few sentences of the speech but with no further commitment to exact wording throughout the main part of the speech. See also IMPROMPTU; MANUSCRIPT; MEMORIZED METHOD OF DELIVERY.

Extended Family. A family consisting of nuclear family (q.v.) members plus other relatives, for example, aunts and uncles, grandparents, cousins.

Extensional Devices. Linguistic devices proposed by Alfred Korzybski (1879–1950) for making language a more accurate means for talking about the world. The extensional devices include the working devices *etc.* (q.v.), *date* (q.v.), and *index* (q.v.), and the safety devices *hyphen* (q.v.) and *quotes* (q.v.).
[Alfred Korzybski, *Science and Sanity: An Introduction to Non-Aristotelian Systems and General Semantics* (Lakeville, Conn.: The International Non-Aristotelian Library, 1933).]

Extensional Orientation. A point of view in which primary consideration is given to the world of experience and only secondary consideration is given to its labels. See also INTENSIONAL ORIENTATION; EXTENSIONAL DEVICES.

Extinction. The process by which a response loses its strength, occurs less frequently, or becomes less likely to occur as a result of its no longer being reinforced.

Extravert. One who is outer- rather than inner-directed; one whose interests are directed toward other things and other people; one who enjoys social interactions and who depends on interactions with others for satisfaction; opposed to introvert (q.v.).

Eyebrow Flash. The quick raising of the eyebrows often used to signal a friendly recognition of another.

Eye Contact. Looking at another person's eyes.

Eye Dialect. A way of writing a word using a modified phonetic spelling to represent its pronunciation, for example, *sez* for *says*.

Eye Gaze. See GAZE.

Eye Rhyme. Words that "rhyme" visually but would not rhyme in spoken form, for example, *lord* and *word* would be eye rhymes.

Fable. A brief allegory (extended metaphor); a story told to teach or illustrate a moral.

Face Engagement. An encounter between people engaged in a focused interaction when each person pays exclusive attention to the other person and is not available for interaction with others.

Face Saving. Behavior designed to reverse some negative impression of oneself due to some mistake or *faux paus*.

Facial Display. The communication of one's feelings through facial expression.

Facial Feedback Hypothesis. An hypothesis holding that our facial expressions "feed back" and influence our emotions.

[J. T. Lanzetta, J. Cartwright-Smith, and R. E. Kleck, "Effects of Nonverbal Dissimulations on Emotional Experience and Autonomic Arousal," *Journal of Personality and Social Psychology* 33 (1976):354–370.]

Facial Management Techniques. The techniques used to express facially what one wants to express and wants others to perceive rather than the emotions actually experienced.

Facial Meaning Sensitivity Test (FMST). A test designed to measure a receiver's ability to identify the meanings communicated through facial expressions.

[Dale G. Leathers and Ted H. Emigh, "Decoding Facial Expressions: A New Test with Decoding Norms," *Quarterly Journal of Speech* 66 (1980):418–436.]

Facilitator. One who facilitates a group's goals and fulfills many of the tasks normally assumed by a group leader; one who assists the group in achieving its goals.

Fact-Inference Confusion. A misevaluation in which one mistakes an inference for a fact and acts on the inference as if it were a fact.

We can make statements about the world that we observe, and we can make statements about what we have not observed. In form or structure these statements are similar and could not be distinguished from each other by any grammatical analysis. For example, we can say, "She is wearing a blue jacket," as well as, "He is harboring an illogical hatred." If we diagrammed these sentences, they would yield identical structures, and yet we know quite clearly that they are very different types of statements. In the first one we can observe the jacket and the blue color. But how do we observe "illogical hatred"? Obviously, this is not a descriptive statement but an inferential statement. It is a statement that we make not solely on the basis of what we observe but on the basis of what we observe plus our own conclusions.

There is no problem with making inferential statements; we must make them if we are to talk about much that is meaningful to us. The problem arises when we act as if those inferential statements were factual statements.

Consider, for example, the following anecdote: A woman went for a walk one day and met her friend, whom she had not seen or heard from or heard of in 10 years. After an exchange of greetings, the woman said, "Is this your little boy?" and her friend replied, "Yes, I got married about 6 years ago." The woman then asked the child, "What is your name?" and the little boy replied, "Same as my father's." "Oh," said the woman, "then it must be Peter."

The question, of course, is how did the woman know the boy's father's name if she had not seen or heard from or heard of her friend in the last 10 years? The answer, of course, is obvious. But it is obvious only after we recognize that in reading this short passage we have made an inference which, although we are not aware of our having made it, is preventing us from answering a simple question. Specifically, we have made the inference that the woman's friend is a woman. Actually, the friend is a man named Peter.

Perhaps the classic example of this type of fact-inference confusion concerns the case of the "empty" gun that unfortunately proves to be loaded. With amazing frequency we find in the newspapers examples of people being so sure that the guns are empty that they point them at another individual and fire. Many times, of course, they are empty. But, unfortunately, many times they are not. Here one makes an inference (that the gun is empty) but acts on the inference as if it were a fact and fires the gun.

Distinguishing Facts and Inferences

Some of the essential differences between factual and inferential statements are summarized in the accompanying table.

DIFFERENCES BETWEEN FACTUAL AND INFERENTIAL STATEMENTS

Factual Statements	Inferential Statements
1. may be made only after observation	1. may be made at any time
2. are limited to what has been observed	2. go beyond what has been observed
3. may be made only by the observer	3. may be made by anyone
4. may only be about the past or the present	4. may be about any time—past, present, or future
5. approach certainty	5. involve varying degrees of probability
6. are subject to verifiable standards	6. are not subject to verifiable standards

Distinguishing between these two types of statements does not imply that one type is better than the other. We need both types of statements; both are useful, both important. The problem arises when we treat one type of statement as if it were the other. Specifically, the problem arises when we treat an inferential statement as if it were a factual statement.

Inferential statements need to be accompanied by tentativeness. We need to recognize that such statements may prove to be wrong, and we should be aware of that possibility. Inferential statements should leave open the possibility of other alternatives. If, for example, we treat the statement, "The United States should enforce the blockade," as if it were a factual statement, we eliminate the possibility of other alternatives. When making inferential statements we should be psychologically prepared to be proven wrong. This requires a great deal of effort, but it is probably effort well spent. If we are psychologically prepared to be proven wrong, we will be less hurt if and when we are shown to be incorrect.

Factual Statement. A statement made by the observer after observation and limited to what has been observed. See also INFERENTIAL STATEMENT.

Failure Events. An offense or wrongdoing; an action (event) that the doer feels the need to repair (q.v.) or justify in some way; an unpopular opinion or belief that the speaker feels needs to be justified. Four stages in the failure event are identified by P. Schonbach: (1) the failure event; (2) the reproach or confrontation as evidenced in, say, disapproving facial expressions; (3) the account or the repair, for example, the excuse or justification; and (4) the evaluation as in acknowledging the repair or perhaps in restating the disapproving reproach. [P. Schonbach, "A Category System for Account Phrases," *European Journal of Social Psychology* 10 (1980):195–200.]

Fairness Doctrine. A Federal Communications Commission (FCC) ruling requiring stations to grant equal time to the various sides of a controversial issue. This doctrine does not apply to cable TV.

Fair Use. Copyright law provision permitting short excerpts from copyrighted material to be used by others without violation of the copyright holder's rights.

Fallacy. An error in reasoning; a fallacious argument.

Falsetto. An abnormally and artificially high voice that overlaps or extends the full range of the voice.

Family Communication Patterns. Each family functions with a unique set of communication patterns. No two relationships will evidence exactly the same interpersonal communication structures. But amid this diversity and uniqueness, there are general patterns that can be identified and that may serve as general classifications or types. Each interpersonal relationship may then be viewed as a variation on one of these basic types. To this end, four major patterns are identified.

The Equality Pattern

The equality pattern probably exists more in theory than in reality, but it is a good starting point for examining communication in primary relationships. In the equality pattern each party shares in the communication transactions equally; the roles played by each are equal. Thus, each party is accorded a similar degree of credibility by the other; each is equally open to the ideas, opinions, and beliefs of the other; each engages in self-disclosure on a more or less equal basis. There is no leader or follower, teacher or student, opinion-giver or opinion-seeker; rather they both play these roles equally for each other. Because of this basic equality, the communication exchanges themselves—over a substantial period of time—are equal. For example, the number of questions asked, the depth and frequency of self-disclosures, the nonverbal behavior of touching and eye gaze would all be about equal.

Both parties share equally in the decision-making processes—the insignificant ones about which movie to attend as well as the significant ones about where to send the child to school, what church to attend, what house to buy, and so on. Conflicts in equality relationships may occur with some frequency, but they are not seen as threatening to the individuals or to the relationship itself. They are seen, rather, as exchanges of ideas, opinions, and values. Even when these individuals disagree, they disagree agreeably. The disagreement is not seen as due to one being stupid and the other being smart, but to the inevitable clash of ideas and differences in values and perceptions that are a part of long-term relationships. These conflicts are content rather than relational in nature; this couple has few power struggles within the relationship domain.

If a communication model of this relationship were drawn in which arrows were used to signify individual messages, there would be an equal number of arrows emanating from each person. Further, if the arrows were classified into different types, the types would likewise be similar. A representation of this is given in the first illustration.

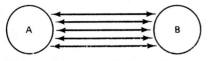

The equality communication pattern.

The Balanced Split Pattern

In the balanced split communication pattern, the equality of the previous type of relationship is maintained, but here each person is in control or in authority over different domains. Each person, for example, is seen as an expert in different areas. For example, in the traditional nuclear family the husband maintains high credibility in business matters and in politics. The wife maintains high credibility with such matters as child care and cooking. Although this is changing, these patterns can still be seen clearly in numerous traditional families. There are also areas of overlap, where both parties have some expertise but neither one has a great deal more than the other. For example, both parties may know the same amount about religion, health, or art, in which case neither would be perceived as more credible than the other.

Conflict with these individuals is generally nonthreatening because each has specified areas of expertise, so the win-lose patterns are more or less predetermined before the conflict begins. To take our traditional example again, if the conflict is over business the husband wins; if the conflict is over child care the wife wins. And neither party is terribly hurt by the conflict. This balanced split pattern is diagrammed in the second illustration.

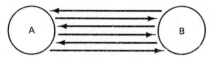

The balanced split communication pattern.

The Unbalanced Split Pattern

In the unbalanced split relationship one person dominates; one person is seen as an expert on more than half of the areas of mutual communication. This pattern is diagrammed in the third illustration. In many unions this expertise takes the form of control. One person is more or less regularly in control of the relationship. In some cases this person is the more intelligent or more knowledgeable, but in many unions it is the one who is more physically attractive. In this case the less attractive one compensates by giving in to the other person, allowing the other person to win the arguments, for example, or have his or her way in decision making.

The person in control makes more assertions, tells the other person what should be and what will be done, gives opinions freely, and seldom asks for opinions in return except perhaps to secure some kind of ego gratification from confirmation or from convincing the other person of the logical sophistication of the argument. The noncontrolling person, conversely, asks questions, seeks opinions, and looks to the other person for decision-making leadership.

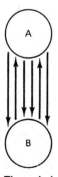

The unbalanced split communication pattern.

The Monopoly Pattern

In a monopoly relationship, one person is seen as the authority. This person lectures rather than communicates, pontificates rather than talks with another person. Rarely if ever does this person ask questions to seek advice, and he or she reserves the right to have the final say. In this type of union the arguments are few because both individuals know who is boss and who will win should an argument arise. When the authority is challenged, perhaps from outside instigation—"Don't let him walk all over you," "Be a man, stand up to her"—there are arguments and bitter conflicts. One reason the conflicts are so bitter here is that these individuals have had no rehearsal for adequate conflict resolution. They do not know how to argue or how to disagree agreeably, so their arguments frequently take the form of hurting the other person.

The controlling person tells the partner what is and what is not to be. The noncontrolling person looks to the other for permission, for opinion leadership, for decisions to be made, almost as would a child to an all-knowing, all-powerful parent. In many cases these unions are more like child-parent relationships. One individual (the "parent") gains gratification from playing the parental role, from ordering, guiding, and caring for the other person. The "child" gains gratification from having his or her needs met and for not having to make decisions and suffering any of the negative consequences attendant on wrong or inadequate decisions. This pattern is diagrammed in the fourth illustration.

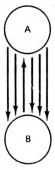

The monopoly communication pattern.

In thinking about these four types of communication patterns, it is easy to identify with the equality or balanced split pattern. Surely most of us would consciously wish to be a part of these unions rather than either of the others. But many of our decisions are based on subconscious factors, and our motivations are not always "logical" and "mature." Further, many people clearly opt for the unbalanced split and the monopoly patterns, some viewing themselves as the controlling agents, others viewing themselves as the controlled. What makes for happiness, satisfaction, and productivity in a relationship varies with the individuals. An equality pattern that might produce satisfaction in one relationship may lead to dissatisfaction among individuals who need to control another person or to be controlled. The pattern that makes you happy might make your father and mother or your son and daughter grossly unhappy. A clear recognition of this relativity seems an essential prerequisite to understanding relationships that exist among others and the role that communication plays in the maintenance of those relationships.

[Sven Wahlroos, *Family Communication,* (New York: New American Library, 1974); Kathleen M. Galvin and Bernard J. Brommel, *Family Communication,* 2d ed. (Glenview, Ill.: Scott, Foresman, 1986).]

Family Script. See SCRIPT.

Family Tree. In linguistics, a model of related languages with a central trunk (or original language) and branches (or languages developed from the parent and are now independent).

[Holger Pedersen, *Linguistic Science in the Nineteenth Century,* John Sprago, trans. (Cambridge: Cambridge University Press, 1931).]

Fantasy Theme Analysis. An approach to the analysis of communication that focuses on how communicators discuss real and fictitious events (past or future).

[Ernest G. Bormann, "The Eagleton Affair: A Fantasy Theme Analysis," *Quarterly Journal of Speech* 59 (1973):143–159.]

FAST (Facial Affect Scoring Technique). Developed by Paul Ekman, FAST is a technique for the analysis of face communication. Here the face is broken up into three main areas: eyebrows and forehead, eyes and eyelids, and the lower face from the bridge of the nose down. Judges then attempt to identify various emotions by observing the different parts of the face and writing descriptions. The technique is designed to enable us to better understand exactly what facial movements communicate what emotions.

[Paul Ekman, W. V. Friesen, and S. S. Tomkins, "Facial Affect Scoring Technique: A First Validity Study," *Semiotica* 3 (1971):37–58.]

Fate Control. Control over the fate of another; the maximum or final control.

[J. W. Thibaut and H. H. Kelley, *The Social Psychology of Groups* (New York: Wiley, 1959).]

Fear Appeals. Persuasive appeals directed at fear in which the speaker attempts to scare the audience into agreement or compliance. Extreme fear appeals are often less effective in persuasion than moderate fear appeals because the audience may ignore or avoid listening to an extreme fear appeal.

Feature Detection. The process of perception in which we perceive elementary or basic units of a stimulus.

Federal Communications Commission (FCC). Created by Congress in 1934 to ensure that broadcasting operates in the public interest. The FCC has concerned itself with the fairness doctrine (q.v.), personal attack law (granting persons attacked via a station's editorial content equal time to respond), advertising, and obscenity. FCC rulings are regarded as law and may only be overturned by Congress or the federal courts.

Federal Trade Commission (FTC). Federal government commission that oversees and regulates advertising and general business practices.

Feedback. Information that is fed back to its source. Feedback may come from the source's own messages (as when we hear what we are saying) or from the receiver in the form of applause, yawning, puzzled looks, questions, letters to the editor, increased or decreased subscriptions to a magazine, and so forth.

Feedback Loop. A system where a particular decision leads to a specific action which results in a change in the system that, in turn, creates new information, which leads to new decisions. The process is a never-ending cycle.

Feedback Regulation. The most popular and perhaps most logical way to explain feedback regulation is with a mechanical analogy. The clearest mechanical feedback system is the thermostat. Let us say that we set the thermostat at the desired temperature of 68 degrees. When the temperature rises above 68 degrees, the thermostat sends information in the form of an electrical signal to the heat-producing mechanism, which decreases the heat production. When the temperature falls below 68 degrees, the thermostat sends information that results in an increase in the heat production. In this way the temperature is maintained at about 68 degrees. This is an example of a negative feedback mechanism; information about the room temperature is fed back to the heat-producing mechanism when the temperature deviates from the predetermined desired level. This negative feedback serves a corrective function. Now consider a thermostat that works in the opposite way: when the temperature rises above 68 degrees, the thermostat sends information to the heat-producing mechanism that raises the temperature. This higher heat then leads the thermostat to send additional information to raise the heat even more, and so on. Alternatively, consider the situation in which the temperature falls below 68 degrees. This would trigger the thermostat to send information to the heat-producing mechanism to lower the heat production, which would further lower the temperature in the room. This then leads the thermostat to instruct the heat-producing mechanism to further lower the heat output, and so on. The result would be either extreme heat or extreme cold. This is an example of a positive feedback system; information about the room temperature is fed back to the heat-producing mechanism to increase the deviation from the established predetermined level.

A Model of the Feedback Cycle

Feedback in human communication is similar to, though by no means identical with, the feedback in the mechanical system of the thermostat. The model presented illustrates the concept of feedback in human communication. The solid arrows going from source to receiver represent the *object messages,* that is, the messages about the people, objects, and events in the world. The dotted arrows going from the receiver to the source represent the messages about the object messages, or the *metamessages.* These messages we call "feedback." Feedback messages are information sent back by the receiver to the source; they are the receiver's responses to the messages of the source. The short arrows going back to the source represent the feedback that the source gets from his or her own message production; for example, we hear ourselves when we speak, we feel ourselves when we gesture.

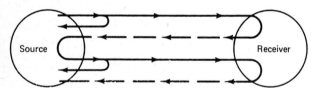

A model of the feedback cycle.

The model is intended to represent visually a number of different characteristics concerning feedback. First, feedback is constantly occurring; it is not something that happens at the end of a public speech or after the television program is over or after we say goodnight. Rather feedback is being emitted throughout the communication encounter in much the same way that object messages are emitted throughout the encounter.

The continuous lines are used to emphasize the fact that the feedback influences the object message, which influences the subsequent feedback message, which in turn influences the next object message, and so on. Object messages and metamessages are interdependent; each influences the other.

The model also illustrates that the feedback from the receiver and the feedback from the self, both of which may be received simultaneously or sequentially, are distinguishable by the source. A normal source does not confuse feedback from the self with that from receivers. Pathological sources frequently do make this confusion, the paranoid being the clearest example.

Finally, the juxtaposition of the object messages and the feedback messages is intended to indicate that feedback may be understood and analyzed in the same general way as object messages. Feedback, like object messages, may come through all channels—auditory, visual, and so on. Feedback is also subject to noise interference and distortion. Feedback represents only a part of the receiver's total response to the object messages, just as the object messages represent only a part of the source's thoughts and ideas.

Positive and Negative Feedback

Both positive and negative feedback occur in other types of systems. Negative feedback is seen clearly in biological systems. When your blood pressure rises, receptors in certain arteries are stretched and send nerve impulses to the brain. The brain then sends signals to dilate the blood vessels, which reduces the blood pressure. Conversely, if blood pressure falls below the acceptable level, messages are sent to constrict the blood vessels and thus to speed up the heart and raise the blood pressure to an acceptable level. One of the most common manifestations of positive feedback is the snowball effect. As a small snowball rolls, it collects snow and becomes larger. In its large size it collects even more snow. As it grows its capacity to collect more snow also grows. The cycle is a continuous positive one. Now consider the operation of negative and positive feedback in communication.

Negative feedback in communication may be manifested in numerous ways, such as looks of disapproval, a lack of interest, negative verbalizations, and disagreements. The major function of negative feedback is to provide the source with information that the message deviates from the predetermined desired effect. This negative feedback provides the source with the information that he or she needs to modify, change, alter, redirect, or revise the messages being sent. Negative feedback also has other effects on the source. For example, when negative feedback is received, mistakes on the part of the source increase (there are more false starts, more sentence changes, more stutters, and more omitted syllables.) There are more linguistic errors—errors of pronunciation, articulation, semantics, and syntax. There are more frequent shifts in topic and focus and a general increase in defensiveness. There is a decrease in the number of verbalizations; the source becomes less willing to talk or communicate in general.

Positive feedback, on the other hand, consists of such manifestations as looks of approval, looks of interest, positive verbalizations, and expressed or implied agreement. When the source receives positive feedback, he or she is in effect informed that the message is being received as intended and that no significant deviations from this intended goal are apparent. On the basis of this information the source may intensify, strengthen, continue, or enlarge upon the message he or she is already sending. The other effects of positive feedback are basically the opposite of those of negative feedback. There is a decrease in linguistic errors and a tendency to continue with the topic and focus that originally led to the positive feedback. There is also a corresponding decrease in defensiveness.

Effective Feedback

Like all message reception processes, feedback may be ineffective, effective, or anywhere in between these two extremes. In an effort to strengthen the chances of our feedback being effective, some suggestions are offered here both for the giving of feedback and for the receiving of feedback.

Giving Feedback Effectively

The process of giving effective feedback seems characterized by at least five qualities: immediateness, honesty, appropriateness, clarity, and informativeness.

Immediateness. The most effective feedback is that which is most immediate. Ideally, feedback is sent immediately after the message is received. Feedback, like reinforcement, loses its effectiveness with time; the longer we wait to praise or punish, for example, the less effect it will have.

Honesty. Feedback should be an honest reaction to a communication. Feedback should not merely be a series of messages that the speaker wants to hear and that will build up his or her ego. Feedback concerning one's understanding of the message as well as one's agreement with the message should be honest. We should neither be ashamed or afraid to admit that we did not understand a message nor should we hesitate to assert our disagreement.

Appropriateness. Feedback should be appropriate to the general communication situation. For the most part we have learned what is appropriate and what is not appropriate from observing others as we grew up. Appropriateness is a learned concept; consequently, what is appropriate for our culture is not necessarily appropriate for another culture.

Feedback to the message should be kept distinct from feedback to the speaker. Make clear, in disagreeing with speakers, for example, that we are disagreeing with what they are saying and not necessarily rejecting them as people. We may dislike what a person says but like the person who is saying it.

Clarity. Feedback should be clear on at least two counts. It should be clear enough so that speakers can perceive that it is feedback to the message and not just a reflection of something you ate that did not agree with you. Feedback should also be clear in meaning; if it is to signal understanding, then it should be clear to the speaker that that is what you are signaling. If you are disagreeing, then that, too, should be clear.

Informativeness. The feedback you send to speakers should convey some information; it should tell them something they did not already know. To always respond in the same way conveys no information. To communicate information, responses must be, in part at least, unpredictable. If speakers are able to completely predict how you will respond to something they say, then your response conveys no information and does not serve any useful feedback function.

Receiving Feedback Effectively

It probably takes a great deal more effort and ingenuity to respond appropriately to feedback than to give feedback to others. The process of receiving feedback effectively is characterized by sensitivity, supportiveness, open-mindedness, helpfulness, and specificity.

Sensitivity. Develop a sensitivity to feedback—a sensitivity that will enable us to perceive feedback in situations where it might normally go unnoticed. Feedback is given to us at all times, through both verbal and nonverbal means. Most often the feedback comes in the form of nonverbal messages—the puzzled face, the wide smile, the limp handshake. These are examples of feedback to which we have to learn to become sensitive. And, of course, verbal feedback also comes in many forms. At times the verbal feedback is obvious; it is said directly and without any attempt at subtlety: "Your humor is gross," "You walk like an elephant," "When you look at me that way, I want to kiss you." But most often verbal feedback comes to us in more subtle ways—the quick, almost throwaway remark about your method of approaching someone; the slow, belabored effort to say something good about your newly decorated apartment. Feedback may also be given by silence, as when someone would normally be expected to say something but says nothing.

Supportiveness. Support the person giving feedback in order to avoid, or at least suspend, any defensive responses. Your own responsiveness to the feedback will in large measure determine the comprehensiveness and depth of the feedback you receive. Defensiveness is usually taken as a sign to stop giving feedback. If the feedback is stopped, we stand to lose a great deal of insight that we might otherwise have gained. If we make the assumption that the person giving the feedback has our own betterment in mind, and this seems a reasonable enough assumption, and if we keep this clearly in mind, our defensiveness should be lessened.

Open-Mindedness. Listen to feedback with an open mind. If the feedback is negative, and especially if it centers on some issue of high ego involvement, then it becomes particularly difficult to accept and we tend to block it out very quickly, even before we hear the entire message. We obviously need to listen to the entire feedback message and to suspend judgment until we have heard it all and understood it all. This is not to say that we must therefore uncritically accept everything anyone else says about us; certainly we should not. We need to evaluate critically what is said, accept what seems reasonable and useful, and reject what seems unreasonable and not useful.

Helpfulness. The task of giving feedback is a difficult one, and the person giving us the feedback needs to be helped along. Often initial feedback will be given in general and highly abstract terms. In this form the feedback is not very useful. Yet most of these general and abstract comments can be made more specific and more useful, and hence some energy may be profitability devoted to enabling the person giving the feedback to become more specific. And so, for example, it might help if, in hearing the feedback, we would say, "Do you mean when I said . . . ?" or "Are you referring to the time I . . . ?" This type of behavior will also demonstrate supportiveness, and the feedback giver will probably be more anxious and more willing to supply additional and more specific feedback.

Specificity. When listening to feedback, translate it into specific, preferably behavioral, terms. Think of the feedback in terms of what it means to our own specific behavior—today's and tomorrow's. That is, we need to ask what we can learn on the basis of this feedback: How can we adjust our verbal and nonverbal messages on the basis of this feedback?

[B. Aubrey Fisher, *Perspectives on Human Communication* (New York: Macmillan, 1978).]

Feedforward. When the distinguished literary critic, author, and semanticist I. A. Richards was asked by *Saturday Review* to contribute to its "What I Have Learned" series—a series of articles in which leading theorists were asked to record their most important insights and learnings—he chose to write on "feedforward." "I am not sure I have learned anything else as important," noted Richards. "I have been able to realize what a prime role what I have come to call 'feedforward' has in all our doings."

Whereas feedback (q.v.) is information that is sent back to the source informing him or her as to the effects of the messages, feedforward is information that is sent prior to the regular messages telling us something about future messages. Feedforward messages are predictions we make concerning what will take place. Perhaps the most important type of feedforward is the information we tell ourselves about the messages we expect to receive or how we expect our own messages to be received by others. For example, whenever we approach a communication situation, we make certain predictions: they won't like me; I'm going to convince mother to give me the car tonight; I'm sure he'll go out with me on Saturday night. These predictions are feedforward. We are in effect identifying for ourselves what messages we expect to receive in the near future.

In scientific analysis and research, feedforward may be seen as the hypothesis-making step in scientific inquiry. The actual results or findings are the feedback that confirm or deny the feedforward predictions or hypotheses.

We also send feedforward messages to others to inform them as to what kinds of messages are to follow and even to provide some guidelines for them in interpreting the messages that do follow. Such examples of feedforward would include a smile as you approach someone at a party which tells that person that the future messages will be positive ones; a scowl on your face as you wait at the door for your spouse to return home communicates that future messages will be unpleasant and negative; a friendly "hello" tells someone that you are pleased to see him or her and wish to communicate further. Feedforward messages are metacommunicational (q.v.); they are comments on other messages, on messages that are yet to be sent.

[I. A. Richards, *Speculative Instruments* (Chicago: University of Chicago Press, 1935); "The Secret of 'Feedforward,'" *Saturday Review* 51 (February 1968):14–17; Bess Sondel, *The Humanity of Words: A Primer of Semantics* (New York: Harcourt Brace Jovanovich, 1958).]

Festschrift. A collection of writings to honor some person or to celebrate some occasion.

Field of Experience. The sum total of an individual's experiences that influence his or her ability to communicate. In some views of communication, two people can communicate only to the extent that their fields of experience overlap.

Field Theory. Theoretical position that holds that behavior is determined by an interaction between environmental and cognitive elements.

Fifth Amendment. The fifth amendment to the Constitution of the United States concerned with self-incrimination, double jeopardy, and due process; it reads:

> *No person shall be held to answer for a capital, or otherwise infamous crime, unless on a presentation or indictment of a Grand Jury, except in cases arising in the land or naval forces, or in the Militia, when in actual service in time of War, or public danger; nor shall any person be subject for the same offence to be twice put in jeopardy of life or limb; nor shall be compelled in any criminal case to be a witness against himself, nor be deprived of life, liberty, or property, without due process of law; nor shall private property be taken for public use, without just compensation.*

Figure Ground Perception. A concept of Gestalt psychology where a *figure* is defined as "any object" and *ground* as "the background or framework in which the figure is seen"; figures are perceived as being separate and apart from the ground.

Figure of Speech. Any figurative use of language; stylistic device in which words are used in other than their literal meanings as, for example, in metaphor (q.v.), hyperbole (q.v.), and personification (q.v.).

Filibuster. Extended speech making used to delay action in a political meeting.

Filled Pause. A vocalized pause filled with such hesitation phenomena as "ah," "er," and the like; opposed to unfilled pause (q.v.). See also HESITATION PHENOMENA.

Filter Theories. A general term for a variety of theories concerned with the development of relationships. These theories have as their common assumtion that we select a relational partner from a field of eligible individuals by filtering out those who are least desirable or who fail to meet selected criteria and are left with one or a few of the most appropriate potential partners.
[A. C. Kerckhoff and K. E. Davis, "Value Consensus and Need Complementarity in Mate Selection," *American Sociological Review* 27 (1962):295–303.]

Finger Spelling. A procedure of spelling with one's fingers to communicate with the deaf; opposed to American Sign Language (q.v.) where signs represent ideas.

FIRO (Fundamental Interpersonal Relations Orientation). A theory of interpersonal relationships built on four major postulates: (1) each person has needs for inclusion (q.v.), control (q.v.), and affection (q.v.); (2) each person's interpersonal behavior reflects his or her earliest interpersonal relationships, generally those with parents; (3) the operation of a group is greatly dependent on compatibility, which increases both cohesiveness and communication and hence productivity; and (4) group development passes through the stages of inclusion, control, and affection, in sequence, while group deterioration passes through the same stages but in reverse; affection, control, inclusion.
[William Schutz, *FIRO: A Three-Dimensional Theory of Interpersonal Behavior* (New York: Rinehart, 1958).]

First Amendment. The first amendment to the Constitution of the United States concerned with free speech, it reads:

> *Congress should make no law respecting an establishment of religion, or prohibiting the free exercise thereof; or abridging the freedom of speech, or of the press; or the right of the people peaceably to assemble, and to petition the Government for a redress of grievances.*

Fisher Divorce Adjustment Scale. A scale designed to measure one's degree of adjustment to the ending of a love relationship.
[Bruce Fisher, *Identifying and Meeting Needs of Formerly Married People Through a Divorce Adjustment Seminar,* doctoral dissertation, University of Colorado, Boulder, Colorado, 1976.]

Five Freedoms. Virginia Satir advances five freedoms that are designed to enhance one's self-esteem and promote meaningful human contact: (1) the freedom to see and hear what is really present rather than what should be, or what was, or what will be; (2) the freedom to say what one thinks and feels instead of what one should think or feel; (3) the freedom to feel as one feels rather than the way one should feel; (4) the freedom to request what one wants rather than to wait for permission; and (5) the freedom to risk in pursuing what one wants rather than to choose only what is secure.
[Virginia Satir, *Making Contact* (Berkeley, Calif.: Celestial Arts, 1976).]

Flooding. Originally introduced as "implosion therapy," a therapeutic procedure in which the patient is confronted rapidly and with prolonged exposure to those elements (situations, ideas, feelings) that cause anxiety. The patient is flooded with the very things that cause distress, sometimes *in vivo* and sometimes in fantasy. See also SYSTEMATIC DESENSITIZATION.
[T. G. Stampfl and D. J. Levis, "Essentials of Implosive Therapy: A Learning-Theory-Based Psychodynamic Behavioral Therapy," *Journal of Abnormal Psychology* 72 (1967):496–503.]

Floppy Disk. The thin, flexible disk that records and stores computer programs and data.

Fluency. Uninterrupted speech; ability to speak and understand a language.

FM (Frequency Modulation). The situation in which the carrier wave frequency is altered when the information wave is superimposed upon it; in television the audio signal is FM. See also AM.

Focal Areas. In language study, that geographical area of linguistic prestige where dialect forms may originate and are transmitted to and accepted by neighboring areas.

Fog Index. A readability (q.v.) index developed by Robert Gunning involving three stages: (1) calculate the number of words per sentence by randomly selecting 100 word sections; (2) calculate the number of words having three or more syllables; express this per 100 words. Do not count proper names, combinations of two easy words (for example, *housekeeper*), or verbs that are three syllables by virtue of their past tense or third-person singular markers; (3) add the mean sentence length (from step 1) and the number of words of three syllables or more per 100 words (from step 2) and multiply by four. The result is the Fog Index, and an index of 13 or higher means that the writing is difficult, around college level. [Robert Gunning, *The Technique of Clear Writing* (New York: McGraw-Hill, 1952).]

Folio. A page number in printed material.

Folk Etymology. Changing spoken or written word forms either to more closely resemble the meaning people have for the words or to more commonly used and familiar forms.

Foot-in-the-Door. A persuasive technique in which one begins with a small request and works up to larger and larger requests. See also DOOR-IN-THE-FACE. [J. L. Freedman and S. C. Fraser, "Compliance Without Pressure: The Foot-In-The-Door Technique," *Journal of Personality and Social Psychology* 4 (1966):195–202.]

Forced Compliance. The procedure of inducing attitude change by forcing individuals to say or do something against their own attitudes. It is often found that attitude change follows the forced verbalization or behavior.

Forensic Rhetoric. One of the three major types of rhetoric (q.v.) identified by Aristotle; rhetoric concerned with the oratory of accusation and defense, with the oratory of the law courts. Also referred to as judicial rhetoric. Also see DELIBERATIVE RHETORIC, EPIDEICTIC RHETORIC.

Forensic Speeches. Legal speeches; speeches concerned with accusation and defense, with justice and injustice.

Formal Operations Stage. The fourth and last of Piaget's stages of child development—occurring around 12 years of age—at which the child is able to deal with abstract concepts and reason deductively.

Formal Organization. The organization as officially structured; the hierarchical structure of an organization with formal lines of responsibility and communication.

Formal Time. Time as divided up by a culture or language, for example, 12 months in a year, 7 days in a week; opposed to technical time (q.v.) and informal time (q.v.). See also TEMPORAL COMMUNICATION.

Formant. An area of acoustic energy concentration shown on a spectrogram as a horizontal band produced by various oral cavities resonating with the production of a particular sound.

Form Class. A part of speech (more traditionally, a *noun, verb, adjective, adverb*), particularly as described by Charles Fries.

[Charles Fries, *The Structure of English: An Introduction to the Construction of English Sentences* (New York: Harcourt, Brace, Jovanovich, 1952).]

Forms of Address. The different modes of addressing people; the titles or names used to address people. See also POWER SEMANTIC; SOLIDARITY SEMANTIC.

FORTRAN. Acronym for "formula translation," a computer language designed for use on scientific materials.

Forum. That part of a small group discussion during which there is a question-and-answer session between the experts who participated in the discussions and the audience.

Foul Copy. Manuscript copy marked up by the copy editor and compositor and used by the compositor to prepare the proofs (galleys) for printed material.

Frame. The information one uses in determining the correct perspective for viewing a behavior or action, for example, seeing a young man waving his hand above his head may prove difficult to understand until you see that he is sitting in a classroom and the instructor has just finished asking a question. This information that the student is in the classroom attempting to answer a question is the "frame" in which to view his hand-waving behavior. By knowing the frame we can make meaningful inferences about what is taking place; without such frames much of what we see would prove meaningless.

[Erving Goffman, *Frame Analysis* (New York: Harper & Row, 1974).]

Frame of Reference. The point of view of a person through which people, objects, and events are perceived.

Freebies. Special gifts (money, services, merchandise) given to media personalities to gain a favorable review, hearing, or free publicity.

Freedom of Information Act. Federal ruling giving the media access to all government information other than that concerned with security, personnel, and the like. Each federal agency must make known (through its publications) how such information may be obtained by the public.

[Harold C. Relyea, "The Freedom of Information Act: Its Evolution and Operational Status," *Journalism Quarterly* 54 (1977):538–544.]

Free Morpheme. A morpheme (q.v.) that can stand alone, for example, *boy, house, love* as opposed to a bound morpheme (q.v.) that cannot stand alone, for example, the suffixes *-ment* and *-ing,* the plural *-s,* and the past tense *-ed.*

Free Information. Information that a person communicates in addition to that which is immediately relevant; information that is communicated in excess of that expected by the maxim of quantity (see also CONVERSATIONAL MAXIMS). Free information may be used to start a conversation or to pursue one along other lines. Free information may be verbal or nonverbal and would include, for example, the incidental mention of one's job, hometown, or political concerns which could then be used as a topic for further discussion.

Freeze Frame. In film, a single picture that is reproduced in the film so that the image projected on the screen is frozen although the film continues to run.

Frequency of Sound. The cycles per second in a sound wave.

Freudian Slip. A speech error motivated subconsciously by some repressed conflict or impulse. Since Freud rejected the idea that any behavior was unmotivated or random, any mistake or error was to be interpreted in terms of subconscious motivation.

Friendship. An interpersonal relationship that is mutually productive, established and maintained through perceived mutual free choice, and characterized by mutual positive regard.

Developmental Stages of Friendship

When we were children, say around 3 to 7 years of age, our friendships might have been characterized as "momentary playmateship," where we valued friends for what they had (the ball, the rope, the tree house) and what they could do (play ball, run fast, jump rope). At this stage of development friends (as we think of them now) really did not exist. As we grew older, say between the ages of 4 and 9, we still had no real understanding of the mutual assistance nature of friendship. A friend, in the young "one-way assistance" relationship, was valued or desired basically for what he or she could give us or for doing what we wanted. Later, around the ages of 6 to 12, we entered our "two-way, fair-weather cooperation" stage where friendship existed to serve our own self-interests rather than interests that were mutually beneficial. Around ages 9 to 15 we developed "intimate, mutually shared relationships"; we were able to step outside the friendship and view it as a third entity—a thing of value for its own sake. Friendship now became a collaborative effort that was entered into in order to achieve some common goals. Here we shared not only objective information but our feelings as well, and we helped each other with problems and conflicts. But at this stage, we were also possessive and resented third parties disturbing these friendships. Still later, from the ages of 12 to adulthood, we developed "autonomous interdependent friendships." These friendships—the ones we now have and the ones from the recent past, were developed and maintained to give mutual emotional and psychological support. Unlike the previous stage, however, the friendships here are not possessive and exclusive; rather, each friend is seen as able to develop other independent relationships and these relationships do not affect the basic structure of the original friendship.

These several stages, identified by psychologists Robert L. and Anne P. Selman, illustrate the development and growth from immature to mature and productive friendships and provide an excellent starting point for examining friendship.

Types of Friendships

Another way of approaching friendship is to look, at least briefly, at some of the different types of friendships that have been defined. The friendship types as distinguished by Aristotle, Reisman, and James and Savary are presented in order to give you a clear picture of the variety of friendships that can and do exist.

Aristotle: Utility, Pleasure, Virtue

In his *Nicomachean Ethics,* Aristotle identified three kinds of friendly relationships, each of which was motivated by a different purpose. Friendships based on *utility* were those in which the individuals formed a relationship in order to profit from the association, for example, financial advantage, prestige, professional advancement, and so on. Self-interests rather than mutual interest motivated the friendship. Friendships based on *pleasure* were those in which the individuals associated for the purpose of increasing their pleasures—whether physical, emotional, intellectual, sexual, and so on. Both of these types of friendships, of course, are motivated by the desire to gain something. Friendships based on *virtue,* however, were those that grew out of a recognition by each person of the good qualities (the virtues) of the other. When we see a person's essential goodness, we grow to like them and wish to form a bond of friendship with them.

Reisman: Reciprocity, Receptivity, Association

John M. Reisman, in his *Anatomy of Friendship,* also distinguishes three types of friendships. The friendship of *reciprocity* is the ideal type of friendship—the kind we think of when we visualize an ideal friendship. It is characterized by loyalty, self-sacrifice, mutual affection, and generosity. A friendship of reciprocity is a friendship based on equality, where each individual shares equally in the giving and in the receiving of the benefits and rewards of the relationship. The friendship of *receptivity,* on the other hand, is characterized by an imbalance of giving and receiving; one person is the primary giver and one person is the primary receiver. This imbalance, however, is a positive one because each person gains something from the relationship—the person who receives affection and the person who gives affection both have their individual (but different) needs satisfied. This is the friendship that often develops between a teacher and a student or between a doctor and a patient; in fact, a difference in status is, according to Reisman, an essential factor for the friendship of receptivity to develop. The friendship of *association* is a transitory one, sometimes more aptly described as a friendly relationship rather than a friendship. These associative friendships are the kind we have with fellow classmates or with various neighbors or even with coworkers. There is here no great loyalty, no great trust, no great giving or receiving. Rather, it is an association that is cordial but not very intense.

James and Savary: Half-to-Whole, Nourishment, Third Self

Muriel James and Louis Savary, in their insightful *The Heart of Friendship,* distinguish among three viewpoints or theories concerning the nature and effects of friendship. These viewpoints provide considerable insight into what friendship is and what it does to people.

The first approach, the *half-to-whole view,* conceives of friendship as a process of making people whole. People without friends, in this view, are incomplete individuals, and it is only through the establishment of a friendship that these people are made whole. Friendship changes you; it makes you complete. But at the same time, it also leads the individual to supplant his or her own identity. Traditional marriages are often viewed in this way; the husband and wife become one; they are no longer as much individuals as they are a team. Here there is no "I" or "you"; there is just "we" and "us."

The second approach, the *nourishment view,* conceives of friendship as enhancing, developing, and nourishing each individual. According to this view, friendship does not destroy individuality but rather heightens it. This approach, as James and Savary note, is clearly typified in the famous and often-repeated observation of Fritz Perls from *Gestalt Therapy Verbatim:*

> *I do my thing, and you do your thing. I am not in this world to live up to your expectations, and you are not in this world to live up to mine. You are you, and I am I: if by chance we find each other, it's beautiful. If not, it can't be helped.*

Whereas traditional views of marriage aligned themselves with the half-to-whole approach, Perls's view of friendship allows the uniqueness and the individuality of each person to grow and to progress. Here they remain "I" and "you."

The third view that James and Savary distinguish is called the *third-self theory* and views friendship as having a life of its own. It is an extension of the nourishment point of view and is not incompatible with it. When two persons experience friendship, a third self emerges—a metaself, a higher-order self. In this view friendship does not destroy or even detract from the uniqueness and individuality of each person but actually enhances it; at the same time, a new self—a third self—emerges. A similar situation occurs with individual notes played on a piano. Each is unique and individual, but when they are played together something new emerges without destroying the integrity or individuality of the individual notes.

According to this view—which James and Savary feel is the most meaningful—each friendship should be treated like a new person, much as a corporation is treated legally as a person. This is similar to teams and gangs having their own identity and even their own names.

One of the implications of this view is that concern and attention must be directed not only to each other but to the relationship as well, that is, to the metaself, the third self. The problem created by the neglect of this third self is seen clearly in those parent-child relationships in which the parent cares for the child's biological and physical needs but ignores the relationship between them. This relationship—this third self—must be cared for and acknowledged just as the individual must be. In this view there are "I," "you," and "we" (the third self).

These different types of friendships may also be seen in the responses of people who were asked to identify the qualities they felt most important in a friend. The responses, presented in the table below are derived from a *Psychology Today* survey of 40,000 respondents. If you examine the list, you will find it easy to fit each one of these qualities into one of the types of friendship noted above.

THE 10 MOST FREQUENTLY MENTIONED QUALITIES OF A FRIEND

Friendship Qualities	Percentage of Respondents
1. keeps confidence	89%
2. loyalty	88
3. warmth; affection	82
4. supportiveness	76
5. frankness	75
6. sense of humor	74
7. willingness to make time for me	62
8. independence	61
9. good conversationalist	59
10. intelligence	57

Based on Mary Brown Parlee and the Editors of *Psychology Today*, "The Friendship Bond," *Psychology Today* 13 (October 1979):43–54, 113.

Friendship Functions

In the previously mentioned *Psychology Today* survey, the 40,000 respondents indicated from a wide number of activities which ones they had engaged in over the past month with friends. The following table presents the 10 most frequently noted activities. As can be appreciated from this list, friendship seems to serve the same functions that all relationships serve but in a unique way. Friendships serve the functions of alleviating loneliness; providing physical, intellectual, and emotional stimulation; and presenting an opportunity to gain self-knowledge. Two general functions—need satisfaction and pleasure/pain functions—are considered by most theorists as basic functions of friendship. These, then, are the functions that friendships serve, as well as the reasons we develop and maintain them.

THE 10 MOST FREQUENTLY IDENTIFIED ACTIVITIES SHARED WITH FRIENDS

Friendship Activities
1. had an intimate talk
2. had a friend ask you to do something for him or her
3. went to dinner in a restaurant
4. asked your friend to do something for you
5. had a meal together at home or at your friend's home
6. went to a movie, play, or concert
7. went drinking together
8. went shopping
9. participated in sports
10. watched a sporting event

Based on Mary Brown Parlee and the Editors of *Psychology Today,* "The Friendship Bond," *Psychology Today* 13 (October 1979):43–54, 113.

Need Satisfaction

Friendships develop and are maintained to satisfy those needs that can only be satisfied by certain people. We select as friends those who, on the basis of our experiences or our predictions, will help to satisfy our basic needs or growth needs, and we cultivate and strive to preserve these relationships.

Selecting friends on the basis of need satisfaction is similar to our choosing a marriage partner, an employee, or any person who may be in a position to satisfy our needs. Thus, for example, if we have the need to be the center of attention or to be popular, we select friends who provide fulfillment of these needs—that is, people who allow us, and even encourage us, to be the center of attention or who tell us, verbally and nonverbally, that we are popular.

As our needs change as we grow older or develop in different ways, the functions that we look for in our friendships also change, and in many instances old friends are dropped from our close circle to be replaced by new friends who better serve these new needs.

Five Friendship Values. Psychologist Paul H. Wright has identified more specifically the needs that we seek to have satisfied through friendships. We establish and maintain friendships, Wright observes, because they provide us with certain "direct rewards."

First, friends serve a *utility value.* A friend may have special talents, skills, or resources that may prove useful to us in achieving our specific goals and needs. We may, for example, become friends with someone who is particularly bright because such a person might assist us in getting better grades, in solving our personal problems, or in getting a better job.

Second, friends serve an *affirmation value.* The behavior of a friend toward us acts as a reflecting mirror that serves to affirm our personal value and enables us to recognize our positively valued self-attributes. A friend may, for example, help us to recognize more clearly our leadership abilities, our athletic prowess, or our sense of humor.

Third, friends serve an *ego-support value.* By behaving in a supportive, encouraging, and helpful manner, friends enable us to more easily view ourselves as worthy and competent individuals.

Fourth, friends serve a *stimulation value.* A friend introduces us to new ideas and new ways of seeing the world and helps us to expand our world view. A friend enables us to come into contact with issues and concepts with which we were not previously familiar—with modern art, foreign cultures, new foods, and hundreds of other new, different, and stimulating things.

Fifth, friends serve a *security value.* A friend does nothing to hurt the other person or to emphasize or call attention to the other person's inadequacies or weaknesses. Because of this security value, friends can interact freely and openly without having to worry about betrayal or negative responses.

Pleasure/Pain Functions

The other function of friendship is to maximize pleasure and minimize pain. This view is actually a special case of the need-satisfaction function.

If you were to ask people to complete the statement, "I most need a friend when . . .," they would probably answer in two ways. One might say, "I most need a friend when I'm down," "I most need a friend when I'm feeling sorry for myself," or "I most need a friend when I'm depressed." Such statements typify the function that friendships serve in the avoidance or the lessening of pain. We want a friend to be around when we are feeling down so that he or she will make us feel a little better, lift our spirits, or in some way alleviate the pain we are feeling.

The other might say, "I most need a friend when I'm happy," ". . . when I want to share my good news," or ". . . when I want someone to enjoy something with me." These statements typify the general function friendships serve to augment one's pleasure. A great part of the pleasure in winning a game, in receiving good news, and in experiencing some good fortune is in telling someone else about it and in many cases sharing it with them.

In the language of operant conditioning, friends provide reinforcement. Friends provide us with positive reinforcement by complimenting us, giving us presents, and providing social support for our ideas and our decisions. Friends provide negative reinforcement by removing painful stimuli, nursing us when we are sick, getting us out of our depressions, alleviating loneliness, and in general minimizing our pain. Goethe expressed much the same idea when he wrote:

> The world is so empty
> if one thinks only
> of mountains, rivers, and
> cities; but to know someone
> who thinks and feels with me,
> and who, though distant
> is close to me in spirit,
> this makes the earth for me
> an inhabited garden.

Communication during the Stages in Friendship Development

Friendship at first sight is even more rare than love at first sight—if it is possible at all. While you may like a person at first sight, you could hardly call that person a friend, at least not until there has been some opportunity for interaction and communication. Friendship, like most things worthwhile, takes time to develop. It may be described according to a number of stages or phases and is best viewed as existing on a continuum. At one end are "strangers" or "the initial meeting of two persons," and at the other end are "intimate friends." We need to consider what happens in between these two extremes so that we might be in a better position to move from initial meetings to real friendships, to encourage the growth of friendship in the right direction, and to introduce correctives in the process should problems, obstacles, or breakdowns occur.

Initial Contact

The first stage of friendship development is obviously an initial meeting of some kind. It may be a meeting by accident or by strategy, planned or unplanned, self-initiated or brought about by some third-party introduction, face-to-face or by letter or telephone. In any event, some interpersonal encounter must take place. This does not mean that what has happened prior to the encounter is unimportant—quite the contrary. In fact, one's prior history of friendships, one's personal needs, and in short, one's readiness or lack of readiness for friendship development is extremely important in determining whether a relationship will develop into a close friendship, will end soon after the first encounter, or will continue for a long period as a mere acquaintanceship.

At this initial contact stage we find the characteristics of effective interpersonal communication (q.v.) only to a small degree. We are guarded, rather than open or expressive, lest we reveal aspects of ourselves that might be viewed too negatively. Because we do not really know the other person our abilities to empathize or to orient ourselves significantly to the other are extremely limited and the "relationship"—at this stage at least—is probably viewed as too temporary to be worth the energy and effort that such empathy and other-orientation would entail. Because we really do not know the other person, supportiveness, positiveness, and equality would all be difficult to manifest in any meaningful sense. The characteristics that are demonstrated are probably done so more out of good manners than out of any genuine expression of positive regard for this relative stranger or this tentative relationship. When conflicts arise, they often function to terminate the relationship rather than to stimulate us to work them through. At this stage the relationship is not important enough for us to work through differences; it is often easier to move on to someone else.

There seems at this stage little genuine immediacy (q.v.); the individuals see themselves as separate and distinct rather than as a unit; there is no real sense of "we-ness" and consequently few verbal or nonverbal immediacy behaviors are in evidence. The confidence that is demonstrated is probably more a function of the individual personalities than of the relationship. Because the relationship is so new and because the individuals do not know each other very well, the interaction is often characterized by a certain awkwardness—overly long pauses, uncertainty in the selection of topics to be discussed, frequent nonfluencies, ineffective exchanges of speaker and listener roles, verbal and nonverbal behaviors that may be misinterpreted, and, in general, a lack of smoothness in the interaction that characterizes more intimate relationships.

Acquaintanceship

If the initial meeting proves at all productive, the individuals progress to the acquaintanceship stage. At this stage personality attractiveness becomes signifi-

cant and in fact greatly determines whether or not the relationship will progress
beyond this point. The dimension of physical attractiveness, however, probably
never fades completely.

At this stage there is a clear recognition of each other, a consistent exchange
of phatic messages, and a definite memory for name, face, and other identifying
data. Put differently, at this stage each person is clearly defined in the mind of
the other person and clearly distinguished from other persons.

At the acquaintanceship stage, and in fact at all subsequent stages, a process
of testing goes on which most people seem reluctant to admit. At this stage we
attempt to determine whether this acquaintanceship should be developed into
a closer relationship or whether it should be terminated. The entire dating system of our culture is essentially one in which each person tests the other person
and attempts to determine whether a long-term or even a lifetime relationship
should be established.

At this acquaintanceship stage we begin to respond more openly and expressively, but still in a mostly guarded manner. The communications are still essentially impersonal. There is little attempt to talk about personal problems, about
fantasies and unfulfilled desires, about family problems, about one's financial
situation. In short, there is little attempt to engage in self-disclosure (q.v.) of any
significance. In fact, should significant self-disclosures occur, they immediately
call attention to themselves and seem intuitively out of place. Empathy (q.v.) and
other-orientation (q.v.) are still extremely difficult to achieve because of our
limited knowledge of the other person. If our initial contact and our acquaintanceship have been positive, then we would probably demonstrate supportiveness and positiveness toward the other person. We begin to see this person as
a potential friend and our positive affect will manifest itself in our communications. Similarly, as we get to know the other person we begin to see him or her
as a unique and contributing individual and so equality begins to be evidenced.

Although confidence is somewhat greater here than at the last stage, it is still
relatively low and, again, more a product of the individuals than of the relationship. There is still no genuine immediacy, although a sense of "we-ness" may be
at a very early stage. The interaction is smoother here than at the earlier stage
and yet there is still a decided lack of synchrony; the questions asked may be
awkwardly phrased and perhaps inappropriate, the eye glances uncoordinated,
and, still, a failure to understand many of the other's verbal and nonverbal
signals.

Casual Friendship

This stage is much like the previous one, except that now there is a dyadic
consciousness, a sense of "we-ness," a sense of togetherness; we communicate
with a clear sense of immediacy. At this stage the individuals participate in
activities as a unit rather than as separate individuals. Most importantly, each
person sees the dyad as a unit—as a whole. The casual friend is the one we
would call to go to the movies, the one we would sit with in the cafeteria or in
class, or the one with whom we would ride home from school. The loss of such
a friendship would disturb us, but only for a relatively short period of time. We
might feel diminished, but only slightly so.

At this casual friendship stage the qualities of effective interpersonal interaction begin to be seen more clearly. We begin to express ourselves openly and
we become interested in his or her disclosures. Prior to this time, disclosures
seem unnatural and premature. We begin to own our own feelings and thoughts

when speaking with this person and respond openly to their communications. Because we are getting to understand this individual we can begin to empathize and demonstrate significant other-orientation. We also demonstrate supportiveness and develop a genuinely positive attitude toward the other person and toward the general communication situation. We know what this person's needs and wants are—to some extent at least—and so can stroke effectively. As we get to know the other person more and more, we see ourselves as both contributing to and deriving benefit from this developing relationship.

Perhaps the most significant change at this stage is that there is now a smoothness, a coordination in the interaction between the two persons. The awkward pauses, the nonfluencies, the misinterpretations of the other's behaviors are now few and, for the most part, go unnoticed. The individuals communicate with confidence; eye contact is appropriately maintained, there is flexibility in body posture and in gesturing, there are few irrelevant responses, and few adaptors (q.v.) signalling discomfort.

Close Friendship

The close friendship is an intensification of the casual friendship; it is a logical progression along the lines of intimacy from the casual friendship. At this stage the individuals know each other well and as a result are able to predict the behaviors of each other with considerable accuracy. In part our predictions are based on our having seen the other person in similar situations and, assuming some consistency on his or her part, we predict that the person will again behave in the same way. But, our predictions are also based on knowing things about the person that enable us to extrapolate beyond anything we have ever observed. We may know the person's values, attitudes, and opinions about specific issues, and so when decisions arc to be made or when actions are to be taken, we use our knowledge of these values and attitudes to predict future, probable behaviors. Because of this knowledge significant interaction management becomes possible.

At this stage we become willing to make significant sacrifices for the other person. We will go far out of our way for the benefit of this friend, and the friend in turn does the same for us. Touching and other nonverbal expressions of intimacy become accepted parts of our friendship behavior. Depending on the sex of the individuals, close friends may kiss, hug, slap each other on the back, put their arms around each other's shoulders, and so on. Touching is not uncomfortable as it often is with a stranger or a mere acquaintance. Instead, it serves a comforting function for both parties; it assures each of the closeness between them. It is nonverbal testimony that this is indeed a close friendship.

Similarly, we begin, at this level, to read accurately the other's nonverbal signals; we know the nonverbal signs that signal the various modes and feelings and we use these as guides to our interactions—avoiding certain topics at certain times, offering consolation before any verbal expression, and, in general, responding appropriately on the basis of mutually shared nonverbal signals.

At this stage we exchange significant messages of affection, messages that express a fondness, a liking, a loving, a caring for the other person. Significant openness and expressiveness are clearly in evidence. Women exchange significantly more affectional messages than do men. In part this difference seems due to the fact that we expect such messages from women and treat such expressions positively whereas in men they are unexpected and are often treated negatively.

At the level of close friendship we see all of the characteristics demonstrated at the previous stage but in increased proportions. The depth of our self-disclosures increases considerably and we disclose things about ourselves and our families, for example, that we normally keep hidden from persons at less intimate levels. We feel that whatever we disclose will not only be kept in confidence but will be accepted. The friendship is felt to be strong enough that our disclosures will not weaken or damage it in any significant way. This confidence is demonstrated throughout our verbal and nonverbal behaviors. This is not to say that we are not at times proven wrong; certainly, there are such times. But generally we correctly make the assumption that we will be accepted and that the relationship will withstand any disclosures. As humanistic philosopher George Santayana put it, "One's friends are that part of the human race with which one can be human."

We empathize and exchange perspectives a great deal more and we expect in return that this friend will also empathize with us. With a genuinely positive feeling for this individual, our supportiveness and our positive stroking become spontaneous. We view this friend as one who is important in our lives and as a result conflicts—inevitable in all close relationships—become important to work out and resolve through compromise and empathic understanding rather than, for example, a refusal to negotiate or a show of force.

Intimate Friendship

An intimate friendship is that very special kind of relationship we might have with one or perhaps two other people. Rarely can we sustain more than a few intimate friendships largely because they take so long to develop and a great deal of time and energy to nurture and maintain.

An intimate friendship possesses all the qualities of the close friendship but goes beyond these. For example, the sacrifices each friend is willing to make at this stage are more extreme than those normally seen at the close friendship stage. A classic example of this is found in the Old Testament, in Ruth's expression of friendship for Naomi (Ruth 1:16–17):

> *Do not ask me to abandon or forsake you! For wherever you go I will go, wherever you lodge I will lodge, your people shall be my people, and your God my God. Wherever you die I will die, and there be buried. May the Lord do so and so to me, and more besides, if aught but death separates me from you!*

The touching that is permitted among close friends is naturally permitted here, as is more intimate touching, again, depending for specifics on the sex of the individuals. Touching between intimates may be more prolonged and more frequent and may focus on more intimate body parts. We may touch each other's faces, breasts, thighs, and so on without any self-consciousness, without any granting of permission. In fact, many of the societal rules that govern touching behavior in our culture, as well as the rules governing other forms of verbal and nonverbal behavior, are disregarded by intimates. Intimates create their own rules of interpersonal interaction. The rules are formed from mutual agreement rather than societal edict. And even the rules that the intimates themselves create may be broken, normally without fear of offending.

At this level of intimate friendship, the characteristics of effective interpersonal interaction are seen almost in their idealized form—total openness, expressiveness, empathy, other-orientation, confidence, supportiveness, immediacy, interaction management, positiveness, and equality. Almost, but not quite. There are still matters that we may keep entirely to ourselves and hidden from this intimate but these would be few in number and very likely extremely important for us to actively keep them from this special friend. Generally, the amount of self-disclosure is considerable; the disclosures themselves are more revealing than those made at the previous levels and an even greater amount of acceptance is expected and is (generally) received. These disclosures pose less of a threat to the friendship than did those disclosed at the level of the close friendship. "A friend," noted Ralph Waldo Emerson, "is a person with whom I may be sincere. Before him I may think aloud." We are willing to respond openly, confidently, and expressively to this person and to own our own feelings and thoughts. We see the relationship as a strong one that will withstand the temporary difficulties and differences that arise from time to time. Empathy is at its height in the intimate friendship. We feel what the other person is feeling with great intensity and similarity. If he or she fails a course or loses a job or has a fight, we know what that friend is going through because we can feel as he or she feels. Sometimes, our empathic abilities are so good that the other person hardly has to talk; we can feel how this person feels solely on the basis of nonverbal cues. Our supportiveness and positiveness are genuine expressions of the closeness we feel for this person. We want to avoid hurting this person because we care but also because it hurts us when our intimate is hurt. Each person in an intimate friendship is truly equal; each can initiate and each can respond; each can be active and each can be passive; each speaks and each listens.

[Robert L. Selman and Anne P. Selman, "Children's Ideas About Friendships," *Psychology Today* 13 (October 1979):71–80; John M. Reisman, *Anatomy of Friendship* (Lexington, Mass.: Lewis Publishing, 1979); Muriel James and Louis Savary, *The Heart of Friendship* (New York: Harper & Row, 1976); Paul H. Wright, "Toward a Theory of Friendship Based on a Conception of Self," *Human Communication Research* 4 (Spring 1978):196–207.]

Frontmatter. The material in a book that precedes the major text (for example, title page, preface, contents).

Frozen evaluation. See STATIC EVALUATION.

F-Scale. A scale designed to measure authoritarianism and fascism.

[T. W. Adorno, E. Frenkel-Brunswick, D. J. Levinson, and R. N. Sanford, *The Authoritarian Personality* (New York: Harper & Row, 1950).]

Functional Analysis. A way of looking at behavior in terms of identifying the external or environmental conditions that may be said to control the occurrence or nonoccurrence of the behavior.

Functional Autonomy. The process by which a goal, originally motivated by a variety of factors, becomes self-sustaining and independent of its original motives.

[G. W. Allport, *Pattern and Growth in Personality* (New York: Holt, Rinehart and Winston, 1961).]

Functional Defect. A defect for which no physical cause can be found.

Functionalism. An approach in psychology concerned with how and why the conscious mind operates as it does.

Function Word. A word that does not make reference to specific content but rather refers to grammatical relationships or functions, for example, prepositions and articles are function words. See also CONTENT WORDS.

Future Shock. As introduced by Alvin Toffler, the effect (shock) resulting from the rapid changes in moral, social, and cultural matters for which the individual has

had little or no preparation. These extensive and rapid changes put people in positions where they have no effective means for coping with and controlling such changes; it leaves people without a sense of purpose or direction.
[Alvin Toffler, *Future Shock* (New York: Random House, 1970).]

Futuristics. The science that deal with the future and the methods for studying the future.

Futurology. The study of the future.

Fuzzy. See WARM FUZZY.

Gain-Loss Theory. A theory hypothesizing that increases in rewards will have a greater impact than will constant invariant rewards.
[Elliot Aronson and D. Linder, "Gain and Loss of Esteem as Determinants of Interpersonal Attractiveness," *Journal of Experimental Social Psychology* 1 (1965):156–171 and Elliot Aronson, *The Social Animal*, 3d ed. (San Francisco, Calif.: W. H. Freeman, 1980).

Galley Proof. Typeset copy that has not yet been divided into pages; used to mark corrections and editorial changes before the text is processed into page proofs and final form.

Game. A simulation of some situation with rules governing the behaviors of the participants and with some payoff (q.v.) for winning. In transactional analysis (q.v.), *game* refers to a series of ulterior transactions (q.v.) that lead to a payoff, a basically dishonest kind of transaction where participants hide their true feelings.

Game Theory. An approach to the study of interpersonal relationships and conflict that utilizes the format of a game complete with players, rules of the game, and outcomes or payoffs.

Gang. A group of individuals who band together for social and other reasons and who are generally viewed negatively by outsiders because of their real or supposed antisocial behavior.

Gatekeeping and Gatekeepers. In the passage of a message from the source of mass media to the actual individual viewer or listener there intervenes what is referred to as a gatekeeper. The term *gatekeeping* was originally used by Kurt Lewin in his *Human Relations* (1947) to refer to (1) the process by which a message passes through various gates as well as to (2) the people or groups that allowed the message to pass (gatekeepers). Gatekeepers may be individual persons or a group of persons through which a message passes in going from sender to receiver. A gatekeeper's main function is to filter the messages that an individual receives. A cameraperson is a clear example of a gatekeeper. From all that he or she can possibly photograph, certain areas are selected for photographing and then are shown to the viewers. Editors of magazines and publishing houses are gatekeepers; they allow certain information to get through and filter other information.

In mass media the term *gatekeeping* is used to refer to individuals or groups operating in relatively formal communication systems (for example, newspapers, television stations, education) whose gatekeeping activities have significant social implications. These gatekeepers are generally from the "preferred" social class—they tend to be highly educated and come from the "right" schools, have high incomes, and are generally white males.

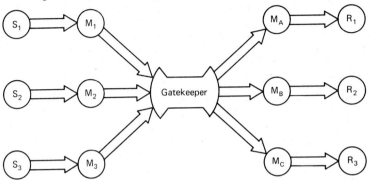

The gatekeeping process.

We might diagram the gatekeeping process as in the accompanying illustration. Note that the messages (M_1, M_2, M_3) received by the gatekeeper come from various different sources (S_1, S_2, S_3), so one of the functions the gatekeeper serves is to select the messages to be communicated and reject the ones that will not be allowed to pass. The gatekeeper then transmits numerous messages (M_A, M_B, M_C) to different receivers (R_1, R_2, R_3) and, it should be noted, may transmit certain messages to some receivers and other messages to other receivers. Teachers, for example, do not pass on the same messages to different classes: advanced courses get very different messages from elementary courses. Perhaps the most important aspect to note about this process is that the messages received by the gatekeeper (M_1, M_2, M_3) are not the same as the messages the gatekeeper sends (M_A, M_B, M_C); the extent to which they differ is the measure of the gatekeeper's changes.

Gaze. The nonverbal behavior of looking, most often used to refer specifically to looking into another person's eyes or face. See also MUTUAL GAZE.

Gemeinschaft. A German term, used to refer to social institutions where individuals treat each other as ends rather than as means; opposed to Gesellschaft (q.v.). Gemeinschaft relationships are emotional and close; there is a strong sense of belonging and solidarity. The major purpose in establishing such relationships is to associate with each other. Gemeinschaft relationships are similar to those of a primary group (q.v.).
[F. Tonnies, *Community and Association* (1887), (East Lansing, Michigan: Michigan State University Press, 1957).]

General Semantics. The study of the relationships among language, thought, and behavior.
[Alfred Korzybski, *Science and Sanity: An Introduction to Non-Aristotelian Systems and General Semantics* (Lakeville, Conn.: The International Non-Aristotelian Library, 1933); Robert Wanderer, "What's General Semantics? A Collection of Definitions," *et cetera* 34 (December 1974):427–439.]

Generation Gap. That division or difference caused by a wide variance in age and usually perception that makes interpersonal communication difficult and interpersonal conflict easy.

Generative Grammar. A type of grammar in which the speaker is regarded as a generator of the sentences of the language, that is, the speaker is viewed as possessing a finite set of rules (a grammar) that enables him or her to generate (to produce and to comprehend) an infinite number of permissible sentences of the language.
[Noam Chomsky, *Syntactic Structures* (The Hague: Mouton, 1957).]

Generative Semantics. A type of grammatical theory in which sentences (surface structures, q.v.) are derived from semantic structures; an approach to grammar that views semantics (rather than syntax) as the generative component.
[George Lakoff, "On Generative Semantics," in *Semantics: An Interdisciplinary Reader,* Leon A. Jakobovits and D. D. Steinberg, eds. (Cambridge, Mass.: M.I.T. Press, 1971).]

Genre. Type or kind. In rhetoric, a type of oratory, for example, forensic or political, or a type of literature, for example, drama or romantic fiction.

Genre Criticism. A form of criticism in which a work is analyzed in light of the essential characteristics of the category of work to which it belongs.

Geriatrics. The science dealing with the clinical problems of the elderly.

Gerontology. The study of the process of aging and its effects.

Gesellschaft. A German term used to refer to social institutions in which individuals treat each other as means rather than as ends; opposed to Gemeinschaft (q.v.). Gesellschaft relationships are formed in order to achieve some common objective, usually ones that are relational and specific; individuals are unequal in authority and power and there is little interpersonal contact. Gesellschaft relationships are similar to those of a secondary group (q.v.).
[F. Tonnies, *Community and Association* (1887), (East Lansing, Michigan: Michigan State University Press, 1957).]

Gestalt Psychology. A school of psychology concerned with explaining behavior as an interdependent whole rather than as isolated parts.
[W. Kohler, *Gestalt Psychology* (New York: Liveright, 1947).]

Gestural Origin Theory. A theory of the origin of language, developed by the German psychologist Wilhelm Wundt, holding that the articulatory movements that accompany gestures came to name the various emotions and ideas that formerly only the gestures named.

Ghostwriting. The procedure by which one writes speeches for someone else while the identity of the real author (the ghostwriter) is undisclosed.
[Lois Einhorn, "The Ghosts Unmasked: A Review of Literature on Speechwriting," *Communication Quarterly* 30 (1981):41–47.]

GIGO. Acronym for "garbage in, garbage out," referring to meaningless or unwanted data in a system.

Glittering Generality. One of the major propaganda techniques that seeks to gain audience acceptance and approval by associating the idea to be accepted with such "virtue words" as *good, love,* and *motherhood,* without any examination of the evidence or reasons for such an association. See PROPAGANDA DEVICES.
[Alfred McClung Lee and Elizabeth Briant Lee, *The Fine Art of Propaganda* (1939) (San Francisco, Calif.: International Society for General Semantics, 1979).]

Global Village. The world of the future in which we are all connected by electronic media. To some theorists, we are already living in the state of a global village, where we can learn very easily everything that is going on throughout the world—much like it would be if the world was a village.
[Marshall McLuhan, *Understanding Media* (New York: McGraw–Hill, 1964).]

Gloss. An explanation or translation of a word, phrase, or extended text.

Glossary. A listing of specific terms and their meanings, usually confined to some specific field or area of interest.

Glossolalia. Incomprehensible speech produced by some people in religious trances or sometimes in schizophrenia; also known as "speaking in tongues." [William J. Samarin, *Tongues of Men and Angels* (New York: Macmillan, 1972); "Glossolalia," *Psychology Today* 6 (August 1972):48–50, 78–80.]

Glottis. The opening between the vocal cords.

Glottochronology. A statistical procedure in which the vocabulary of a language is examined in an effort to identify the time when the language split from its parent language.
[S. C. Gudschinsky, "The ABC's of Lexicostatistics," *Word* 12 (1956):175–210.]

Gobbledygook. A general term for double-talk; the communication of information in a confusing and unnecessarily complex manner.

God Term. See ULTIMATE TERMS.

Good Will, The Speech to Secure. A speech designed to secure the audience's favorable attitude toward a person, idea, institution, way of life, or, in fact, anything to which one may have an attitude.

Gossip. Interpersonal, public, or mass communication by one person to another or others about a third person or group of persons; most often used to refer to informal and interpersonal communication situations. Rosnow defines *gossip* as communication between A and B about C that is undertaken for some gain, for example, more gossip or increased status. Gossip often includes evaluation and judgment.
[Sally Yerkovich, "Gossiping as a Way of Speaking," *Journal of Communication* 27 (1977); R. L. Rosnow, "Gossip and Marketplace Psychology," *Journal of Communication* 27 (1977): 158–163; Sissela Bok, *Secrets: On the Ethics of Concealment and Revelation* (New York: Vintage Books, 1983).]

Graduated Reciprocation Initiative in Tension Reduction (GRIT). A conflict resolution strategy in which one side unilaterally makes a small concession that is followed by a small concession from the other side, and so on with the result that the tension and conflict is reduced.
[Charles E. Osgood, *An Alternative to War or Surrender* (Urbana, Ill.: University of Illinois Press, 1962).]

Graffiti. Norman Mailer once characterized graffiti—the scrawlings on toilet walls, fences, and subway trains and stations—as "some of the best prose in America." And the widely syndicated columnist Norton Mockridge in his *The Scrawl of the Wild* notes that "a great deal of the finest, keenest, and most satirical and witty writing being done today is not necessarily in books, magazines, and newspapers—but on fences and walls!" Graffiti seems firmly established; whitewash and cleanser may remove some of it some of the time but as a form of communication it seems here to stay, as firmly etched on American edifices as on the American psyche.

    Graffiti comes from the Italian verb *graffiare,* meaning "to scratch," and its noun form, *graffio,* meaning "scratch." *Graffito* is the diminutive form, meaning "little scratch"; the English word *graffiti* is simply the plural form. Its meaning has been generalized to refer to the scratches, scrawlings, and writings in public places—toilets, subway cars, billboards, buildings, fences, rocks, and just about any place where one can write and another can read.

    Some would argue that graffiti is an aggressive act. Richard Freeman, for example, in *Graffiti,* argued that writing graffiti evidenced aggressiveness in at least two ways. First, and perhaps most obvious, is that with most graffiti there is a defacement involved; the wall is smeared with paint, the toilet stall is scratched with a nail, or the train is attacked with a marking pen. The second way graffiti evidences aggressiveness is that the writer—in the very act of writing the graffiti—is saying something that he or she would not normally say, usually something aggressive.

Others would argue that the graffiti writer is psychologically unbalanced. The graffiti writer, in this view, is someone who cannot deal with reality, cannot be assertive on an interpersonal level, and therefore retreats to anonymous writing on subway walls or toilet stalls.

And of course many would claim that the graffiti writer represents a cross section of the general public, that the graffiti writer is no different from anyone else, and that he or she merely chooses to express some thoughts, sometimes, through graffiti.

Graffiti serves a number of important communicative functions. Perhaps the most obvious function is that it establishes the identity of someone in a visible and relatively permanent way. Many scrawlings on subway cars, on billboards, and on walls merely contain the individual's name, sometimes accompanied by a "was here" or "will return" notation. The name itself is probably the most important part of such graffiti. Often this identification function is served by noting a romantic connection between oneself and another person. This "Pat loves Chris" type of graffiti is especially prevalent where young people congregate.

Another function is to comment on some political, social, religious, or economic issue—perhaps to show off one's knowledge, perhaps to communicate something without the threat of being refuted, perhaps to assist one in thinking out his or her own thoughts, perhaps to serve as a persuasive message to influence the thinking and behaving of others. "Black Power" and "Gay Power" slogans are perhaps the clearest examples of such writings.

An additional function—almost always restricted to toilets—is that of sexual solicitation. Such solicitations leave little to the imagination. They state what the writer wants in no uncertain terms. These solicitations come in two basic forms—the "I am looking for" and the "I am available" types. Both serve essentially the same basic function of bringing together persons who want to be brought together. Actually, such solicitations probably result in relatively few such interpersonal meetings. The most important outcome of such writing is probably the fantasies of such interpersonal encounters by their writers and readers. Still another function of graffiti is to tell a story, usually a sexual one. In college toilets, however, many of these stories concern themselves with academic issues—the problems of registering, in getting a fair grade, in being treated as an individual rather than as a computer number.

Grammar. The rules of a language for forming sentences and pertaining to phonological, semantic, and syntactic dimensions. These rules enable the users to comprehend and to produce an infinite number of sentences. In popular usage, correct or socially acceptable usage. See also DESCRIPTIVE GRAMMAR; PRESCRIPTIVE GRAMMAR.

Grammatical Relation(ship). The relationships among subject, verb (predicate), and objects (direct and indirect) in a sentence.

The Grapevine. The term *grapevine* seems to have originated during the Civil War, when telegraph wires were hung from tree to tree and resembled grapevines and now refers to messages that travel through no organized structure. The grapevine, according to organizational theorist Keith Davis, seems most likely to be used when: (1) there is great upheaval or change within the organization; (2) the information is new (no one likes to spread old and well-known information); (3) face-to-face communication is physically easy; and (4) workers "cluster in clique-groups along the vine." The grapevine is most active immediately after the event that is to be communicated and is most likely to be activated when the news concerns one's intimates, friends, and associates. We seem less concerned with grapevine information when it concerns those about whom we know or care little.

Although the grapevine is part of every large organization's informal communications, it is not used as frequently as many would have us believe. It is unlikely to grow in climates that are stable and comfortable; change and ambiguity, it seems, nourish the grapevine. Even more surprising than its relative infrequency of usage, however, is its reported accuracy. Keith Davis, for example, found that 75 to 95 percent of the grapevine information is correct. Even though many details are omitted, the stories are basically true.

Although many managers may view the grapevine as a great inconvenience and would, if they could, wish it out of existence, it actually serves some useful purposes. Keith Davis, for example, observes: "A lively grapevine reflects the deep psychological need of people to talk about their jobs and their company as a central life interest. Without it, the company would literally be sick." Its speed and accuracy make it an ideal medium to carry a great deal of the social communications that so effectively bind together workers in an organization.
[Keith David, "Management Communication and the Grapevine," *Harvard Business Review* 31 (September–October, 1953):43–49, and "The Care and Cultivation of the Corporate Grapevine," *Dun's Review* (July 1973):44–47.]

Grapheme. The smallest element of the written language composed of letters or alphabetic characters. A, b, c, and so on, are graphemes of written English; analogous to the phoneme (q.v.) of the spoken language.

Graphic Indicator. A peculiar characteristic of one's handwriting that may prove significant in handwriting analysis or graphology (q.v.).

Graphology. The study of personality as revealed through an analysis of one's handwriting. Also known as "graphoanalysis."
[Karla G. Roman, *Encyclopedia of the Written Word: A Lexicon for Graphology and Other Aspects of Writing,* Rose Wolfson and Maurice Edwards, eds. (New York: Frederick Ungar, 1968).]

Graphomania. Pathological impulse to write or scribble; often used to refer to the tendency of the paranoid to write letters of protest or persecution.

Graphophobia. An unreasonable fear of writing.

Graphotherapy. A therapeutic approach based on the theory that handwriting and personality are intimately connected. In some systems, one attempts to change one's personality by changing one's handwriting; in other systems, the handwriting is analyzed in an attempt to increase understanding of the individual.
[Rhoda Riddell, "Writing Personalities," *Human Behavior* (July 1978):18–23.]

Grice's Maxims. See CONVERSATIONAL MAXIMS.

GRIT. See GRADUATED RECIPROCATION INITIATIVE IN TENSION REDUCTION.

Group Communication: Analysis Guidelines.
In offering an analysis or an evaluation of any small group member or of the group as a whole, a number of guidelines will prove helpful.

Be Positive
All participants and all groups have undoubtedly done something right; mention this. If you have trouble finding something positive to say, look again. This does not mean that negative aspects should not be stated, but only that something positive should also be said. Generally it will be helpful if you state the positive first.

Be Descriptive First
Describe what you think happened in the group and then offer your evaluation of why you think this aspect should be viewed positively or negatively. Instead of saying, for example, that effective leadership was not exercised, start by noting that the group seemed to go off the track a number of times and that no one directed the group back to its main task. In this way, you will be stating in clear terms the basis for your evaluation and the reasoning you used in arriving at your conclusion. By stating description first you also force yourself to anchor your critical comments to the specifics of the group rather than to some abstract or general feeling.

Be Specific
Be as specific as you can in offering any critical comment. Instead of saying that leadership was poorly exercised, state exactly what aspect of leadership was poorly exercised. Was it that the leader failed to provide an effective definition of the problem? Was it that members argued over who was to be the leader? Was it that the leader was too autocratic? Try to focus your critical comments on specific principles of small group communication rather than on generalities. Try to support your statements with specific examples.

Be Improvement Oriented
Your critical comments should function to improve the group's performance. Therefore, try to phrase those comments in as constructive a way as possible. If you offer a negative evaluation, try to specify how the event could have been avoided or how something could have been improved. For example, instead of saying that participation was not spread evenly among members, you might say that it would have helped if the leader had asked some open-ended questions to draw out the more silent members or that the leader might have provided the more reticent members with an opportunity to express what they thought. With these comments, the group will be able to see what could have been done to spread participation more evenly rather than simply being told that participation was uneven.

Be the Owner of Your Evaluations
When stating an opinion, make it clear that that opinion is yours and that it emanates from your perception of the group. It should be clear that your evaluation is *your* evaluation and that what you are saying may not be true in any objective sense. For example, in evaluating a group discussion, you might say (when not owning your own thoughts and feelings): "The discussion rambled," "The leadership was ineffective," or "The group members were ill prepared." Or

you might say (owning your own thoughts and feelings): "I was bored," "I thought the leader should have done X, Y, and Z instead of A, B, and C," or "I felt the members should have had more specific knowledge of the topic."

In the former cases, you imply that boredom, ineffective leadership, and lack of preparation were somehow characteristic of the group. Actually, these are your perceptions. And these comments are valuable precisely because they are the perceptions of one careful analyst—you.

See also DELPHI METHOD; INTERACTION DIAGRAMS; INTERACTION PROCESS ANALYSIS; INTERPERSONAL COMMUNICATION EFFECTIVENESS; NOMINAL GROUP; QUALITY CIRCLES.

Group Communication: Leader Guidelines. In relatively formal small group situations such as politicians planning a campaign strategy, advertisers discussing a campaign, or teachers considering educational methods, the leader has a number of specific functions. These functions are not the exclusive property of the leader; rather they are functions that when performed are performed by a person serving a leadership role. Put differently, it is more important that these functions be served than who serves them. In situations where a specific leader is appointed or exists by virtue of some position or prior agreement, these functions are generally expected to be performed by him or her. Leadership functions are performed best when they are performed unobtrusively—when they are performed in a nonobvious, natural manner. Leaders perform six major functions.

Activate the Group Interaction

In many situations the group needs no encouragement to interact. Certainly this is true of most groups with definite goals and an urgency about their mission. On the other hand, there are many groups which for one reason or another need some prodding, some stimulation to interact, perhaps the group is newly formed and the members feel a bit uneasy with one another. Here the leader serves an important function by stimulating the members to interact. This function needs to be served when the individuals of a group are acting as individuals rather than as a group. In this case the leader must do something to make the members recognize that they are part of a group rather than of a collection of individuals.

Maintain Effective Interaction Throughout

The leader should see that the members maintain effective interaction throughout the discussion and throughout the membership. Discussions have a way of dragging after the preliminaries are over and before the meat of the problem is addressed. When this happens it is necessary for the leader to again prod the group to effective interaction. Problems are created when disproportionate participation is extreme or when members feel an uneasiness about entering the group interaction.

Keep Members on the Track

The leader should recognize that most individuals are relatively egocentric and have interests and concerns that are unique to them. Because of this, each individual will tend to wander off the track a bit. It is the leader's task to keep all members on the track—perhaps by asking relevant questions, by interjecting internal summaries as the group goes along, or perhaps by providing suitable transitions so that the relationship between the issue just discussed and the one about to be considered is made clear. In some problem-solving and educational groups a formal agenda may be used to assist in this function.

Ensure Member Satisfaction

The leader should recognize that all members have different psychological needs and wants and many people enter groups because of these needs and wants. Even though a group may, for example, deal with political issues, the various members may have come together for reasons that are more psychological than political or intellectual. If a group such as this is to be effective, it must not only meet the surface purposes of the group (in this case political) but also the underlying or psychological purposes that motivated many of the members to come together in the first place.

Encourage Ongoing Evaluation and Improvement

All groups will encounter obstacles as they attempt to solve a problem, reach a decision, or generate ideas. No group is totally effective. All groups have room for improvement. It is the responsibility of the group members (encouraged by the leader) to seek out these obstacles and to improve the process of group interaction. If the group is to improve, it must focus some attention on itself and, along with attempting to solve some external problem, must attempt to solve its own internal problems as well.

Prepare the Group Members for the Discussion

Groups form gradually and need to be eased into any discussion that is meaningful. It is the function of the leader to prepare the group members for the discussion, and this involves preparing the members for the small group interaction as well as for the discussion of a specific issue or problem.

Diverse members should not be expected to just sit down and discuss a problem without becoming familiar with each other at least superficially. Similarly, if the members are to discuss a specific problem, it is necessary that a proper briefing be introduced. Perhaps materials need to be distributed to group members before the actual discussion, or perhaps members need to be instructed to read certain materials or view a particular film or television show. Whatever the prediscussion preparations, it should be organized and coordinated by the leader.

Group Communication: Member Guidelines. Here are several guidelines that will help make the participation of members in small group communication both more effective and more enjoyable.

Be Group Oriented

The most general and the most important suggestion to keep in mind is that in the small group communication situation, you are a member of a group, a member of some larger whole. Your participation is of value to the extent that it advances the goals of the group with effectiveness and with member satisfaction. Your responsibility is toward the group rather than to any one individual or yourself. The effective participant is one who cooperates with others to achieve some mutually satisfying goal. In the small group situation your task is to pool your talents, knowledge, and insight so that a solution may be arrived at that is more effective than a solution that could have been reached by any one individual.

This call for group orientation is not to be taken as a suggestion for abandoning one's individuality or giving up one's personal values or beliefs for the sake of the group. This is clearly an undesirable extreme but one seen frequently in many contemporary cults and small groups. Individuality with a group orientation is what is advocated here.

Center Conflict on Issues

Conflict in small group communication situations is inevitable. If some form of conflict does not occur, the group is probably irrelevant or the members are so bored they do not care what is going on. Conflict is a natural part of the exchange of ideas; it is not something that should be feared or ignored. Conflict should be recognized as a natural part of the small group communication process, but it should be centered on issues rather than on personalities. Conflict creates problems in small group communication when it is person-centered rather than issue-centered.

When you disagree with what someone has said, make it clear that your disagreement, your conflict, is with the proposal advanced, the solution suggested, the ideas expressed, and not with the person. Similarly, when someone disagrees with what you say, do not take this as a personal attack but rather as an opportunity to discuss issues from an alternative point of view. Often conflict does center on personalities, and when this happens members of the group have a responsibility to redirect that conflict to the significant issues and should try to get the conflicting individuals to see that the goals of the group will be better advanced if the conflict is pursued only insofar as it relates to the issues under consideration.

Be Critically Open-Minded

One of the most detrimental developments in a small group occurs when members come to the group with their minds already made up. When this happens, the small group process degenerates into a series of individual debates, each person arguing for his or her own position. The small group process is a cooperative venture where each member contributes something to the whole and where the resultant decision or solution emerges from the deliberations of all members. Each member therefore should come to the group equipped with relevant information—facts, figures, and ideas that will be useful to the discussion—but should not have decided on the solution or conclusion they will accept. Thus, any solutions or conclusions that are advanced should be done so with tentativeness rather than definiteness. Discussants should be willing to alter their suggestions and revise them in the light of the discussion.

Ensure Understanding

Most discussions that fail probably do so because of a lack of understanding. We need to make sure that our ideas and our information are understood by all participants. If something is worth saying, it is worth making sure that it is clearly understood. And so when in doubt, ask the members if what you are saying is clear—not with "Can you understand that bit of complex reasoning?" but rather with "Is that clear?" or "Did I explain that clearly?"

Make sure too that you understand fully the contributions of the other members, especially before you take issue with them. In fact, it is often wise to preface any extended disagreement with some kind of statement such as "As I understand you, you want to exclude Martians from playing on the football team, and if that is correct then I want to say why I think that would be a mistake." Then you would go on to state your objections. In this way you give the other person the opportunity to clarify, deny, or otherwise alter what was said and thus frequently save yourself a long argument and the group's time and energy.

Group Dynamics. The study of small group interaction and social relationships. Dorwin Cartwright and Alvin Zander identify four major characteristics of this field of study. In group dynamics there is (1) an emphasis on empirical research that is of theoretical significance; (2) an interest in the dynamics and inter-dependence of events and behaviors; (3) interdisciplinary research and applica-tion; and (4) potential application of its findings to the improvement of group functioning.

[*Group Dynamics: Research and Theory,* 3d ed., Dorwin Cartwright and Alvin Zander, eds. (New York: Harper & Row, 1968).]

Group Interview. An interview (q.v.) conducted between an interviewer and a group of persons instead of the more popular and familiar one-to-one situation.

Group Therapy. Therapy that takes place in a group rather than on an individual one-to-one basis. Frequently, patients with similar problems meet together with a therapist who acts as a group leader while the group members interact and share their experiences and insights. One of the assumptions in group therapy is that people can learn from the experiences of others and that people without special training can provide insight into the problems of others.

Groupthink. After examining the decisions and the decision-making processes of large government organizations—the catastrophic decisions of the Bay of Pigs and Pearl Harbor, the decision processes that went into the development of the Marshall Plan, and President Kennedy's handling of the Cuban missile crisis—Irving Janis developed a theory he calls "groupthink." Groupthink, according to Janis, may be defined as "the mode of thinking that persons engage in when *concurrence seeking* becomes so dominant in a cohesive ingroup that it tends to override realistic appraisals of alternative courses of action." The term itself is meant to signal a "deterioration in mental efficiency, reality testing, and moral judgments as a result of group pressures."

There are many specific behaviors of the group members that may be singled out as characteristic of groupthink. One of the most significant behaviors is that the group limits its discussion of possible alternatives to only a small range. It generally does not consider other possibilities as alternatives. Once the group has made a decision, it does not reexamine its decisions even when there are indications of possible dangers. Little time is spent in discussing the reasons why certain of the initial alternatives were in fact rejected. Similarly, the group members make little effort to obtain expert information even from people within their own organization.

The group members are extremely selective in the information they consider seriously. Facts and opinions contrary to the position of the group are generally ignored, while those facts and opinions that support the position of the group are welcomed. The group members generally limit themselves to the one decision or one plan. They fail to discuss alternative decisions or plans in the event that their initial decision fails or encounters problems on the way to implementation.

The following symptoms should help in recognizing the existence of group-think in the groups we observe or in which we participate.

1. Group members think the group and its members are invulnerable to dan-gers.
2. Members create rationalizations to avoid dealing directly with warnings or threats.
3. Group members believe their group is moral.
4. Those opposed to the group are perceived in simplistic stereotyped ways.

5. Group pressure is put on any member who expresses doubts or questions the group's arguments or proposals.
6. Group members censor their own doubts.
7. Group members believe all members are in unanimous agreement, whether such agreement is stated or not.
8. Group members emerge whose function it is to guard the information that gets to other members of the group especially when such information may create diversity of opinion.

[Irving L. Janis, *Groupthink: Psychological Studies of Policy Decisions and Fiascoes,* 2d ed. (Boston: Houghton Mifflin, 1983).]

Gunnysacking. An unproductive conflict strategy in which an imaginary "gunnysack" is loaded with the accumulated misdeeds and mistakes of one person to be used against them by another person with whom he or she is fighting. See also CONFLICT STRATEGIES.

[George R. Bach and Peter Wyden, *The Intimate Enemy* (New York: Avon, 1968).]

Hack. A writer whose style is trite; a writer who hires himself or herself out to write insignificant (but perhaps popular) material; from *hackney,* a horse for hire.

Hacker. An expert computer user.

Hackneyed. Overused and unoriginal, used mostly in reference to an uninspired and stale style.

Halo Effect. The tendency for one's generally positive impression of a person to be applied to a specific individual characteristic, or a positive impression of a specific characteristic to be generalized concerning the entire person. For example, the tendency to think that being an expert in one field makes one an expert in other unrelated fields.

Handout. Any written document distributed to an audience; often used in reference to official press releases issued by, for example, a politician or a political organization.

Hands-On. An experiential activity; an activity or experience in which an individual is actually physically involved.

Haplography. A writing error in which a portion of written material is omitted. See also HAPLOLOGY.

Haplology. A type of speech error in which a portion of speech is deliberately omitted. Technically, haplology is the omission of one or two consecutive identical groups of sounds, for example, saying "Posties" instead of "Post Toasties."

Happiness. A relatively stable state of satisfaction involving both active dimensions (fun, excitement) and passive dimensions (peace of mind, tranquility). Close, loving, and supportive relationships seem to be the most important determinant of personal happiness.

[Jonathan Freedman, *Happy People: What Happiness Is, Who Has It, and Why* (New York: Ballantine Books, 1978).]

Haptics. The study of the role of touch in communications.

Haptometer. A device for measuring sensitivity to touch.

Harangue. A long speech of criticism; a tirade.

Hard Copy. The printed computer copy that can be read and handled; opposed to soft copy (q.v.).

Hard Disk. An aluminum or ceramic computer disk encased in a sealed container which functions faster and can store a great deal more information than a floppy disk (q.v.).

Hard News. A form of news that focuses on real life, on events that impact directly on the listener or reader.

Hard Sell. A persuasive technique of salespeople and advertisers characterized by high pressure, repetition of a point, and increased speaking volume.

Hatchet Job. A malicious attack against a person, idea, or institution.

Hawthorne Effect. An effect observed in the Hawthorne studies which showed that worker performance improved simply as a result of the increased self-esteem that accompanied their being studied. The workers' improved perform-ance was observed regardless of what variables were manipulated or in what way they were altered. See also SCIENTIFIC APPROACH TO ORGANIZATIONS.
[F. Roethlisberger and W. J. Dixon, *Management and the Worker* (Cambridge, Mass.: Harvard University Press, 1941).]

Headlinese. The form of compressed, abbreviated writing found in newspaper headlines.

Health Communication. An area of communication concerned with the trans-mission of messages among health professionals and between health profession-als and the public.
[Gary L. Kreps and Barbara C. Thornton, *Health Communication* (New York: Longman, 1984); Dennis Klinzing and Dene Klinzing, *Communication for Allied Health Profes-sionals* (Dubuque, Iowa: Brown, 1985).]

Hearing Aid. A device that amplifies or helps to focus incoming sound.

Hearing Conservation. The processes or programs involved in preventing hear-ing loss through, for example, identifying persons who might need special atten-tion or eliminating the causes of hearing impairment.

Heckling. Abusive or negative commentaries by audience members during a speech.

Hedge. See LICENSE.

Hedge Word. A qualifying term used to disclaim responsibility as in, for example, "The president *reportedly*. . . ."

Hedging. A type of disclaimer (q.v.) in which the speaker voices some doubt concerning the effect an utterance will have on the audience or notes his or her own uncertainty or lack of association with the statement, for example, "I didn't read the entire report" or "I'm not sure about how this should be taken, but. . . ." See also DISCLAIMER.

Helping Relationship. An interpersonal relationship in which one (or both) per-sons helps the other to grow, develop, progress, improve, and so on.
[Carl Rogers, *On Becoming a Person* (Boston: Houghton Mifflin, 1961).]

Hermeneutics. The methodological interpretation of some literary, and especially a scriptural, text; the study of the interpretation of human behaviors, including communication messages of all kinds, through an interpretation of a text, for example, by studying it from the perspective of the communicator. In hermeneut-ics the part must be understood in relationship with the whole and the whole in the light of its various parts.
[Z. Bauman, *Hermeneutics and Social Science* (London: Hutchinson, 1978).]

Hertz (Hz). Named after Heinrich Rudolf Hertz (1857–1894), German physicist, a unit of sound wave frequency equal to one cycle per second. Hertz has been adopted internationally to replace *cycles per second*.

Hesitation Phenomena. Vocalized or silent pauses in speech. Maclay and Osgood identify four main types of hesitation phenomena: (1) repeats: "It it was . . .," (2) false starts: "It was a tall, a really tall guy . . .," (3) the filled pause: pauses filled by *a, er, mm,* and so on, and (4) the unfilled pause: a silent pause or lengthening of a sound.
[Howard Maclay and Charles E. Osgood, "Hesitation Phenomena in Spontaneous English Speech," *Word* 15 (1959):19–44; Jane Blankenship and Christian Kay, "Hesitation Phenomena in English Speech: A Study in Distribution," *Word* 20 (1964):360–371.]

Heterography. Inconsistent or incorrect spelling; the use of the same letter or group of letters to represent different sounds (as in thro*ugh* and bo*ugh*) or the use of different letters to represent the same sounds (as in ro*ugh* and ree*f*).

Heterophemy. A speech error involving the incorrect use of one word for another that is similar in sound or spelling, for example, the use of "magician" for "musician."

Heterophily. The degree of difference between individuals. See also HOMOPHILY.

Heuristic Approach. An approach that leads to or encourages new ideas and new ways of looking at things.

Hiatus. A pause in sound between two vowels as in "deemphasize"; a missing element (for example, a word, sentence, or even entire pages) in a written text.

Hidden Agenda. A goal or purpose that is not revealed to certain members of the group but to the achievement of which the group's efforts are directed.

Hidden Self. In the Johari model (q.v.), the self that is known only to oneself and is kept hidden from others.

Hierarchical Organization. A structured arrangement of people, objects, or roles according to relative status.

Hierarchical Structure. The structure of many organizations in which individuals are accorded status in terms of their relative importance to the organization.

Hieroglyphics. A writing system utilizing pictures to represent words and used by the ancient Egyptians; a form of sacred writing. Because of the difficulty in deciphering hieroglyphics, the term has been generalized to mean writing that is illegible or difficult to decipher or understand.

Hirmos. A figure of speech in which a long series of nouns is used for emphasis, for example, "She gathered the animals of the field—the lions, the leopards, the elephants, the birds, the dogs, the cats, the bears, the horses. . . ."

Hoarseness. A vocal quality characterized by a huskiness or a noise-filled voice, and brought about by a swelling of the vocal cords as when there is a physical infection.

Holistic Processing. Perception of a stimulus as a whole rather than broken down into its elementary features. See also FEATURE DETECTION.

Hologram. A photograph or film with an image that appears to the viewer in three dimensions.

Holograph. A written message in the handwriting of its author.

Holophrase. A one-word utterance of a child that is assumed to stand for an entire sentence or thought; in adult speech, the use of one word in place of an entire sentence in a context where the one word communicates the meaning of the entire sentence, for example, "Coffee?" instead of "May I please have more coffee?"

Homeostasis. A condition of balance or equilibrium in either a physical, psychological, or social system.

Homiletics. The art of religious speech making; the theory of preparing and delivering homilies. See HOMILY.

Homily. A sermon; a religious speech addressed to a congregation for the purpose of explaining scripture or giving instruction.

Homograph. Words that have the same spelling but have different meanings and often of different pronunciations, for example, *lead* meaning "to guide others" or a type of metal.

Homonym. Words that have the same pronunciation and written form but have different meanings, for example, *bear* meaning "to carry" or the animal.

Homophily. The degree of similarity between individuals. See HETEROPHILY.

Homophobia. Unreasonable fear of or dislike for homosexuals (gay men and lesbians).

Homophone. Words having the same pronunciation but different meanings and often a different spelling, for example, *I* and *eye, wood* and *would.*

Honorific. Descriptors expressing high regard or respect. In some languages certain pronouns of address are honorific and are used to address those of high status. In English such titles as "Dr.," "Professor," and "the Honorable" are honorific.

Hook. A stylistic element that captures the receiver's attention at the beginning of a literary work.

Hot Line. A telephone communication system established for dealing with a variety of different crises, for example, suicide, alcoholism, rape.

Hot Medium. See COOL MEDIUM.

Humanistic Psychology. An approach to psychology concerned especially with the human qualities of dignity and self-actualization and with identifying the differences between humans and the lower animals.

Human Potential Movement. A movement in psychology that focuses on personal growth and development and that greatly influenced the study of small group communication away from an almost exclusive concern with problem-solving, task-oriented groups to a concern with personal development and sensitivity training.

Human Relations Approach to Organizations. The human relations approach developed as a reaction against the exclusive concern with the physical and the exclusion of psychological and social factors in measuring organizational success.

One of the principal assumptions of the human relations approach is that increases in worker satisfaction lead to increases in productivity: A happy worker is a productive worker. Management's function, therefore, is to keep the workers happy.

Since leaders establish the norms that group members follow, control of the leadership is considered one of the best ways to increase satisfaction and production. Management is to influence the leaders, who then influence the workers to be happy and hence productive. But not just any leader is to be developed; the human relations approach strongly favors the democratic leader—the leader who encourages members to participate in the running of the organization by offering suggestions, giving feedback, and sharing their problems and complaints. What is desired, in Rensis Likert's terms, is "participatory management." All members of the organization are to participate in the decisions that ultimately affect them. Communication is one of management's main tools in this endeavor. The human relations approach acknowledges the importance of the social, informal groups within the organization and gives special consideration to the interpersonal communications within these groups.

But even in this seemingly best of all possible worlds, where the communication is free and the leadership democratic, the human relations school encountered difficulties. The major one was that the approach was based on an invalid assumption—namely, that satisfaction and productivity were positively related. They were in some cases, but certainly not in all. Yet another problem with the human relations approach is that it gives too much attention to agreement and fails to note the very real and important contribution conflict and competition make to an organization.

Humpty Dumpty. The use of impressive sounding but meaningless words; gobbledygook (q.v.); one who uses words to mean whatever he or she wants them to mean as Humpty Dumpty did in Lewis Carroll's *Alice in Wonderland.*

Hybrid. A term composed of words from two languages, for example, *automobile* comes from the Greek *autos* and the Latin *mobilis.*

Hypacusis. The condition of being hearing impaired; hard of hearing.

Hypallage. A figure of speech in which a modifier, appropriate to one noun, is transferred to another technically inappropriate noun, as in "a cheerful morning" where, technically, it is not the morning that is cheerful.

Hype. Exaggerated and excessive praise used to promote films, television shows, records, and the like. Hype is often used to distort (increase) audience ratings of a particular program during ratings measurement periods.

Hyperacusis. An abnormally acute sense of hearing.

Hyperbole. A figure of speech in which there is extreme exaggeration, as in "your obedient and humble servant" or "I'm so hungry I could eat a cow."

Hypercorrect Form (Hyperforms). Expressions that are technically incorrect but which appear correct through constant misuse and are used as attempts to avoid common errors or to imitate the "prestige dialect," for example, "between you and I" instead of the grammatically correct "between you and me." Also known as *hyperurbanisms* since many such expressions were in imitation of the higher status urban speaker.

Hyperurbanism. See HYPERCORRECT FORM.

Hyphen. An extensional device (q.v.) used to illustrate that what may be separated verbally may not be separable on the physical or nonverbal level. Although one may talk about body and mind, for example, as if they were separable, in reality they are more accurately referred to as body-mind.

Hypothesis. A proposition that tentatively assumes how variables are related to each other in order to guide the collection and analysis of the data.

Hysterical Deafness. A hearing loss caused by psychological rather than physical factors. Also referred to as conversion deafness.

I

Icon. A sign that is similar to the thing it represents.

Iconic Memory. A type of short-term memory (q.v.) in which one retains a mental picture of the stimulus for a brief time; visual sensory memory.

Iconic Signals. Signals that bear real or nonarbitrary relationships to their referents, for example, an accurate map is iconic with the territory; opposed to arbitrariness (q.v.).

Ideal Managerial Climate (IMC). As defined by Charles Redding, a prescriptive model of what organizations should strive for, consisting of: supportiveness (q.v.); participative decision making; trust, confidence, and credibility; openness and candor; and an emphasis on high performance goals.
[Charles Redding, *Communication Within the Organization* (New York: Industrial Communication Council, 1972); Phillip K. Tompkins, "The Functions of Human Communication in Organization," in *Handbook of Rhetorical and Communication Theory,* Carroll C. Arnold and John Waite Bowers, eds. (Boston: Allyn and Bacon, 1984), pp. 659–719.]

Ideal Self. The self that an individual would like to be.

Identification. In Freudian terms, a process in which an individual assumes the characteristics of a person with whom one has a close bond in an attempt to reduce or eliminate his or her own anxieties and conflicts. In general semantics, a misevaluation whereby two or more items are considered as identical and thus denying the characteristic of nonidentity. In Kenneth Burke's theory, a process of becoming similar to another individual; a process of aligning one's interests to those of another, an essential process for persuasion. One of the processes of opinion change occurs when an individual adopts the behaviors of another person or group because these behaviors are closely related to one's self-definition. See also COMPLIANCE; INTERNALIZATION.
[Herbert C. Kelman, "Processes of Opinion Change," *Public Opinion Quarterly* 25 (1961): 57–78.]

Identity, Need For. The need for an individual to learn about oneself, one's capabilities and competencies.

Ideogram. A picture or graphic symbol representing a specific meaning, for example, %, $, #; a written symbol standing for an idea or concept. Also referred to as an "ideograph."

Ideograph. Bodily movements that sketch the path or direction of a thought.

Ideographic Writing. A system of writing in which a graphic symbol ideogram (q.v.) stands for an idea, as in Chinese ligatures.

Idioglossia. Speech that is so distorted that it is unintelligible by those unfamiliar with it; often used by mentally retarded children or twins to communicate with each other.

Idiolect. An individual's manner of speaking; an individual's personalized, unique treatment of the sound, meaning, and structural systems of the language.

Idiom. A phrase whose actual meaning is significantly different from the literal meanings of the individual words. The meaning of an idiom cannot be inferred from the meanings of the individual words, for example, "to kick the bucket" is an idiom meaning "to die" but its meaning cannot be deduced from an analysis of the words in the phrase. Also used to refer to the general nature or characteristics of a language or sublanguage, as in "He speaks the idiom of the people."

Idiot Card. Cue card from which the performer reads his or her lines.

I–It Relationship. Defined by Martin Buber (1878–1965), a relationship between two people in which one treats the other as an object or where one controls or uses the other.
[Martin Buber, *I and Thou,* 2d ed. (New York: Scribners, 1958).]

Illeism. The practice of using the third person pronoun excessively, especially in referring to oneself.

Illiteracy. Inability to read or write. Also used to refer to unacceptable or ungrammatical expressions.

Illiterate. One who cannot read or write; unlearned; ungrammatical.

Illocutionary Act. That part of the speech act (q.v.) whereby the statement or utterance itself performs or accomplishes some act as in, for example, "I promise. . . ." or "I confess. . . ."

Illocutionary Force. The effect that a sentence is designed to have on the hearer. Five types of effects or speech acts are distinguished: (1) to get the hearer to perform a certain behavior (directive); (2) to have the hearer believe that what the speaker says is true (representative); (3) to get the hearer to understand the speaker's psychological state (expressive); (4) to get the hearer to understand the speaker's future actions as in promises and pledges (commissive); and (5) to get the hearer to understand the speaker's desire to create a new or different situation as in "You're fired" (declarative).
[J. R. Searle, "A Taxonomy of Illocutionary Acts," in *Minnesota Studies in the Philosophy of Language,* K. Gunderson, ed. (Minneapolis: University of Minnesota Press, 1975), pp. 344–369.]

Illustration. A form of amplification consisting of a relatively long and detailed example or specific instance told in a narrative or storylike form. See also EXAMPLE.

Illustrators. Nonverbal behaviors that accompany and literally illustrate the verbal messages, for example, upward movements of the hand and head that accompany the verbalization "It's up there."

Imagery. Visually descriptive.

I-Messages. Messages that describe the speaker's feelings or thoughts; messages in which the speaker takes responsibility for his or her own feelings; opposed to you-messages (q.v.).

Imitation. The process of copying another's behavior as a way of learning; an early stage in the child speech acquisition process whereby a large part of the child's utterances are imitations of the speech of the adult community.

Immanent Reference. A principle of communication that refers to the notion that all messages make some reference to the present, to the immediate context, and to the speaker himself or herself.
[Robert E. Pittenger, Charles F. Hockett, and John Danehy, *The First Five Minutes: A Sample of Microscopic Interview Analysis* (Ithaca, N.Y.: Paul Martineau, 1960).]

Immediacy, Theory of. An approach to interpersonal relationships that holds that people approach and become involved with those people and objects they like and avoid people and objects they do not like. Immediacy is a reflection of closeness and may be measured by such nonverbal and verbal behaviors as amount and intimacy of touching, eye contact, physical closeness, use of such expressions as "we" instead of "you and me," directness in speech, owning one's thoughts (q.v.).
[M. Wiener and A. Mehrabian, *Language Within Language: Immediacy, a Channel in Verbal Communication* (New York: Appleton-Century-Crofts, 1968); A. Mehrabian, *Silent Messages: Implicit Communication of Emotions and Attitudes,* 2d ed. (Belmont, Calif.: Wadsworth, 1981).]

Implicature. An implication that can be drawn or an assumption that is made on the basis of the form of a statement, for example, an implicature of the statement "It's chilly in here" is that one should close the window. Implicatures are based on the conversational maxims (q.v.) derived from the cooperation principle (q.v.).

Implicit Personality Theory. The assumptions one makes in judging the personality of self or others; generally used to refer to that set of personality characteristics that seem to go together, and with a recognition of one of the characteristics of that set, the other characteristics indicative of that set are assumed to also exist. Thus, if eagerness, energetic, and aggressive are thought to go together, and eagerness and energy are observed in a person, we assume that that person is also aggressive.

Impostor Phenomenon. A psychological syndrome in which one feels like a failure and a fake in spite of the achievement of success.
[Joan Harvey with Cynthia Katz, *If I'm So Successful, Why Do I Feel Like a Fake?* (New York: St. Martin's Press, 1985); Pauline Rose Clance, *The Impostor Phenomenon: Overcoming the Fear That Haunts Your Success* (Atlanta: Peachtree, 1985).]

Imprecation. Expression of a curse; malediction.

Impression Formation. The process through which we formulate impressions of others.

Impressionistic Criticism. See CRITICISM.

Impression Management. The tendency or techniques by which one presents oneself in the best possible light to various others. See also SELF-MONITORING.

Imprimatur. From the Latin, "Let it be printed," a seal of approval given by the Roman Catholic Church (through its bishops) that states that the work (usually a book or monograph) is free of doctrinal error. Often used more generally to refer to a work that is approved or sanctioned by some authority.

Imprinting. Irreversible, rapid, and relatively permanent learning acquired very early in life (during the organism's "critical period") and usually released by some triggering stimulus, for example, ducklings will follow the first moving object they see immediately after hatching and will treat this object as though it was their mother.

Impromptu Method of Delivery. A method for delivering a public speech that involves no prior specific preparation for the speech. See also EXTEMPORANEOUS METHOD; MANUSCRIPT METHOD; MEMORIZED METHOD.

Improvisation. Impromptu acting used as a technique in psychodrama (q.v.) where a subject acts out a situation without any prior preparation or rehearsal.

Inartistic Proofs. In Aristotelian rhetoric (q.v.), those proofs that exist independently of the speaker, for example, laws, witnesses, and contracts; opposed to artistic proofs (q.v.).

Incantation. The expression of words thought to have some magical power.

Incidental Learning. Knowledge obtained without actively seeking it; opposed to intentional learning (q.v.).

Inclusion. One of the three interpersonal needs in Schutz's Fundamental Interpersonal Relations Orientation (FIRO, q.v.) theory; the need for togetherness, for association with others.
[William C. Schutz, *FIRO: A Three-Dimensional Theory of Interpersonal Behavior* (New York: Holt, Rinehart and Winston, 1958).]

Incongruence. A psychological state in which the individual is at odds with oneself; a condition of tension, defensiveness, and maladjustment and where one's interpersonal relationships are ineffective and unsatisfying; opposed to congruence (q.v.).
[Carl Rogers, *On Becoming a Person* (Boston: Houghton Mifflin, 1961).]

Independent Clause. See CLAUSE.

Index. An extensional device (q.v.) used to emphasize the notion of nonidentity (that no two things are the same) and symbolized by a subscript, for example, politician$_1$ is not politician$_2$; a sign that is caused by or affected by what it signifies or represents, for example, lipstick on one's collar is an index of kissing or a romantic encounter.

Index of Communication. See COMMUNICATION, INDEX OF.

Index of Communicativity. See COMMUNICATIVITY, INDEX OF.

Index, The. More formally, the *Index Librorum Prohibitorum,* formally published by the Roman Catholic Church, a list of books that Catholics were forbidden to read without the permission of their bishop.

Indiscrimination. A misevaluation that occurs when we focus on classes of individuals or objects or events and fail to see that each is unique, each is different, and each needs to be looked at individually. This misevaluation is at the heart of the common practice of stereotyping (q.v.) national, racial, and religious groups.

Induction. Reasoning from specific instances to some general conclusion.

Inevitability of Communication. A commonly accepted principle of communication that holds that in any interaction situation, one cannot not communicate; all behavior is communicational.

Infatuation. A term used to denote a romantic relationship that only appears to be love; usually, infatuation is thought to be short lived, immature, anxiety provoking, and foolish in comparison to love which is usually defined as being lasting, mature, comforting, and meaningful.

Inferential Statement. A statement that can be made by anyone, is not limited to the observed, and can be made at any time and about any time (past, present, or future). See also FACTUAL STATEMENT.

Infix. See AFFIX.

Inflection. A linguistic change in the form of a word, for example, by adding a suffix, a prefix, a plural form, or a tense marker.

Informal Organization. The structure established by the individuals of an organization apart from and perhaps in contradiction to the formally established structure; the informally established subgroups and communication patterns within an organization.

Informal Time. Time conceived in general and approximate categories, for example, *soon, a while, as soon as possible, right away;* opposed to formal time (q.v.) and technical time (q.v.). See also TEMPORAL COMMUNICATION.

Information. That which reduces uncertainty; that which is new to the receiver.

Information Feedback. A therapeutic procedure that focuses the client's attention on his or her interpersonal behavior and its effects on others with the goal of identifying new behavioral choices. The "therapist" functions to help explain the various behavior patterns a person uses and their effects on self and others. It is up to the client to select or reject the desired behavior changes.

[J. W. Kaswan, et al., "Information Feedback as a Method of Clinical Intervention and Consultation," in *Current Topics in Clinical and Community Psychology,* 3d ed., C. Spielberger, ed. (New York: Academic Press, 1971).]

Information Input. The data that are fed into a computer or into any information storage system.

Information Output. The data that are retrieved from a computer or any information storage system.

Information Overload. That condition in which the quantity of information exceeds the receiver's capacity to process it or to deal with it in any meaningful way.

Today, with the explosion of technology, information overload is becoming one of our greatest problems. Information is being generated at such a rapid rate that it is becoming extremely difficult (actually, impossible) to keep up with all that is relevant to one's job or interests. Invariably, each person must select certain information to attend to and must omit other information.

Information is so easily and quickly generated and disseminated throughout an organization that we often forget that it still takes time to digest the information and to make use of it in a meaningful way. The junk mail that seems to grow every day is a perfect example of the results of the technological advances that make this sending of information so easy, so quick, and so inexpensive. Now what we need is the corresponding technology to enable us to read and use the information just as quickly.

Another major cause of overload is that many organizational managers disseminate information as a substitute for doing something about a problem or issue. A department head confronted with a problem may choose to write a memo on the problem and distribute it to all workers. The manager has thus bought time, but has also added to the information overload. Action on the problem can now be delayed until responses from the workers or other managers are received, that is, until they can digest, think about, and respond to the memo.

Information overload has probably crept into all organizations of any size. And of course this is the major reason why so many organizations have computerized their operations; putting everything on the computer is a relatively easy and efficient way to deal with vast amounts of information. But putting it on the computer isn't the entire answer. Some human being must still do something about the information—at least usually. And under conditions of information overload, errors are more likely simply because the person cannot devote the needed time to any one item. The more rushed we are, the more likely we are to make mistakes. There are also likely to be great delays between the sending of the message and the taking of the required action, and delays are inefficient and costly to an organization.

Sometimes we confront information overload by avoiding it; we simply refuse to deal with any additional information. We may simply discard junk mail without even opening it, so tired are we of going through the motions of opening the envelope and reading all about the new house or car we will win if we just scratch off the seven numbers on the enclosed card. At other times, we respond by developing generalized responses for large amounts of data—surely an inefficient method for dealing with any situation.

Information, Principles for Communicating. Technically, "information" is something that the receiver does not already know. To tell listeners something they know is not communicating information. A speech devoted to what listeners already know is not an informative speech. In preparing and presenting informative speeches, you need to communicate something new to your receivers. It may be a new way of looking at old things or an old way of looking at new things; it may be a theory not previously heard of or a familiar one not fully understood; it may be devoted to events that the audience may be unaware of or may have misconceptions about. The following principles should refine your informative speech-making skills.

Limit the Amount of Information

There is a limit to the amount of information that a listener can take in at one time. Beginning speakers tend to present a great deal of information and, when they are limited to say five or six minutes, that information is so tightly packed that it is impossible for anyone to understand and retain more than a very small part of it. It is generally best, especially during your beginning efforts, to limit the amount of information that you will communicate and, instead, expand its presentation. Thus, it is better to present two new items of information and explain these with examples, illustrations, descriptions, and the like than to present five new items without this needed amplification.

Stress Relevance and Usefulness

Information is best attended to and retained when it is perceived as relevant and useful to some need, want, or goal. If you want the audience to listen to your speech, you must make that information relevant to their needs, wants, or goals.

Present Information in a Nonthreatening Manner

Information will be listened to more fairly and will be better retained when it is perceived as nonthreatening; alternatively, information will be avoided and resisted when it is perceived as threatening. Generally, we seek out information that supports rather than contradicts what we think we already know.

Present Information at the Appropriate Level

Information is best received and retained when it is presented on an appropriate level. The speaker has to be careful to steer a middle course between being too simple—thus boring or insulting the audience—and being too sophisticated—thus confusing the audience.

Relate New Information to Old

We seem to learn information more easily and retain it longer when it is related in some way to what we already know. As a general rule, relate the new to the old, the unfamiliar to the familiar, the unseen to the seen, the untasted to the tasted. In this way the audience will be able to visualize more clearly or somehow perceive what they have never seen or experienced before.

Information Retrieval. The process of recovering or recalling information from a storage system; usually used in reference to computers but also used in reference to human memory systems.

Information Society. A society dominated by the information sciences and occupations and in which a major part of the work force is employed in acquiring, storing, retrieving, and utilizing information; opposed to agrarian or industrial societies in which people work on farms or in the manufacture of goods.

Information Theory. An approach to communication based on the measurement of information carried by a particular medium or channel. See also MATHEMATICAL THEORY OF COMMUNICATION.
[Claude E. Shannon and Warren Weaver, *The Mathematical Theory of Communication* (Urbana, Ill.: University of Illinois Press, 1949); Wilbur Schramm, "Information Theory and Mass Communication," *Journalism Quarterly* 32 (1955):131–146.]

Information Wave. A low-frequency wave that carries information but which is not powerful enough to travel through the air by itself and so is superimposed on the higher frequency carrier wave (q.v.).

Ingratiation. A technique in which a person makes himself or herself more attractive to another in an attempt to persuade the person; verbal and nonverbal behavior that has as its goal the attainment of the approval or positive regard of another person.

In-Group. A group to which an individual belongs; a group with which one identifies strongly and feels loyalty toward; a cohesive, tightly knit group in which members feel closely united and where membership in the group is restricted or guarded; opposed to out-group (q.v.). Also referred to as "we-group."

Initial Teaching Alphabet. Developed by Sir James Pitman and used in teaching children to read, an alphabet with close correspondence between the written symbol and the sounds of the language.

Innate Predisposition. An inborn, biologically determined tendency to acquire a certain behavior or competency as opposed to acquiring it through learning.

Inner Speech. Inaudible talk with oneself, generally in sentence fragments and phrases; intrapersonal communication designed to enable the individual to draw connections among concepts rather than to serve any interpersonal function.
[Lev S. Vygotsky, *Thought and Language,* Eugenia Hanfmann and Gertrude Vakar, trans. and eds. (Cambridge, Mass.: M.I.T. Press, 1962).]

Innovation. A new idea, process, or method of doing things that is adopted by the community over time and in various stages. See also DIFFUSION OF INNOVATION.

Innovativeness. A personality construct referring to one's willingness to change or to adopt new modes of behavior, new developments, and new technologies. See also DIFFUSION OF INNOVATION.
[H. Thomas Hurt, Katherine Joseph, and Chester D. Cook, "Scales for the Measurement of Innovativeness," *Human Communication Research* 4 (1977):58–65.]

Innuendo. An indirect implication, especially a negative one.

Inoculation. See PERSUASION, PRINCIPLES OF.

Input. That which the computer operator stores in the computer, for example, instructions or data.

Input Overload. See INFORMATION OVERLOAD.

Insight. Sudden understanding of oneself or of some problem or situation.

Instinct. An innate, unlearned behavior pattern.

Instrumental and Expressive Communication. See EXPRESSIVE AND INSTRUMENTAL COMMUNICATION.

Instrumental Conditioning. See OPERANT CONDITIONING.

Intelsat. International Telecommunications Satellite Consortium, a satellite communication system established in 1964.

Integrity Group. A therapeutic group, developed by O. Hobart Mowrer, focusing on the development of personal integrity (consistency between one's beliefs and actions; the absence of secrecy and duplicity) with the aim that one's identity (a wholeness, an authenticity, a personal integration) is enhanced.
[O. Hobart Mowrer, "Integrity Groups: Basic Principles and Procedures," *The Counseling Psychologist* 3 (1972):7–32.]

Intensional Orientation. Intensional orientation refers to the tendency to view people, objects, and events in terms of the way in which they are talked about or labeled rather than in terms of the way in which they actually exist and operate. *Extensional orientation,* on the other hand, is the tendency to look first at the actual people, objects, and events and only then to their labels. It is the tendency to be guided by what we see happening rather than by the label used for what is happening.

Intensional orientation is seen when we act as if the words and labels are more important than the things they represent—when we act as if the map were more important than the territory. In its extreme form intensional orientation is seen in the person who is afraid of dogs and begins to sweat when shown a picture of a dog or when hearing people talk about dogs. Here the person is responding to the labels (maps) as if they were the actual thing (territory).

Intensive. A word that gives emphasis; emphatic expression.

Intention. One of the characteristics or qualities of credibility; the motivation that a speaker is perceived as possessing, whether, for example, to benefit the audience or to benefit some selfish personal aim.

Intentional Fallacy. The misconceptions resulting from judging a work, especially a literary work, on the basis of the author's stated purpose.
[W. K. Wimsatt, Jr. and Monroe C. Beardsley, "The Intentional Fallacy," in W. K. Wimsatt, Jr., *The Verbal Icon* (New York: Noonday Press, 1962).]

Intentional Learning. Knowledge acquired by deliberate effort, for example, studying (learning) in anticipation of an examination; opposed to incidental learning (q.v.).

Interaction Diagrams. Interaction diagrams are useful for recording the number of messages addressed to one person from another. They enable us to quantify who speaks to whom. There are various ways to draw these diagrams. Perhaps the most popular method is to represent each member by a circle and draw arrows from the source of the message to the receiver, as shown in the first diagram. The arrows drawn to "group" indicate that the comments were addressed to all members of the group. Alternatively, we might begin with a model of the group with arrows connecting each possible dyad and simply mark off each comment on the appropriate line, as illustrated in the second diagram.

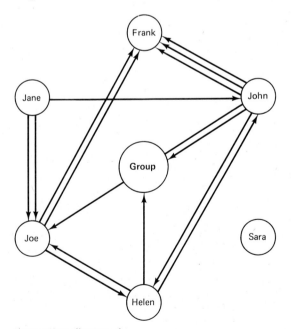

Interaction diagram 1.

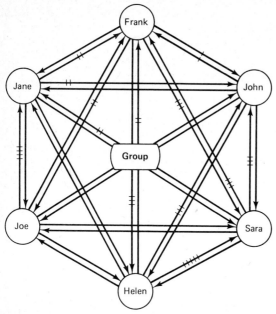

Interaction diagram 2.

In each of these cases we have a record of who spoke to whom and how often. The diagrams can become pretty messy if there is much communication or if there are many members. Therefore the communication matrix for recording interactions such as the one presented in the third diagram seems more workable. With slash marks we can easily record the various messages. Viewing the names on the left as the sources and those at the top as receivers, we can easily separate, for example, those messages from Joe to Helen (second column, top row) from those from Helen to Joe (first column, second row). Also included is a slot for messages addressed to the group as a whole.

	Joe	Helen	Sara	John	Frank	Jane	Group
Joe		//////	//	///			//
Helen	///			//////			//////
Sara	////						
John	////// ///						
Frank	///						
Jane	/	///	////	//////			//

Communication matrix for recording interactions.

This model seems the most practical of the three since it allows for a clear recording of the messages regardless of how many members there are or how many messages are communicated.

Interaction Management. The process by which an interpersonal interaction is orchestrated, coordinated, or regulated; the process by which an interaction is initiated, maintained, and terminated; the extent to which an interaction, in all its phases, is satisfactorily controlled.

[Michael Argyle, *Social Interaction* (Chicago, Ill.: Aldine Atherton, 1969).]

Interaction Process Analysis. Perhaps the most widely used system of analysis is that proposed by Robert Bales known as interaction process analysis, or IPA. Interaction process analysis is a form of content analysis, a method that classifies messages into 4 general categories: (1) social-emotional positive, (2) social-emotional negative, (3) attempted answers, and (4) questions. Each of these 4 areas contains 3 subdivisions, giving us a total of 12 categories. It is assumed that all the messages occurring in small groups may be classified into one of these 12 categories:

Social-Emotional Positive
   to show solidarity
   to show tension release
   to show agreement
Social-Emotional Negative
   to show disagreement
   to show tension
   to show antagonism
Attempted Answers
   to give suggestions
   to give opinions
   to give information
Questions
   to ask for suggestions
   to ask for opinions
   to ask for information

Note that the categories under social-emotional positive are the natural opposites of those under social-emotional negative, and those under attempted answers are the natural opposites of those under questions. With even brief experience in using this system, one can categorize the various messages with relative ease.

Generally, charts are constructed to record the type and frequency of messages communicated in the small group. A typical chart would look something like that presented in the accompanying process analysis form.

From this chart, which represents the messages communicated in a relatively short period of time, we can see that certain members are taking on various roles. Grace seems negative; she is high on antagonism, tension, and disagreement. Linda seems particularly positive with numerous messages showing solidarity and asking for suggestions and opinions. Helen, on the other hand, seems particularly tense but does nothing to relieve the tension or to display positive feelings. We can make more significant observations after observing a longer period of interaction.

[Robert F. Bales, *Interaction Process Analysis* (Reading, Mass.: Addison-Wesley, 1967).]

Interchangeability. The feature of language that makes possible the reversal of

	Judy	Helen	Linda	Grace	Rhoda	Diane
Shows Solidarity	I		卌 I			I
Shows Tension Release						
Shows Agreement	III		II			II
Shows Antagonism				卌 II		
Shows Tension		卌		III		
Shows Disagreement	III			卌		
Gives Suggestions				II	III	
Gives Opinions		II				
Gives Information	III				I	
Asks for Suggestions			IIII			卌
Asks for Opinions			III			
Asks for Information	卌					

Interaction process analysis form.

roles between senders and receivers of messages. Because of interchangeability all adult members of a speech community may serve as both senders and receivers, that is, persons may produce any linguistic message they can understand.

Interchange Compatibility. A condition that exists between two persons when they have similar desires (goals) in terms of their expression of inclusion (q.v.), control (q.v.), and affection (q.v.). There would be interchange *in*compatibility if the two persons differed in their desires concerning the expression of these needs.

[William C. Schutz, *FIRO: A Three-Dimensional Theory of Interpersonal Behavior* (New York: Holt, Rinehart and Winston, 1958).]

Intercultural Communication. Communication between members of different cultures or subcultures. Also called "cross-cultural communication."

[Larry A. Samovar, Richard E. Porter, and Memi C. Jain, *Understanding Intercultural Communication* (Belmont, Calif.: Wadsworth, 1981).]

Interface. The point at which two systems meet; as a verb, it refers to the process by which two systems confront each other and form a common boundary.

Interior Monologue. Expression of a character's inner thoughts and feelings.

Interlingua. A proposed universal language developed by an American, Alexander Gode. The words were taken from existing languages making Interlingua understandable by persons speaking one of these other languages with little specific training.

Internalization. One of the processes of opinion change occurring when one accepts persuasion because it is consistent with one's own value system.

[Herbert C. Kelman, "Processes of Opinion Change," *Public Opinion Quarterly* 25 (1961): 57–78.]

Internal Justification. A means of resolving cognitive dissonance (q.v.) in which we change our attitudes toward one of the attitude objects. The dissonance reduction or elimination is achieved through persuading oneself to change one's attitude.

International Phonetic Alphabet (IPA). A written representation of the spoken language in which each sound in the language is given a separate symbol.

Interpersonal Attraction. See ATTRACTION.

Interpersonal Communication. Communication between individuals as distinguished from mass communication and public communication. Often used as a general term to include intrapersonal, two-person or dyadic, and small group communication. At times the term is used synonymously with dyadic communication or to designate communication that is personal and intimate rather than impersonal.

Interpersonal Communication Effectiveness. Effectiveness in interpersonal communication may be approached in at least two ways. First, there is the humanistic perspective that stresses openness, empathy, supportiveness, and, in general, those qualities that foster meaningful, honest, and satisfying interactions. Second, there is the pragmatic or behavioral perspective that stresses interaction management, immediacy, and, in general, those qualities that contribute to achieving a variety of desired goals. Five qualities derived from each perspective may be offered as a comprehensive summary of those qualities that are currently assumed to contribute to effectiveness in interpersonal communication.

Five qualities from the humanistic perspective are: openness, empathy, supportiveness, positiveness, and equality.

Openness

The quality of openness refers to at least three aspects of interpersonal communication. First, effective interpersonal communicators must be open to the people with whom they are interacting. There should be a willingness to self-disclose—to reveal information about oneself that might normally be kept hidden. Second, communicators should be willing to react honestly to incoming stimuli, to give open and honest feedback to others. Third, communicators should own their own feelings and thoughts—they should be willing to take responsibility for these thoughts and feelings, to say "This is how I feel," "This is what I think."

Empathy

Empathy refers to the ability to feel as the other individual feels, to "walk in the same shoes," to feel the same feelings in the same way. Effective interpersonal communicators need to empathize with the person with whom they are interacting and see the world from that person's perspective.

Supportiveness

Effective interpersonal communicators are supportive of the people with whom they interact: they describe rather than evaluate; they are spontaneous rather than strategic; and they are provisional and tentative rather than certain.

Positiveness

Effective interpersonal communicators are positive toward the interaction; they express positive feelings (verbally and nonverbally) about the interaction and the process of interacting. Likewise, they express positiveness toward the other person as well as for themselves.

Equality

Effective communicators seem to approach the interpersonal interaction with the belief that each person can contribute to the success of the interaction. There should be a tacit recognition that both parties are valuable and worthwhile human beings and that each has something important to contribute. Equality should also characterize the interaction in terms of speaking versus listening.

The five qualities derived from the pragmatic or behavioral perspective are: confidence, immediacy, interaction management, expressiveness, and other-orientation.

Confidence

The effective communicator has social confidence; any anxiety that is present is not readily perceived by others. There is, instead, a comfortableness with the other person and with the communication situation generally.

Immediacy

The effective communicator conveys a sense of immediacy, a sense of contact, of togetherness. This person communicates to others a feeling of interest, an attentive attitude, a liking for and an attraction toward the other person.

Interaction Management

The effective communicator controls the interaction to the satisfaction of both parties. Neither person feels ignored or on stage; each contributes to the total communication interchange. Verbal and nonverbal messages are consistent and reinforce one another. Contradictory signals are rarely in evidence. The conversation keeps flowing and is relatively fluent without long and awkward pauses that make everyone uncomfortable. The effective interaction manager is a high self-monitor (q.v.).

Expressiveness

The effective communicator evidences genuine involvement in the interaction; this person plays the game instead of just watching it as a spectator. This communicator takes responsibility for both talking and listening and states his or her position directly and with I-messages (q.v.). Both vocally and facially this person demonstrates expressiveness by using appropriate variations in vocal rate, pitch, volume, and rhythm to convey involvement and interest and allows the facial muscles to reflect and echo this inner involvement.

Other-Orientation

The effective interpersonal communicator focuses on the other person through focused eye contact, smiles, head nods, leaning toward the other person, and displaying appropriate effect. Verbally, interest is shown through such comments as "I see," "Really," or "I get it"; through requests for further information ("What else did you do in Vegas?"); and through expressions of empathy ("I can understand what you're going through; my father died just recently too.").

[Joseph A. DeVito, *The Interpersonal Communication Book,* 4th ed. (New York: Harper & Row, 1986); Brian H. Spitzberg and William R. Cupach, *Interpersonal Communication Competence* (Beverly Hills, Calif.: Sage, 1984).]

Interpersonal Conflict. A disagreement between two persons; a discordant state within an individual caused by his or her relationships with other people. See also CONFLICT RESOLUTION; CONFLICT STRATEGIES.

Interviewing. Interviewing is a particular form of interpersonal communication in which two persons interact largely through a question-and-answer format for the purpose of achieving rather specific goals. Interviews *usually* involve two persons, but numerous interviews take place among three, four, and even more people. At conventions, for example, where many people apply for the few available jobs, interviewers often interview several persons at once. The idea is to present the general nature of the job, to answer some of the more common questions, to learn something about the candidates, and perhaps to weed the numbers down. Similarly, therapy situations, although normally involving only two persons, frequently involve entire families, groups of co-workers, or other related individuals. Nevertheless, the two-person type of interview is certainly the most common and is the focus of this essay.

The interview is distinctly different from other forms of communication because it proceeds through questions and answers. The content of the interview is guided and, in fact, rather rigidly structured on the basis of the specific questions asked and the answers given. Both parties in the interview ask and answer questions, but most often the interviewer asks the questions and the interviewee answers them.

The interview has rather specific goals. The achievement of these goals constitutes the reason for the interview, and they guide and structure the interview in terms of both content and format. In an employment interview, for example, the goal for the interviewer is to find an applicant who can fulfill the tasks of the position and the interviewee's goal is to get the job. These goals guide the behaviors of both parties. Note that these goals are relatively specific and usually quite clear to both parties.

Kinds of Interviews

The various types of interviews are often distinguished on the basis of the goals of interviewer and interviewee. Discussions of some of the most important types follow.

The Information Interview

In the information interview, the interviewer attempts to learn something about the interviewee and asks the interviewee, usually a person of some reputation and accomplishment, a series of questions designed to elicit his or her views, beliefs, insights, perspectives, predictions, life history, and so on. Popular examples of the information interview are those published in such popular magazines as *Psychology Today* and *Playboy,* the TV interviews conducted by Johnny Carson, Ted Koppel, and Barbara Walters, and the interviews conducted by a lawyer during a trial. All are designed to elicit specific information from someone who supposedly knows something that others do not know.

The Persuasive Interview

In the interview designed to change an individual's attitude or behavior, the goal is persuasion. The interviewer usually puts himself or herself into the position of answering the interviewee's questions, and in doing so hopes to change his or her attitude and/or behaviors. If you go into a showroom to buy a new car, you are the interviewer and the salesperson is the interviewee. The salesperson's goal is to persuade you to buy a particular car, and he or she attempts to accomplish it by answering your questions persuasively. You ask about mileage, safety features, finance terms; the salesperson discourses eloquently on the superiority of this car over all others.

All interviews contain elements of both information and persuasion. When, for example, a guest appears on "The Tonight Show" and talks about a new movie, television show, or record album just completed, there is information being communicated. But there is also a considerable amount of persuasion intended. In fact, the performer is being interviewed primarily to persuade the audience to see the movie or television show or to buy the record album. Information and persuasion are the two major functions of communication, and there is probably no type of communication that does not in part serve one or both functions. The interview is clearly no exception.

The Appraisal Interview

In the appraisal or evaluation interview, the interviewee's performance is assessed by management or, in the case of teaching, by more experienced colleagues. The general aim is to discover what the individual is doing well (to praise it), and what he or she is not doing well and why (and to correct it). These interviews are particularly important because they are a means for the new member of the organization to find out what the rules of the game are and how they can be played more effectively. It is a way for the new member to see how his or her performance matches up with the expectations of management or of those making promotion and firing decisions.

The Exit Interview

Another type of interview, reportedly used by some 80 percent of companies in the United States, is the exit interview. When an employee leaves the company of his or her own accord, it is important for the company to know why. All organizations compete in one way or another for superior workers, and if an organization is losing its workers, it must discover the reasons to prevent others from leaving as well.

Another function of this interview is to provide a way of making the exit as pleasant and as efficient as possible for both employee and employer.

The interviewer must be especially careful in this type of interview to be supportive of the individual leaving and of the reasons for the leaving. Otherwise, the departing employee will fail to reveal the real reasons for the exit and the company will be the loser.

The Employment Interview

Perhaps of most concern is the employment interview. Here you are in the position of looking for a job. Interviewers from various companies will attempt to interest superior persons to enter their firms. Your task is to convince them that you are one of these superior people and that they should offer you a position. In such an employment interview, a great deal of information and attempts at persuasion will be exchanged. The interviewer will learn about you, your interests, your talents—and, if the interviewer is clever, some of your weaknesses and liabilities. You will be informed about the nature of the company, its benefits, its advantages—and, if you are clever, some of its disadvantages and problems.

The Counseling Interview

Another popular type of interview is that designed to provide guidance. Usually this type of interview is conducted by someone trained in psychology, guidance, education, communication, or some other field concerned with personal and interpersonal adjustment. The goal here is to help the individual deal more effectively with his or her problems; to work more effectively; to get along better with friends, relatives, children, or lovers; and to cope more realistically and effectively with day-to-day living. Like the employment interview, this interview also contains elements of both information and persuasion. For the interview to be of any value, the guidance counselor (the interviewer) must learn a considerable amount about the person—habits, problems, self-perceptions, goals, and so on. With this information, the counselor then attempts to persuade the person to alter certain aspects of his or her thinking and/or behavior. The counselor may attempt to persuade you, for example, to listen more attentively when your spouse argues, to devote more time and energy to your classwork, to avoid seeing certain people who might have a disturbing influence on you, and so on.

The Interview Sequence

The interview sequence might, for convenience, be divided into three main periods: a preparatory period, in which the individual does some preparation; the interview itself; and the postinterview period, in which the person reflects on and follows up on the interview. Each of these periods is explained with a view to providing you with some specific suggestions to make the interview work more effectively for you.

Before the Interview

The preinterview period has no clear beginning. If, for example, you are to be interviewed for an accounting job, your preparation might logically be said to have begun when you enrolled as an accounting major or when you entered college. For our purposes, however, the preinterview period may be said to start at the time you begin specific preparation for a specific interview.

Prepare Yourself. This is perhaps the most difficult aspect of the entire interview process. And it is probably the step that is most often overlooked. Preparation (or lack of it) can prevent (or cause) considerable trouble.

Intellectual Preparation. We should prepare ourselves intellectually; we should seek to educate ourselves as much as possible about the relevant topics. We should, for example, learn something about the company and their specific product or products. If possible, we should also try to learn something about the person who will interview us.

Although it is difficult in most instances to research the interviewer, you can generally find out something about the person who will interview you. In teaching positions, at least on the college level, this is quite simple. All the interviewee has to do is to look up the chairperson's name and then consult the various indexes in the appropriate field and the various biographical dictionaries to discover what this person's special interests, talents, and background are. With this as a foundation, the person can build rapport and more effectively discuss matters of mutual concern, and in general talk with at least some knowledge of the person behind the desk.

Attitudinal Preparation. Prepare yourself attitudinally. Many interviewees go into the interview with the idea that it is a contest, a competitive bout. They assume it is a fight to prove they are worthy of the position or whatever is at stake. If you are applying for a job, both you and the company want something. You want a job that will meet your needs, and the company wants an employee who will meet its needs. In short, you each want something that perhaps the other has. So the interview should not be thought of as a contest; both interviewer and interviewee stand to gain something from the experience. Try to view the interview as an opportunity to engage in a joint effort to gain something beneficial to both.

Physical Preparation. Physical preparation is always difficult to give advice about, especially because the type of physical preparation that will be helpful in one situation will not matter much in another. And yet we do know that a great number of jobs are won or lost on the basis of physical appearance alone, so considerable attention should be given to the physical dimensions of the interview. Clearly you should dress in a manner that shows that you care enough about the interview to make a good impression. At the same time, your dress should be comfortable. It should not make you strain at the collar each second. To avoid extremes is perhaps the most specific advice that can be given. If in doubt, it is probably best to err on the side of formality: Wear the tie or the high heels or the dress.

Another form of physical preparedness is to make sure you bring with you the appropriate materials, whatever they may be. At the very least you should bring a pen and some paper so that you can take down any information the interviewer may wish to give you—an address or a reference book to consult, for example.

Establish Objectives. All interviews have specific primary objectives. As part of your preparation, fix these objectives firmly in mind and use them as guides to the remainder of your preparation and also as guides to your behavior during and even after the interview. Many interviews also have secondary objectives; these too should be established and figure in your preparation and behaviors. For example, you may enter an interview with the primary objective of getting the particular job offered. But there may also be secondary objectives, such as learning to relax during an interview or making enough of an impression so that you are asked back for a more extensive interview.

Prepare Answers and Questions. If the interview is at all important to you, you will probably think about it for some time. In fact, you will probably devote a considerable amount of "worry time" to it. While this is often inevitable, part of that time might more profitably be directed to rehearsing the predicted course of the interview and attempting to predict the questions that will be asked and the answers you will most likely give.

Some questions are obvious. You might want to devote some time to thinking about these inevitable questions and how you will answer them. Other questions might not seem so obvious at first, but if you think about the specific interview enough, you may be able to predict at least some of them. If you accurately predict the questions that will be asked, you will be that much ahead because you will have had the time to think of intelligent answers. But even if you do not succeed in predicting any of the questions, the rehearsal of the interview process will have the beneficial effect of helping you to relax once you get into the interview.

Even though the interviewer will ask most of the questions and you will be answering most of the time, in any interview both parties ask and both answer at least some questions. In addition to rehearsing some answers to predicted questions, you should also fix firmly in your mind the questions you want to ask the interviewer and the ways in which you will respond to any of the predicted answers he or she may give.

During the Interview

After the preliminary preparations, you are ready for the interview proper. Several suggestions may guide you through this sometimes difficult procedure.

Make an Effective Presentation of Self. Obviously the first step is to present yourself, an aspect of the interview process that many persons claim is the most important part of the entire procedure. If you fail here, if you make a bad initial impression, it will be difficult to salvage the rest of the interview. So devote special care to the way in which you present yourself.

Arrive on time, which in interview situations generally means five to ten minutes early. This is advisable since the interviewer may be running ahead of schedule and your being there early would be appreciated; it will also allow you time to relax, to get accustomed to the general surroundings, and perhaps to fill out any forms that may be required; and it gives you a cushion should something delay you on the way. But do not arrive at the office too early and certainly do not arrive late. If you arrive late to the interview, the interviewer may reasonably conclude that you are not interested in the job and/or that you are not responsible or organized.

Establish a Relationship with the Interviewer. At the very beginning of the interview, try to establish some interpersonal relationship with the interviewer. Try to make the interviewer, who sees perhaps 10 or 20 people in one day, see you as unique and different from everyone else.

Be sure you know the name of the company, the job title, and the interviewer's name. Although you will have much on your mind when you go into the interview, the interviewer's name is not one of the things you can afford to forget (or mispronounce).

In presenting yourself, be sure that you do not err on the side of too much casualness or too much informality. When there is any doubt, act on the side of increased formality. Slouching back in the chair, smoking, gum or candy chewing are obvious behaviors to avoid when you are trying to impress an interviewer.

Demonstrate Effective Interpersonal Communication. Throughout the interview, be certain that you demonstrate the skills of effective interpersonal communication. The interview is the ideal place to put into practice all the skills you have learned. (See also INTERPERSONAL COMMUNICATION EFFECTIVENESS.)

Be especially alert to feedback from the interviewer. Take note of the small movements that tell you he or she has heard enough and those movements that say "what else?" Distinguish between the nod that says "I'm listening" and the nod that says "I agree."

Avoid being defensive. This is especially difficult to do, and yet it often distinguishes an effective interview. When an interviewer asks you a particular question, assume that that question is asked to determine your suitability for the position and is not a personal attack. Some interviewers are not terribly effective in asking questions and often ask them in ways that sound like personal attacks. In some cases they might be, but most often they are not. The interviewer does not know you and probably has little desire to insult you in any way. So treat without defensiveness questions such as "Do you think you could really do this job?" or "You have no experience with this type of product, are you sure you could handle it?" or "What makes you think that we should hire you?"

Demonstrate Competence and Self-Esteem. This is a difficult suggestion to follow since it involves steering a clear course between appearing overly confident and cocky (the "I know everything" type of response) and insecure (the "I'm not sure I could do this job" type of response). The interviewer wants to hire a competent and self-confident individual; the company probably has enough of the other kind. So, throughout the interview demonstrate that you have the relevant knowledge (but that you could certainly learn more and that you intend to learn more), that you are self-confident (but not overly so), and that you have a positive image of yourself (but not that you are blind to your faults or that you cannot improve).

After the Interview
Even after the interview, you still have work to do.

Mentally Rehearse the Interview. By rehearsing the interview, you will be able to fix it firmly in your mind. Go over what happened—what questions were asked and what answers were given. Review any especially important information the interviewer gave. Write down any significant information. (The pen and paper you took to the interview will come in handy now since it is best to write down what happened as soon after you leave the interview as possible.) Although immediately after an interview you will be convinced that you will not forget what happened, after three or four interviews you will probably find that they all blend into one another and that it becomes increasingly difficult to distinguish one from the other. Analyze your strengths and weaknesses as these manifested themselves during the interview and consider how you might correct your weaknesses and capitalize on your strengths in future interviews.

Follow Up. The most important aspect of the postinterview period is the follow-up. In most cases, you should follow up an interview with a thank you note to the interviewer. In this brief, professional letter, you thank the interviewer for his or her time and consideration, reiterate your interest in the company, and perhaps add that you hope to hear from him or her soon.

This letter serves a number of useful and important purposes. On the most general level, the letter provides you with an opportunity to resell yourself, to reiterate those qualities you possess and wish to emphasize, but may have been too modest to say at the time. It will help to make you stand out in the mind of the interviewer since not many interviewees write letters of thanks. It will help to remind the interviewer of your interview and perhaps fix it in his or her mind a bit more firmly. It will also help to convince the interviewer that you are still interested in the position. Finally, the letter will help to further demonstrate your sophistication in the employment world. A short letter that serves all these functions seems surely worth the small effort required.

[Charles J. Stewart and William B. Cash, Jr., *Interviewing: Principles and Practices,* 4th ed. (Dubuque, Iowa: Brown, 1985); H. Anthony Medley, *Sweaty Palms: The Neglected Art of Being Interviewed* (Belmont, Calif.: Lifetime Learning Publications, Wadsworth, 1978); Cal W. Downs, G. Paul Smeyak, and Ernest Martin, *Professional Interviewing* (New York: Harper & Row, 1980).]

Interpretative Reporting. A form of journalism in which the interpretations of the reporter are included along with the descriptive information.

Intimate Distance. The closest proxemic (q.v.) distance, ranging from touching someone to being 6 to 18 inches away from them.

Intimate Stranger. As used by Richard Schickel, one who we feel we know well but who knows us not at all; celebrities are, to most people, intimate strangers—we feel we know them but they do not know us.

[Richard Schickel, *Intimate Strangers* (New York: Doubleday, 1985).]

Intonation. The relative highness or lowness of pitch.

Intrapersonal Communication. Communication with oneself.

Introduction, Speech of. A speech designed to introduce another speaker or to introduce a general topic area and a series of speakers at, for example, a convention or symposium.

Introspection. A procedure whereby an individual looks into oneself—into one's thoughts and feelings—in an attempt to gain a better understanding of the self.

Introversion. A psychological orientation to the inner world of the self as opposed to the external, outer world; opposed to extroversion (q.v.).

Introvert. One who is primarily concerned with introspection (q.v.), with looking inward to his or her own thoughts and feelings; one who withdraws from social interactions and who is generally self-sufficient; opposed to extrovert (q.v.).

Invective. Abusive language; denunciation.

Invention. One of the canons of classical rhetoric (q.v.) concerned with locating the major issues and arguments for a speech.

Inversion. Reversal of normal word order, for example, "in full bloom was love"; anastrophe.

Investigative Journalism. A form of journalism in which the reporter seeks out and uncovers information relevant to the story being written.

Invocation. The act of calling on a deity for inspiration or guidance.

Iridology. The study of the iris of the eye as an indicator of the health or illness in other parts of the body.
[Evan Marshall, *Eye Language: Understanding the Eloquent Eye* (New York: New Trend, 1983); J. Dobson, "A Closer Look at Eyes," *The Atlanta Journal and Constitution Magazine* (July 1978):10–19.]

Irony. A figure of speech in which the real or intended meaning is the opposite of the literal meaning, for example, a teacher handing back failing examinations might say "So pleased to see how many of you studied so hard."

Irreversibility. That characteristic of communication referring to the inability to uncommunicate or to reverse the process of message reception.

Isogloss. A boundary line drawn on a map demarking the area in which a certain linguistic feature is used.

Isomorphism. Similarity in form with or without similarity in content or substance, for example, a photograph of a person and the actual person.
[Kurt Koffka, *Principles of Gestalt Psychology* (New York: Harcourt, Brace, Jovanovich, 1935).]

Italicize. To print certain words or passages in a scriptlike type to give them emphasis or distinction.

I-Thou Relationship. Defined by philosopher Martin Buber (1878–1965), a relationship between two people (both subjects) that is reciprocal, where each trusts the other and each is concerned with the other's well-being; opposed to I-it relationships (q.v.).
[Martin Buber, *I and Thou,* 2d ed. (New York: Scribners, 1958).]

J

Jabberwocky. Unintelligible discourse; meaningless talk or writing.

James–Lange Theory of Emotion. A theory of emotion combined from the theories of William James and C. G. Lange which holds that our perception of emotions results from our awareness of physiological changes. Thus, according to this theory, we are happy because we smile, are sad because we cry, and not that we smile because we are happy or cry because we are sad; opposed to the Cannon–Bard Theory (q.v.).

Jargon. A kind of sublanguage (q.v.) common to a specific group; the language of any special group, often a professional class, that is unintelligible to individuals not belonging to the group; "shop talk."
[Don Ethan Miller, *The Book of Jargon: An Essential Guide to the Inside Languages of Today* (New York: Macmillan, 1981).]

Jealousy. A feeling of dissatisfaction and anxiety resulting from the fear that someone or something belonging to one may be lost or taken away by another.

Johari Model (Window). A visual device or model depicting the four selves: the open, blind, hidden, and unknown selves. The first diagram is divided into four equal quadrants, each representing one of the selves.

	Known to Self	Not Known to Self
Known to Others	Open Self	Blind Self
Not Known to Others	Hidden Self	Unknown Self

The Johari Window. The name "Johari" was derived from the first names of the two persons who developed the model: Joseph Luft and Harry Ingham. *Source:* **Joseph Luft,** *Group Processes: An Introduction to Group Dynamics* **(Palo Alto, Calif.: National Press Books, 1970, p. 11.)**

The Open Self

The open self represents all the information, behaviors, attitudes, feelings, desires, motivations and ideas that are known to the self and also known to others. The type of information included here might vary from one's name, skin color, and sex to one's age, political and religious affiliations, and batting average. Each individual's open self will vary in size depending upon the time and upon the individuals he or she is dealing with. We are more likely to open ourselves up at some times than at other times. If, for example, we opened ourselves and got hurt because of it, we might then close up a bit more than usual. Similarly, some people make us feel comfortable and support us; to them, we open ourselves wide, but to others we prefer to leave most of ourselves closed.

"The smaller the first quadrant," says Joseph Luft, "the poorer the communication." Communication is dependent upon the degree to which we open ourselves to others and to ourself. If we do not allow others to know us (that is, if we keep the open self small), communication between them and us becomes extremely difficult, if not impossible. We can communicate meaningfully only to the extent that we know each other and know ourselves. To improve communication, we have to work first on enlarging the open self.

A change in the open area—or in any of the quadrants—will bring about a change in the other quadrants. We might visualize the entire model as being of constant size but each section as being variable, sometimes small, sometimes large. As one section becomes smaller, one or more of the others must become larger. Similarly, as one section becomes larger, one or more of the others must become smaller. For example, if we enlarge the open self, this will shrink the hidden self. Further, this revelation or disclosure in turn will function to lead others to decrease the size of our blind selves by revealing to us what they know and we do not know.

In the second diagram, two models of the self are presented to illustrate the different sizes of the four selves, depending upon the particular interpersonal situation. In section A of the diagram let us assume that we are with a friend to whom we have opened up a great deal. Consequently, our open self is large and our hidden self is small. In section B let us assume that we are with a new employer who we do not know very well and with whom we are still a bit uncomfortable. Thus our open self is relatively small and our hidden self is large.

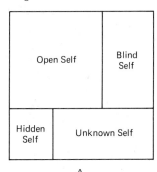 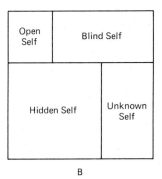

A   B

Two models of the four selves.

The Blind Self

The blind self represents all those things about ourselves that others know but of which we are ignorant. This may vary from the relatively insignificant habit of saying "you know" or rubbing your nose when you get angry or having a peculiar body odor to something as significant as defense mechanisms or fight strategies or repressed past experiences.

Some people have a very large blind self and seem to be totally oblivious to their own faults and sometimes (though not as often) their own virtues. Others seem overly concerned with having a small blind self, wanting to know what everyone thinks of us. In between these extremes lie most of us.

Interpersonal communication depends in great part on both parties sharing the same basic information about each other. To the extent that blind areas exist, communication will be made difficult. Yet blind areas will always exist for each of us. Although we may be able to shrink our blind areas, we can never totally eliminate them.

The Hidden Self

The hidden self contains all that you know of yourself and of others but that you keep to yourself. This area includes all your successfully kept secrets about yourself and others. In any interaction this area includes all that is relevant or irrelevant to the conversation but that you do not want to reveal.

At the extremes we have the overdisclosers and the underdisclosers. The overdisclosers tell all. They keep nothing hidden about themselves or others. They will tell you their family history, their sexual problems, their marital difficulties, their children's problems, their financial status, their strategies for rising to the top, their goals, their failures and successes, and just about everything else. For them this area is very small, and had they sufficient time and others sufficient patience, it would be reduced to near zero. The problem with these overdisclosers is that they do not discriminate. They do not distinguish between those to whom such information should be disclosed and those to whom it should not be disclosed, nor do they distinguish among the various types of information that should be disclosed or not be disclosed.

The underdisclosers tell nothing. They will talk about you but not about themselves. Depending upon one's relationship with these underdisclosers, we might feel that they are afraid to tell anyone anything for fear of being laughed at or rejected. Or we may feel somewhat rejected for their refusal to trust us. To never reveal anything about yourself comments on what you think of the people with whom you are interacting. On one level, at least, it is saying, "I don't trust you enough to reveal myself to you."

The vast majority of us are somewhat between these two extremes. We keep certain things hidden and we disclose certain things. We disclose to some people and we do not disclose to others. We are, in effect, selective disclosers.

The Unknown Self

The unknown self represents those truths that exist but that neither we nor others know about. One could legitimately argue that if neither we nor anyone else knows what is in this area, we cannot know that it exists at all. Actually, we do not *know* that it exists; rather, we *infer* that it exists.

We infer its existence from a number of different sources. Sometimes this area is revealed to us through temporary changes brought about by drug experiences or through special experimental conditions such as hypnosis or sensory deprivation. Sometimes this area is revealed by various projective tests or dreams. There seem to be sufficient instances of such revelations to justify our including this unknown area as part of the self.

Although we cannot easily manipulate this area, recognize that it does exist and that there are things about ourselves and about others that we simply do not and will not know.

[Joseph Luft, *Group Processes: An Introduction to Group Dynamics* (Palo Alto, Calif.: National Press Books, 1970).]

Johnny Carson Technique. A technique to divert attention and concern from oneself to the other person. As used by David Burns, the technique involves three steps: (1) paraphrasing what the other person has said, (2) asking questions to follow up what the other has said, and (3) expressing support or agreement for what has been said.

[David D. Burns, *Intimate Connections* (New York: Morrow, 1985).]

Journal. A record or diary (q.v.) of one's thoughts, feelings, and experiences. One aim of keeping a journal is to gain a greater understanding of oneself and to increase creativity and various other abilities.

[Tristine Rainer, *The New Diary* (Los Angeles, Calif.: J. P. Tarcher, 1978); Curtis W. Casewit, *The Diary: A Complete Guide to Journal Writing* (Allen, Texas: Argus Communications, 1982).]

Journalese. The jargon of the journalism profession.

Journalism. The profession concerned with the collecting, writing, and reporting of news and events of interest to the public.

Judicial Criticism. See CRITICISM.

Judicial Debate. A debate designed to defend or prosecute alleged offenders that is conducted in a court of law or similar assembly according to the rules governing the specific court.

Juncture. A linguistic pause. In some cases the juncture is phonemic (q.v.) and distinguishes one word from another, for example, *lighthouse* versus *light house.*

Just World Hypothesis. The belief or assumption, held by many, that people get what they deserve; the belief that people who are stigmatized for some physical or mental disorder are also morally defective and, conversely, that those without such disorders are morally righteous; the belief that because the world is a just one, those who suffer deserve to suffer and those who prosper deserve to prosper.

[M. J. Lerner, *The Belief in a Just World: A Fundamental Delusion* (New York: Plenum, 1980).]

K. 1024 bytes; a term used to express the number of bytes in computer memory, 128K = 131,072 bytes, for example.

Kicker. The punchline of a story or joke; an unexpected ending.

Kill Fee. A fee, usually a percentage of the agreed-upon fee for the completed work, paid to an author who has contracted to write a speech, article, or book but whose contract has been cancelled.

Kine. An individually produced bodily motion, analogous to the phone (q.v.), the individually produced sound.

Kineme. The range of movements which have the same meaning, analogous to the phoneme (q.v.) which is the range of sounds having the same meaning.

Kinemorph. A combination of kines which, taken together, communicate a meaning.

Kinesics. The study of the movements of the body, developed and systematized by Ray L. Birdwhistell.

[Ray L. Birdwhistell, *Kinesics and Context: Essays on Body Motion Communication* (New York: Ballantine, 1970).]

Kinesthetic Factors. A category of proxemic behavior denoting the closeness of one person to another and the potential that exists for touching and holding. Eight main subcategories are identified: (1) within body contact distance, (2) just outside this distance, (3) within touching distance with forearm extended, (4) just outside this distance, (5) within touching distance with arm extended, (6) just outside this distance, (7) within touching distance by reaching, and (8) just outside this distance. See also PROXEMICS; PROXEMIC BEHAVIOR CATEGORIES.

Kinetographs. Nonverbal movements that depict a bodily action or some nonhuman physical action; for example, the sun rising.

King's English. Grammatically correct English; language properly and eloquently spoken; English as spoken by the educated and upper classes.

Kitchensinking. An unproductive conflict strategy in which the participants include everything and anything that can be used against the other.
[George Bach and Peter Wyden, *The Intimate Enemy* (New York: Avon, 1968).]

Kitsch. Low quality "art" forms; poor imitations of more artistic creations.

Labeling Theory. An approach to explaining and accounting for deviant behavior. This theory focuses on the reactions of those who have labeled the deviance (doctors, parents, friends) and attempts to explain the behavior by the labels and the reactions to the labels. See also SEMANTOGENIC.

Laissez-Faire Leader. A type of small group leader who allows the group to develop and progress on its own and even allows it to make its own mistakes. This leader gives up or denies any real leadership authority and takes no initiative in directing or suggesting alternative courses of action. See also AUTHORITARIAN LEADER; DEMOCRATIC LEADER.

Lallation. A self-imitation stage in language acquisition characterized by the repetition of syllables.

Lalophobia. An unreasonable fear of speaking.

Lampoon. Unrestrained satire or spoof, usually in fun and directed at people or institutions.

Language. The rules of syntax (q.v.), semantics (q.v.), and phonology (q.v.); a potentially self-reflexive structure system of symbols that catalogue the objects, events, and relations in the world. *A Language* refers to the infinite set of grammatical sentences generated by the grammar of any language, for example, English, Italian, Bantu, Chinese.

Language Acquisition Device (LAD). The assumed innate component that enables a child to acquire language without explicit teaching and over a very short period of time. Some theorists view LAD as containing (1) linguistic universals or those characteristics that all languages have in common, (2) a hypothesis maker, and (3) a hypothesis tester so that alternative grammars may be analyzed, discarded, and the correct one eventually selected.

Language Family. A group of related languages that developed from a common origin or source, for example, French, Italian, and Spanish belong to the same language family or linguistic group, having all originated from Latin.

Language Intensity. The degree of positiveness or negativeness of a speaker's attitudes as revealed in the language or style used in speaking; the degree to which language deviates from neutrality.
[John Waite Bowers, "Language Intensity, Social Introversion, and Attitude Change," *Communication Monographs* 30 (1963):345–352, and "Language and Argument," in *Perspectives on Argumentation*, Gerald R. Miller and Thomas R. Nilsen, eds. (Glenview, Ill.: Scott, Foresman, 1966).]

Language Planning. The making of explicit choices concerning the use of the available languages in a society or culture.
[Joan Rubin and Roger Shuy, eds., *Language Planning: Current Issues and Research* (Washington, D.C.: Georgetown University Press, 1973).]

Langue. According to Ferdinand de Saussure (1857–1913), it is the grammatical system that is used by most speakers of a particular language as distinguished from *parole* which is the individual use of the language. See also PAROLE.

Latency. The period of inactivity between a stimulus and its corresponding response.

Latent. Hidden, not visible.

Latent Content. The hidden meaning in a message, usually used in reference to dreams; the "deep structure" of a dream. See also MANIFEST CONTENT.

Latent Functions of Mass Communication. The hidden (nonobvious) functions of the media; opposed to manifest functions of the media (q.v.).

Latent Learning. Knowledge of some kind that is not obvious or demonstrated in one's behavior.

Lateral Communication. Lateral communication refers to messages sent by equals to equals—manager to manager, worker to worker, faculty member to faculty member. Such messages may move within the same subdivision or department of the organization or across divisions. Lateral communication may refer to the communication that takes place between two history professors at Illinois State University as well as that which takes place between the psychologist at Ohio State and the communicologist at Kent State.

Lateral communication facilitates the sharing of insights, methods, and problems and thus enables the organization to avoid some problems and to more easily solve others. Lateral communication also facilitates worker satisfaction and builds morale. Good relationships and meaningful communication between workers are among the main sources of worker satisfaction. Lateral communication serves the purpose of coordinating the various activities of the organization and enables the various divisions to pool insights and expertise.

But, there are barriers. One obvious example is the specialized languages that different divisions within an organization may develop. Such languages are often mutually unintelligible. To communicate with the psychologist, for example, it is essential to speak the language of psychology—to know the meaning of such terms as *reinforcement schedules, egoism, catharsis, STM,* and *free association;* not everyone does. And as specialization increases in every field, it is becoming increasingly difficult for the behavioral psychologist to understand the clinical psychologist and even within clinical psychology for the Freudian to understand the Jungian.

Related to this problem is the tendency of workers in a specialized organization to view their area as the one crucial to the health and success of the company. This prevents us from seeing the value in the work of others and often prevents a meaningful exchange of ideas.

Another barrier is that effective lateral communication is a sharing, a pooling of insights and resources. Yet we live in a competitive society and work in competive organizations. If there is only one promotion available and that promotion is to be made on the basis of quality of work accomplished, it really does not benefit workers to share their best insights with those who may, because of these added insights, secure that one promotion.

Lateralization. The specialization of one hemisphere of the brain in dealing with different cognitive or behavioral abilities (speech is specialized in the left hemisphere).

Lateral Lisp. An articulatory defect in which the sibilant sounds (those made with hissing sounds such as [s] and [z]) are made incorrectly and in which there is an excessive escaping of air around the sides of the tongue.

Latitude of Acceptance. The range of attitudes that an individual would find acceptable. See also SOCIAL JUDGMENT-INVOLVEMENT THEORY.

Latitude of Noncommitment. The range of attitudes that an individual would neither reject nor accept; attitudes about which one has no strong feelings. See also SOCIAL JUDGMENT-INVOLVEMENT THEORY.

Latitude of Rejection. The range of attitudes that a person would find unacceptable. See also SOCIAL JUDGMENT-INVOLVEMENT THEORY.

Leader. Defined variously as (1) the group member who is the focus of the members' behaviors, the one to whom the group's messages are addressed, the one who is given the greatest attention by the members of the group; (2) the one who leads the group to some specific goal(s); (3) the one who occupies the titular position of leadership, for example, the president or chair; and (4) the one who performs the functions of leadership, the one who engages in leadership behaviors.

Leaderless Group. A group of people who interact for a variety of reasons (for example, problem solving or self-help) without any designated leader. The tasks normally served by an appointed or elected leader are generally shared by a number of members.

Leadership Style. The manner in which leadership is exerted. Generally three styles of leadership are distinguished: the laissez-faire leader (q.v.) who allows the group to do as it wants; the democratic leader (q.v.) who allows the group to make its own decisions but provides guidance and direction; and the authoritarian leader (q.v.) who makes the decisions for the group.

Leading Question. A query that encourages the listener to give a specific answer.

Leakage. Verbal or nonverbal behaviors that reveal the truth that a liar is attempting to conceal. See also SPEECH ERROR; DECEPTION CLUE.
[Paul Ekman, *Telling Lies: Clues to Deceit in the Marketplace, Politics, and Marriage* (New York: Norton, 1985).]

Learnability. The feature of language that refers to the fact that any normal human being is capable of learning any language as a first language. Learnability is dependent upon and follows from language being traditionally or culturally transmitted. This feature refers to the outer, surface features of language and does not deny an innate component in language acquisition.

Learned Helplessness. A condition of helplessness created in people through repeated exposure to negative stimuli over which they have no control and from which they cannot escape and as a result give up trying.
[M. E. P. Seligman and S. F. Maier, "Failure to Escape Traumatic Shock," *Journal of Experimental Psychology* 74 (1967):1–9.]

Learning. Relatively permanent cognitive or behavior change brought about by exposure and experience; the process of acquiring responses through practice and experience.

Least Effort, Principle of. A principle—originally formulated to account for language changes over time—that holds that we will seek to expend the least amount of effort possible to accomplish a task.
[George Kingsley Zipf, *The Psycho-Biology of Language: An Introduction to Dynamic Philology* (Boston: Houghton Mifflin, 1935).]

Least Interest, Principle of. In interpersonal relationships, the principle that holds that the person least interested in maintaining the relationship is the person who maintains the power and who controls the relationship. The person who can most easily endure the punishments and who is least interested in the rewards controlled by the other person is the person who controls the relationship. The more a person wants the rewards or fears the punishments controlled by the other person, the less power that person has in the relationship.

Least Preferred Coworker Test (LPC). A test of leadership effectiveness in which an individual rates his or her least preferred coworker on a variety of characteristics, for example, friendliness, productiveness, supportiveness. A person who rates the LPC most highly is judged the most effective leader and the one who derives considerable personal satisfaction from interpersonal relationships.
[F. E. Fiedler, *A Theory of Leadership Effectiveness* (New York: McGraw-Hill, 1967).]

Leave Taking. The process of removing oneself from an interaction.

Leave Taking Cues. Verbal and nonverbal hints that the individual desires to end the interaction.

Left Movers. Persons whose eye gestures move to the left when answering questions or solving problems and who therefore allegedly use their right brain more extensively. See also RIGHT MOVERS.

Legalese. The jargon of the legal profession.

Legibility. The ease with which handwriting can be read; in graphology (q.v.), legibility is taken as a sign of a willingness to communicate.

Leveling. A process of message distortion in serial communication (q.v.) where successive versions omit details and become shorter and easier to remember; a technique used in therapy that encourages the expression of aggression as a means of reducing tension and the possibility of physical aggression. See also SHARPENING; ASSIMILATION.

Level of Abstraction. The relative distance of a term or statement from the referent or perception; a low-order abstraction would be a description of the perception, whereas a high-order abstraction would consist of inferences about inferences about descriptions of a perception.

Lexeme. The semantically meaningful elements in a language; morphemes (q.v.) or words.

Lexical Access Process. The process by which one locates a term in one's mental dictionary.

Lexicographer. One who authors or compiles a dictionary.

Lexicography. The area of linguistics concerned with dictionaries.

Lexicology. The area of linguistics concerned with the meaning and derivation of words.

Lexicon. An inventory of the words of a language.

Lexicostatistics. See GLOTTOCHRONOLOGY.

Libel. A written statement that defames or causes some damage to an individual's reputation; the publication of statements that are false or harmful to a person's reputation; opposed to slander (q.v.) which is spoken defamation.

License. A linguistic device (phrase or sentence) that informs the listener that a conversational rule may appear to be broken but is actually being adhered to, or it is to be broken for a very special reason, for example, "I don't want to appear gross but, to use the director's own words, ..." Also called a "hedge." See also COOPERATIVE PRINCIPLE.
[S. S. Mura, "Licensing Violations: An Investigation of Legitimate Violations of Grice's

Conversational Maxims," in *Conversational Coherence: Studies in Form and Strategy,* Robert T. Craig and Karen Tracy, eds. (Beverly Hills, Calif.: Sage, 1983).]

Lie Detector. An instrument for determining whether one is telling the truth by measuring changes in galvanic skin responses, heart rate, and other bodily responses as indicators of stress, while a series of questions are being answered with the aim of drawing inferences concerning lying. Also referred to as a "polygraph."

Life Positions. One of the basic tenets of Transactional Analysis (q.v.) is that we live our lives largely according to "scripts" (q.v.). These scripts are very similar to dramatic scripts, complete with a list of characters and roles, stage directions, dialogue, and plot.

Our culture provides us with one kind of script. This cultural script provides us with guides to proper dress; rules for sexual conduct; roles for men and women; a value system pertaining to marriage, children, money, and education; the concepts of success and failure; and so on. Families provide another kind of script. Family scripts contain more specific instructions for each of the family members—the boys should go into politics, the girls should get involved in social work; this family will always have its own business; this family may not earn much money but will always have adequate insurance; the oldest son takes over the father's business; the oldest daughter gets married first, and so on.

From our early experiences, particularly from the messages received from our parents (both verbal and nonverbal), we develop a psychological script for ourselves and, for the most part, follow this throughout our lives. Individual scripts are generally "written" by the age of 3; they provide us with specific directions for functioning within the larger cultural script. Should we play the victim or the persecutor, the slave or the master, the clown or the intellectual?

Some children, for example, are told they will be successes. Nonverbally, they are given love and affection; verbally, they are reinforced for numerous actions. Other children have been told they will never succeed. Statements such as, "No matter what you do, you'll be a success" as well as "You'll never amount to anything" are extremely important in determining the script the child will assume in later life. Generally, people follow the scripts their parents have written for them. But such scripts can be broken—we do not *have* to follow the script written for us by our parents. One of the major purposes of Transactional Analysis is to break the negative and unproductive scripts, to substitute positive and productive scripts in their places, and to prevent destructive messages from being written into the script.

These scripts, which we all have, are the bases on which we develop what are called "life positions." In Transactional Analysis there are four basic life positions.

I'm Not O.K., You're O.K.

This person sees others as well-adjusted and effective (you're O.K.) but sees himself or herself as maladjusted and ineffective (I'm not O.K.). This is the first position we develop as very young children. This is the position of the child who sees himself or herself as helpless and dirty and sees the adult as all-powerful and all-knowing. This person feels helpless and powerless in comparison to others and withdraws from confrontations rather than competing. This life position leads one to live off others, to make others pay for their being O.K. (and for oneself's being not O.K.). Such people are frequently depressed; at times they isolate themselves, lamenting, "If only . . ." or "I should have been. . . ."

I'm Not O.K., You're Not O.K.

People in this category think badly of themselves (I'm not O.K.) as well as of other people (you're not O.K.). They have no real acceptance of either themselves or others. They give themselves no support (because they are not O.K.), and they accept no support from others (because others are not O.K.). These people have given up. To them, nothing seems worthwhile, and so they withdraw. Interpersonal communication is extremely difficult since they put down both themselves and others, and intrapersonal communication does not seem particularly satisfying either. Attempts to give such people help are generally met with refusals since the would-be helpers are seen as being not O.K.

Such people seem to have lost interest in themselves, in others, and in the world generally. Living seems a drag. In the extreme they are the suicides and homicides, the autistics and pathologicals.

I'm O.K., You're Not O.K.

Persons in this position view themselves as effective (I'm O.K.) but see others as ineffective (you're not O.K.); "I am good, you are bad." These people have little or no respect for others and easily and frequently find fault with both friends and enemies. They are supportive of themselves but do not accept support from others. They are independent and seem to derive some satisfaction from *intra*personal communication but reject *inter*personal interaction and involvement. Literally and figuratively they need space, elbow room; they resent being crowded by those "not O.K." Criminals are drawn with disproportional frequency from this class, as are the paranoids who feel persecuted and who blame others for their problems.

I'm O.K., You're O.K.

This is the adult, normal, healthy position. This, says Eric Berne in *What Do You Say After You Say Hello?,* is "the position of genuine heroes and princes, and heroines and princesses." These people approach and solve problems constructively. They have valid expectations about themselves and others and accept themselves and others as basically good, worthy, and significant human beings. These people feel free to develop and progress as individuals. They enter freely into meaningful relationships with other people and do not fear involvements. They feel neither inferior nor superior to others. Rather, they are worthy and others are worthy. This is the position of winners.

It is impossible to say how many people are in each class. Many pass through the "I'm not O.K., you're O.K." position; few arrive at the "I'm O.K., you're O.K." position—few people are winners in this sense. Very probably the vast majority of people are in the "I'm not O.K., you're O.K." and "I'm O.K., you're not O.K." positions. It should be clear, of course, that these are general classes and that human beings resist classification. Thus these four positions should be looked at as areas on a continuum, none of which have clear-cut boundaries and yet all of which are different.

See also TRANSACTIONAL ANALYSIS.

Likert Scale. An attitude scale, developed by Rensis Likert, in which subjects indicate their agreement or disagreement with specific attitude statements categorized on a three- or five-point scale.

Limerick. Humorous and usually bawdy verse of five lines, for example, from *The Harper Handbook to Literature:*

> The limerick's an art form complex,
> Whose contents run chiefly to sex;
>   It's famous for virgins
>   And masculine urgins
>   And vulgar erotic effects.

Limiting Effects Model of Mass Communication. A theory or set of assumptions about the power of the media to persuade. The basic notion is that the media's effects are limited and contribute toward persuasion (interacting with a wide variety of other forces, for example, interpersonal interactions) but are not the sole causes of persuasion.

[Joseph Klapper, *The Effects of Mass Communication* (New York: Free Press, 1960).]

Linear Models of Communication. A left-to-right model of the communication process; a model that describes communication in a linear fashion, originating with the source and ending with the receiver's response; a model of communication that fails to take into consideration the transactional (q.v.) nature of communication and especially the notion that the source and the receiver each serve both source and receiver functions.

Lingua Franca. Any language (natural or artificial) that is used by speakers of different languages to communicate; a language understood by persons speaking different and mutually unintelligible languages.

Lingo. Jargon; specialized vocabulary.

Linguistic Analysis. The scientific analysis of language in terms of its sound (phonology), meaning (semantics), and/or structural (syntax) systems.

Linguistic Determinism. A view of language holding that our language determines what we can and cannot see or think or imagine. Language, it presumes, forces us to have certain perceptions and prevents us from having others. See also LINGUISTIC RELATIVITY.

Linguistic Relativity. A theory, developed largely by Benjamin Lee Whorf (1897–1941), that proposes that the language we speak influences what we perceive, how we think, and how we behave. Since different languages catalogue the world differently, speakers of different languages will see the world differently. The theory focuses on differences in perception, thought, and behavior that result from differences in language.

[John B. Carroll, ed., *Language, Thought, and Reality: Selected Writings of Benjamin Lee Whorf* (New York: Wiley, 1956); Joshua Fishman, "A Systematization of the Whorfian Hypothesis," *Behavioral Science* 5 (1960):323–339.]

Linguistics. The study of language and languages; the study of language competence encompassing the system of rules that native speakers know but cannot necessarily verbalize, and which enable them to produce and understand an infinite number of sentences of the language.

Linguistic Universal. A characteristic of language that is shared by all languages of the world; usually used to refer to characteristics shared by all natural, human languages.

[Joseph H. Greenberg, ed., *Universals of Language* (Cambridge, Mass.: M.I.T. Press, 1963).]

Linus Blanket Relationship. One of four cohabitation patterns common among students and identified by C. A. Ridley and colleagues, a relationship in which one partner has an overwhelming need to be in a relationship with emotional security being the primary objective; opposed to emancipation (q.v.), convenience (q.v.), and testing (q.v.) relationships.

[C. A. Ridley, D. J. Peterman, and A. W. Avery, "Cohabitation: Does It Make for a Better Marriage?" *The Family Coordinator* 27 (April 1978):129–137).]

Lipreading. The process of comprehending speech largely through watching the way the lips of the speaker move. Lipreading also makes use of interpreting facial gestures and because of this it is often referred to as "speech reading."

Lisp. An articulatory defect in which the sibilant sounds (those made with hissing sounds such as [s] and [z]) are made incorrectly due to some improper placement of the tongue.

Listenability. The relative difficulty of an orally presented message. See also READABILITY.

Listening. An active process of receiving aural stimuli. Contrary to popular conception, listening is an active rather than a passive process. Listening does not just happen; we must make it happen. Listening takes energy and a commitment to engage in often difficult labor.

Listening involves receiving stimuli and is thus distinguished from hearing as a physiological process. The word *receiving* is used here to imply that stimuli are taken in by the listener and are in some way processed or utilized. For at least some amount of time, the signals received are retained by the listener.

Listening involves aural stimuli, that is, signals (sound waves) received by the ear. Listening therefore is not limited to verbal signals but encompasses all signals sent by means of fluctuations in air—noises as well as words, music as well as prose.

Listening, Principles of

In *How to Speak, How to Listen,* philosopher Mortimer J. Adler criticizes our educational system for ignoring the teaching of listening: "How utterly amazing is the general assumption that the ability to listen well is a natural gift for which no training is required. How extraordinary is the fact that no effort is made anywhere in the whole educational process to help individuals learn how to listen well—at least well enough to close the circuit and make speech effective as a means of communication." The following principles should help significantly to "close the circuit." Listening comprehension will be facilitated if you listen actively, listen for total meaning, listen with empathy, listen with an open mind, and listen critically.

Listen Actively

The first step in improving listening comprehension is the recognition that it is not a passive activity; it is not a process that will happen if you simply do nothing to stop it. You may hear without effort but you cannot listen without effort.

Listening is a difficult process; in many ways it is more demanding than speaking. In speaking you are in control of the situation; you can talk about what you like in the way you like. In listening, however, you are forced to follow the pace, the content, and the language of the speaker.

Perhaps the best preparation for active listening is to act like an active listener. Recall, for example, how your body almost automatically reacts to important news. Almost immediately you assume an upright posture, cock your head to the speaker, and remain relatively still and quiet. You do this almost reflexively because this is how you listen most effectively.

Listen for Total Meaning

When listening to another individual listen for total meaning. However, the total meaning is not only in the words used. The meaning is also in the nonverbal behavior of the speaker. Sweating hands and shaking knees communicate just as surely as do words and phrases.

Along with the verbal and nonverbal behaviors, the meaning of any speech lies also in what is omitted. The speaker who talks about racism solely in the abstract, for example, and who never once mentions a specific group is communicating something quite different from the speaker who talks in specifics.

Listen with Empathy

It is relatively easy to learn to listen for understanding or for comprehension. But this is only a part of the communication encounter. You also need to *feel* what the speaker feels—to empathize with the speaker. To empathize with others is to feel what they feel, to see the world as they see it, to walk in their shoes. Only when you achieve this will you be able to fully understand another's meaning.

Listen with an Open Mind

Listening with an open mind is difficult. It is not easy to listen to arguments against some cherished belief. It is not easy to listen to statements condemning what you so fervently believe. It is not easy to listen to criticisms of what you think is just great.

It is difficult for most people to continue listening fairly after some signal has gone up in the form of an out-of-place expression or a hostile remark. Listening often stops when such a remark is made. Admittedly, to continue listening with an open mind is difficult; yet, it is when hostile feelings first develop that it is particularly important that listening continues.

Listen Critically

Although you should listen with an open mind and with empathy, you also should listen critically. You need to listen fairly but critically if meaningful communication is to take place.

See also ACTIVE LISTENING.

Listening Tendencies To Avoid

Your listening effectiveness should improve if you do not prejudge the speech or speaker, do not rehearse your responses, do not filter out unpleasant messages, and do not focus attention on style and delivery.

Don't Prejudge the Speech or Speaker

Whether in a lecture auditorium or in a small group of people there is a strong tendency to prejudge the conversation of others as uninteresting or irrelevant to our own needs or to the task at hand.

By prejudging any message as uninteresting, you are in effect lifting the burden of listening from your own shoulders. If you have already determined that what will be said will be uninteresting, for example, there is no reason to listen. So you may just tune out the speaker and let your mind recapture last Saturday night.

Don't Rehearse Your Responses

For the most part we are, as Wendell Johnson put it, our own most enchanted listeners. No one speaks as well or on such interesting topics as we do. If we could listen just to ourselves, listening would be no problem.

It often happens that a speaker may say something with which you disagree; for the remainder of that speaker's time you may rehearse your response or rebuttal or question. You then imagine his or her reply to your response and then your response to his or her response and so on and on. Meanwhile, you have missed whatever else the speaker had to say—perhaps even the part that would make your question unnecessary or irrelevant or which might raise other and more significant questions.

Don't Filter Out Unpleasant Messages

Many of the messages we confront will need careful consideration and in-depth scrutiny. Listening will be difficult, but the alternative—to miss out on what is said—seems even less pleasant than stretching and straining our minds.

Perhaps more serious than filtering out difficult messages is filtering out unpleasant ones. None of us want to be told that something we believe in is untrue, that people we care for are unpleasant, or that ideals we hold are self-destructive. And yet, these are the very messages we need to listen to with great care. These are the very messages that will lead us to examine and reexamine our implicit and unconscious assumptions. If we filter out this kind of information we will be left with a host of unstated and unexamined assumptions and premises that will influence us without our influencing them. That prospect is not very pleasant.

Don't Focus Attention on Style or Delivery

Focusing on style and delivery diverts time and energy away from the message itself. This is not to say that such behaviors are not important, but only that you can fall into the trap of devoting too much attention to the way the message is packaged and not enough to the message itself.

[Lyman K. Steil, Larry L. Barker, and Kittie W. Watson, *Effective Listening: Key to Your Success* (Reading, Mass.: Addison-Wesley, 1983); Andrew D. Wolvin and Carolyn Gwynn Coakley, *Listening* (Dubuque, Iowa: Brown, 1982).]

Listening Apprehension. Apprehension (q.v.) or fear concerning listening.

[Michael J. Beatty, Ralph R. Behnke, and Linda S. Henderson, "An Empirical Validation of the Receiver Apprehension Test as a Measure of Trait Listening Anxiety," *Western Journal of Speech Communication* 44 (Spring 1980):132–136.]

List Processing. An advanced computer language used especially for list manipulation and analysis.

Litotes. A figure of speech in which emphasis is achieved through understatement and a denial of its opposite, for example, "King Kong was no small monkey."

Little Professor. See CHILD EGO STATE.

Livre à Clef. See ROMAN À CLEF.

Lloyd Morgan's Canon. Named after psychologist Lloyd Morgan who proposed this specific application of Occam's Razor (q.v.), the principle holding that animal behavior should be accounted for with the simplest possible mechanisms—that we should attribute to animals the least abilities needed to account for the observed behaviors.

Loan Word. A word from one language incorporated into the vocabulary of another language.

Localism. Word or phrase whose meaning is restricted to a particular geographical area.

Localization. The particular areas of the brain that govern specific cognitive and behavioral functions; the process of locating the source or origin of a message or stimulus.

Loci. Places; the places where arguments are to be found, for example, the arguments for establishing one's credibility are to be found in the character, competence, and reputation of the speaker.

Locutionary Act. That part of a speech act (q.v.) that communicates the speaker's meaning.

Locutionary Force. The meaning that a sentence communicates.

Logic. The science of reasoning; the study of the principles governing the analysis of inference making.

Logical Implication. The natural or necessary consequence or implication of a statement, for example, the logical implication of the statement "He has a fever of 104°" is that he is ill; opposed to pragmatic implication (q.v.).

Logical Positivism. A school of philosophy that attempted to apply the concepts and theories of logic and mathematics to empiricism. This philosophy emphasized the application of factual knowledge and the language of science to philosophical concepts and problems.

Logical Proof. See LOGOS.

Loglan. An artificial logical language designed to examine the theory of linguistic relativity (q.v.).
[James Cooke Brown, "Loglan," *Scientific American* 206 (June 1960):53–63.]

Log Off. To deactivate a computer; to end one's interaction with the computer system.

Logogram (Logograph). Written symbol that represents one or more words. Commonly referred to as a "logo."

Logography. Writing system employing logograms (q.v.).

Logology. The study of words.

Logomachy. A dispute over words and their meanings; the game of making up words.

Log On. To begin computer operations by putting the computer into active operation.

Logophobia. Fear of words.

Logorrhea. Pathologically uncontrollable and repetitive speech.

Logos. The logical dimension of invention (q.v.); that area of rhetoric (q.v.) concerned with the finding of arguments necessary to prove the validity of a proposition.

Loneliness. A state of dissatisfaction with one's interpersonal relationships, particularly with one's level of involvement in interpersonal relationships.
[L. Anne Peplau and Daniel Perlman, eds., *Loneliness: A Sourcebook of Current Theory, Research, and Therapy* (New York: Wiley-Interscience, 1982); Carin Rubenstein and Philip Shaver, *In Search of Intimacy* (New York: Delacorte Press, 1982).]

Long-Term Memory. Relatively permanent memory. See also SHORT-TERM MEMORY.

Looking-Glass Self. That part or view of the self that is formed on the basis of the judgments and reactions of other people. As developed by Charles Cooley, the three-part process through which one develops a self-image: (1) an idea of how one appears to others; (2) an idea of others' judgments of one's appearance;

and (3) the feelings one has about oneself. More generally, used to refer to that part of an individual's self-image that develops as a result of and is based on the reactions and evaluations of others.

[Charles H. Cooley, *Human Nature and the Social Order* (New York: Scribners, 1902).]

Loose Sentence. A sentence that continues beyond the point at which it is grammatically complete; a sentence in which the main clause is presented first with the dependent clauses following; opposed to periodic sentence (q.v.).

Loudness. The perception of the relative intensity or volume of sound.

Love. Of all the types of interpersonal relationships, none seems as important as love. "We are all born for love," noted Disraeli, "It is the principle of existence and its only end." Cyril Bibby, in his essay "The Art of Loving," suggests that *loving* may be a better term to use than *love* and in so doing gets at some of the important qualities of this interpersonal relationship. So long as love is treated as a thing, to be built up mechanically by the addition of this piece of social relationship to that piece of amatory technique, it can never really flourish. To make the most of the human capacity for loving, it is necessary to treat it as an activity of the whole person, in which body and mind and emotions are all actively involved. This is not to deny the importance of social factors or of sexual techniques but merely to put them in their proper place as aids to an essentially outgiving activity.

The Natures of Love

Loving and *love* are not easy terms to define. On the one hand, we have poets who extol love's virtues: "Come live with me and be my love, And we will all the pleasures prove," wrote Christopher Marlowe, and who could resist the promise of such a reward? On the other hand, there are cynics, spoken for eloquently by Ambrose Bierce in *The Devil's Dictionary.* Love, says Bierce, is "a temporary insanity curable by marriage or by removal of the patient from the influences under which he incurred the disorder. This disease, like caries and many other ailments, is prevalent only among civilized races living under artificial conditions; barbarous nations breathing pure air and eating simple food enjoy immunity from its ravages."

Perhaps it's the variety of ways in which people may love that makes definition difficult. In *How Do You Feel?* four different approaches to loving are presented. Among the words the writers use in describing the feelings and the behaviors of loving are: *warmth, contentment, excitement, oneness, limitless, infinite, boundless, totally encompassing, lucky, faith, trust, dynamic, effort, commitment, tender, multicolored, active, healthy, energetic, courageous, forward-looking, patient, robust, openness, honesty, understanding,* and *fun.* Throughout these words there is a clear emphasis on activity rather than passivity. Loving is an active process. Larry Carlin, in one of the essays in *How Do You Feel?,* puts it this way: "When I feel loving it seems like I can't keep what's inside inside; I have to reach out, touch, embrace, hold, kiss."

Five Dimensions of Love

Pitirim Sorokin further explains love by identifying five major dimensions or variables.

1. *Intensity.* Loving feelings or behavior can vary in intensity from nothing to slight to some undefined extreme. Love can vary in intensity from giving a dime to a beggar to sacrificing one's life for one's loved ones.

2. *Extensity.* Love can vary in terms of the degree to which it extends from outside the individual and may be solely a love of oneself (low extensity) or may range to the love of all humankind (high extensity).
3. *Duration.* Like any emotion, loving can vary in duration from seconds to a lifetime.
4. *Purity.* By "purity" Sorokin means the degree to which the love is motivated by considerations for the self or by considerations for the other person. "Impure" love, in this system, refers to love motivated by selfish considerations without concern for the other person. Pure love is the love of an individual for the sake of the beloved.
5. *Adequacy.* Love may vary from wise to blind. In inadequate or blind love there is a huge difference between the purposes or motives in loving and the consequences. An example of inadequate or blind love might be the excessive love a father and a mother have for their child which leads the child to become totally dependent upon them. Adequate or wise love, on the other hand, has consequences that are positive for the beloved.

Types of Love

In addition to describing love in terms of its significant dimensions or variables, we may also describe love in terms of a kind or type. In *The Colors of Love,* John Alan Lee distinguishes a number of types or kinds of love: ludus, storge, mania, pragma, eros, and agape as well as various combinations of these. A brief explanation of these various types should help to clarify further the nature of love.

Ludus

Ludus love is experienced as a game. The ludic lover sees love as fun, a game to be played. The better he or she can play the game, the more the love is enjoyed. To the ludic lover, love is not to be taken too seriously; emotions are to be held in check lest they get out of hand and make trouble; passions never rise to the point where they get out of control. Ludic love is a self-controlled love—a love that the lover carefully manages and controls rather than allowing it to control him or her. This lover is consciously aware of the need to remain in control and uses this awareness to guide his or her own behaviors.

The ludic lover retains a partner only so long as he or she is interesting and amusing. When the partner is no longer interesting enough, it is time to change. And ludic lovers do change partners frequently. Perhaps because love is a game, sexual fidelity is not something that is of major importance in a ludic love relationship. The ludic lover expects his or her partner to have had (and probably to have in the future) other partners and does not appear to get upset if occasional partners are experienced during their relationship.

Storge

Like ludus, *storge* lacks passion and intensity. But whereas the ludic lover is aware of passion but keeps it under control, the storge lover is unaware of any intensity of feeling. The storgic lover does not set out to find a lover but rather seems to establish a storge relationship with someone who he or she knows and shares similar interests and activities. Storgic love develops over a period of time rather than in one mad burst of passion. Sex in storgic relationships comes late, and when it comes it assumes no great importance. One advantage of this is that storgic lovers are not plagued by sexual difficulties as are so many other types of lovers.

Storgic lovers rarely say "I love you" or even remember what many would consider romantic milestones such as the first date, the first weekend alone, the first time we said "I love you," and so on. Storgic love is a gradual process of unfolding one's thoughts and one's feelings; the changes seem to come so slowly and so gradually that it is often difficult to define exactly where the relationship is at any point in time. Storgic love is sometimes difficult to separate from friendship; it is often characterized by the same qualities that characterize friendship: mutual caring, compassion, respect, and concern for the other person.

Not only is storgic love slow in developing and slow burning, it is also slow in dissolving. Storgic lovers can endure long periods of time away from each other without feeling that there is any problem with the relationship. Similarly, they may endure long periods of relative inactivity or lack of excitement without feeling there is any relationship problem.

Mania

The quality of *mania* that separates it from all other loves is its extremes of both highs and lows, of ups and downs. The manic lover loves intensely and at the same time intensely worries and fears the loss of the love. And this intense fear prevents the manic lover in many cases from deriving as much pleasure as might be derived from the relationship. At the slightest provocation, for example, the manic lover experiences extreme jealousy. Manic love is obsessive; the manic lover has to possess the lover completely—in all ways, at all times. And in return the manic lover wishes to be possessed, to be loved intensely. It seems almost as if the manic lover is driven to these extremes by some outside force or perhaps by some inner obsession that cannot be controlled.

Manic lovers are often unhappy with life and so devote a great deal of energy to love. The manic lover's poor self-image seems only capable of being improved by being loved; self-worth seems to come only from being loved rather than from any sense of inner satisfaction. Because love is so important, danger signs in a relationship are often ignored; the manic lover really believes that if there is love, nothing else matters.

Pragma

The *pragma* lover is the practical lover who seeks a relationship that will work. Pragma lovers seek compatibility and a relationship in which their important needs and desires will be satisfied. Computer matching services seem based largely on pragmatic love. The computer matches persons on the basis of similar interests, attitudes, personality characteristics, religion, politics, hobbies, and a host of other likes and dislikes. The assumption here is that persons who are similar will be more apt to establish relationships than will persons who are different. This assumption is generally supported by research.

In its extreme, pragma love may be seen in the person who writes down the qualities wanted in a mate and actively goes about seeking someone to match these stated qualities. As might be expected, the pragma lover is concerned with the social qualifications of a potential mate even more so than with personal qualities; family and background are extremely important to the pragma lover who does not rely on feelings as much as on logic. The pragma lover wants to marry and settle down and get on with the business of living. In pragma, a love relationship is a means to the achievement of other ends, unlike the manic lover to whom love is the end and all else are means to its attainment. The pragma lover views love as a necessity—or certainly as a useful relationship—that makes the rest of life easier. And so the pragma lover asks such questions of a potential mate as "Will this person earn a good living?," "Can this person cook?," and "Will this person help me advance in my career?"

Not surprisingly, relationships rarely deteriorate among pragma lovers. This is true in part because pragma lovers have chosen their mates carefully and have emphasized similarities. Perhaps they have intuitively discovered what experimental research has confirmed, namely that relationships between similar people are much less likely to break up than are relationships among those who are very different. Another reason for the less frequent breakups seems to be that their romantic expectations are realistic. They seem willing to settle for less and, consequently, are seldom disappointed.

Eros
One version of the Narcissus legend is that Narcissus, a beautiful Greek boy, fell in love with his own reflection in the water. So absorbed was he with his own beauty that he ignored the love of the beautiful nymph, Echo. One day, while admiring his own reflection and attempting to get closer and closer to it, he fell into the water and drowned. Another way of looking at this legend, as John Lee suggests, is to look at Narcissus as the classic erotic lover. In this view Narcissus was punished for his total absorption with a beauty and perfection that he could never possess. His own reflection was more beautiful than the fountain nymph Echo, or than anyone else he could possibly love. The erotic lover focuses on beauty and physical attractiveness, sometimes to the exclusion of qualities we might consider more important and more enduring. And like Narcissus, the erotic lover often has an ideal image of beauty that is unattainable in reality. Consequently, the erotic lover often feels unfulfilled. Erotic lovers are particularly sensitive to physical imperfections in their beloveds—a nose that is too long, a complexion that is blemished, a figure that is a bit too full, and so on—all cause difficulties for the erotic lover, which is one reason why the erotic lover wants to experience the entire person as quickly in the relationship as possible.

Eros is an ego-centered love, a love that is given to someone because that person will return the love. It is in this sense a utilitarian, rational love because it is a calculated love with an anticipated return. Eros is essentially hedonistic; it is a sensual love of the physical qualities of an individual. In Eros physical attraction is paramount. Eros is a discriminating type of love; it is selective in its love objects. It is directed at someone because he or she is valuable and can be expected to return the love in kind.

Agape
Agape is a compassionate love; it is an egoless, self-giving love. Agape is nonrational and nondiscriminative. Agape creates value and virtue by its love rather than bestowing love only on that which is valuable and virtuous. The agapic lover loves even those he or she does not have any close ties with. This lover loves the stranger on the road, and the fact that they will probably never meet again has nothing to do with it. Jesus, Buddha, Gandhi, and similar people practiced and preached agape, an unqualified love.

Agape is a spiritual love. One cannot love altruistically if one loves with the thought that one will be rewarded in some way for this love or compassion. Agapic love is offered with no concern for any kind of personal reward or gain. The agapic lover loves without even expecting that the love will be returned or reciprocated. The agapic lover gives to the other person the kind of love the person needs even though there may be great difficulties or personal hardships involved.

In one sense agape is more of a philosophical kind of love than a love that most of us have the strength to achieve. In fact, John Lee notes that "unfortunately, I have yet to interview any respondent involved in even a relatively short-term affiliative love relationship which I could classify without qualification as an example of agape. I *have* encountered brief agapic episodes in continuing love relationships."

Sex Differences in Loving

In our culture, the differences between men and women in love are considered great. In poetry, in novels, and in the mass media women and men are depicted as acting very differently when falling in love, in being in love, and in ending a love relationship. Women are seen as totally absorbed with love whereas men are seen as relegating love to one part of their lives. Or, as Lord Byron put it in *Don Juan,* "Man's love is of man's life a thing apart,/'Tis woman's whole existence." Women are portrayed as being emotional whereas men are portrayed as being logical. Women are supposed to love intensely while men are supposed to love with some detachment. Noted the military leader Giorgio Basta: "Man loves little and often, woman much and rarely." While the folklore on sex differences is extensive, the research is meager.

Degree of Love

In their responses to a questionnaire designed to investigate love, social psychologist Zick Rubin found that men and women were quite similar; men and women seem to experience love to a similar degree. Women do, however, indicate greater love for their same-sex friends than do men. This may reflect a real difference between the sexes or it may be a function of the greater social restrictions under which men operate. Men are not supposed to admit their love for another man, lest they be thought homosexual or somehow different from their fellows. Women are permitted a greater freedom to communicate their love for other women.

Romantic Experiences and Attitudes

In an attempt to investigate the number of romantic experiences and the ages at which these occur, sociologist William Kephart surveyed over 1000 college students from 18 to 24 years of age. The women indicated that they had been infatuated more times than the men. The median times infatuated for women was 5.6 and for men was 4.5. For love relationships, there is greater similarity. The median number of times in love for these same women was 1.3 and for the men was 1.2. As expected, women had their first romantic experiences earlier than men. The median age of first infatuation for women was 13 and for men was 13.6; median age for first time in love for women was 17.1 and for men was 17.6.

In this same study men, contrary to popular myth, were found to place more emphasis on romance than women. For example, the college students were asked the following question: "If a boy (girl) had all the other qualities you desired, would you marry this person if you were not in love with him (her)?" Approximately two-thirds of the men responded "no," which seems to indicate that a high percentage were concerned with "love" and "romance." However, less than one-third of the women responded "no." Further, when sociologist D. H. Knox surveyed men and women concerning their views on love—whether it is basically realistic or basically romantic—it was found that married women had a more realistic (less romantic) conception of love than did married men. It is also interesting to note that married persons had a more realistic view of love than did unmarrieds.

Romantic Breakups

Popular myth would have us believe that when love affairs break up, the breakups are the result of the man developing some outside affair. But the research does not seem to support this. When surveyed on the reasons for breaking up, only 15 percent of the men indicated that it was because of their interest in another partner, but 32 percent of the women noted this as a reason for the breakup. And these findings are consistent with the perceptions of the partners regarding the causes of the breakups as well: 30 percent of the men but only 15 percent of the women noted that their partner's interest in another person was the reason for the breakup. The most popular reason reported was a mutual loss of interest: 47 percent of the men and 38 percent of the women noted this as a reason for breaking up.

In their reactions to broken romantic affairs there are both similarities and differences between women and men. For example, both women and men tended to remember only the pleasant things and to revisit places with past remembrances about equally. On the other hand, men engaged in more dreaming about the lost partner and in more daydreaming generally as a reaction to the breakup.

What will happen in the next decades with regard to sex differences in loving is hard to gauge. On the one hand, as the sexes become more equal socially and economically, the differences in love and loving may be lessened considerably, maybe even eliminated. On the other hand, as the socioeconomic differences are eliminated, the sexual-romantic-loving differences may be accentuated and may well take on added significance and relevance.

Loving and Communication

Herbert A. Otto, one of the leaders in the human potential movement, notes in *Love Today* the paradoxical conclusions made about communication in love. Communication in love, says Otto, is characterized by two features: "(1) confusion and lack of clarity; and (2) increased clarity and comprehension." While some lovers note the extreme difficulty in understanding what the other person means, many others note the exceptional ability they now seem to possess in understanding the other person.

Effectiveness Characteristics and Love

Empathic communication is naturally increased in any love relationship since, on the basis of our more open communication, we can understand how the other feels and want to feel what he or she feels. This increased empathy enables us to know much more accurately what messages are appropriate and when. We know what arouses our loved one into anger and into ecstasy. Consequently, we can easily offend, not only because we are important to our loved one and hence have great power to hurt but also because we know the person's soft spots, the forbidden areas that can only be discussed at great risk. Fortunately, we also know how to soothe and calm our loved one. In short, when people become lovers and develop a strong empathic ability, they learn what buttons to push with what effect.

In many ways, to love someone is to support him or her. We naturally support those we love, in part because we want them to be secure and unafraid. Our supportiveness helps them and theirs helps us. Love is an emotion that is not only good to receive but good to give as well; it makes us feel pleased to love and, consequently, the positiveness we feel for ourselves, for our beloved, and for the relationship itself is increased. Normally, we love persons whom we respect and regard as good; we like them as well as love them. If we love someone, we want to become a part of him or her. This is perhaps the best way to encourage the feeling of equality.

But loving implies the taking of risks. We run the risk of not having our love returned or being rejected outright. The alternative we often take is to conceal our love or perhaps never even admit it to ourselves. Communicating our love also involves the risk of self-disclosure. In any love relationship mutual self-disclosure is important. As Otto says, "This helps to establish a relationship characterized by optimal personality growth for both lovers."

Much as loving relationships are helped by self-disclosure, love also encourages openness and honesty. We seem to have a need to express ourselves, to let other people know who we "really" are. And yet perhaps because of the fear of rejection, we conceal our "true selves." In a love relationship we have someone to whom we can reveal ourselves without fear of being rejected or thought foolish. Not every relationship is quite so simple, of course. In many instances it is with the people we love that we are most on guard. If, for example, we initially pretended to be strong, we might conceal weakness for fear that it was our strength that made us attractive. It is often with people we love that we hide aspects of ourselves that we might readily reveal to strangers if we were sure of never meeting them again.

Verbal Indicators of Love

In addition to these general communication characteristics, we may also note a number of more specific ways in which we communicate when in love. Verbally, there is an exaggeration of the virtues and a minimization of the faults of the one we love. We share emotions and experiences and speak tenderly (using labels such as "honey," "baby," and "sweetheart") and with an extra degree of kindness to each other; "please," "thank you," and similar terms abound.

Lovers also develop private codes; they speak in a way that only each other can understand, a phenomenon that Truman Capote referred to when he defined *love* as never having to finish your sentences. Likewise, lovers have private names for each other, pet names that are sometimes sweet and sometimes silly but always appropriate to the lovers exclusively. When outsiders use these terms—as sometimes they do—they seem inappropriate at best and at times an unwarranted invasion of privacy.

Nonverbal Indicators of Love

We have all seen movies of the star struck lovers staring into each other's eyes. This prolonged and focused eye contact is perhaps the clearest nonverbal indicator of love. Lovers lean toward each other in an attempt, it would seem, to keep physical distance at a minimum and any possible intruders outside the privacy of the relationship. The physical closeness echoes the emotional closeness. In deteriorating relationships, when emotional closeness fades, so does physical closeness—the closeness of bodies as well as the closeness that is achieved psychologically by direct and prolonged eye contact.

Lovers not only become more conscious of their loved one but also of their physical selves. There seems a certain muscle tone that is heightened when people are in love, a tendency to engage in preening gestures, especially immediately prior to meeting the loved one, and an arrangement of the body (insofar as that is possible) into its most attractive position—stomach pulled in, shoulders square, legs arranged in masculine or feminine positions. And perhaps the most obvious nonverbal behavior of all is the elimination of the socially taboo adaptors (at least in the presence of the loved one): scratching one's head, picking one's teeth, or cleaning one's ears seem avoided. Interestingly enough, these adaptors often (though foolishly, I think) return after the lovers have achieved a permanent relationship.

[Pitirim A. Sorokin, "Altruistic Love," and Cyril Bibby, "The Art of Love," in *The Encyclopedia of Sexual Behavior,* Albert Ellis and Albert Abarbanel, eds. (New York: Hawthorn Books, 1967); John Wood, ed., *How Do You Feel?* (Englewood Cliffs, N.J.: Prentice-Hall, 1974); John Alan Lee, *The Colors of Love* (New York: Bantam Books, 1977); Ellen Berscheid and Elaine Walster, "A Little Bit about Love," in *Foundations of Interpersonal Attraction,* T. L. Huston, ed. (New York: Academic Press, 1974); Herbert A. Otto, "Communication in Love," in *Love Today: A New Exploration,* Herbert A. Otto, ed., (New York: Delta Books, 1972); Elaine Walster and G. William Walster, *A New Look at Love* (Reading, Mass.: Addison-Wesley, 1978); Glenn Wilson and David Nias, *The Mystery of Love* (New York: Quadrangle/The New York Times Book Co., 1976).]

Lying. According to the *Random House Dictionary,* a *lie* is "a false statement made with deliberate intent to deceive; a falsehood; something intended or serving to convey a false impression." As these definitions make clear, lying may be both overt and covert. Although usually done by overt statements, lying may also be committed by omission. When we omit something relevant to the issue at hand which leads others to draw incorrect inferences, we have lied just as surely as if we had made a false statement.

Similarly, although most lies are verbal, some are nonverbal and most seem to involve at least some nonverbal elements. The innocent facial expression—despite the commission of some punishable act—and the knowing nod instead of the honest expression of ignorance are common enough examples of nonverbal lying. Lies may range from the "white" lie where one "stretches the truth" to the big lie where one formulates falsehoods that are so enormous everyone comes to believe they are true.

Lying occurs in all communication contexts. In interpersonal contexts people lie about their virtues and vices, generally maximizing the former and minimizing the latter, their marital status, their sexual prowess, their financial resources, and their emotional state. In group situations people lie to colleagues and co-workers about their contribution to the organization, their dedication to the job, and their feelings concerning relevant issues and third parties. In public communication situations, people lie about their facts, figures, and the claims drawn from them, their plans to help the voters, and their dedication to openness and honesty. In mass communication, people lie about the benefits to be derived from a new frozen food or a new diet plan, about the help to be derived from the new magazine article, horoscope, or advice columnist. Even on the intrapersonal level, people frequently lie to themselves—telling themselves that what they have done is justified, that this "small" unethical act they now engage in will be rectified later, and that they couldn't possibly give up smoking, stick to a diet, or exercise—so why bother trying to start.

There are probably as many reasons for lying as there are lies; each situation is different and each situation seems to be governed by a different reason or set of reasons. But if we boiled it down, we would probably find that people lie for two main reasons: (1) to gain some reward or (2) to avoid some punishment. Carl

Camden, Michael Motley, and Ann Wilson, in their study of white lies in inter-personal communication, have identified four major reward categories that seem to motivate lying behavior:

Basic needs: Lies told to gain or to retain objects that fulfill basic needs—for example, money or various material possessions.

Affiliation: Lies told to increase desired affiliations or to decrease undesired affiliations—for example, lies told to prolong desirable social interactions and to avoid interpersonal conflicts or to avoid granting some request and to avoid prolonged interaction. Also included here are lies told to gain or maintain conversational control during interpersonal interaction—for example, lies told to avoid certain self-disclosures or to manipulate the conversation in a desired direction.

Self-esteem: Lies told to protect or increase the self-esteem of oneself, the person one is interacting with, or some third party—for example, lies told to increase one's perceived competence or taste or social desirability.

Self-gratification: Lies told to achieve some personal satisfaction—for exam-ple, lies told for the sake of humor or to exaggerate for some desired effect.

Very likely an in-depth analysis of the avoidance of punishment would yield categories similar to those identified for gaining rewards. That is, we probably lie *to avoid* such punishments as having our basic needs taken away (losing money, for example), decreasing desired affiliations and increasing undesirable affiliations, decreasing self-esteem, and losing or decreasing personal satisfac-tion.

Generally, people lie in order to achieve some reward or avoid some punish-ment for themselves, although some lies are motivated by a desire to benefit the person with whom one is interacting or some third party. From an analysis of 322 lies, Camden, Motley, and Wilson found that 75.8 percent benefited the liar, 21.7 percent benefited the other interactant, and 2.5 percent benefited some third party.

Generally, we know when we are lying and when we are not lying. No one has to tell us. And yet there are many grey areas where it is not clear when a statement is a lie and when it is not. Sometimes it is difficult to tell, for example, when someone is asking for an honest opinion or merely asking for a compliment. "What do you think of my new apartment?" may be designed to get a needed pat on the back and not an honest opinion of the decoration. Sometimes there is a tacit agreement between people to avoid telling the truth about certain issues. A couple, for example, may agree that extrarelational affairs are not to be disclosed and that the acceptable procedure is to make up some kind of innocent excuse—working late at the office and its variants—to cover. Some-times people have made it known that they do not want to be told if they are terminally ill. In each of these instances, the context and the intent of the mes-sage would define whether something is or is not a lie. Thus, if in response to the question about the apartment, one said "It's really beautiful" because of the belief that the question was asking for a compliment, then I think there was no lie. Similarly, if the individuals have made it known that they do not want to deal with the truth about certain issues, then it seems it is not a lie to conform to this expectation or wish.

Communication messages are sent and received as packages—lies are no exception. It is often difficult to lie nonverbally with any degree of conviction. Often our lies are betrayed nonverbally, as nonverbal researchers Paul Ekman and Wallace Friesen have demonstrated. It is far easier to lie with our mouths than with our faces and our bodies. And when the contradiction is observed, it is the nonverbal that is generally believed. The end result is that we have lied, but it has been to no avail. Our reputation may suffer without our having achieved the reward or avoided the punishment. Perhaps the main disadvantage of lying is that it influences who we are and what we think of ourselves. When we have the internalized belief that lying is wrong and yet lie ourselves, we are creating psychological imbalance and intrapersonal conflict, neither of which is particularly healthy. We seem to be designed to function as a consistent whole with our thinking and our behavior echoing each other. When we believe one thing and do something else, we begin to develop various internal conflicts.

As a result of lying, one has to expend a considerable amount of energy to maintain the lie. We realize, like F. M. Knowles, who wrote in his *A Cheerful Year Book:* "There is nothing so pathetic as a forgetful liar." The more people we lie to, and the more complex the lie, the more energy we have to devote to keeping things straight in order to preserve that lie. This leaves us with that much less energy to use for other matters. This is similar to the case of self-disclosure; the more secrets we keep, the more energy has to be exerted to maintain those secrets.

Perhaps the most obvious disadvantage is that there will be social disapproval when the lie is discovered. Although the vast majority of people lie—at some times and with some issues—the vast majority dislike lying and condemn it, consequently, when our lie is discovered, we incur social disapproval. It may range from mild disapproval to total ostracism from the group or organization. It is interesting to note in this connection that Mark Comadena found that intimates are better lie detectors than are friends; further, women seem to be somewhat better at detecting lies than men. The general upshot of all this is that the liar's communication effectiveness will have been drastically impaired. "The principal difference between a cat and a lie," observed Mark Twain, "is that a cat has only nine lives." When an individual is known to have lied or to be a liar, that person is seldom believed, even when telling the truth—because, after all, even liars tell the truth most of the time. We not only disbelieve the information this individual might wish to communicate, we give no persuasive force to his or her arguments, frequently discounting them as lies. Even more important, it seems, is that one's relational messages and relational interactions generally become less meaningful. The most important messages an individual can communicate—the "I love you," "I enjoy being with you" messages—are discounted since we can no longer ascertain whether or not they are true.

[Sissela Bok, *Lying: Moral Choice in Public and Private Life* (New York: Pantheon Books, 1978); Paul Ekman, *Telling Lies: Clues to Deceit in the Marketplace, Politics, and Marriage* (New York: Norton, 1985).]

M. A measure of meaningfulness; the average number of word associations produced by a group of persons in a specified amount of time—the more word associations, the higher the M value and the greater the meaningfulness.

[C. E. Noble, "An Analysis of Meaning," *Psychological Review* 59 (1952):421–430.]

McCarthyism. The approach and tactics of the late Senator Joseph McCarthy (1908–1957) of Wisconsin of finding and weeding out people who were thought to be communists or communist sympathizers. Such an accusation from McCarthy during the 1950s was sufficient to get the person fired and put on a blacklist; numerous people in the communications field (film, television, radio) were thus ruined by these accusations.

Machiavellianism. Of all the manipulators throughout history the name of Niccolo Machiavelli (1469–1527) stands out. In *The Prince,* Machiavelli provided an indepth analysis of political power, how it is secured and how it is maintained. Because of the cynicism and the detachment with which he wrote *The Prince,* "Machiavelli" has come to mean control without concern.

In communication *Machiavellianism* refers to the techniques or tactics by which control is exerted by one person over another. A great deal of research has been directed at analyzing Machiavellianism in people.

Much of this research has utilized a test in which subjects are asked to respond to various items on a scale ranging from much agreement, to neutral, to much disagreement. Items include, for example, "There is no excuse for lying," "The best way to handle people is to tell them what they want to hear," and "One should take action only when it is morally right."

Richard Christie has noted some general characteristics of "high Machs"— people who exhibit a high degree of Machiavellianism. Machiavellianism is generally not concerned with moral issues, at least not as we normally think of them. Interpersonally, high Machs are rather uninvolved, detached, and cool. High Machs become involved in the art of manipulation and seem to enjoy it and engage in it almost for its own sake. They are, in other words, more concerned with the means of conning another individual than with the ends to be achieved with this conning. Lastly, and contrary to what some might assume, Machiavellians are not at all pathologically disturbed. Since they must be cool and detached and must function effectively in the real world, they have an undistorted view of the world and at times are overly logical in their interactions with others.

In one experiment Christie and Geis worked with groups of three college students. One student had scored high on the Machiavellian (Mach) test, one scored low, and one scored near the middle. The three members were seated around a table where 10 one-dollar bills were placed. Their instructions were to divide up the money among any two of them in any way they wished. The only restriction was that no deals be made to include the third person in the payoff. The results showed that the high Machs won significantly more money than the middle or low Machs. Even children have been found to perform differently depending on their Mach score. In one case, children were divided into high, low, and middle Machs (on the basis of an adaptation of the Mach test suitable for children). The high and low Machs were used as subjects while the middle Machs were used as "targets." All the children were given an unpleasant-tasting cracker to eat. After eating it the subjects (high and low Machs) were asked to try to convince the targets (middle Machs) to eat another cracker. For each cracker they persuaded a child to eat they would receive a nickle. As predicted, the high Machs were significantly better than the low Machs at persuading the children to eat these quinine-soaked crackers.

In another study, when high Machs were caught cheating—in a specially rigged experiment—they resisted confessing more than did the low Machs. They also engaged in more direct eye contact with the accusing instructor than did the low Machs.

Machiavellians do not always perform at higher levels than low Machs. Christie and his colleagues have found that for high Machs to perform at significantly better levels than low Machs, three conditions are helpful. First, when the interaction is face-to-face high Machs have a decided advantage. Machiavellians are particularly effective in influencing attitudes and behavior when they are in face-to-face contact. Second, high Machs perform better when there is room for improvisation. If a high Mach is restricted to pushing buttons or marking items on a test he or she is not likely to do any better than a low Mach. But when there is an opportunity for free behavior he or she will usually perform at a more effective level. Third, the high Mach is more influential when emotions can be brought into play and when the consequences of an action are serious. If high Machs participate in an experiment where they could merely win points they will be less effective than if they could win money.
[Richard Christie and Florence Geis, *Studies in Machiavellianism* (New York: Academic Press, 1970).]

Machine Translation. The translation of a text from one language to another by computer. Programs are constructed to perform a grammatical analysis of the sentence and then substitute the appropriate translation equivalents.

Macroscopic Approach to Communication. The focus on broad and general aspects of communication. See also MICROSCOPIC APPROACH TO COMMUNICATION.

Maintenance Synergy. The amount of energy that must be used by the group to maintain cohesiveness and harmony among its members.
[Raymond B. Catell, "Concepts and Methods in the Measurement of Group Syntality," *Psychological Review* 55 (1948):48–63.]

Malapropism. From Mrs. Malaprop, a character in Richard B. Sheridan's *The Rivals,* who frequently used words (usually elegantly sounding words) in the wrong places; the incorrect substitution of one word for another that is similar in sound but different in meaning. Archie Bunker of "All in the Family" is probably the clearest contemporary example of one who uses malaprops and thus displays his ignorance.

Management by Objectives. An approach to management in which both management and worker establish goals, work plans, and methods for measuring performance.

Management Style. See LEADERSHIP STYLE.

Managerial Grid. A two-dimensional analysis of managerial style including the interpersonal relationship and productivity dimensions. See also CONFLICT GRID.

Mand. A verbal operant (q.v.) under the control of a drive state, as when a thirsty person asks for water. If the drive state of thirst motivates the verbal request for water, the person may be said to be "manding" water. A mand benefits the speaker and specifies the desired behavior of the listener, the reinforcement necessary (which will reduce the drive state), or both. Coined by B. F. Skinner on the basis of such words as *demand* and *command.*
[B. F. Skinner, *Verbal Behavior* (New York: Appleton-Century-Crofts, 1957).]

Manifest Content. The "visible" portion in a message, usually used in reference to dreams; the content of the dream as it is experienced by the dreamer; the "surface structure" of a dream. See also LATENT CONTENT.

Manifest Functions of Mass Communication. Obvious and clearly observable functions of the media. See also LATENT FUNCTIONS OF MASS COMMUNICATION.

Manipulation. A process by which one attempts to change the attitudes and/or behaviors of another in a covert and generally underhanded manner, for example, putting a person into a receptive mood before asking for a favor or before disagreeing or arguing.

Manner, Maxim of. See CONVERSATIONAL MAXIMS.

Mantra. A secret word or phrase used in transcendental meditation, the frequent and prolonged repetition of which is designed to produce a relaxed and meditative state and to eliminate competing thoughts.

Manuscript Method of Delivery. A method of delivering the public speech in which the entire speech is written out word for word and is read to the audience. See also EXTEMPORANEOUS METHOD; IMPROMPTU METHOD; MEMORIZED METHOD.

Map-Territory Analogy. An analogy used in general semantics (q.v.) to emphasize the distinction between the way in which something is labeled or described (the map) and the actual reality (the territory); the word is not the thing as the map is not the territory. To confuse the word and the thing (the map and the territory) distorts our evaluative processes.

Marathon Group. A self-help group (q.v.) that meets for an extended period of time, sometimes days, on the assumption that interpersonal issues can best be dealt with through concentrated and prolonged encounters.

Marked Relationship. A relationship in which one or both parties possesses a potentially discrediting characteristic (the mark); for example, physical abnormality, mental disorder, alcoholism. Using the terminology of Edward Jones and associates, a *markable person* is one who bears the mark; the *marker* is the one who perceives the mark; and the *marked person* is the target or object of a marking act.
[Edward E. Jones, Amerigo Farina, Albert H. Hastorf, Hazel Markus, Dale T. Miller, and Robert A. Scott, *Social Stigma: The Psychology of Marked Relationships* (New York: W. H. Freeman, 1984).]

Market Research. A type of applied communication research that seeks to discover why people buy certain products. The ultimate objective is to utilize this information to increase advertising effectiveness and eventually sales.

Masking. The blocking out of one sense stimulation by another, for example, playing a radio to block out (mask) the conversation in the next room or using perfumes to block out (mask) body odor; substituting the display of one emotion for the emotion actually being experienced, for example, smiling to hide the disappointment at receiving bad news.

Mass Action. A principle, articulated by Karl Lashley, referring to the fact that the entire brain functions as a whole in learning. Together with the concept of equipotentiality (q.v.), mass action refuted the notion of localization (q.v.). See also EQUIPOTENTIALITY.

Mass Communication. Communication mediated by some medium, for example, television, newspapers, billboards, or movies. Charles Wright observes three major characteristics of mass communication: (1) the mass communication audience is a relatively large one; (2) the audience is a heterogeneous one composed of people from varied social groups and with varied and different characteristics; and (3) the audience is an anonymous one, that is, the audience member and the communicator are generally not personally known to each other.
[Charles Wright, *Mass Communication*, 2d ed. (New York: Random House, 1975).]

Mass Communication Functions. A variety of functions may be identified:

> to entertain,
> to reinforce or strengthen existing attitudes, opinions, and values,
> to change or persuade,

to educate or teach,

to confer status and to focus attention on selected people and issues,

to activate or move to action,

to narcotize or provide the viewer with information that he or she confuses with doing something about something,

to create ties of union or make the viewer feel a part of some larger group, and

to ethicize or provide viewers with a collective ethic or ethical system.

Matching Hypothesis. An hypothesis stating that persons of relatively equal attractiveness (or other qualities) will become partners, will choose each other as potential dating partners, for example.
[Elaine Walster and G. William Walster, *A New Look at Love* (Reading, Mass.: Addison-Wesley, 1978).]

Mathematical Theory of Communication. This theory had its origin in the work on channel capacity by Claude Shannon. In this model or theory, communication follows a simple left-to-right process (see the accompanying illustration). The information source selects a desired message from all possible messages. The message is sent through a transmitter, for example, a microphone, and is changed into signals. The signals are received by a receiver, for example, an earphone of some kind, changed back into a message, and delivered to the destination, say a listener. In the process of transmission certain things are added to the signal which were not intended by the information source and these added distortions constitute "noise." The actual theory on which this elementary view of communication is based is, in essence, extremely complex and allows for great precision in the measurement of information. Its great weakness is that it describes communication as a simple linear process going from speaker to listener; furthermore, it does not provide any mechanism for meaning.

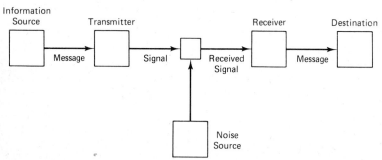

The mathematical theory of communication. *Source:* From Claude E. Shannon and Warren Weaver, *The Mathematical Theory of Communication* (Urbana: University of Illinois Press, 1949). p. 5. Copyright © The University of Illinois Press.

[Claude E. Shannon and Warren Weaver, *The Mathematical Theory of Communication* (Urbana, Ill.: University of Illinois Press, 1949); Wilbur Schramm, "Information Theory and Mass Communication," *Journalism Quarterly* 32 (1955):131–146; Fred Attneave, *Applications of Information Theory to Psychology: A Summary of Basic Concepts, Methods, and Results* (New York: Holt, Rinehart and Winston, 1959).]

Mature Love. A love that is concerned with the other person rather than with oneself; a love that is given to the other person for the other person's benefit without any expectation of any return; a love that accepts the other person as is, with weaknesses and imperfections.
[Erich Fromm, *The Art of Loving* (New York: Harper & Row, 1956).]

Maxim. A brief statement of some commonly accepted truth: A bird in the hand is worth two in the bush.

Maxims of Conversation. See CONVERSATIONAL MAXIMS.

Meaningfulness. A principle of perception that refers to the fact that we assume that the behavior of people is sensible and stems from some logical antecedent and that it is consequently meaningful rather than meaningless or random.

Mean Length of Utterance (MLU). The average length of a child's utterances, measured in syllables and considered a valid measure of a child's language development.

Media Access Movement. Attempts to gain a hearing in the media for a particular viewpoint.

Mediation. A psychological process whereby two things are cognitively connected. In communication, the process of conflict resolution where some neutral third party assesses the sources of conflict and makes recommendations for its resolution.

Medicalese. The jargon of the medical profession.

Medical Model. A theoretical position that views abnormal behavior as similar to (and as a result of) physical disease.

Meiosis. A figure of speech in which something is minimized (made less important, smaller, lighter, shorter), for example, "the lion was a pussy cat."

Memorable Messages. Certain interpersonal messages that are remembered over long periods of time and which exert considerable influence on a person's life.
[Mark L. Knapp, Cynthia Stohl, and Kathleen K. Reardon, " 'Memorable' Messages," *Journal of Communication* 31 (Autumn 1981):27–41.]

Memoria. One of the canons of classical rhetoric concerned with the ways and means of remembering the speech.

Memorized Method of Delivery. A method of delivering the public speech in which the speech is written out, memorized, and recited to the audience. See also EXTEMPORANEOUS METHOD; IMPROMPTU METHOD; MANUSCRIPT METHOD.

Memory. The total of one's remembered experiences; the process by which one receives, stores, and later retrieves information. See also REPRODUCTIVE MEMORY; RECONSTRUCTIVE MEMORY.

Mentalism. An approach in psychology that focuses on cognitive processes or mental operations as explanations for human learning, memory, language; opposed to behaviorism (q.v.).

Mere Exposure Hypothesis. A hypothesis holding that repeated or prolonged exposure to a stimulus may result in an attitude change toward the stimulus object, generally in the direction of increased positiveness.
[Robert B. Zajonc, "Attitudinal Effects of Mere Exposure," *Journal of Personality and Social Psychology Monograph Supplement* 9, no. 2, part 2 (1968).]

Mesomorphy. The muscular dimension of body build; characterized by strong bones and muscular development. As defined by William Sheldon, the mesomorph is identified as having a somatotonia (q.v.) temperament characterized by assertiveness, love of physical adventure, love of dominating and a lust for power, boldness and directness of manner, physical courage, and goal orientation.
[William H. Sheldon, *The Varieties of Human Physique* (New York: Harper & Row, 1940).]

Message. Any signal or combination of signals that serves as a stimulus (q.v.) for a receiver.

Message Sidedness. A general term for the strategy of persuasion concerned with the relative effectiveness of presenting only one side as opposed to both sides of the argument.

Meta-. Prefix designating a higher order, for example, a *metatheory* is a theory about theories. See also METACOMMUNICATION; METALANGUAGE.

Metacommunication. Communication about communication, for example, talking about the way one talks.

Metalanguage. Language used to talk about language.

Metaphor. A figure of speech in which two normally unlike things are compared as in, for example, "He's a lion when he wakes up" or "He's a real bulldozer."

Metathesis. The transposition of sounds, syllables or letters; one of the processes through which changes in language are brought about, for example, the Old English *brid* was changed through metathesis to give us the modern *bird.*

Metonymy. A figure of speech in which a name for one thing is substituted for something else with which it is closely associated, for example, "City Hall issued the following news release" where "City Hall" is used in place of "the mayor" or "the city council."

Microfiche. Pieces of film containing perhaps 100 frames on approximately 4 $\times$ 6-inch cards that can be read through a projection system. Ultramicrofiche contains perhaps 1200 pages of text on a 2 $\times$ 2-inch card.

Microfilm. Reels of film containing documents of various kinds (for example, newspapers, magazines) that can be read through a projection system.

Microkinesics. The area of kinesics (q.v.) concerned with bodily movements that communicate different meanings.

Micromomentary Expressions. Facial expressions that occur so rapidly and in such subtle ways that they are not perceived consciously but probably subconsciously—they seem only to be seen on film played at slow speeds.
[E. A. Haggard and K. S. Isaacs, "Micromomentary Facial Expressions as Indicators of Ego Mechanisms in Psychotherapy," in *Methods of Research in Psychotherapy,* L. A. Gottschalk and A. H. Auerback, eds. (New York: Appleton-Century-Crofts, 1966).]

Microscopic Approach to Communication. The focus on minute and specific aspects of communication. See also MACROSCOPIC APPROACH TO COMMUNICATION.

Mind-Body Problem. The controversy in psychology and philosophy concerning the influence of the mind on the body and of the body on the mind.

Mind Reading. Interpreting the motivations of others without any attempt to verify, especially seen in conflict situations where one person tries to mind read the reasons and motives for specific behaviors, for example, "This is the second time you missed my birthday; you obviously don't care about me, I'm just not important to you."
[George R. Bach and Ronald M. Deutsch, *Pairing: How to Achieve Genuine Intimacy* (New York: Avon, (1970).]

Mini-Comm. Communications that possess the characteristics of mass communications but which are addressed to a small specific mass audience, as seen, for example, in the rise of magazines and newspapers addressed to narrowly defined audiences. Also see DEMASSIFICATION.
[Gary Gumpert, "The Rise of Mini-Comm," *Journal of Communication* 20 (1970):280–290.]

Mini-Docs. Short documentary films or videos presented in a series of say five or six. Many news programs feature a series of five or six installments on one topic during the week, for example, drug addiction in the cities or unemployment.

Minutes. The record of the transactions of a meeting.

Mirroring. Imitating the nonverbal behaviors of another person, usually a sign of attraction; a technique used in psychodrama (q.v.) in which one person mirrors or imitates the behavior of the subject in an attempt to illustrate how he or she appears and how others react.

Misderivation. A type of speech error in which an inappropriate morpheme (q.v.) is used instead of the intended one, for example, saying "ambigual" instead of "ambiguity."

Mixed Metaphor. An unlikely comparison containing two elements that differ so greatly that attention is drawn to the absurdity of the implied comparison, for example, "We need to work harder to put our noses where our mouths are" or "We have to commit ourselves, we can no longer sit on the wall." See also METAPHOR.

Mnemonics. Aids to memory; devices that enable one to remember more effectively and efficiently.

Modality. One of the senses, for example, touch, sight, taste, vision, smell; a sensory channel through which messages are received.

Model. A visual or verbal description of a process; a type of elementary theory.

Modeling. A form of learning (used widely in behavior modification programs) in which an individual observes the behaviors of another and acquires them through observation and subsequent imitation. Those demonstrating the behavior to be learned are the models.

[Albert Bandura, ed., *Psychological Modeling: Conflicting Theories* (Chicago: Aldine-Atherton, 1971).]

Modem. Coined from the joint terms *modulator* and *demodulator,* a device that converts computer signals into sounds that can be carried over telephone lines and then translates them back into computer signals so they can be received by another computer since telephone lines are not capable of carrying digital computer signals.

Modulated. The situation in which the information wave is superimposed on the carrier wave.

Monaural. Pertaining to one ear; sound emitted by a single output device such as one loudspeaker.

Monitor. The screen or display unit in a computer system. See also TELLER.

Monochronism. A time orientation of a society or culture in which only one event is scheduled at a time; opposed to polychronism (q.v.). See also TEMPORAL COMMUNICATION.

Monolingual. The state of speaking and understanding only one language; one who knows only one language; opposed to bilingual (q.v.).

Monologue. A form of communication in which one person speaks and the other person listens; opposed to dialogue (q.v.). In monologue there is no interaction among participants, the focus is clearly and solely on the person doing the speaking. The term *monologic communication* is an extension of this basic definition and refers to communication in which there is no genuine interaction, in which one speaks without any real concern for the other person's feelings or attitudes, in which one is concerned only with his or her own goals and is interested in the other person only insofar as he or she can benefit the speaker.

Monomorphism. See OPINION LEADER.

Montage. A visual illustration or picture composed of a combination of several pictures. In film, sequences blending into each other.

Mores. The standards of behavior sanctioned by a society or culture.

Morgan's Canon. See LLOYD MORGAN'S CANON.

Morpheme. The minimum unit of meaningful speech; a unit of speech that cannot be subdivided without destroying or drastically altering its meaning. Morphemes may be of any length and vary from one phoneme (q.v.), for example, *I* or *a,* to several phonemes or syllables, for example, *Mississippi.*

Morphology. The study of the morphemes (q.v.) of a language.

Morse Code. A system of dots and dashes that represent the letters of the alphabet. Invented by Samuel F. B. Morse (1791–1872), it is the language of the telegraph.

Mother-in-Law Research. Research based on small samples whose subjects are usually known to the experimenter or polltaker, such as friends and relatives.

Motivated Sequence. Developed by Alan H. Monroe in the 1930s and widely used in all sorts of oral and written communications, the motivated sequence is a pattern of arranging information to be conveyed in a speech so as to motivate your audience to respond positively to your purpose. In fact, it may be reasonably argued that all effective communications follow this basic pattern whether it is called the motivated sequence or given some other name. There are in the motivated sequence five steps: attention, need, satisfaction, visualization, and action.

1. Attention

In this step you gain the attention of your listeners through any of a variety of methods: a provocative quotation, a little-known fact, some startling statistics, a personal or humorous anecdote, and so on. These methods are identified in more detail under "Attention, Securing and Maintaining." The important function of this step is to make the audience give you their undivided attention. If you execute this step effectively, your audience should be anxious and ready to hear what you have to say.

2. Need

Here the demonstration that a need exists is the major point. There may be a need to know something, to change some existing beliefs or attitude, or to recognize that some existing institution is creating difficulties and that something must be done. As a result of this step the audience should feel that they need to know something or that some action needs to be taken.

3. Satisfaction

Here you would present the "answer" or the "solution" to satisfying the need that you demonstrated existed in step 2. You want the audience to understand that what you are informing them about or persuading them to do will in fact satisfy the demonstrated need. In other words, after this step the audience should feel that your information or proposal will correctly and effectively satisfy the need.

4. Visualization

Visualization functions to intensify the audience's feelings or beliefs. It takes the audience beyond the present time and place and enables them to imagine the situation as it would be if the need was satisfied as suggested in step 3. This might be done, for example, by showing the positive benefits to be derived if this advocated proposal was put into operation or if your audience understands and remembers the information you convey. Another method would be to show the negative consequences if your plan is not put into operation, then follow this with the benefits to be derived from implementing your plan. Thus, you will demonstrate not only the negative consequences of not taking action, but also the positive benefits of your plan as well.

5. Action

In this step tell the audience members what they should do to ensure that the need demonstrated in step 2 is satisfied as stated in step 3 and as visualized in step 4. Here you would move the audience to act in a particular way, to speak in favor of X or against Y, to attend the next student government meeting, and so on.

Not all speeches will necessarily contain all five steps. For example, informative speeches need only the first three steps but may continue to include the fourth and perhaps even the fifth step. Let us say you wanted to inform your audience about the workings of home computers. Your steps might look something like this:

Attention:	By the time we graduate, there will be more home computers than automobiles.
Need:	Much like it is now impossible to get around without a car, it will be impossible to get around the enormous amount of information without a home computer.
Satisfaction:	Learning a few basic principles of home computers will enable us to process our work more efficiently, in less time, and more enjoyably.
Visualization:	With these basic principles firmly in mind (and a home computer), you'll be able to stay at home and do your library research for your next speech by just punching in the correct code.
Action:	These few principles should be supplemented by further study. Probably the best way to further your study is to enroll in a computer course. Such a course. . . . Another useful way is to read the brief paperback, *The Home Computer for the College Student.*

Notice that an informative speech could have stopped after the satisfaction step because the speaker would have accomplished his or her goal of informing the audience about some principles of home computers. But, in some cases, you may feel it helpful to complete the steps to emphasize your point in detail.

In a persuasive speech, on the other hand, you must go at least as far as visualization (if your purpose is limited to strengthening or changing attitudes or beliefs) or to the action step (if you are attempting to motivate behavior). [Douglas Ehninger, Bruce E. Gronbeck, and Alan H. Monroe, *Principles of Speech Communication,* 9th ed. (Glenview, Ill.: Scott, Foresman, 1984).]

Motivation. An intervening variable used to describe the process or condition that directs or stimulates an individual to behave in certain ways with respect to some goal.

Motivation Theory. The theory concerned with motives (those factors that direct us toward or away from some object or goal), and the ways in which they may be aroused and influenced.

Motive. An inner force that directs or stimulates one's behavior toward the achievement of some goal or attainment of some object.

MS-DOS. Microsoft disk operating system; the standard operating system for 16-bit computers. IBM chose MS-DOS for their computers and this has led it to become the industry standard.

Muckraking. The process of exposing corruption. President Theodore Roosevelt, in his famous speech, "The Man with the Muckrake" (April 14, 1906), used this term to refer negatively to those writers who attempted to expose corruption and social injustice through sensationalism, to those "who could look no way but downward."
[Judson A. Grenier, "Muckraking and the Muckrakers: An Historical Definition," *Journalism Quarterly* 37 (1960):552–558; Harry H. Stein, "American Muckrakers and Muckraking: The 50-Year Scholarship," *Journalism Quarterly* 56 (1979):9–17.]

Multichanneled Nature of Communication. Communication that is sent and received through a number of sensory channels at the same time, for example, vocal-auditory, gestural-visual, cutaneous-tactile.

Multilingual. One who speaks and understands several languages.

Multiordinality. In general semantics (q.v.), a condition whereby a term may exist on different levels of abstraction (q.v.), for example, the italicized words in "*hate* of hate" and "*hate* of a person" exist on different levels of abstraction.

Multiple Access Hypothesis. The hypothesis holding that in analyzing a linguistic ambiguity, all meanings are accessed and the correct one selected; opposed to the single access hypothesis (q.v.).

Multiple Product Announcements. See PIGGYBACKING.

Multivalued Orientation. A point of view that emphasizes that there are many sides to any issue (rather than only one or two sides).

Mutual Gaze. The time both people in an interaction simultaneously maintain eye contact.

Name Calling. A persuasive device in which one's opponent is criticized and discredited by calling him or her names that carry strong negative meanings. See also PROPAGANDA DEVICES.

Narcissism. The love of oneself; an excessive love of self. In psychoanalytic theory, narcissism is one of the early stages of development characterized by an excessive concern for oneself and little if any for others.

Narcotize. See MASS COMMUNICATION FUNCTIONS.

Narrowcasting. Programming that is directed to a specific group of viewers (a narrowly defined audience).

Narratio. In classical rhetoric, the second major part of the speech consisting of the statement of facts. See also PARTS OF THE SPEECH.

Narration. The act or art of storytelling, of relating a sequence of events. See also EXPOSITION.

Nasality. Vocal quality characterized by "speaking through your nose" where the expelled air is emitted through the nose rather than through the mouth. In English only [m], [n], and [ng] are properly articulated with nasal resonance. See also DENASALITY.

National Language. A language that is the official language of a country; the language that is taught in the schools and in which official state business is conducted.

Nativism. A theoretical position that emphasizes innateness (inborn knowledge) rather than deliberate learning in the development of cognitive and/or behavioral processes. A nativist position has been used extensively in theories of language acquisition.

Natural Child. See CHILD EGO STATE.

Naturalistic Observation. Observations of behaviors as they occur in nature without any outside manipulation.

Nature-Nurture Controversy. The controversy revolving around the relative importance of the contributions made by nature, heredity, or innate factors on the one hand, and those made by nurturing or through learning and experience on the other hand in the development of cognitive processes such as language.

Nay. A "no" vote at a meeting.

Need. A physiological or psychological desire that provides frequent motivation (q.v.) for specific behaviors, for example, the need for food or for status.

Need Hierarchy. According to some theorists needs are hierarchically structured such that needs at the lower and more basic levels must be satisfied before higher order needs can be addressed. Perhaps the most influential of these need hierarchies is that proposed by Abraham Maslow. In Maslow's system five orders of needs are identified (as illustrated). Thus, for example, people do not concern themselves with the need for security or freedom from fear if they are starving (that is, if their food need has not been fulfilled). Similarly, they would not be concerned with friendship or affectional relationships if their need for protection and security has not been fulfilled.

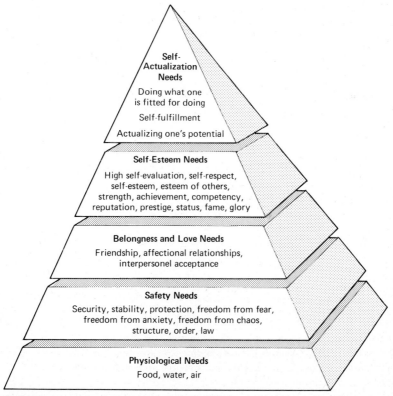

Maslow's "hierarchy of needs." *Source:* **Based on Abraham Maslow,** *Motivation and Personality* **(New York: Harper & Row, 1970).**

Negative Attitude Change. Attitude change in the direction opposite to that being advocated.

Negative Feedback. Feedback that serves a corrective function by informing the source that his or her message is not being received in the way intended. Negative feedback serves to redirect the source's behavior. Looks of boredom, shouts of disagreement, letters critical of newspaper policy, and the teacher's instructions on how to better approach a problem would be examples of negative feedback. See also POSITIVE FEEDBACK; FEEDBACK REGULATION.

Negative Reinforcement. The strengthening of a particular behavioral response by removing an aversive or painful stimulus. See also POSITIVE REINFORCEMENT.

Negativity Effect. The process in which negative information is given greater weight than positive information in the formation of interpersonal and social evaluations. See also POLLYANNA HYPOTHESIS.
[Kathy Kellermann, "The Negativity Effect and Its Implications for Initial Interaction," *Communication Monographs* 51 (1984):37–55.]

Negotiation. A conflict resolution procedure where the parties discuss the relevant issues in an attempt to reach a mutually satisfying agreement.
[D. G. Pruitt, *Negotiating Behavior* (New York: Academic Press, 1981); Michael Schatzki, *Negotiation: The Art of Getting What You Want* (New York: New American Library, 1981).]

Neo-Aristotelian Rhetorical Criticism. An approach to rhetorical criticism that focuses on the speaker as the most essential element, uses the classical canons of rhetoric (q.v.) as the major categories, and evaluates the speech in terms of its effectiveness in achieving the speaker's purpose.

Neologism. A newly coined word; a word newly introduced into the language.

Nerve Deafness. The inability to hear due to damage to the auditory nerve or the cochlea mechanism.

Network. A group of connected radio or television stations that broadcast many of the same programs. See also COMMUNICATION NETWORKS; NETWORKING.

Networking. The design or interaction between or among two or more networks; the making of contacts with other people, especially those who can help or provide some assistance, guidance, or direction.

Neurosis. A general term for personality disorders characterized by unrealistic anxieties and distortions of reality. Neurotics are usually aware of their disturbances.

Neurotic Lock. The condition whereby two people are bound together by neurotic needs rather than by free choice.
[Theodore Isaac Rubin, *One to One: Understanding Personal Relationships* (New York: Viking, 1983).]

Neutrality. A response pattern lacking in personal involvement; encourages defensiveness (q.v.); opposed to empathy (q.v.).

New Criticism. Literary analysis that focuses on the text rather than on the author or the historical period.
[John Crowe Ransom, *The New Criticism* (Norfolk, Conn.: New Directions, 1941); Cleanth Brooks and Robert Penn Warren, *Understanding Poetry* (New York: Holt, Rinehart, Winston, 1960).]

New Journalism. A personalized style of journalism that became popular during the 1960s. Many of the techniques of the novelist were used by the new journalists and may best be illustrated by Tom Wolfe and Norman Mailer.

Newspeak. The fictional language used in *1984,* George Orwell's futuristic novel set in Oceania. The aim of the language was to eliminate thoughts and feelings that were contrary to the Party; by containing only approved words, speakers, it was reasoned, would only be able to entertain approved thoughts and feelings. The "language" of Newspeak is explained in the appendix to *1984*.

Nibble. One-half of a byte (1 byte = 8 bits); four bits of information.

Nickelodeon. An early "moving picture" theater where one would look through a viewer and see a short film for a nickle.

Nielsen Rating. Compiled by A. C. Nielsen, ratings of television programs on the basis of the households viewing them. These ratings are in turn used to determine advertising costs and they greatly influence the networks' programming decisions.

Nihil Obstat. Latin for "nothing stands in the way"; a phrase used by the Roman Catholic Church to indicate that a book or pamphlet is free of moral or doctrinal error; contrary to popular perception, it does not mean that the Church is in agreement with the content of the work.

Noise. Anything that distorts the message intended by the source, anything that interferes with the receiver's receiving the message as the source intended the message to be received. Noise is present in a communication system to the extent that the message received is not the message sent. Three major types of noise may be identified.

Physical Noise

Physical noise interferes with the physical transmission of the signal or message. The screeching of passing cars, the hum of an air conditioner or computer, the lisp of a speaker, and sunglasses may all be regarded as physical noise since they interfere with the transmission of signals from one person to another. Physical noise is also present in written communication and would include blurred type, the print that shows through from the back of the page, creases in the paper, and anything that prevents a reader from getting the message sent by the writer.

Psychological Noise

Psychological noise refers to any form of psychological interference and includes biases and prejudices in senders and receivers that lead to distortions in receiving and processing information, and closed-mindedness—perhaps the classic example of psychological noise preventing information from being received or being received fairly.

Semantic Noise

In semantic noise the interference is due to the receiver failing to grasp the meanings intended by the sender. Semantic noise in its extreme occurs between people speaking different languages. In more common form, semantic noise is created by the speaker's use of jargon, technical, or complex terms not understood by the listener or in the assignment by the listener of meanings different from those intended by the speaker (as would frequently be the case with ambiguous or highly emotional terms and sentences).

Nominal Group. Members of a nominal group are grouped together but they do not communicate with one another; the group is a group in name only. Such a group is composed of a number of members of the organization who meet but do not talk. The group's task is accomplished in three main stages, all of which take place in about one hour. First, each member writes down the major issues concerning the problem on which the group is to focus. For example, if the question was whether or not a communications department should be established at ABC, Inc., each member would attempt to identify the advantages and disadvantages of such a proposal. Next, a chairperson records the responses on a board so that all can see them by having each person read her or his ideas aloud. This continues until all contributions from all members are duly recorded. Members are instructed to eliminate duplicates and to withhold any evaluation or, in fact, any comments at all until the three stages are complete. Third, members study the lists and rank-order each list in terms of importance. These individual rank-orders are then collected and tabulated and a combined master list is made. At this point, we have a rank-ordered list of the advantages and a rank-order list of the disadvantages of establishing a communications department at ABC, Inc. The task of the nominal group is now complete. A regular problem-solving discussion may then follow or some other method may be used to implement any suggestions or problem solutions.

Note that although the group members do not profit from the interaction that usually characterizes the small group, there are a number of advantages to this approach. For example, there is likely to be great openness and honesty and less inhibition since the lists are made privately. Since criticism and evaluation are postponed, all facets of the problem are identified. This prevents the all too frequent situation in which one argument is advanced and the group debates this one issue for the entire hour without ever introducing other issues.
[Richard C. Huseman, James Lahiff, and Robert Wells, "Communication Thermoclines: Toward a Process of Identification," *Personnel Journal* (February 1974):124–135.]

Nonallness. An attitude or point of view in which it is recognized that one can never know all about anything and that what we know or say or hear is only a part of what there is to know or say or hear.

Nonce Word. A word coined for a specific occasion but which does not enter the general vocabulary.

Nondirective Therapy. A therapeutic approach in which the therapist is supportive and accepting of the client and in which the client determines the goals and processes of therapy.

Nonfluency. A break in the stream of speech. See also HESITATION PHENOMENA; PRIMARY STUTTERING.

Nongroup Organization. Term used in business to refer to an organization that has little or no structure.

Non-U. See U.

Normative Grammar. See PRESCRIPTIVE GRAMMAR.

Norms. The rules of a social group that guide the behavior of its members.

Nonsense Syllable. A syllable, developed and used extensively by Hermann Ebbinghaus (1850–1909), composed of a consonant-vowel-consonant combination of sounds that does not exist in the language and is used in experimental studies of learning and memory, for example, *deg, gol, mok.*

Nonverbal Communication. Communication without words. See also PROXEMICS; TACTILE COMMUNICATION; FACIAL COMMUNICATION, COLOR COMMUNICATION; TEMPORAL COMMUNICATION; EYE COMMUNICATION; BODY COMMUNICATION; BODY TYPE.

Nonverbal Leakage. See LEAKAGE.

Nuclear Family. The members of a family consisting of mother, father, and their children. See also EXTENDED FAMILY.

Nurture. The learning process of an individual acquired through their experiences; opposed to nature (q.v.) or innateness.

Nurture-Nature Controversy. See NATURE-NURTURE CONTROVERSY.

O

Object Adaptors. Nonverbal behaviors that make use of some kind of prop that in itself does not serve any instrumental function, for example, scratching your head with a pencil or chewing on your necklace. See also ADAPTORS.

Objective Abstracting. A form or type of abstracting (q.v.) in which one groups individual units into a class of which they are all members as, for example, all chapters being grouped into a book. See also CLASSIFYING ABSTRACTING; EVALUATIVE ABSTRACTING; RELATIONAL ABSTRACTING.

Object Language. Language used to talk about the objective world of people, objects, and events; opposed to metalanguage (q.v.) which is used to talk about language itself.

Object Permanence. See SENSORY MOTOR PERIOD.

Obligatory Linguistic Category. A concept that *must* be expressed in the language; a concept to which reference must be made in all sentences, for example, in English the concepts of time (past, present, and future) and number (singular or plural) are obligatory categories.

Obscenity. The portrayal (in sound, print, or graphics) of sexually explicit material that is judged to appeal to "purient interests" and to be without serious literary or artistic merit.

Observational Adequacy of a Grammar. That criterion of a grammar by which it must generate all and only the sentences of the language. See also DESCRIPTIVE ADEQUACY OF A GRAMMAR.
[Noam Chomsky, *Current Issues in Linguistic Theory* (The Hague: Mouton, 1964).]

Obsolete. A word or phrase that is no longer used.

Obstinate Audience. A view of the audience, particularly the public and mass communication audience, as critical, selective, and active.
[Raymond Bauer, "The Obstinate Audience," *American Psychologist* 19 (1964):319–328.]

Occam's Razor. Named after William of Occam (c. 1285–1349), a Franciscan monk and philosopher, the principle holding that the preferred explanation is the simplest one; the explanation requiring the least number of unproven assumptions. Also referred to as the "law of parsimony." See also LLOYD MORGAN'S CANON.

Off-Line. In computer terminology, closed to any communication functions; opposed to on-line (q.v.).

Oldspeak. Standard English before the advent of Newspeak (q.v.).

Olfaction. A category for the analysis of proxemic distance, denoting the type of body odor that can be detected. Five major categories are identified: differentiated body odor detectable, undifferentiated body odor detectable, breath odor detectable, olfaction probably present, and olfaction not present. The sense of smell or act of smelling. See also PROXEMICS; PROXEMIC BEHAVIOR CATEGORIES.

Olfactory Communication. Communication signals received through one's sense of smell.
[Ruth Winter, *The Smell Book: Scents, Sex, and Society* (Philadelphia: Lippincott, 1976).]

One-Step Flow Model. A theoretical position which holds that the media influence people directly rather than through any intermediaries. See also TWO-STEP FLOW; MULTISTEP FLOW.

On-Line. In computer terminology, ready to communicate; open for sending and receiving information; opposed to off-line (q.v.).

Onomatopoeia. The phenomenon of words sounding like their meaning, for example, *snap* and *babble* are considered onomatopoeic because they sound like their meanings.

Onomatopoeic Theory. A theory of the origin of language that holds that speech began when people imitated the sounds made by animals and objects. Also referred to as the "bow-wow" or "echoic theory."

Open-Ended Question. A question that provides the answerer considerable freedom in the type and length of response; opposed to closed question (q.v.).

Open Line Program. A method for improving organizational communication in which a channel is established for anyone who wishes to complain, offer an opinion, or advance an idea. First, this channel is confidential; the individual's identity is known only to the coordinator of the open line program. Workers are informed of this confidentiality, which must be rigorously maintained. Second, a frank, written reply from management is guaranteed and is sent to the worker's home. Or, if the employee wishes, he or she is guaranteed an interview with an officer of the company to discuss the issues raised. In this way workers may be assured that they have an avenue for voicing their opinions and that management will listen to and respond to their opinions.
[Robert M. Wendlinger, "Improving Upward Communication," *Journal of Business Communication* (Summer 1973):17–23.]

Open Marriage. A marital arrangement in which extramarital relationships are permitted and may even be encouraged and where such extramarital relationships are openly discussed with the marital partner rather than hidden.
[Nena O'Neill and George O'Neill, *Open Marriage* (New York: Avon, 1972).]

Openness. See PRODUCTIVITY.

Open Self. In the Johari model (q.v.), the self that is known both to oneself and to others; the self containing that information known to both self and others.

Open System. A system that can be changed, one in which elements and relationships are not fixed but may be added or subtracted.

Open Words. A class of words used in the child's two- and three-word utterances that refer to things rather than to grammatical or other relationships. In such utterances as "more juice," "more cookie," "more milk," "allgone milk," "allgone truck," "allgone Daddy," the open words are the second words of the phrases, the words that refer to content; the pivot words (q.v.) are the first words of the phrases. Open words generally occur with pivot words in either first or second position but may also occur with other open words.
[Martin D. S. Braine, "The Ontogeny of English Phrase Structure: The First Phrase," *Language* 39 (1963):1–13, and "On Learning the Grammatical Order of Words," *Psychological Review* 70 (1963):323–348.]

Operant. A bit of behavior that is emitted rather than elicited and that is controlled by reinforcement (q.v.). There is no identifiable stimulus (q.v.) for this type of behavior; verbal behavior is considered operant behavior in the Skinnerian analysis of language.

Operant Conditioning. A type of conditioning (q.v.) in which the reinforcement (q.v.) is contingent upon the desired response, for example, the pigeon is rewarded (receives a food pellet as reinforcement or reward) after it pecks the metal plate (performs the desired behavior).

Operational Definition. A method of defining a concept in which the procedures that would be used to produce or measure the element are identified, for example, defining *intelligence* by noting the test used to measure it and the resulting score obtained.

Opinion. A tentative conclusion concerning some object, person, or event; a belief rather than a proven fact.

Opinion Leader. An opinion leader is a person who influences the opinions of others. The opinion leader is different from the people who are influenced in a number of important ways, ways that clearly distinguish this person from others. Opinion leaders have been found to have more formal education, to have greater wealth, to be of higher social status, and to have greater exposure to mass communications than those they influence. They also participate in social activities to a greater extent and are more innovative, cosmopolitan, competent, and accessible than those they influence.

Possessing these characteristics does not ensure that someone will become an opinion leader, and yet, when opinion leaders are studied, they are found to possess these characteristics. These characteristics are relative. The opinion leader does not possess these characteristics in an absolute sense but rather possesses them to a greater extent than the individual who is influenced.

Much as opinion leaders differ from the people they influence, they also differ from one another. Some opinion leaders, for example, are cosmopolitan, whereas others are local. The cosmopolitan leader is concerned with national and international issues. Today the cosmopolitan leader would be concerned with such issues as the Middle East conflicts, economic problems in Europe, and trade regulations. The local opinion leader, on the other hand, is concerned with issues that are more immediate, more localized. The issues with which a local opinion leader would be concerned today would depend on where that leader was. If in New York this leader might be concerned with rent increases, fuel costs, Yankee Stadium, and millions of possible issues that are less than national or international in scope. These issues are not unimportant; rather, they are simply of concern to less people than the issues the cosmopolitan leader deals with. The cosmopolitan leader is generally restricted to one field of expertise, whereas the local leader is generally more broadly based, extending through several different and diverse fields of knowledge. A cosmopolitan leader might, for example, be restricted to economic issues, to Central American affairs, or to Soviet-American relations. A local opinion leader is looked to for guidance and information on a broad variety of issues. Robert Merton introduced the terms *monomorphism* (q.v.) and *polymorphism* (q.v.) to highlight this distinction. The terms are, in a way, self-explanatory. *Monomorphism* refers to the tendency to serve as a leader for one topic (for example, national politics, contemporary fiction, carpentry); monomorphism generally characterizes cosmopolitan leaders. *Polymorphism,* on the other hand, refers to the tendency for a leader to serve as a leader for a number of different topics; polymorphism generally characterizes local opinion leaders.

[Elihu Katz and Paul F. Lazarsfeld, *Personal Influence: The Part Played by People in the Flow of Mass Communications* (New York: Free Press, 1955); Robert K. Merton, *Social Theory and Social Structure,* rev. ed. (New York: Free Press, 1959).]

Optimal Heterophily. That degree of difference between people that facilitates the interpersonal influence that causes a change in one's behavior. If people are extremely different—for example, one is extremely competent and one is extremely incompetent—there will be little mutual understanding and hence little interpersonal change. Similarly, if two people are very similar (homophilous, q.v.), neither will exert much influence over or change the other because of this great similarity. But, when people are optimally heterophilous—where one is optimally more competent than the other, for example—she or he will be able to effect a change in the other.

Oral Gesture Theory. A theory of language origin holding that when primitives' hands were occupied with tools or other objects, they began to gesture vocally and that the resulting sounds became names for a variety of objects, actions, and people.
[Richard Paget, *Human Speech* (London: Routledge and K. Paul, 1930).]

Oralism. A method for teaching the deaf to communicate which concentrates not on finger spelling but on lipreading and talking.

Oral Style. A quality of spoken language that clearly differentiates it from written language. The words and grammatical constructions you use differ depending on whether you are speaking or writing. The major reason for this difference is that you compose speech instantly; you select your words and construct your sentences as you think your thoughts with very little time in between the thought and the utterance. When you write, however, you compose your thoughts after considerable reflection and even then often rewrite and edit as you go along. Another reason for the difference (and this one from the point of view of the listener) is that the listener hears a speech only once and therefore it must be made instantly intelligible. The reader can reread an essay, look up an unfamiliar word, and otherwise spend a great deal of time understanding the meaning of the written communication. The listener, however, is forced to move at the pace of the speaker. Temporary attention lapses may force the reader to reread a sentence or paragraph but such lapses can never be made up by the listener.

Thus, the two forms of communication differ in the way in which they are produced and in the way in which they are received. These differences lead speakers and writers to compose differently. At the same time, the differences in reception demand that speakers and writers employ different rules or principles to guide them in composing messages for their particular mode of expression and reception.

On a purely descriptive level, spoken language differs from written language in a number of important ways. Generally, spoken language consists of shorter, simpler, and more familiar words than the written language. There is a great deal more qualification in speech than in writing. For example, speakers will make greater use of such expressions as *although, however, perhaps, to me,* and so on. Writers probably edit out such expressions before their copy is published. Spoken language also contains a greater number of self-reference terms (terms that refer to the speaker himself or herself) and a greater number of "allness" terms (for example, *all, none, every, always, never*). Spoken language is also significantly less abstract than written language; spoken language contains more finite verbs and less abstract nouns (two major ingredients in abstraction) than does written language.

The specific suggestions that follow are designed to guide you in styling your speech that will retain the best of the oral style while maintaining comprehension and persuasion.

Principles of Oral Style

To achieve clarity and maintain interest in the development of an oral style, (1) use simple terms and sentence patterns; (2) vary the levels of abstraction; (3) use guide phrases; (4) use repetition, restatement, and internal summaries; (5) personalize your language; (6) use moderate rather than extreme language; (7) use familiar terms; and (8) be sure that your language does not offend any members of your audience. Although these suggestions are applicable to all oral communication situations, they are most often considered in connection with styling a public speech. Hence, this particular form will be emphasized here.

Simple Terms and Sentence Patterns

Because a speech in normal circumstances is only heard once, it is not possible for members of the audience to look up an unfamiliar word or unwind complicated sentence patterns in order to get at the meaning you wish to convey. On the other hand, overly simplified language can turn off the audience and lead them to think that you have nothing of value to communicate. Even more important is that you should never "talk down" to the audience; condescension impedes communication. Simple language and grammatical constructions result in immediate comprehension but will not insult the audience. Generally simple, active, declarative sentences are preferred to the more complex, passive sentences because these forms are easier to understand and grasp with just one exposure. It has been found, for example, that active sentences ("The dog caught the ball") are easier to comprehend than passive sentences ("The ball was caught by the dog"). Affirmatives ("The circle follows the square") are easier to understand than negatives ("The square doesn't follow the circle"). With questions, nontags ("Does the circle follow the square?") are easier to comprehend than tag questions ("The circle follows the square, doesn't it?"). The "tag" is the short phrase that asks for agreement: doesn't it? didn't he? wasn't it? It is interesting to note that women use a significantly greater number of tag questions than men—it is one of the ways in which women frequently dilute the strength of their messages.

Levels of Abstraction

Most people seem to prefer a mixture of the abstract and the concrete, the specific and the general. By mixing these levels of abstraction you communicate in a clearer, more interesting, and more meaningful fashion. By mixing the levels of abstraction you can more actively involve the audience in your speech. If a speech concentrates solely on low-level abstractions, that is, on concrete terms and sentences, the audience will probably become bored. Similarly, if you only talk in terms of high-order abstractions, using highly abstract and all-inclusive terms, the audience will again become bored.

Active Words and Sentence Patterns

In all forms of communication, active words and sentence patterns are to be preferred over more passive words and patterns. When styling your speech, use language that makes your people and even your objects move. To say "The elephant was chased by the mouse" or "The lawyer was thrown out of court by the judge" is to phrase your ideas in the passive mode, a relatively static and unmoving state. To say, on the other hand, "The mouse chased the elephant" and "The judge threw the lawyer out of court" creates the feeling of movement, of activity. Similarly, in selecting individual words, select words that convey activity. Instead of saying "The students are here," it would be more effective to replace the relatively inactive *are* with *arrived* or *barged in* or whatever term best suits your meaning. "The old couple went up the street" conveys little action, but we get a much clearer image of movement when we hear "The old couple struggled up the street" or "The old couple raced up the street."

Guide Phrases

Listening attentively to a speech is difficult work and consequently you should assist the audience in any way you can. One of the most effective ways is to use frequent transitional phrases that provide a kind of bridge between one set of ideas and another or between one piece of evidence and another. Phrases such as "Now that we have seen how . . ., let us consider how . . .," will help to keep the audience on the right track. Even terms such as *first, second, and also, although,* and *however* help the audience to better follow your thought patterns. Much like transitions, "markers" will help audience comprehension. Make frequent use of marker terms that will provide signposts to the audience. Numbers and letters are perhaps the most obvious examples, but phrases such as "The second argument is . . ." or "The last example I want to provide . . ." help to focus the audience's thinking on the kind of outline you are using.

Repetition, Restatement, and Internal Summaries

Much like transitions and marker phrases help to keep the audience on the same track with you, repetition (repeating something in exactly the same way), restatement (rephrasing an idea or statement), and internal summaries (summaries or reviews of subsections of the speech) all help the listeners to better follow what you are saying.

All this is not to imply that tautologies are therefore to be welcomed in the public speech. (A *tautology* is a needlessly redundant expression, an expression that says the same thing twice.) Here are a few of the more common examples: *absolutely sure, actual truth, again reiterate, cash money, clearly unambiguous, crazy maniac, I myself personally, most unique, new innovation, personal opinion, recline back, overexaggerate,* and *written down.* Avoid these and similar expressions.

Personalized Language

The best guide to what is personalized language is to focus on the language of everyday conversation and note its characteristics; this is invariably personalized language. It makes frequent use of personal pronouns, *I, you, he, she;* it makes use of contractions, simple sentences, and short phrases; it makes use of repetition and restatement. It avoids long, complex, and passive sentences. It avoids the use of the pronoun *one* or phrases such as *the speaker, the former/the latter* (which are difficult to retrace), and, in general, those expressions that are more popular and more expected in the language of written prose than in the language of everyday communication.

Moderation

Extremism in style is generally best avoided. Specifically, extremism in the use of what are called "allness" terms is generally misleading. The use of such terms as *all, every, none, always, never,* and the like are seldom descriptive of reality. You can seldom know *all* or *every* of anything and so it is best to more accurately reflect reality with terms that are less extreme but more descriptive. *Some, seldom, often, rarely,* and the like are generally more descriptive of reality and are to be preferred, especially in public speaking where listeners are not afforded the luxury of asking for clarification on such terms. (See also ALLNESS.)

Another type of extremism to avoid is what is called "polarization" (q.v.) or "either/or" language. Polarization refers to the tendency to divide the world, its objects, and its people into two classes, two extremes—the bad and the good, the ugly and the beautiful, the rich and the poor. Extremes represent a small portion of the real world; the vast majority of people, objects, and events fall in between these extremes. And yet many speakers persist in categorizing people as "for us" or "against us," "liberal" or "conservative," "pro-*X*" or "con-*X*." One reason for this tendency is that our language provides an abundant source of easy-to-use labels for the extremes. For example, it is easier to think and to communicate about someone as "rich" or "poor," as "healthy" or "sick," or as "sane" or "insane," than to qualify such statements with *somewhat, moderately, fairly.*

Familiar Terms

As a speaker, you may fall into a pattern of using terms that are jargon within the subject matter being discussed but which are unfamiliar to your listeners. And while this usage often gives the listener the impression that you may be something of an expert on the topic, it also creates a number of negative impressions. One impression is that you are putting yourself above the listener, and this is generally resented. Another impression is that you really do not care to communicate but are more concerned with the subject of the speech than with the listener, and this too is generally resented. But perhaps the most significant implication is that it prevents clear and accurate communication and often draws the listener's attention to the words used rather than focus on the subject.

A preference for the familiar should not be taken as a license to use timeworn cliches. Expressions such as "green with envy," "to be in hot water," "pretty as a picture," "the writing on the wall," "the whole ball of wax," and numerous others communicate nothing or very little. At the same time they have the effect of drawing attention to themselves and giving the listener the impression that you are unimaginative and uncreative and therefore must resort to these cliches.

Nonoffensive Language

The sexist aspect of language has become the center of a great deal of interest. Basically, the masculine pronoun or professions designated by masculine names should not be used generically, nor should the term *man* be used to refer to human beings. Many, of course, will disagree with this and yet with a bit of reflection you can easily see why these constructions should be avoided. Why should a hypothetical doctor, dentist, or lawyer be referred to with masculine pronouns and references? Similarly why should the hypothetical individual be called *he?* That this is traditional and convenient are not satisfactory answers although these seem the only arguments ever used. It is probably best to use *he and she* or *person* instead of just *he* or *man.* Similarly, terms such as *chairman* should be replaced by *chairperson.* In a similar vein, terms that were at one time used to refer to a woman in a specific position (normally originating from a masculine term) should be avoided; for example, *poetess, Negress, Jewess, heroine, actress,* and the like.

Oration. A formal public speech.

Oratory. Speech making; the art of public speaking.

Ordinary Language. A school of language philosophy that focuses on philosophical problems as they arise from the inappropriate use of ordinary language.
[C. E. Caton, ed., *Philosophy and Ordinary Language* (Urbana, Ill.: University of Illinois Press, 1963).]

Organizational Chart. An illustration of an organization's hierarchy, especially designed to show who reports to whom and who has responsibility for what.

Organizational Communications. Organizational communication refers to the messages sent and received within the organization—within the organization's formally structured and informally established groups. As the organization becomes larger and more complex, so do the communications. In a three-person organization communication is relatively simple, but in organizations of thousands it becomes a highly complex and often specialized function. In such complex organizations, even the communication roles become specialized, and each exerts considerable influence on the organization. Rogers and Rogers have identified four such crucial communication roles.

The Gatekeeper. This person controls the messages that get into the system or that get to any one member of the organization. The secretary who screens phone calls or who sorts the mail serves this function every day, as does a line manager who passes or conceals certain information received from the executive level to the workers.

The Liaison. This person connects two subgroups within the organization but does not belong to either. The liaison serves as a link between, say, students and faculty within a college organization but is neither a student nor a faculty member, but perhaps a student counselor, a coach, or a dormitory director.

The Opinion Leader. This person is the one to whom others look for guidance and direction. This is the person who influences others.

The Cosmopolite. This person is the one who communicates often with many individuals from various subgroups throughout the organization.

Organizational communication may be both formal and informal. The formal communications are those sanctioned by the organization itself and are organizationally oriented; they deal with the workings of the organization, with productivity, and the various jobs done throughout the organization. The informal communications are socially sanctioned; they are oriented not to the organization itself, but to the individual members.

Although we have defined *organizational communication* as that which occurs within the organization, organizations spend considerable time and energy and money on securing information from outside and on disseminating information to other organizations or to the general public. Although these outgoing messages are organizationally motivated, they are probably best treated as examples of public or mass or even interpersonal communication—depending on the situation.
[Everett Rogers and Rekha Agarwala-Rogers, *Communication in Organizations* (New York: Free Press, 1976).]

Orientation. The relationship existing between a person and some part of the environment such that the person attends to it, is directed to it, and is selective in attending to it; an individual's attitude toward a person or thing.

Originator Compatibility. A condition that exists when the expression of inclusion (q.v.), control (q.v.), and affection (q.v.) of one person corresponds to the desire of the other person to receive such expressions.

[William C. Schutz, *FIRO: A Three-Dimensional Theory of Interpersonal Behavior* (New York: Holt, Rinehart and Winston, 1958).]

Orthography. The written representation of spoken language forms—sounds, syllables, and words.

Other Orientation. The quality by which one is attentive to and adapts to the other person in the relationship or interaction.

Otology. The study of the ear.

Outgroup. Those persons not members of or excluded from an ingroup (q.v.); a group thought to be in opposition to an ingroup. Also referred to as "they-group."

Output. That which the computer sends out.

Oxymoron. A figure of speech in which contradictory terms are combined to produce a paradox, for example, "a bitter sweet romance."

Pair Stigma. A stigma (q.v.) that only exists when paired. A stigma that is created by the pairing of two individuals, neither of whom would be stigmatized individually, for example, a short man and a tall woman do not individually have stigmas; together, however, they may be stigmatized. Similarly, a very young and a very old person are not stigmatized individually but would be if they were romantically paired.

Paleography. The science of writing, especially those inscriptions on paper, papyrus (q.v.), or skin; generally dealing with writing from a more recent period than epigraphy (q.v.) represents.

Palmer Method. A system of writing or penmanship developed by A. N. Palmer (1859–1927) and used widely in the late nineteenth- and early twentieth-century schools. Students were taught to write through exercises in which they developed free-flowing writing movements.

A. N. Palmer, *The Palmer Method Plan of Teaching Practical Writing in Graded Schools* (New York: A. N. Palmer, 1910–1911).]

Panegyric. An oration in praise of a person or institution; speech of commendation.

Papyrus. Parchment made from the pressed stalks of the papyrus plant and used by the ancient Egyptians and later civilizations as writing material.

Parable. A story designed to teach a moral and built around an extended metaphor.

Paradigm. A set of assumptions, methods and procedures, and hypotheses that generally guide research and theory.

Paradigmatic Relationship. The relationship existing between elements of the same paradigm or class. In linguistics, the relationship between linguistic elements of the same form class or part of speech, for example, two nouns. See also SYNTAGMATIC RELATIONSHIP.

Paradigmatic Response. A word association based on similarity of class or part of speech, for example, giving *radio* or *film* as a response to *television.* See also SYNTAGMATIC RESPONSE.

Paradiorthosis. A figure of speech in which a well-known quotation is reworded, for example, "Ask not what you can do for your country, but what your country can do for you."

Paradox. A self-contradictory statement that has some truth to it; a logical impossibility; that which exhibits a contradictory nature.

Paralanguage. The vocal (but nonverbal) dimension of speech; the manner in which something is said rather than what is said.

Paralanguage Structure

An outline of a classification offered by George L. Trager is presented in the accompanying table. More important than the specifics of this table, though, is that paralanguage encompasses a great deal of vocal expression and can be classified and analyzed rather precisely for various different purposes.

PARALANGUAGE: A CLASSIFICATION

I. Voice Qualities
   A. Pitch Range
      1. Spread
         a. Upward
         b. Downward
      2. Narrowed
         a. From above
         b. From below
   B. Vocal Lip Control
      1. Rasp
      2. Openness
   C. Glottis Control
      1. Sharp transitions
      2. Smooth transitions
   D. Pitch Control
   E. Articulation Control
      1. Forceful (precise)
      2. Relaxed (slurred)
   F. Rhythm Control
      1. Smooth
      2. Jerky
   G. Resonance
      1. Resonant
      2. Thin
   H. Tempo
      1. Increased from norm
      2. Decreased from norm
II. Vocalizations
   A. Vocal Characterizers
      1. Laughing/crying
      2. Yelling/whispering
      3. Moaning/groaning
      4. Whining/breaking
      5. Belching/yawning

   B. Vocal Qualifiers
      1. Intensity
         a. Overloud
            (1) somewhat
            (2) considerably
            (3) very much
         b. Oversoft
            (1) somewhat
            (2) considerably
            (3) very much
      2. Pitch Height
         a. Overhigh
            (1) slightly
            (2) appreciably
            (3) greatly
         b. Overlow
            (1) slightly
            (2) appreciably
            (3) greatly
      3. Extent
         a. Drawl
            (1) slight
            (2) noticeable
            (3) extreme
         b. Clipping
            (1) slight
            (2) noticeable
            (3) extreme
   C. Vocal Segregates
      1. Uh-uh
      2. Uh-huh
      3. Sh
      4. (Pause)

Adapted from George L. Trager, "Paralanguage: A First Approximation," *Studies in Linguistics* 13 (1958): 1–12; George L. Trager, "The Typology of Paralanguage," *Anthropological Linguistics* 3 (1961): 17–21; and Robert E. Pittenger and Henry Smith, Jr., "A Basis for Some Contributions of Linguistics to Psychiatry," *Psychiatry* 20 (1957):61–78.

The four major classes of paralinguistic phenomena are *voice qualities, vocal characterizers, vocal qualifiers,* and *vocal segregates.* The sounds used in vocal segregates are not the same as those same letters when used in words—that is, the *sh* that means "silence!" is not the same as the *sh* sound in *sh*ed. The "pause" noted as a vocal segregate is classified in a somewhat different area by many contemporary researchers. This area, generally referred to as "hesitation phenomena," is concerned with all forms of hesitations, the pause being only one of these. Some of the classifications are actually continuous scales; vocal lip control may be analyzed as ranging from "rasp" through "openness" rather than simply as either "rasp" or "open."

If we assume the validity of the proposition that nothing never happens, that all behavior serves a communicative function, then we must further assume that each of these paralinguistic features also communicates meaning. Thus the speaker who speaks quickly communicates something different from the one who speaks slowly. Even though the words might be the same, if the speed differs, the meaning we receive will also differ. And we may derive different meanings from "fast talk" depending on the speaker. Perhaps in one person we might perceive fear, feeling that he or she is hurrying to get the statement over with. In another we might perceive annoyance or lack of concern, inferring that he or she speaks rapidly so that not too much time is wasted. In still another we might perceive extreme interest, feeling that the person is speaking quickly so that he or she can get to the punch line and hear our reaction.

Parallelism. The similarity of structure among phrases and sentences.

Parallel Port. See PORT.

Parallel Processing. The analysis of a number of items simultaneously.

Parallel Structure. The use of similarly structured or composed phrases or sentences; usually a preferred way of wording the main points of a speech.

Paranormal Communication. Communication taking place through means other than the "normal" sensory channels.
["Paranormal Communication: A Symposium," *Journal of Communication* 25 (Winter 1975):96–194.]

Paraphrase. A sentence or phrase that conveys the same meaning but is presented in a different form from another sentence or phrase: "The boy hit the ball" and "The ball was hit by the boy" are paraphrases of each other. The ability to paraphrase is often taken as an indication of comprehension.

Parasocial Relationship. A perceived or imagined (rather than a real) relationship, for example, a relationship that a viewer might develop with some media personality.

Parasocial Speech. A type of intrapersonal communication that children engage in in interpersonal situations.

Parent Effectiveness Training (PET). An approach to child rearing developed by Thomas Gordon emphasizing the development of authentic communication, active listening (q.v.), no-lose conflict resolution, and I-messages (q.v.).
[Thomas Gordon, *P.E.T.: Parent Effectiveness Training* (New York: New American Library, 1975).]

Parent Ego State. The ego state (q.v.) of Parent is one that is borrowed from one's real or substitute parents and may take the form of "mothering" or controlling. In the ego state of Parent, the individual acts and speaks like a real parent; verbally and nonverbally he or she assumes the role of the parent. The Parent makes frequent use of such expressions as "don't," "should," "shouldn't," "Don't touch," "Be good," "Eat this," "I'll do it," "You'll get hurt," "Don't bother me now," "I'll get it," "Stop that," "Don't move from here," "Don't worry," "I'll fix everything," and so on. The Parent is especially evaluative and frequently uses such labels as good and bad, beautiful and ugly, healthy and sick, and similar terms to define an individual or group of individuals. Nonverbally the Parent uses his or her body to supplement the words and makes frequent use of the accusing finger, the tapping foot (indicating impatience), the head shake (indicating "no"), the disapproving arms folded in front of the abdomen, the consoling arm on the shoulder, the approving cheek pinch, and so on.

The behaviors in which we engage while in the Parent state are behaviors we learned from our real parents or from others who played significant roles in our lives or who served as parent figures—for example, a family doctor, an older brother or sister, an aunt or uncle. When we emit these behaviors we are functioning in our Parent state. Thus, when we say to someone, "That's a great job," or "You should have taken more time and done a better job," we are "repeating" the evaluative comments of our own parents.

In attempting to determine whether or not we are in the Parent state, it may help to try to find critical or demanding behaviors ("That's wrong"; "Don't do that"; "Get over here fast") or nurturing behaviors, behaviors that make it known that we will take care of everything and that the other person does not have to worry ("I'll fix it"; "I'll take care of it"; "I'll look after you"). Another good clue is to analyze the ego state of the person with whom we are interacting. If that person is in the Child state, it is likely that we are in the Parent state, because the Parent tends to stimulate and arouse the Child. If, for example, you find that your boyfriend or girlfriend is frequently in the Child state, you should probably examine your own behaviors to see if you are frequently in the Parent state and if you are bringing out the Child in your partner.

See also ADULT EGO STATE; CHILD EGO STATE.

Parliamentarian. One who functions to inform the group members of proper parliamentary procedure (q.v.).

Parliamentary Debate. A debate designed to pass, amend, or defeat motions that is conducted under the rules of parliamentary procedure.

Parole. An individual's use of language; speech.
[F. de Saussure, *Course in General Linguistics,* W. Baskin, trans. (New York: Basic Books, 1959).]

Parsimony, Law of. See OCCAM'S RAZOR.

Partito. In classical rhetoric (q.v.), the third part of the speech in which the orator states what issues were agreed upon, what issues remain to be proven, and what he intends to demonstrate in his speech. See also PARTS OF THE SPEECH.

Part of Speech. A type or class of words that performs a specific function in a sentence, for example, a noun, verb, adjective, adverb, pronoun, preposition, conjunction, article (determiner), and expletive.

Parts of the Speech (Partes Orationis). In classical rhetoric (q.v.), the speech was viewed as having six parts: exordium (q.v.) or introduction; narratio (q.v.) or statement of facts; partito (q.v.) or statement of resolved and unresolved issues; confirmation (q.v.) or arguments to prove the case; confutatio (q.v.) or refutation of opposing arguments; and peroration (q.v.) or conclusion (conclusio).

Pascal. Named for the French mathematician Blaise Pascal (1623–1662), a relatively easy to learn computer language.

Passive Listening. A form of listening that is attentive but not intrusive; listening that allows the speaker to discuss his or her thoughts and feelings without directing or influencing the speaker's messages. Used extensively in psychotherapy encounters.

Passive Vocabulary. See VOCABULARY.

Pathetic Fallacy. Using human characteristics to describe inanimate things; describing inanimate things with human emotions and cognitive abilities. See also PERSONIFICATION.

Pathogenic Secret. A secret that can cause the holder to experience psychological problems.
[Henri F. Ellenberger, *The Discovery of the Unconscious* (New York: Basic Books, 1970).]

Pathos. The quality in a message that evokes such strong emotions as pity and sympathy in the receiver; emotional appeal particularly as a method of persuasion.

Pattern Recognition. The psychological process whereby we categorize stimuli by comparing them with information stored in memory.

Pay-Off. The reward one gets from accomplishing some task. Used in transactional analysis (q.v.) to denote the reward obtained from playing a game (q.v.).

Payola. A contraction of "pay" and "Victrola," the practice of paying a disk jockey to play a specific record. The term was coined in the 1960s, after disclosures that certain disk jockeys were accepting large fees to promote certain records and artists. As a result Congress enacted laws making such payments illegal.

Pay TV. Television for which the viewer must pay directly, as opposed to free TV where the viewer pays indirectly by purchasing the advertised products.

PB Words. A phonetically balanced list of monosyllabic words that contain sounds in about the same relative frequency or proportion as they occur in ordinary speech. PB lists contain the phonemes (q.v.) of English in the same proportion to their frequency in connected discourse.

Peak Experience. An experience of intense happiness, ecstasy; an experience that makes an individual feel at one with the self and with the world; a self-actualizing experience.
[Abraham Maslow, *Motivation and Personality,* rev. ed. (New York: Harper & Row, 1970).]

Pecking Order. A status hierarchy; a hierarchy found in most formal organizations where most persons (like chickens) may be pecked by others (that is, those above them in status) and may peck others (that is, those below them in status).

Pedantry. Ostentatious demonstration of learning; the rigid following of rules and details to the neglect of commonsense principles. Applied to those communications containing elaborate figures, foreign expressions, philosophical quotations, and references to obscure authors and works.

Pedolalia. See BABY TALK.

Peer Group. A collection of equals; a group made up of persons all of whom are of equal status in regard to the functions of the group.

Peer Group Learning. A group in which members learn from their equals (their peers).

Peer Pressure. Social pressure exerted by one's associates in the direction of group conformity.

Penetration. See SOCIAL PENETRATION.

Pen Name. A name, other than one's own, used by a writer. Also known as a *nom de plume.*

Penny Press. The earliest newspapers which sold for one penny.

Pentad. A set of five elements proposed by rhetorical theorist Kenneth Burke as a framework for analyzing human motivation or any rhetorical act: act (q.v.), scene (q.v.), agent (q.v.), agency (q.v.), and purpose (q.v.).
[Kenneth Burke, *A Grammar of Motives* (Englewood Cliffs, N.J.: Prentice-Hall, 1950).]

Perception. The process of becoming aware of objects and events from the senses.

Perceptual Defense. The process or mechanism by which threatening stimuli are suppressed; a raising of one's perceptual threshold so as to prevent certain stimuli from being perceived; opposed to perceptual vigilance (q.v.).

[Elliott McGinnies, "Emotionality and Perceptual Defense," *Psychological Review* 56 (1949):244–251.]

Perceptual Vigilance. The process or mechanism by which certain stimuli are actively searched for; a lowering of one's perceptual threshold. See also PERCEPTUAL DEFENSE.

Performance. The actual utterances made by a speaker and heard by a listener. See also COMPETENCE.

Performance Appraisal. The evaluation of a worker designed to reward effectiveness and to correct ineffectiveness.

Performance Standards. The criteria by which workers are evaluated.

Performative. A statement that simultaneously performs some act, for example, "I promise . . ." or "I now pronounce you husband and wife."; opposed to constative (q.v.). See also SPEECH ACT.

Performative Analysis. An approach to the analysis of sentences that seeks to represent the underlying performative structure of all sentences. The assumption made here is that all sentences are, at the level of their underlying structure, performative sentences, that is, sentences that perform some act. See also PERFORMATIVE.

[J. R. Ross, "On Declarative Sentences," in *Readings in English Transformational Grammar,* R. A. Jacobs and P. S. Rosenbaum, eds. (Waltham, Mass.: Blaisdell, 1970).]

Performative Verb. A class of verbs whose utterance performs an act, for example, *promise, confess, convict, love.*

Periodic Sentence. A sentence in which the main clause is presented last; a sentence that becomes grammatically complete with its last word or words; opposed to loose sentence (q.v.).

Perlocutionary Act. That part of a speech act (q.v.) that has effects on the person addressed even beyond those understood by the person addressed, for example, embarrassing or consoling the person.

Perlocutionary Force. The function that is accomplished in the expression of a sentence.

Permission. Consent; allowing freedom of choice. In communication, giving oneself or another the freedom to do as one wishes in order to satisfy some need or want. For example, workaholics often refuse to give themselves permission to relax and to play; men often refuse themselves permission to cry or to express fear.

Peroration (Conclusio). In classical rhetoric (q.v.), the conclusion of a speech consisting of recapitulation, the arousing of indignation, and appealing to pity. See also PARTS OF THE SPEECH.

Perseveration. Inappropriate repetition of certain words or phrases; an inability to change the behavior one is engaging in.

Persona. The role an individual plays, usually in public. From the Latin meaning "mask," the mask or image presented to the public, but not a true representation of one's inner feelings.

Personal Construct. A belief or attitude that defines or influences the way an individual perceives and gives meaning to the world. Constructs are like hypotheses that people develop on the basis of experience or hearsay, test through their own experience, and then (perhaps) abandon, revise, or strengthen them. See also COGNITIVE COMPLEXITY.

[George A. Kelly, *The Psychology of Personal Constructs* (New York: Norton, 1955).]

Personal Distance. The second-closest proxemic (q.v.) distance, ranging from 1.5 to 4 feet.

Personality. One of the characteristics or qualities of credibility; the pleasantness of an individual; a composite of an individual's characteristics that make the person distinctive; an individual's ways of thinking and behaving. Friendly, positive, forward-looking persons are generally viewed as having a pleasing personality and are thought to be more credible.

Person, Effect of. The changes in physiological functioning brought about by the presence and the behavior of another person.

[W. H. Gantt, "Analysis of the Effect of Person," *Conditional Reflex* 7 (1972):67–73.]

Personification. A figure of speech in which human characteristics are attributed to inanimate objects as in, for example, "This room cries for activity" or "My car is tired and wants a drink." In psychology, according to Harry Stack Sullivan's theory, the image a person has of himself or herself or of some other person.

[Harry Stack Sullivan, *The Interpersonal Theory of Psychiatry* (New York: Norton, 1953).]

Perspective-Taking. Taking the viewpoint of another person; seeing the world through the eyes of another person; an empathizing ability regarded as one of the major determinants of effective interpersonal communication.

[David L. Swanson and Jesse G. Delia, *The Nature of Human Communication* (Chicago, Ill.: Science Research Associates, 1976).]

Persuasion. Persuasion is the process of influencing attitudes and behavior.

Principles of Persuasion

Thousands of articles and books—crammed with theories, descriptions, observations, and experimental tests—have been written about persuasion. Offered here is only a very small sampling of the principles of persuasion.

The Credibility Principle

A speaker will be more persuasive if she or he is perceived as credible by the audience. This means that the audience should perceive the speaker as being competent or knowledgeable, of good character, and charismatic or dynamic. If you project these characteristics, you will have a much greater chance of being believed than if you are seen not to possess them. You know this is true from your own experience; there are certain people that you believe and others that you do not believe, and that these decisions to believe or not to believe exist apart from any consideration of what is being said. (See also CREDIBILITY.)

The Attractiveness Principle

A speaker will be more persuasive if he or she is perceived as attractive and well-liked. The more attractive (physically and in personality) the speaker, the better the chance of being successful in persuasion. Physical and personality attractiveness—as perceived by the audience—are helpful components of the persuasion transaction. The obvious implication is that any speaker who wishes to effectively persuade an audience should give some attention to his or her own attractiveness.

The Selective Exposure Principle

Audiences will generally follow the "law of selective exposure." It has at least two parts: (1) that listeners will actively seek out information that supports their opinions, beliefs, values, decisions, behaviors, and the like and (2) that listeners will actively avoid information that contradicts their existing opinions, beliefs, attitudes, values, behaviors, and so on. There are a few qualifications to this "law" that are interesting to note. For example, if a person is very sure of himself or herself (that is, very sure that the opinions and attitudes held are logical, valid, and productive), then this person might not bother to seek out the support of others or may not actively avoid nonsupportive messages. Selective exposure is exercised most often when confidence in one's opinions and beliefs is weak.

This principle of selective exposure suggests a number of implications for the speaker. For example, if you are attempting to persuade an audience that holds very different attitudes from your own, anticipate selective exposure operating and proceed inductively; that is, hold back on your main purpose until they have assimilated some of your evidence and argument and only then relate it to your main (and initially contrary) proposition. If you were to present them with your thesis first, they might just "tune you out" without giving your position a fair hearing. Another implication is that you must be thoroughly knowledgeable about the attitudes of your audience if you are to succeed in making the necessary adjustments and adaptations. Still another implication is that if you, as a speaker, have been successful in weakening the confidence of the listeners in their initial position, they will seek out other sources of information to restore that confidence. In many instances they will seek out the very information that will contradict what you have been persuading them to accept. Thus, at the end of your speech, it may appear that you have been successful. But you may find that the additional information exposure subsequent to the speech convinces the listeners even more of their initial position than before you began speaking. In this instance it is necessary to reinforce your point of view repeatedly—like advertisers do—or to somehow make the audience feel comfortable with their potentially new attitudes and beliefs.

The Inoculation Principle

The principle of inoculation may be explained with the biological analogy on which it is based. Suppose you lived in a germ-free environment. Upon leaving this germ-free environment and upon exposure to germs, you would be particularly susceptible to infection because your body has not built up an immunity—it has no resistance. Resistance, the ability to fight off germs, might be achieved by the body, if not naturally, through some form of inoculation. You would, for example, be injected with a weakened dose of the germ so that your body begins the fight by building up antibodies that create an "immunity" to this type of infection. Your body, then, because of its production of antibodies, is able to fight off even powerful doses of this germ.

The situation in persuasion is similar to this biological process. Some of our attitudes and beliefs have existed in a "germ-free" environment, in an environment in which these attitudes and beliefs have never been attacked or challenged. For example, many of us have lived in an environment in which the values of a democratic form of government, the importance of education, and the traditional family structure have not been challenged. Consequently, we have not been "immunized" against attacks on these values and beliefs. We have no counterarguments (antibodies) prepared to fight off these attacks on our beliefs, so, if someone were to come along with strong arguments against these beliefs, we might be easily persuaded.

Contrast these "germ-free" beliefs with issues that have been attacked and for which we have a ready arsenal of counterarguments: our attitudes on the draft, nuclear weapons, college athletics, and thousands of other issues have been challenged in the press, on television, and in our interpersonal interactions. As a result of this exposure, we have counterarguments ready for any attacks on our beliefs concerning these issues. We have been inoculated and immunized against attacks should someone attempt to change our attitudes or beliefs.

The major implications of the inoculation principle for persuasion should be clear. First, if you are addressing an inoculated audience you must take into consideration the fact that they have a ready arsenal of counterarguments to fight your persuasive assault. Be prepared, therefore, to achieve only small gains; don't try to totally reverse the beliefs of a well-inoculated audience.

Second, if you are trying to persuade an uninoculated audience, your task is much simpler in that you do not have to penetrate a fully developed immunization shield. You also must recognize that even when an audience has not immunized itself, they take certain beliefs to be self-evident and may well tune out any attacks on such cherished beliefs or values. Again, proceed slowly and be content with small gains. Further, an inductive approach would suit your purposes better here. Attacking cherished beliefs directly will create impenetrable resistance; instead, build your case by first presenting your arguments and evidence and gradually work up to your conclusion.

Third, if you are attempting to strengthen an audience's belief, give them the antibodies they will need if ever under attack. Consider raising counterarguments to this belief and then demolishing them. Much like the injection of a small amount of a germ will enable the body to build an immunization system, presenting counterarguments and then refuting them will enable the listeners to effectively immunize themselves against future attacks on these values and beliefs. This procedure has been found to confer greater and longer-lasting resistance to strong attacks than by merely providing the audience with an arsenal of supporting arguments.

[William J. McGuire, "Inducing Resistance to Persuasion: Some Contemporary Approaches," in *Advances in Experimental Social Psychology*, I, Leonard Berkowitz, ed. (New York: Academic Press, 1964), pp. 191–229; Mary John Smith, *Persuasion and Human Action: A Review and Critique of Social Influence Theories* (Belmont, Calif.: Wadsworth, 1982).]

The Magnitude of Change Principle

The greater and more important the change desired by the speaker, the more difficult its achievement will be. The reason for this is simple enough: We normally demand a greater number of reasons and lots more evidence before we make important decisions—career changes, moving our families to another state, or investing our life savings in certain stocks. On the other hand, we may be more easily persuaded (and demand less evidence) on relatively minor issues.

Generally, people change gradually, in small degrees over a long period of time. And although there are cases of sudden conversions, this general principle seems to be valid more often than not. Persuasion, therefore, is most effective when it strives for small changes and works over a considerable period of time. Persuasion that attempts to convince the audience to radically change their attitudes or to engage in behaviors to which they are initially opposed will frequently backfire on the speaker. During this type of situation, the audience will frequently tune out the speaker, closing its ears to even the best and most logical arguments.

The Audience Participation Principle

Persuasion is greatest when the audience participates actively. In experimental tests, for example, the same speech is delivered to different audiences. The attitudes of one audience are measured before and after the speech, the difference being a measure of the speech's effectiveness. The attitudes of another group are measured before and after the speech, but they are also asked, for example, to paraphrase or summarize the various arguments of the speaker. It is consistently found that those listeners who participated actively (as in paraphrasing or summarizing) were more persuaded than those who passively received the message. Demagogues and propagandists who succeed in arousing huge crowds often have the crowds chant slogans, repeat catch phrases, and otherwise participate actively in the persuasive experience.

The Motivational Principle

Listeners are best persuaded when your propositions are positively linked to their motives—their desires, wants, wishes, and needs. You will be persuasive to the extent that you can relate the attitudes and behaviors you wish the audience to exhibit with such motives as status, financial gain, affection, love, friendship, sex, attraction, self-esteem, individuality, independence, competition, and so on.

Persuasive Definition. A definition that functions to persuade; a definition biased so as to create a positive or a negative impression.

PERT (Program Evaluation and Review Technique). A technique of problem solving by which a problem is divided into small steps in order to best analyze and evaluate it.
[Gerald M. Phillips, *Communication and the Small Group* (Indianapolis: Bobbs-Merrill, 1966).]

PET. See PARENT EFFECTIVENESS TRAINING.

Peter Pan Syndrome. Also known as Peter Panism, the inability or refusal to relinquish the role of the child and assume a mature adult role.
[Dan Kiley, *The Peter Pan Syndrome* (New York: Avon, 1985).]

Phatic Communion. The small talk that precedes the big talk, the talk that opens the channels of communication so that the important and significant issues may be discussed.

In terms of content, phatic communion is trivial—"Hello," "How are you?" "Fine weather, isn't it?" "Have a nice day," and the like. But in terms of establishing and maintaining relationships, phatic talk is extremely important. For one thing, phatic communication assures us that the social customs are in effect; the general rules of communication that we expect to operate will operate here also.

In first encounters, phatic communion enables us to reveal something of ourselves and at the same time to gain some preliminary information about the other person. Even if it is only to hear the tone or quality of voice, something is gained. Sometimes the important benefit is that phatic talk allows us time to look each other over and to decide on our next move. Phatic communion also shows us that the other person is willing to communicate, that in fact the channels of communication are open, that there is some willingness to pursue the interaction.

Phatic communion, by its nature and because of the purposes it serves, is noncontroversial; with phatic talk there is little chance for conflict or fighting. Similarly, the topics considered are unemotional and hence not ego-involving. They are neither intellectually demanding nor too personal. In phatic talk the parties avoid extreme positions; rather, they seem to engage in what appears to be rather bland chatter. But we need to see that what on the surface is shallow is actually a foundation for later and more significant communication.

All of the ways of making verbal contact may well sound trite, but they are for the most part examples of phatic communion. They are messages whose importance and usefulness should not be measured by their originality or their profundity; they should rather be taken simply as attempts to establish some kind of verbal contact.

The person who says, "Haven't I seen you here before?" is probably asking not if you have been here before but rather "Would you like to talk with me?" To answer the literal question and fail to respond to the underlying and more significant question is a clear example of miscommunication.

[Bronislaw Malinowski, "The Problem of Meaning in Primitive Languages," in *The Meaning of Meaning,* C. K. Ogden and I. A. Richards, eds. (New York: Harcourt, Brace, Jovanovich, 1923), pp. 296–336.

Phenomenal Field. In Carl Rogers's system, the total of all one's experiences.

Phileme. As used by Murray Davis, "the smallest distinguishable unit of a person's behavior that indicates his level of intimacy with whomever he is interacting." A *phileme family* is a set of related philemes; *philemics* is the scientific study of philemes: "the study of all the behaviors through which interacting individuals construct as well as communicate their relationship."

[Murray Davis, *Intimate Relations* (New York: Free Press, 1973).]

Phonation. The process of producing sound through the vibration of the vocal folds.

Phoneme. The smallest unit of sound; a bundle of sound features.

Phoneme Monitoring Task. A psycholinguistic research procedure in which linguistic forms are presented to a subject who listens for (monitors) a particular phoneme (q.v.) or sound. The time between the presentation of the sound and its identification by the subject (for example, with a buzzer press) is taken as a measure of processing difficulty.

Phonemic Restoration Effect. A perceptual phenomenon that refers to a hearer's "restoring" (or perceiving that he or she heard) a sound that is physically absent but which the context strongly suggests, for example, when the parenthesized sound was omitted in the following sentence, listeners reported hearing the sound: "The state governors met with their respective legi(s)latures convening in the capital city."

[R. M. Warren, "Perceptual Restoration of Missing Speech Sounds," *Science* 167 (1970): 392–393.]

Phonemics. The area of linguistics concerned with phonemes (q.v.), their identification and characterization, and the rules for the combination of individual phonemes into larger units of the language, for example, syllables and words.

Phonemic Transcription. A written representation of speech in which there is a different symbol for each phoneme (q.v.), each functionally different sound. See also PHONETIC TRANSCRIPTION.

Phonetics. The area of linguistics concerned with phones (q.v.) or individual speech sounds.

Phonetic Symbolism. The theory that sounds and meanings are not arbitrary. The universal phonetic symbolism hypothesis suggests that these meanings are the same in all languages while the relative phonetic symbolism hypothesis proposes that these meanings are valid within one language but differ between languages.
[Insup Kim Taylor, *Psycholinguistics* (New York: Holt, Rinehart and Winston, 1976).]

Phonetic Transcription. A written representation of speech in which each written symbol stands for an individual sound. In phonetic transcription the individual variations of a phoneme—the allophones (q.v.)—are noted whereas in phonemic transcription (q.v.) these variations are ignored.

Phonics. An approach to teaching reading based on sounds.

Phonology. The study of the sound system of a language.

Phrase. A group of words without a subject and a predicate. See also CLAUSE.

Phrase Structure Rules. Rewrite rules; rules that provide equivalences such that one may be rewritten as the other, for example, $S \rightarrow NP + VP$ and $NP \rightarrow det + N$ are phrase structure rules and are to be interpreted as instructions to rewrite sentence *(S)* as noun phrase *(NP)* plus verb phrase *(VP)* and to rewrite noun phrase as determiner *(det)* plus noun *(N)*. In generative grammar (q.v.), these rules generate the deep structure (q.v.) of a sentence.

Physiological Acoustics. See ACOUSTICS.

Pictics. The study of the pictorial code of communication (for example drawings).

Pictogram (Pictograph). A graphic symbol that pictures an object, person, or event; a pictorial symbol.

Pictograph. Bodily movement that "draws" pictures in the air of the general shape of the thing being talked about.

Pictography. A writing system using pictograms (q.v.).

Pidgin Language. A language with a simplified syntax and vocabulary. All speakers of pidgin also speak another language as their native language but unlike creole (q.v.), which derives from pidgin and which has native speakers, pidgin has no native speakers.
[Dell Hymes, ed., *Pidginization and Creolization of Languages* (Cambridge: Cambridge University Press, 1971).]

Piggybacking. The practice of running several unrelated commercials one right after the other. Also called "multiple product announcements."

Pilot Show. A sample television show created to test the popularity of a proposed series.

Pitch. The highness or lowness of the vocal tone.

Plagiarism. Using the written material of another as if it were one's own without proper acknowledgment.

Plain Folks. A persuasive or propaganda device (q.v.) in which the speaker makes himself or herself appear to be like the members of the audience—the speaker is "just plain folk."

Playing the Dozens. An interpersonal linguistic interchange that originated among blacks in which each person ridicules the other's family, especially the other's mother. Some such games utilize obscene language and sexual references while others are essentially "clean."
[Thurmon Garner, "Playing the Dozens: Folklore as Strategies for Living," *Quarterly Journal of Speech* (1983):47–57.]

Play Theory. The play theory of mass communication was formulated by British theorist William Stephenson in his *The Play Theory of Communication*. Stephenson draws a contrast between work and play. *Work* he defines as activity dealing with earning a living and with meeting the needs of one's body for food, clothing, and shelter. Work is a productive activity; it results in tangible benefits that are needed or desired by the individual. *Play,* on the other hand, is an unproductive activity; it accomplishes nothing other than the enjoyment or satisfaction it provides—it is fun.

Communication may be viewed in a similar way. In communication pleasure, nothing is accomplished; the participants are just having fun—they're playing. In communication unpleasure or communication pain, communications are intended to do work, to accomplish something—for example, to change opinion, to raise money, to solicit support.

According to Stephenson, the mass media are pleasure-oriented; their primary function is to allow us to escape work and to enjoy ourselves. Audiences look to the mass media for entertainment or play, not for information or improvement or education. The popularity of any mass medium is directly related to the degree to which it serves this function. If it allows us to escape work and gives us pleasure, it will prove popular. If it fails in this, it will prove unpopular and eventually fade out of existence.

By arguing that the mass media are used for entertainment, Stephenson is not claiming that they are useless. Play (and communication play is no exception) is an extremely important part of a healthy and well-balanced life. The media allow us to achieve this balance by providing an inexpensive and readily available supply of play materials. This theory explains a great deal about the popularity of media and may be used to explain why most current television news shows have become playful, why the personality of the newscaster is so important to viewers and ultimately to the networks and to advertisers, and why even the most sophisticated newspapers and magazines are devoting more and more space to playful items—advice columns, cartoons, human interest stories, pictures.

The play theory does not explain the whole of media influence and media viewing. It does, however, draw our attention to the role of play in the success and survival of any mass communication program or system. Theories that fail to take into consideration the importance of play are sure to be inadequate and incomplete explanations.

[William Stephenson, *The Play Theory of Communication* (Chicago, Ill.: University of Chicago Press, 1967).]

Pleasure Centers. Areas of the brain that when stimulated result in pleasurable sensations.

Pleasure Principle. The principle, articulated by Sigmund Freud (1856–1939), which assumes that people seek immediate gratification and are motivated by the achievement of pleasure.

Plot. The sequence of events in a work of literature; the scheme or plan of events in works of fiction.

Plug. Free advertisement.

Plugola. The practice of paying writers and directors for using a particular product on their shows.

Polarization. The tendency to look at the world and to describe it in terms of extremes—good or bad, positive or negative, healthy or sick, intelligent or stupid, rich or poor, and so on. It is often referred to as the fallacy of "either-or" or "black-and-white." Although it is true that magnetic poles may be described as positive or negative and that certain people are extremely rich while others are extremely poor, the vast majority of cases are clearly in the middle, between these two extremes. Most people exist somewhere between the extremes of good and bad, healthy or sick, intelligent or stupid, rich or poor. Yet there seems to be a strong tendency to view only the extremes and to categorize people, objects, and events in terms of these polar opposites.

This tendency may be easily illustrated by attempting to fill in the polar opposites for the following words:

tall   →   _____
heavy →   _____
strong →   _____
happy →   _____
legal   →   _____

Filling in these opposites should have been relatively easy and quick. The words should also have been fairly short. Further, if a number of people supplied opposites, we would find a high degree of agreement among them.

Now attempt to fill in the middle positions with words meaning, for example, "midway between tall and short," "midway between heavy and light," and so on. These midway responses (compared to the opposites) were probably more difficult to think of and took more time. The words should also have been fairly long or phrases of two, three, four, or more words. Further, we would probably find rather low agreement among different people completing this same task.

It might be helpful to visualize the familiar bell-shaped curve. Few items exist at either of the two extremes, but as we move closer to the center, more and more items are included. This is true of any random sample. If we selected 100 people at random, we would find that their intelligence, height, weight, income, age, health, and so on would, if plotted, fall into a bell-shaped or "normal" distribution. Yet our tendency seems to be to concentrate on the extremes, on the ends of this curve, and ignore the middle, which contains the vast majority of cases.

It is legitimate to phrase certain statements in terms of two values. For example, this thing that you are holding is either a book or it is not. Clearly the classes of book and not-book include all possibilities. And so there is no problem with this kind of statement. Similarly, we may say that the student will either pass this course or will not pass it; these two categories include all possibilities.

We create problems, however, when we use this basic form in situations in which it is inappropriate, for example, "The politician is either for us or against us." Note that these two possibilities do not include all possibilities; the politician may be for us in some things and against us in other things, or he or she may be neutral.

Pollyanna Hypothesis. The Pollyanna hypothesis states that "there is a universal human tendency to use evaluatively positive (E+) words more frequently, diversely, and facilely than evaluatively negative (E−) words." Put differently, we all tend to say the positive rather than the negative thing more often, in more different situations, and with greater ease. Some examples of the kind of evidence used to formulate this hypothesis might make this clearer still. In one situation the experimenters gave 100 high school boys in 13 different language communities a list of 100 culture-common nouns. The boys were instructed to write down the first qualifier that occurred to them for each of the 100 nouns. In

12 of the 13 language communities, more E+ words were supplied than E– words.

In the language of children this Pollyanna effect is also present. When the vocabularies of children are analyzed it is found that the frequency and diversity of the usage of E+ terms is much higher than that of E– terms. Although this difference gets smaller as the child grows older, E+ words are still more frequently and more diversely used in adult language.

Numerous studies have shown that E+ words are easier to learn than E– words. E+ words can be learned in less time and with fewer errors than can E– words. Also, it has been demonstrated repeatedly that E+ words can be recognized at lower recognition thresholds than can E– words. That is, the stimulus has to be more intense (brighter, louder) for E– words to be recognized than for E+ words.

Two major theories have been advanced to account for this effect. One position argues that the positive evaluation leads to the high frequency of usage; that is, the words are used more frequently because they are of positive evaluation. The other position argues that the high frequency leads to positive evaluation; that is, the words that are used most frequently become more positive in evaluation. This position is also known as the "mere exposure" (q.v.) hypothesis, and although at first it may appear totally inaccurate and illogical, there is much experimental support in its favor. In terms of language usage, however, the first position seems the more accurate. See also NEGATIVITY EFFECT.
[Jerry Boucher and Charles E. Osgood, "The Pollyanna Hypothesis," *Journal of Verbal Learning and Verbal Behavior* 8 (1969):1–8.]

Polychronism. A time orientation of a society or culture in which several events may be scheduled at the same time; opposed to monochronism (q.v.). See also TEMPORAL COMMUNICATION.

Polyglot. One who speaks and understands a number of different languages.

Polymorphism. See OPINION LEADER.

Polysemy. Having several different meanings.

Pons. See PROFILE OF NONVERBAL SENSITIVITY TEST.

Pooh-Pooh Theory. Also referred to as the "interjectional theory," a theory of language origin holding that language began with utterances made as instinctive reactions to emotional strain, and these exclamations soon came to be used as names for the emotions or feelings that gave rise to these sounds.

Popular Culture. Forms of entertainment that enjoy widespread popularity such as films, television, and comics.

Pornography. Messages judged to be primarily sexual; messages designed to arouse sexual excitement and which are judged to be contrary to the community's acceptable standards.

Port. A channel through which data are sent and received by a computer. Parallel ports can send or receive several bits of information at the same time; serial ports can only send or receive one bit of information at a time.

Portmanteau Word. A blend; a word formed from the combination of other words, for example, Lewis Carroll's *"slithy"* from *lithe* and *slimy.*

Positive Feedback. Feedback (q.v.) that supports or reinforces behavior along the lines that it is already proceeding, for example, applause during a speech. See also NEGATIVE FEEDBACK; FEEDBACK REGULATION.

Positive Regard. See UNCONDITIONAL POSITIVE REGARD.

Positive Reinforcement. The strengthening of a particular response by making a reward contingent upon it. The process may be visualized in three stages: (1) a response is emitted, for example, a child says "daddy"; (2) a reward is given, for example, a smile or candy or touching; (3) the response, "daddy," is strengthened, that is, it is more likely to occur under similar circumstances. See also NEGATIVE REINFORCEMENT.

Positive Sum Game. A game in which the winnings exceed the losses; a game in which the winners outnumber the losers. See also NEGATIVE SUM GAME; ZERO SUM GAME.

Postural Sex Identifiers. A proxemic category denoting the sex and posture of the interactants. Six main divisions are noted: man prone, man sitting or squatting, man standing, woman prone, woman sitting or squatting, woman standing. See also PROXEMICS; PROXEMIC BEHAVIOR CATEGORIES.

Potency Meaning. A kind of connotative meaning that may be indexed in terms of such scales as strong–weak, potent–impotent.

Power. A relationship between or among people such that the one with power has the ability or potential to control the behaviors of the other(s). Thus, if A has power over B and C, then A (by virtue of this power and through the exercise of this power or the threat of it being exercised) can control the behaviors of B and C. John French and Bertram Raven, and later Raven and his associates, identified six power bases or types of power.

Referent Power. Person A may be said to have power over person B when B wishes to be like A or to be identified with A. For example, an older brother may have power over a younger brother because the younger brother wants to be like the older brother.

Legitimate Power. Person A has legitimate power over person B when B believes that A has a right—by virtue of A's position—to influence or control B's behavior. If I believe that someone has the right to control my behavior, then that person may be said to have control over me.

Reward Power. Person A has reward power over person B if A has the ability to reward B. Reward may be material (for example, money, promotion, jewelry) or social (for example, love, friendship, respect).

Coercive Power. Person A has coercive power over person B when A has the ability to administer punishment or to remove rewards from B should B not yield to the influence of A.

Expert Power. Person A has expert power over person B if A is regarded by B as having expertise or knowledge—the knowledge that A has gives A expert power.

Information or Persuasion Power. Person A has information or persuasion power over person B when B attributes to A the ability to communicate logically and persuasively. We generally attribute persuasion power to someone we see as possessing significant information and the ability to use that information in presenting a well-reasoned, well-thought out argument.

John Kenneth Galbraith offers a three-part classification of the types of power: (1) Condign power is the ability to punish—by inflicting or threatening punishment, power is exerted and submission is achieved; (2) compensatory power is the ability to reward someone with something of value, submission is achieved; (3) conditioned power is exerted by persuasion—power is exerted by changing beliefs (for example, through education) so that the individual conforms or submits because he or she believes it is right and just to do so.

[John R. P. French, Jr. and Bertram Raven, "The Bases of Social Power," in *Group Dynamics: Research and Theory,* 3d ed., Dorwin Cartwright and Alvin Zander, eds. (New York: Harper & Row, 1968), pp. 259–269; B. Raven, C. Centers, and A. Rodrigues, "The Bases of Conjugal Power," in *Power in Families,* R. E. Cromwell and D. H. Olson, eds. (New York: Halsted Press, 1975), pp. 217–234; John Kenneth Galbraith, *The Anatomy of Power* (Boston: Houghton Mifflin, 1983).]

Power Games. Patterns of interaction that are basically unfair and dishonest and in which one person attempts to control the behaviors of another through manipulation (q.v.) rather than reason or persuasion.
[Claude M. Steiner, *The Other Side of Power* (New York: Grove, 1981).]

Practical Criticism. Sometimes called "applied criticism"; the evaluation of specific works and writers. See also CRITICISM: THEORETICAL CRITICISM.

Pragmatic Implication. The probable consequence or implication of a statement, for example, the pragmatic implications of the statement "She has a fever of 104°" would indicate that a thermometer was used to take the temperature, that a doctor should or will be called, and that measures will be or are being taken to reduce the fever.

Pragmatics. That division of semiotics (q.v.) concerned with the uses and effects of language; an approach to communication that focuses on the behavioral aspects.
[Charles Morris, *Signs, Language and Behavior* (New York: George Braziller, 1955); Paul Watzlawick, Janet Beavin, and Don Jackson, *Pragmatics of Human Communication: A Study of Interactional Patterns, Pathologies, and Paradoxes* (New York: Norton, 1967).]

Predispositions Toward Verbal Behavior Scale (PVB). A 25-item self-report scale designed to measure an individual's predisposition to engage in verbal behavior.
[C. David Mortensen, Paul H. Arntson, and Myron Lustig, "The Measurement of Verbal Predispositions: Scale Development and Application," *Human Communication Research* 3 (1977):146–158.]

Preening Behavior. Primping gestures; nonverbal behaviors aimed at making oneself more attractive or more desirable to another person and that basically rearrange or fix one's hair or clothing. Popular preening gestures include running one's fingers through one's hair, fixing a tie, straightening one's socks or stockings.

Prefix. See AFFIX.

Prejudice. Negative attitude toward some particular group of people, for example, a racial, ethnic, or religious group.

Prekinesics. The area of kinesics (q.v.) concerned with the physiological aspects of bodily movements.

Premack Principle. See DIFFERENTIAL PROBABILITY HYPOTHESIS.

Premise. An assumption underlying an argument and from which conclusions may be deduced.

Preoperational Stage. In Piaget's theory of child development, a stage occurring from around 2 to 7 years of age at which the child learns speech and how to use speech to manipulate and control the environment.

Prescriptive Grammar. The rules speakers of a language should follow in order to speak correctly or in an acceptable manner; opposed to descriptive grammar (q.v.). Also called "normative grammar."

Present-Moment Living. The tendency to live in the present, to devote primary attention to one's present experiences rather than living in the past or for the future.
[Richard S. Ruch, "Present-Moment Living," *Humanist* 39 (January–February, 1979):32–35.]

Prestige Dialect. That dialect of a language that is regarded as superior to others; the dialect spoken by persons regarded as better educated and more socially prominent.

Prestige Suggestion. A persuasive technique in which a high prestige source (for example, a noted scientist or writer) is positively connected to a thesis or proposition. A form of intensional orientation (q.v.).

Presumption. A concept developed by Richard Whately in his *Rhetoric* (1828), the assumption that something should remain as it is until sufficient proof is advanced against it. According to Whately and contemporary theorists, there is a presumption in favor of the status quo. In most legal systems there is a presumption of innocence and the burden of proof (q.v.) rests on those who would refute or argue against this presumed innocence.

Prevarication. The feature of human language that makes lying possible.

Primacy. The tendency to remember best (and to be most influenced by) what is heard first. See also RECENCY.

Primacy Effect. The condition by which what comes first exerts greater influence than what follows. See also RECENCY EFFECT.

Primary Group. A group whose members have an intimate and long-lasting relationship with each other, for example, a family. See also SECONDARY GROUP.

Primary Reinforcement. A stimulus that increases the likelihood of behavior occurring without prior learning and which determines the strength of a response or the frequency of the response; opposed to secondary reinforcer (q.v.) whose reinforcing value is acquired through learning. Food, for example, is a primary reinforcer. See also REINFORCEMENT.

Primary Stuttering. Disfluencies in speech that are normal in children and that are produced without any conscious awareness that these are nonfluences and without any attempt to suppress them. See also SECONDARY STUTTERING.

Primary Territory. An area or territory that is regularly used by an individual in his or her everyday activities.
[I. Altman, *The Environment and Social Behavior* (Monterey, Calif.: Brooks/Cole, 1975).]

Prime Time. The time during which the media have their largest audiences. Television prime time is 7:30 to 11:00 P.M. EST and 6:30 to 10:00 P.M. CST.

Prior Residence Effect. The advantage one has in power and effectiveness when in one's own territory.

Prisoner's Dilemma. A game used in the study of numerous communication variables such as conflict, cooperation, competition, trust. In this game two "convicts" are interrogated separately. If both confess to the "crime," both will serve lenient sentences. If both claim innocence, both will go free. If one confesses and one does not, the one that confesses is set free and the one who does not confess is "convicted."
[Anatol Rapoport, *Fights, Games and Debates* (Ann Arbor, Michigan: University of Michigan Press, 1960).]

Problem Orientation. A focus on a problem and its possible solutions rather than on controlling the group processes; opposed to control (q.v.). Problem orientation encourages supportiveness (q.v.).

Problem-Solving Group. Perhaps the type of group most familiar to us when we think of small group communication is the problem-solving group—a group of individuals meeting to solve a particular problem or to at least reach a decision that may be a preface to the solution.

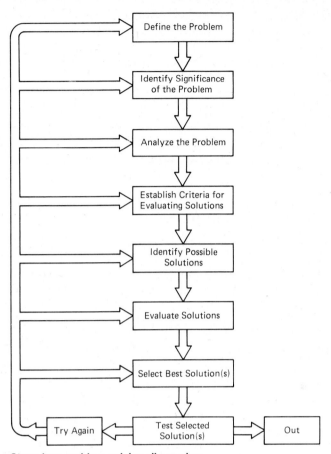

Steps in a problem-solving discussion.

In a problem-solving discussion it is useful to identify approximately eight steps that should be followed. These steps are designed to make problem-solving more efficient and more effective. Although some of the initial steps may at first seem unnecessary and there may be a temptation to short-circuit this process, it has been found repeatedly that this does not in fact save time; rather it wastes time in the long run. These steps to be followed are:

1. Define the Problem

In many instances the nature of the problem is clearly specified, and everyone in the group knows exactly what the problem is, for example, what color the new soap package should be or what the name for the new candy bar should be. In other instances, however, the problem may be vague, and it remains for the group to define it in concrete, unambiguous, specific terms. The problem should also be limited in some way so that it identifies a manageable area for discussion. Generally, it is best to define the problem as an open-ended question ("How can we improve the student newspaper?") rather than as a statement ("The student newspaper needs to be improved") or a yes/no question ("Does the student newspaper need improvement?"). The open-ended question allows for greater freedom of exploration and does not restrict the ways in which the problem may be approached. Further, the statement of the problem should not suggest possible solutions, as would, for example, "How can faculty supervision improve the student newspaper?" Here we are stating that faculty supervision is the solution to the problem of improving the student newspaper rather than leaving the solutions open for discussants to identify and evaluate.

2. Identify the Significance of the Problem

In many groups all the participants will be aware of the importance or significance of the problem. In other groups it may be helpful for the significance of the problem to be stressed. Sometimes the importance of an issue is recognized only in the abstract, and it may be helpful for its importance to be made more concrete. Sometimes it is recognized that the problem is important for others, and it remains to be pointed out how the problem affects the members of the group themselves. Group members need to be aware of what the implications of the problem are, how this problem may lead to other problems, in what ways this problem blocks goals that group members value, how this problem impinges on the lives of group members, and so on. The more important the problem is perceived to be by the group members, the more importance they will give to the problem-solving process and the more energy they will be willing to expend in dealing with the problem.

3. Analyze the Problem

In the analysis of the problem the group members seek to identify the ramifications of the problem. Given a general problem, we seek in this analysis stage to identify its particular dimensions. Although there are no prescribed questions to ask of all problems, appropriate questions (for most problems) seem to revolve around the following issues: (1) *Duration*. How long has the problem existed? Is it likely that it will continue to exist in the future? What is the predicted course of the problem?, for example, will it grow or lessen in influence? (2) *Causes*. What are the major causes of the problem? How certain may we be that these are the actual causes? (3) *Effects*. What are the effects of the problem? How significant are these effects? Who is affected by this problem? How significantly are they affected by the problem? Is this problem causing other problems? How important are these other problems?

4. Establish Criteria for Evaluating the Solutions

Before any solutions are proposed, the group members should identify the standards that will be employed in evaluating the possible solutions, the criteria that will be used in selecting one solution over another. After the solutions are identified (step 5), the members go back to these standards to make certain that the new solution does meet these criteria.

5. Identify Possible Solutions

At this brainstorming (q.v.) stage the members attempt to identify as many solutions as possible. It is best to focus on quantity rather than quality. Try to identify as many solutions as possible. Brainstorming may be particularly useful at this point. *Brainstorming* is a technique for literally bombarding a problem and generating as many ideas or solutions as possible.

6. Evaluate Solutions

After all the solutions have been proposed, the members evaluate each of them according to the criteria for evaluating solutions established in step 4. Each solution should be matched against the criteria for evaluating solutions.

7. Select the Best Solution(s)

At this stage the best solution or solutions are selected and put into operation.

8. Test Selected Solutions

After we put the solution(s) into operation, we attempt to test their effectiveness. If these solutions prove ineffective, then it is necessary to go back to one of the previous stages and go through part of the process again. Often this takes the form of selecting other solutions to test, but it may involve going further back to, for example, a reanalysis of the problem, an identification of other solutions, or a restatement of criteria.

These eight steps may seem at first to be rather rigidly prescribed, but for most problem-solving discussions it would probably not be a bad idea to follow the pattern with some precision. When discussants become more adept at the problem-solving process, the steps may be approached with greater flexibility, where participants go back and forth and may skip a step and come back to it after a normally later step has been covered. Even with such flexibility, however, the problem-solving process is generally fairly clearly prescribed.

Process. Ongoing activity; nonstatic. Communication is referred to as a process to emphasize that it is always changing, always in motion.

Productivity. The feature of language that makes possible the creation and understanding of novel utterances. With human language we can talk about matters that have never been talked about before, and similarly we can understand utterances that we have never heard before. Productivity also allows for the creation of new words. Also referred to as "openness" and "creativity."

Profile of Nonverbal Sensitivity Test (Pons). A test in which a subject views a film consisting of 220 segments. These 220 segments are made up of 20 scenes, each of which is represented by 11 nonverbal communication channels (for example, face alone, no voice; body from the neck to the knees, no voice). The subject's task is to indicate the label that correctly describes the scene.
[Robert Rosenthal, Judity A. Hall, Dane Archer, M. Robin DeMatteo, and Peter L. Rogers, "The Pons Test: Measuring Sensitivity to Nonverbal Cues," in Shirley Weitz, ed., *Nonverbal Communication: Readings with Commentary* (New York: Oxford, 1979), pp. 357–370.]

Progymnasmata. A series of elementary exercises, graduating in difficulty, that were used in ancient Greece and Rome as preparatory to the study of rhetoric (q.v.) and oratory (q.v.). In some exercises the student learned alternative ways of expressing an idea; in more advanced exercises, the students developed short speeches of praise or blame or argued for or against a particular issue.

Projection. A defense mechanism whereby individuals "see" in others characteristics they themselves possess.

Prolegomenon. An introduction or preface, of any length, to a work that sets forth the work's purpose or point of view.

Propaganda. Organized persuasion; the spreading of ideas and values through a variety of persuasive devices; popularly viewed as persuasion that is unethical and relies on unfair tactics and concerned with ideas that are often thought harmful. See also PROPAGANDA DEVICES.
[Alfred McClung Lee and Elizabeth Briant Lee, *The Fine Art of Propaganda* [1939] (San Francisco: International Society for General Semantics, 1979).]

Propaganda Devices. In *The Fine Art of Propaganda,* prepared for the Institute for Propaganda Analysis, seven propaganda devices are identified—seven ways in which the propagandist (the unethical persuader) attempts to gain our compliance without logic or evidence.

Name Calling

Here the propagandist gives an idea, a group of people, or a political ideology a bad name ("Communist," "Nazi") and in this way attempts to make us condemn the idea without analyzing the argument and evidence.

Glittering Generality

This is the opposite of name calling. Here the propagandist attempts to gain our acceptance of some idea by associating it with things we value highly ("democracy," "Americanism"). By using "virtue words," the propagandist attempts to get us to ignore the evidence and simply approve of the idea.

Transfer

Here the propagandist associates his or her idea with something we respect (in order to gain our approval) or with something we detest (in order to gain our rejection).

Testimonial

This device involves using the authority of some person to gain our approval (if we respect the person) or our rejection (if we do not respect the person). This is the technique of advertisers who use testimonials of famous and well-liked people to get us to buy everything from soft drinks to cereal to designer jeans.

Plain Folks

With this propaganda device, the speaker identifies himself or herself and their propositions with the audience. The speaker and the proposition are good—the "reasoning" goes—because they are one of the people, just "plain folks" like the rest of us.

Card Stacking

The persuader here selects only the evidence and arguments that build a case (even falsifies evidence and distorts the facts). Although there is a deliberate attempt to distort the available evidence or to select only that which would fit the speaker's conclusions, the "evidence" is presented as being a fair and unbiased representation.

Band Wagon

Using this device, the speaker persuades the audience to accept or reject a particular idea or proposal because "everybody is doing it," or perhaps because the "right" people are doing it. The propagandist persuades by convincing us to jump on the band wagon.

[Alfred McClung Lee and Elizabeth Briant Lee, *The Fine Art of Propaganda* [1939] (San Francisco: International Society for General Semantics, 1979).]

Propinquity. Physical proximity (q.v.); closeness.

Proposition. A minimal sentence; a linguistic unit containing a verb and its arguments (q.v.).

Propositional Analysis. The analysis of a text into its minimal linguistic units (propositions, q.v.) or subject and predicate units.

Prose. Direct writing that is based on and imitates normal speech; writing that is unrestricted as to, for example, rhyme or rhythm.

Prosocial Behavior. Behavior that benefits others rather than the person performing the behavior and may even involve personal risk or loss.

Prosody. The study or art of metrical structure or versification that concentrates on, for example, rhyme, rhythm, and meter.

Proto-. When used as a prefix—as in proto-IndoEuropean—it refers to the earliest known form of the language.

Proverb. A short statement of some generally accepted truth.

Provisionalism. An attitude of open-mindedness (q.v.) that leads to the creation of supportiveness (q.v.); opposed to certainty (q.v.).

Proxemic Behavior Categories. Eight categories identified by Edward T. Hall for the analysis of proxemic (q.v.) or spatial behavior: postural-sex identifiers (q.v.); sociofugal–sociopetal axis (q.v.); kinesthetic factors (q.v.); touch code (q.v.); visual code (q.v.); thermal code (q.v.); olfaction (q.v.); and voice loudness (q.v.). Each of these categories is subdivided into smaller categories or classes.
[Edward T. Hall, "A System for the Notation of Proxemic Behavior," *American Anthropologist* 65 (1963):1003–1026.]

Proxemics. In "A System for the Notation of Proxemic Behavior," Edward T. Hall defines *proxemics* as the "study of how man unconsciously structures microspace—the distance between men in the conduct of their daily transactions, the organization of space in his houses and buildings, and ultimately the layout of his towns."

Proxemic Dimensions

Eight general classes of proxemic behaviors have been identified: postural-sex identifiers (q.v.), sociofugal-sociopetal orientation (q.v.), kinesthetic factors (q.v.), touch (q.v.), vision (q.v.), thermal factors (q.v.), loudness (q.v.), and smell or olfaction (q.v.).

Proxemic Distances

One of the earliest references to space as communication occurs in the Gospel of Luke (14:1–11):

When thou are invited to a wedding feast, do not recline in the first place, lest perhaps one more distinguished than thou have been invited by him. And he who invited thee and him, come and say to thee, "Make room for this man"; and then thou begin with shame to take the last place. But when thou art invited, go and recline in the last place; that when he who invited thee comes in, he may say to thee, "Friend, go up higher!" Then thou wilt be honored in the presence of all who are at table with thee. For everyone who exalts himself shall be humbled, and he who humbles himself shall be exalted.

This brief passage illustrates one of the concepts or meanings that space communicates, namely, status. We know, for example, that in a large organization status is the basis for determining how large an office one receives, whether that office has a window or not, how high up the office is (that is, on what floor of the building), and how close one's office is to that of the president or chairperson.

Space is especially important in interpersonal communication, although we seldom think about it or even consider the possibility that it might serve a communicative function. Hall distinguishes four distances that he feels define the type of relationship permitted. Each of these four distances has a close phase and a far phase, giving us a total of eight clearly identifiable distances. These four distances, according to Hall, correspond to the four major types of relationships: intimate, personal, social, and public.

Intimate Distance

In intimate distance, ranging from the close phase of actual touching to the far phase of 6 to 18 inches, the presence of the other individual is unmistakable. Each individual experiences the sound, smell, and feel of the other's breath. The close phase is used for lovemaking and wrestling, for comforting and protecting. In the close phase the muscles and the skin communicate, while actual verbalizations play a minor role. In this close phase whispering, says Hall, has the effect of increasing the psychological distance between the two individuals. The far phase allows us to touch each other by extending our hands. The distance is so close that it is not considered proper in public, and because of the feeling of inappropriateness and discomfort (at least for Americans), the eyes seldom meet but remain fixed on some remote object.

Personal Distance

Each of us, says Hall, carries around with him or her a protective bubble defining our personal distance, which allows us to stay protected and untouched by others. In the close phase of personal distance (from 1.5 to 2.5 feet) we can still hold or grasp each other but only by extending our arms. We can then take into our protective bubble certain individuals—for example, loved ones. In the far phase (from 2.5 to 4 feet) two people can only touch each other if they both extend their arms. This far phase is the extent to which we can physically get our hands on things, and hence it defines, in one sense, the limits of our physical control over others. Even at this distance we can see many of the fine details of an individual—the gray hairs, tooth stains, clothing lint, and so on. However, we can no longer detect body heat. At times we may detect breath odor, but generally at this distance etiquette demands that we direct our breath to some neutral corner so as not to offend.

This distance is particularly interesting from the point of view of body odor and the colognes designed to hide it. At this distance we cannot perceive normal cologne or perfume. Thus it has been proposed that cologne has two functions: First, it serves to disguise the body odor or hide it; and second, it serves to make clear the limits of the protective bubble around the individual. The bubble, defined by the perfume, signals that you may not enter beyond the point where you can smell me.

Social Distance

At the social distance we lose the visual detail we had in the personal distance. The close phase (from 4 to 7 feet) is the distance at which we conduct impersonal business, the distance at which we interact at a social gathering. The far phase (from 7 to 12 feet) is the distance we stand when someone says, "Stand away so I can look at you." At this level business transactions have a more formal tone than when conducted in the close phase. In offices of high officials the desks are positioned so that the individual is assured of at least this distance when dealing with clients. Unlike the intimate distance, where eye contact is awkward, the far phase of the social distance makes eye contact essential, otherwise communication is lost. The voice is generally louder than normal at this level, but shouting or raising the voice has the effect of reducing the social distance to a personal distance. It is at this distance that we can work with people and yet not constantly interact with them and not appear rude. At certain distances, of course, one cannot ignore the presence of another individual. At other distances, however, we can ignore the other individual and keep to our own business.

This social distance requires that a certain amount of space be available. In many instances, however, such distances are not available; yet it is necessary to keep social distance, at least psychologically if not physically. For this we attempt different arrangements with the furniture. In small offices in colleges, for example, professors sharing an office might have their desks facing in different directions so that each may stay separated from the other. Or they may position their desks against a wall so that each will feel psychologically alone in the office and thus be able to effectively maintain a social rather than a personal distance.

Public Distance

In the close phase of public distance (from 12 to 15 feet) an individual seems protected by space. At this distance one is able to take defensive action should one be threatened. On a public bus or train, for example, we might keep at least this distance from a drunkard so that should anything come up (literally or figuratively) we could get away in time. Although at this distance we lose the fine details of the face and eyes, we are still close enough to see what is happening should we need to take defensive action.

At the far phase (more than 25 feet) we see individuals not as separate individuals but as part of the whole setting. We automatically set approximately 30 feet around public figures who are of considerable importance, and we seem to do this whether or not there are guards preventing us from entering this distance. This far phase is, of course, the distance from which actors perform on stage; consequently, their actions and voices will have to be somewhat exaggerated.

[Edward T. Hall, *The Silent Language* (Garden City, N.Y.: Doubleday, 1959); *The Hidden Dimension* (Garden City, N.Y.: Doubleday, 1966).]

Proximity. Physical closeness; one of the qualities influencing interpersonal attractiveness (q.v.). In perception, the law of proximity holds that the objects that are physically close to each other will be perceived as a unit or group.

Proxy. A statement granting one individual the right to act for another.

Pseudocommunication. A form of miscommunication in which each party incorrectly assumes that the other understands the meanings intended to be communicated.

Pseudoevent. Events that would normally be considered unimportant but to which the media gives extensive coverage and thus makes them appear important.

Psychodrama. A therapeutic experience developed by J. L. Moreno where the individual participates in or acts out a psychological drama. The acting out, together with feedback from other group members, is considered helpful in enabling the individual to better understand the problem, accept the problem situation as it is, or change some attitude or behavior.

Psychogrammatical Factors. Linguistic elements that are thought to have significant psychological correlates.

[Wendell Johnson, *People in Quandaries: The Semantics of Personal Adjustment* (New York: Harper & Row, 1946); Joseph A. DeVito, "Psychogrammatical Factors in Oral and Written Discourse by Skilled Communicators," *Communication Monographs* 33 (1966): 73–76.]

Psycholinguistics. The study of the psychological processes of speaking and hearing, and of language acquisition and development in the child.

[Joseph A. DeVito, *The Psychology of Speech and Language: An Introduction to Psycholinguistics* (Washington, D.C.: University Press of America [1970], 1981); Danny D. Steinberg, *Psycholinguistics: Language, Mind and World* (New York: Longman, 1982); Donald J. Foss and David T. Hakes, *Psycholinguistics: An Introduction to the Psychology of Language* (Englewood Cliffs, N.J.: Prentice-Hall, 1978).]

Psychological Acoustics. See ACOUSTICS.

Psychomotor Domain. That area of learning (behavioral objectives, q.v.) concerned with motor or perceptual motor skills, for example, gross and finely coordinated bodily movements and verbal and nonverbal behaviors such as reading Braille, playing a piano, communicating one's wants by gesture, communicating one's ideas in a public speech. See also BEHAVIORAL OBJECTIVE.

Public Distance. The farthest proxemic (q.v.) distance, ranging from 12 to over 25 feet.

Public Domain. Material that may be used freely by the public; material that has not been copyrighted or whose copyright has expired and thus may now be used without securing anyone's permission.

Public Speaking. That form of communication in which a speaker addresses a relatively large audience with a relatively continuous discourse, usually in a face-to-face situation. Here eight principles or steps for constructing an effective public speech are identified.

1. Select the Topic and Purpose

The first step in preparing a public speech is to select the subject on which you will speak and the general and specific purposes you hope to achieve. Each of these is considered in turn.

The Topic

Select a topic that is worthwhile and will prove relevant and interesting to both the audience and to you. After all, you will invest a great deal of time and energy in studying and organizing the topic, and you should derive something of value from the topic itself as well as from the application of the public speaking principles.

If your speech is to be persuasive, one in which you attempt to influence the attitudes or behaviors of your audience, it would be best to select a topic about which both you and the audience agree and attempt to strengthen rather than to change their existing attitudes. Or you might select a topic about which the audience is relatively neutral and attempt to persuade them to feel either positively or negatively, as you think best. Be certain to limit and narrow your topic to manageable proportions; do not try to cover too much. It would be much better to cover a limited aspect of a topic in depth than to attempt to cover a broad topic but only superficially.

The Purpose

Generally, three types of speeches are distinguished. The type of speech selected will depend on your purpose in making the speech, although in many instances the dividing lines between the different types are not always easy to draw. Recognize that some of the distinctions are made for practical and pedagogical purposes rather than because these distinctions always exist in clear form. The three purposes of speeches are to inform, to persuade, and to serve some ceremonial or special occasion function.

The *informative speech* is designed to create understanding—to clarify, to enlighten, to correct misunderstandings, to demonstrate how something works, to explain how something is structured. In this type of speech we rely most heavily on materials that amplify—on examples, illustrations, definitions, testimony, visual aids, and the like.

The *persuasive speech,* on the other hand, is designed to influence attitudes or behaviors—to strengthen existing attitudes or to change the beliefs of the audience; to motivate behavior or redirect the way in which audience members act. In this type of speech we rely most heavily on materials that offer proof—on evidence, argument, and psychological appeals, for example. Any persuasive speech is in part an informative speech and as such contains materials that amplify, illustrate, define, and so on. It would probably be impossible to persuade an audience of something without informing them as well. But in its concern with strengthening or changing attitudes and behaviors, the persuasive speech must go beyond amplification to the use of evidence, argument, motivational appeals, and the like.

The *special occasion speech* contains elements of information and persuasion; yet it is distinctive enough to merit a special division. "Special occasion" means speeches designed, for example, to introduce another speaker or a group of speakers; to present a tribute to some individual, institution, or event; and, perhaps most importantly, to secure good will—for an individual, for an institution, for a way of life, for a point of view. This special occasion speech, as you can easily appreciate, is most closely related to the persuasive speech.

Whether you intend to inform, to persuade, to praise, or to introduce, you must narrow your specific purpose. Too many speakers attempt to cover too much in too little time. If your specific purpose is narrow enough, you can go into some depth on those aspects of the topic you do choose to cover. The audience benefits most from a speech that covers a small area in some depth. Otherwise, you will find that you will be telling them essentially what they already know or will be giving them so many new facts and data that they could not possibly retain even a small part of them. Select a few main issues within the topic and illustrate, explain, describe, and support them in a variety of ways.

2. Analyze the Audience

If you are to inform or persuade your audience, you must know them. Who are they? What do they already know? What would they want to know more about? What special competencies do they have? What opinions, attitudes, and beliefs do they have? Where do they stand on the issues you wish to address? What needs do they have? Specifically, you might wish to focus on some of the following variables, asking yourself what are their implications for your subject, purpose, and method of construction and presentation, and, in fact, for any and all aspects of public speaking.

Age. What is the general age of the audience? How wide is the range? Are there different age groups that will have to be addressed differently? Does the age of the audience impose any limitations on the topic? On the language that will be used? On the examples and illustrations to be selected?

Sex. What is the predominant sex of the audience? Do men and women view the topic differently? If so, how? Do men and women have different backgrounds and experiences and knowledge about the topic? How will this influence the way in which the topic is developed?

Cultural and Subcultural Factors. How does the audience break down in terms of ethnic and racial background? What implications are there for the topic?

For the purpose? For the method of development? Do the experiences, back-grounds, and knowledge of these groups differ so that adjustments must be made in the way in which the speech is constructed? Will the audience identify with you or see you as an outsider—as one outside their own cultural or subcultural group—and what are the implications of this?

Occupation, Income, and Status of the Audience. What are the main occupations of the audience? How might this influence your speech? Does the income of the audience have any implications for the subject chosen, or the way in which it will be developed? What about the general status of the audience members? Might this influence the speech in any way?

Religion and Religiousness. What is the dominant religious affiliation of the audience? What are the implications of this for the speech? What is the strength of their belief? How might this relate to the speech topic?

Other Factors. What other factors will influence the way in which your speech is prepared and presented? Is marital status relevant? Does the audience have special interests that might be noted in the speech?

Occasion. Is it a special occasion? Does it impose any restrictions on what may or may not be considered appropriate? Are there any implications for the way in which the speech is prepared or presented?

Context. Will the context influence what you discuss or the way in which your speech is presented? Will the context impose any restrictions? Are there appropriate facilities for showing slides? Is there a blackboard? Is there adequate light? Are there enough seats? Is there a podium? Is a microphone necessary?

3. Research the Topic

If the speech is to be worthwhile and if you and the audience are to profit from it, you must research the topic. This will probably entail research in the library. First read some general source—an encyclopedia article or a general article in a journal or magazine. You might pursue some of the references in the article or seek a book or two on the topic from the card catalog. You might also consult one or more of the guides to periodical literature for recent articles in journals, magazines, and newspapers. For some topics, you might want to consult individuals—professors, politicians, physicians, or any person or group of persons with specialized information of value to the development of your speech.

4. Formulate Your Thesis and Identify the Major Propositions

The thesis of your speech is simply the main assertion; it is the essence, the core, of what you want your audience to derive from your speech. If your speech is an informative one, then your thesis is the main idea that you want your audience to understand. For example: "Human blood consists of four major elements," or "Speeches may be delivered in four general ways."

If your speech is to be a persuasive one, then your thesis is the main proposition that you wish your audience to accept, to believe in, or to follow. For example: "We should buy Brand X," or "We should contribute to the college athletic fund."

Once the thesis statement is formulated, ask yourself—as would an audience—questions about the thesis in an attempt to identify its major components. In an informative speech, the questions that seem most relevant are What? or How? So, to the thesis "Human blood consists of four major elements," the logical question seems to be: *What are they?* To the thesis "Speeches may be delivered in four general ways," the logical question seems to be: *How?* or *What are they?* In answering these questions, you, in effect, identify the major propositions that should be covered in your speech. The answer to the question *What are the major elements of the blood?,* in the form of a brief public speech outline, would look something like this:

   Thesis: "There are four major elements in the human blood." *(What are they?)*

   I. Plasma
  II. Red blood cells (erythrocytes)
 III. White blood cells (leukocytes)
 IV. Platelets (thrombocytes)

In the persuasive speech, the questions an audience would ask would be more often of the *Why?* type. If your thesis is "We should buy Brand X," then the inevitable question is *Why should we buy Brand X?* Your answers to this question will then enable you to identify the major parts of the speech, which might look something like this:

   Thesis: "We should buy Brand X." *(Why should we buy Brand X?)*

   I. Brand X lasts longer.
  II. Brand X is cheaper.
 III. Brand X does a better job.

5. Support the Major Propositions

Now that you have identified your thesis and your major propositions, you must support each of them. You now need to devote attention to telling the audience what it needs to know about plasma and white blood cells. You need to convince the audience that Brand X does in fact last longer and does a better job.

In the informative speech, your support primarily amplifies—describes, illustrates, defines, exemplifies—the various concepts being discussed. You want the "causes of inflation" to come alive to the audience, to stand out as real, significant, and relevant. Amplification accomplishes this. Specifically, you might use examples and illustrations and the testimony of various authorities or of eyewitnesses to reconstruct an event, for example, a crime of some sort. Presenting definitions especially makes the audience conversant with what you are talking about and breathe life into concepts that may otherwise be too abstract or vague. Statistics (summary figures that explain various trends) are essential for certain topics. Audiovisual aids—charts, maps, actual objects, slides, films, audiotapes, records, and so on—will enliven normally vague concepts.

In a persuasive speech your support is proof—material that offers evidence, argument, and motivational appeal and that establishes the credibility and reputation of the speaker—designed to convince the audience to agree with you. If you want to persuade the audience that Brand X should be their choice and if you are going to accomplish this, in part, by demonstrating that Brand X is cheaper, then you must give them good reasons for believing that this is true. You might, for example, compare the price of Brand X with five or six other brands and/or you might demonstrate that the same amount of Brand X will accomplish twice the work as other brands selling at the same price.

Generally, we support our propositions with reasoning from specific instances, from general principles, from analogy, and from causes and effects. These may be thought of as logical support. Also, we support our position through the use of motivational appeals—to the audience's desire for status, for financial gain, for increased self-esteem. We also add persuasive force to our propositions through our own personal reputation or credibility. If the audience members see us as competent, of high moral character, and as charismatic, they are more likely to believe what we say.

6. Organize the Speech Materials

The material must be organized if the audience is to understand and retain it. You might, for example, select a simple *topical pattern*. This involves taking the main points of your speech, treating them as coordinate and equal items, and organizing the various supporting materials under the appropriate items. The body of the speech, then, might look like this:

I. Main point I
   A. Supporting material for I
   B. Supporting material for I
II. Main point II
   A. Supporting material for II
   B. Supporting material for II
   C. Supporting material for II

III. Main point III
   A. Supporting material for III
   B. Supporting material for III

Or you might, in describing the events leading up to a specific happening, choose a temporal pattern, arranging the main issues in chronological order. Say, for example, your topic is war movies and you want to explain some of the changes that have taken place in them. A temporal organizational pattern might be appropriate and might look like this:

I. Movies about World War II
   A. *The Best Years of Our Lives*
   B. *From Here to Eternity*
   C. *Sands of Iwo Jima*
II. Movies about the Korean War
   A. *M*A*S*H*
   B. *The Manchurian Candidate*
   C. *Pork Chop Hill*
III. Movies about the Vietnam War
   A. *Coming Home*
   B. *The Deer Hunter*
   C. *Apocalypse Now*

For a persuasive speech you may wish to consider other organizational patterns. For example, a *problem-solution pattern* might be effective for a number of topics. Let us say you want to persuade your listeners that communication courses should be required in high schools. You might use a problem-solution pattern; your speech in outline form might look like this:

I. Students cannot communicate. (problem)
   A. They are inarticulate in expressing ideas. (problem 1)
   B. They are ineffective listeners. (problem 2)
   C. They are not critical. (problem 3)
II. Communication courses should be established in high school. (solution)
   A. Communication courses will train students to express themselves. (solution 1)
   B. Communication courses will train students in listening skills. (solution 2)
   C. Communication courses will train students to be critical. (solution 3)

In general, the pattern for a persuasive speech looks like this:

I. Assertion 1
   A. Reason for accepting I
   B. Reason for accepting I
      1. Reason for accepting B
      2. Reason for accepting B
II. Assertion 2
   A. Reason for accepting II
      1. Reason for accepting A
      2. Reason for accepting A
   B. Reason for accepting II

The two assertions (I and II) would, in turn, support the general purpose of the speech. Thus, for example, your specific purpose might be to persuade the audience that they should invest in real estate. Assertions I and II would be reasons why people should invest in real estate. Support A and B would be reasons why we should accept assertions I and II. In short, each item should persuade the audience to accept the item it supports.

7. Word the Speech

It is obvious that you cannot simply read the outline to the audience. You have to put flesh on the bones and that is the function of language and wording the speech. This step should not be taken as a suggestion to write out your speech word for word; this would result in a stilted and artificial speech, something you clearly want to avoid and something the audience likewise wants to avoid. Rather, in wording the speech you should be concerned with putting your main ideas as well as your supporting materials into language that will be readily understood by your audience. The audience will hear your speech only once. Consequently, make what you are saying instantly intelligible. Do not speak down to your audience but make your ideas, even complex ones, easy to understand at one hearing.

Use words that are simple rather than complex, concrete rather than abstract. Use personal and informal rather than impersonal and formal language. Use simple and active rather than complex and passive sentences. In wording the speech be careful that you do not offend members of your audience. Remember that not all doctors are men and not all secretaries are women; not all persons are or want to be married. Not all persons love parents, dogs, and children. The hypothetical person does not have to be male.

In wording the persuasive speech try to phrase your main assertions in a convincing manner. Be forceful. If the audience you are addressing is hostile or holds a position very different from yours, your wording might be more conciliatory. If you wish to strengthen the position of an already favorable audience, you might be more direct at the start.

See also ORAL STYLE.

8. Construct the Conclusion and the Introduction

You may wish to outline the conclusion or write it out word for word. As you develop greater facility in speech preparation, you will construct the conclusion in the way that works best for you. Although conclusions may serve a number of different functions, you should try in the initial speeches to have your conclusion serve two major purposes. First, summarize the speech. Identify the main points again and recapitulate essentially what you have told the audience. Second, try to wrap up your speech in some way; seek some kind of closure, some crisp ending. Do not let the speech hang. End the speech clearly and distinctly. For a persuasive speech you may also wish to provide one final push in the direction you want, one final motivational appeal.

The introduction should be the last major part to be constructed because you must know in detail all that you are going to say before you prepare it. It will also be easier to prepare once you have constructed the major part of the speech. Your introduction should first gain the attention of the audience. Most often, your coming to the front of the room will attract their attention; however, as you start to speak you may lose them if you do not make a special effort to hold their attention. A provocative statistic, a little-known fact, an interesting story, or a statement explaining the significance of your topic will secure this attention. Second, try to establish some kind of relationship with the topic and the audience. That is, tell the audience why you are speaking on this topic—why you are concerned with the topic, why you are addressing the audience on this topic, why you are competent to address them, and so on. These are questions that most audiences will automatically ask, and as a speaker you should tell them before they ask. Lastly, the introduction should orient the audience: prepare them for what you are going to say in the order you are going to say it.

[Joseph A. DeVito, *The Elements of Public Speaking,* 2d ed. (New York: Harper & Row, 1984).]

Pulp Magazine. A magazine, originally printed on cheap, pulp paper, and devoted to escapist articles; now usually used to refer to a magazine specializing in the printing of sensationalized articles.

Pun. A humorous play on words involving using a word with two meanings.

Punctuation. Written symbols that break a sequence of written language into smaller units; in English, punctuation marks consist of the period, comma, colon, semicolon, dash, parentheses, and the use of capitalization.

Punctuation of Communication Events. Communication events are continuous transactions. They are broken up (or punctuated) into short sequences only for purposes of convenience. What is stimulus and what is response is not very easy to determine when we, as analysts of communication, enter after the communication transaction is under way.

Consider, for example, the following incident. A couple is at a party. The husband is flirting with the other women and the wife is drinking; both are scowling at each other and are obviously in a deep nonverbal argument with each other. In explaining the situation the husband might recall the events by observing that the wife drank and so he flirted with the sober women. The more she drank the more he flirted. The only reason for his behavior was his anger over her drinking. Notice that he sees his behavior as the response to her behavior; her behavior came first and was the cause of his behavior.

In recalling the "same" incident the wife might say that she drank when he started flirting. The more he flirted, the more she drank. She had no intention of drinking until he started flirting. To her, his behavior was the stimulus and her's was the response; he caused her behavior. Thus he sees the behavior as going from drinking to flirting, and she sees it as going from flirting to drinking. This example is depicted visually in the accompanying illustration.

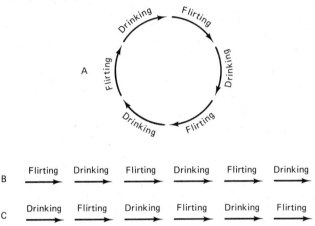

Punctuation of communication events.

In part (a) we see what we assume to be the actual sequence of events. We see this as a continuous series of events with no absolute beginning and no absolute end. Each action (drinking and flirting) stimulates another action, but there can be no initial cause identified. In part (b) we see the same sequence of events, but this time it is punctuated by the wife. She sees the sequence as beginning with the husband's flirting. She sees her drinking behavior as a response to her husband's stimulus (flirting). In part (c) the same sequence of events is portrayed, but this time from the husband's point of view. He sees the sequence beginning with the wife's drinking. He sees his flirting as a response to his wife's stimulus (drinking).

This tendency to divide up the various communication transactions into sequences of stimuli and responses is referred to as the punctuation of the sequences of events. Because we each see things differently, we each punctuate events differently. To the extent that these differences are significant, the possibility for a communication breakdown exists.

[Paul Watzlawick, Janet Helmick Beavin, and Don D. Jackson, *Pragmatics of Human Communication: A Study of Interactional Patterns, Pathologies, and Paradoxes* (New York: Norton, 1967).]

Punishment. A stimulus that reduces the strength, frequency, or likelihood of a response.

Pupil Dilation. Enlargement of the pupils of the eyes. Pupil dilation occurs in response to positive emotions and to viewing pleasant and appealing scenes;

dilated pupils are perceived generally as more attractive (and as more interested) than constricted pupils.

[Ekhard H. Hess, *The Tell-Tale Eye* (New York: Van Nostrand Reinhold, 1975).]

Pupillometer. Device for measuring pupil constriction and dilation as indexes of a person's attitudes and enjoyment while viewing varied scenes.

[Berkeley Rice, "Rattlesnakes, French Fries and Pupillometric Oversell," *Psychology Today* 8 (February 1974):55–59; Ekhard H. Hess, *The Tell-Tale Eye* (New York: Van Nostrand Reinhold, 1975).]

Pupillometrics. The study of pupil constriction and dilation as indexes of cognitive and emotional states.

[Ekhard H. Hess, *The Tell-Tale Eye* (New York: Van Nostrand Reinhold, 1975).]

Pupillometry. See PUPILLOMETRICS.

Purple Patch. An unnecessarily flowery passage that is irrelevant to the purpose of the entire work and incongruous with the work's overall style.

Purpose. In Kenneth Burke's terminology, the purpose or reason for a rhetorical act; answers the question, "Why was the act performed?," "For what reason was this done?" See also PENTAD.

Purr Words. Words of endearment and positive expression; positive words that appear to be descriptive but actually express one's opinions or feelings. See also SNARL WORDS.

[S. I. Hayakawa, *Language in Thought and Action* (New York: Harcourt, Brace, Jovanovich, 1972).]

Pygmalion Effect. The condition in which one makes a prediction and then proceeds to fulfill it; a type of self-fulfilling prophecy (q.v.) but one that refers to others and to our evaluation of others rather than to ourselves.

[Robert Rosenthal and L. Jacobson, *Pygmalion in the Classroom* (New York: Holt, Rinehart and Winston, 1968).]

Pygmalion Gift. A gift that would be used and appreciated by the kind of person the giver wants the receiver to become, for example, giving a child a doctor's play kit because the giver wants the child to become a doctor.

Q

Quadrivium. The four advanced subjects taught in the medieval university: arithmatic, geometry, astronomy, and music. See also TRIVIUM.

Qualification Terms. Terms that limit or qualify the meaning of an expression or statement such as *however, if, but.*

Qualifier. A modifying term that qualifies or somehow limits the meaning of another term or phrase, for example, *although, but, unless.*

Quality. The general characteristic of voice that refers to a variety of factors by which one voice is distinguished from another, for example, nasality and denasality, breathiness, hoarseness.

Quality Circles. Quality circles are small groups of organizational members who meet voluntarily to solve some specific problem. Originally developed in the United States, quality circle programs were exported to Japan where they were widely adopted, and have now been returned to the United States where they are used by such organizations as Chrysler, R. J. Reynolds, J. C. Penney, General Motors, Bendix, and numerous others. The structure and function of quality circles may be explained by identifying the major participants.

Circle participants—usually numbering 15 or less—may address any number of issues relating to the operation of the organization, for example, ways to reduce costs, methods of improving communication, error reduction, safety improvement, and any other issues considered significant by workers and/or management. A number of quality circles may operate at the same time within the same company, each addressing itself to a somewhat different issue.

A *circle leader* functions to energize, but not to dominate, the group. (See also GROUP COMMUNICATION: LEADER GUIDELINES.)

A *program facilitator* coordinates the quality circle program. The facilitator keeps others informed about the circle's workings, secures outside experts as needed by the circle, coordinates interaction among the several circles, and organizes the presentation of the circle's findings to top management.

The *advisory committee*—consisting of persons from all the relevant functions of the organization—helps the facilitators, leaders, and participants by providing additional perspectives to explore and by demonstrating how the issues under consideration affect the different divisions of the organization.

There are also workers and members of management, who although they are *noncircle participants,* need to be kept informed of circle developments because the circle's findings or conclusions will be relevant to their work, as well as to the organization as a whole. Although nonmembers, these persons are encouraged to communicate their thoughts, ideas, and feelings to circle members.

Quality circles involve workers in the decision-making processes of an organization, thereby bringing management and employees closer together.

John Baird, upon whose work on quality circles I have been drawing, identified 12 main events that make up the quality circle program. These events should complete our understanding of what a quality circle is, how it is developed, and how it operates.

1. A decision to institute a quality circle program is made by management.
2. An advisory committee is formed.
3. A facilitator is chosen.
4. The facilitator is trained in small group communication skills.
5. The areas where quality circles will be instituted are selected.
6. The quality circle program is announced.
7. Participants are selected from the volunteers.
8. Quality circle leaders are selected.
9. Leaders are trained in small group skills and in leadership skills.
10. Participants are trained.
11. Meetings begin: the problems are identified; information is collected; problems are analyzed; solutions are proposed, analyzed, and accepted; and presentation of findings is prepared.
12. Findings are presented to management.

[John E. Baird, Jr., *Quality Circles* (Prospect Heights, Ill.: Waveland Press, 1982).]

Quality, Maxim of. See CONVERSATIONAL MAXIMS.

Quantifier. A modifying term denoting quantity, for example, a numeral.

Quantity, Maxim of. See CONVERSATIONAL MAXIMS.

Quasicourtship Behaviors. Unconsciously emitted nonverbal behaviors that are flirtatious.

[Albert E. Scheflen, "Quasi-Courtship Behavior in Psychotherapy," *Psychiatry* 28 (1965): 245–257.]

Questionnaire. A list of questions designed to collect data. Usually the questionnaire is designed to collect a great deal of information from a large number of informants in a relatively short period of time.

Quiz Show Scandals. Scandals in the 1950s that centered on the rigging of big money quiz shows such as "The $64,000 Question." The scandal focused both on the contestants being prompted and helped with their answers (since the big money questions drew the big audiences) and on the producers, writers, network executives, and others denying this to a Grand Jury; eventually the rigging was proven and a number pleaded guilty to perjury; the scandals resulted in the networks removing such shows from their lineups.

Quorum. The number of members of an organization needed to be present at a meeting for business to be conducted.

Quotes. An extensional device (q.v.) used to emphasize that a word or phrase is being used in a special sense and should therefore be given special attention.

Racism. Negative attitudes or behaviors toward members of a particular race.

RAM. See RANDOM ACCESS MEMORY.

Ramistic Rhetoric. Based on the educational theories of Peter Ramus (1515–1573), an approach to defining rhetoric (q.v.) as concerned only with style and delivery whereas invention, disposition, and memory were assigned to dialectic to avoid duplication.
[Walter J. Ong, *Ramus: Method and the Decay of Dialogue* (Cambridge, Mass.: Harvard University Press, 1958).]

Random Access Memory (RAM). The memory banks of a computer; the internal memory of the computer.

Rapid Eye Movements (REM). A stage of deep sleep during which the eyes move rapidly; a sleep stage during which the person is assumed to be dreaming.

Rapid Fading. The evanescent (fleeting) or nonpermanent quality of speech signals.

Rate. The speed with which we speak, generally measured in words per minute. The average speech rate is approximately 140 words per minute.

Rating Services. Research organizations that provide information on the audiences (types, sizes, incomes, ages) of various communications media, generally with a view toward providing data that will be used to determine the cost per unit of media advertising.

Rational Emotive Therapy (RET). Formulated by Albert Ellis, a therapeutic approach which assumes that people make irrational assumptions that create emotional and behavioral problems. Therapy consists of substituting logical and rational premises for the irrational ones.
[Albert Ellis and Robert A. Harper, *A New Guide to Rational Living* (North Hollywood, Calif.: Wilshire Book Co., 1972).]

Rationalization. A defense mechanism whereby the individual attempts to justify his or her behavior by providing "reasonable sounding" reasons that are, in reality, inaccurate.

Reactance. The process of resisting persuasive attempts to change attitudes and behaviors by maintaining attitudes and behaving in ways that are opposite to those being advocated; a negative reaction brought on by one's belief that excessive pressure is being exerted and that one's personal freedom is being restricted. When this is experienced the individual often behaves in a way opposite to that being advocated, a reaction known as "negative attitude change."

Reaction Formation. A defense mechanism whereby an individual acts out the opposite of his or her anxious feelings.

Reaction Time. The time intervening between stimulus and response, for example, the time between the presentation of a verbal stimulus and the subject's response of, say, pressing the required button.

Readability. A measure of the reading ease or ease of comprehension of a written text.

[George R. Klare, *The Measurement of Readability* (Ames, Iowa: Iowa State University Press, 1963).]

Read Only Memory (ROM). A computer memory chip, the contents of which can be read but not written on.

Reality Principle. The assumption that communicators make that each will talk about reality. In psychoanalytic theory, the understanding that there is a reality apart from what one might wish it to be and that one needs to behave on the basis of this reality if one is to behave rationally.

Rebus. A puzzle consisting of linguistic symbols (letters, syllables, words) and pictures which, when deciphered correctly, can be read as a complete sentence or phrase.

Receiver. Any person or thing that takes in messages. Receivers may be individuals listening to or reading a message, a group of persons hearing a speech, a scattered television audience, or a machine that stores information.

Recency. The tendency to remember best and to be most influenced by what is heard most recently. See also PRIMACY.

Recency Effect. The condition in which what we perceive last (that is, most recently) exerts greater influence than input received first. See also PRIMACY EFFECT.

Recess. A "time out" or intermission during a meeting or event.

Reciprocal Compatibility. A condition which exists when each person in an interpersonal relationship satisfies the other person's preferences for the expression or nonexpression of inclusion (q.v.), control (q.v.), and affection (q.v.). For example, if one person wants to express a great deal of affection and the other person desires this expression then the two persons are reciprocally compatible; if, on the other hand, one person wishes to express affection and the other person does not wish it, then they are reciprocally incompatible.

[William C. Schutz, *FIRO: A Three-Dimensional Theory of Interpersonal Behavior* (New York: Holt, Rinehart and Winston, 1958).]

Reconstructive Memory. A view of memory as an active process whereby stimuli are reorganized, worked over, and integrated with existing information; opposed to reproductive memory (q.v.).

Recto. The right hand page of a book.

Recurrence, Principle of. The principle of verbal interaction that holds that individuals will repeat many times and in many different ways who they are, how they see themselves, and, in general, what they think is important and significant.

[Robert E. Pittenger, Charles F. Hockett, and John J. Danehy, *The First Five Minutes: A Sample of Microscopic Interview Analysis* (Ithaca, N.Y.: Paul Martineau, 1960).]

Redundancy. The quality of a message that makes it totally predictable and therefore lacking in information. A message of zero redundancy would be completely unpredictable; a message of 100 percent redundancy would be completely predictable. All human languages contain some degree of redundancy built into them, generally estimated at about 50 percent.

Redundancy Rule. A rule that specifies the way in which one semantic feature incorporates or necessitates another, for example, *animate* implies "living," *human* implies "animate," and *male* implies "animate."

Reference. The thought one holds about an object, person, or event.

Reference Group. A group to which an individual looks for behavior and attitude guidelines but does not necessarily belong to and from which he or she derives standards or norms of behavior, for example, the church.

Referent. The person, object, or event to which a word refers or about which one has a thought.

Referential Meaning. See DENOTATION; TRIANGLE OF MEANING.

Reflective Thinking Process. See DEWEY'S REFLECTIVE THINKING PROCESS.

Reflexiveness. The features of language that refer to the fact that human language can be used to refer to itself, that is, we can talk about our talk and create a metalanguage (q.v.), a language for talking about language. See also SELF-REFLEXIVENESS.

Regional Dialect. A variant of a language used in a particular region; opposed to social dialect (q.v.). See also DIALECT.

Regulative Rule. In speech act (q.v.) theory, a rule that states how a person should behave within a specific context.

Regulators. Nonverbal movements that control or monitor (or "regulate") the flow of communication. Regulators inform the speaker what the listener expects or wants the speaker to do as they are communicating, for example, to keep on going, to slow down, to speed up; regulators would also include such gross movements as turning one's head, leaning forward in one's chair, and even walking away.

Reification. Treatment of an abstraction as though it were a real, concrete object.

Reinforcement. A stimulus which increases the strength, frequency, or likelihood of a response. See also POSITIVE REINFORCEMENT; NEGATIVE REINFORCEMENT; PRIMARY REINFORCEMENT; SECONDARY REINFORCEMENT.

Reinforcement/Packaging, Principle of. The principle of verbal interaction that holds that in most interactions, multiple messages are transmitted simultaneously through a number of different channels that normally reinforce each other; messages come in packages.

[Robert E. Pittenger, Charles F. Hockett, and John J. Danehy, *The First Five Minutes: A Sample of Microscopic Interview Analysis* (Ithaca, N.Y.: Paul Martineau, 1960).]

Reinforcer. A stimulus that increases the strength, frequency, or likelihood of a behavior occurring.

Rejection. A response by an individual that rejects or denies the validity of another individual's self view.

Relatedness, Need for. The need for an individual to share his or her experiences with another human being. This need develops, according to Erich Fromm (1900–1980), because humans have the ability to reason but have lost their relationship with nature. The most satisfying of these relationships is love yielding mutual respect and understanding. One of the five major psychological needs identified by Erich Fromm, the others being the needs for transcendence, rootedness, identity, and frame of orientation.

[Erich Fromm, *Man for Himself* (New York: Rinehart, 1947).]

Relational Abstracting. A form or type of abstracting (q.v.) in which relationships among items are abstracted and represented in some kind of formula, equation, or diagram, for example, the formula $a^2 = b^2 + c^2$ expressing the relationship among the sides of a right triangle is the result of relational abstracting. See also CLASSIFYING ABSTRACTING; EVALUATIVE ABSTRACTING; OBJECTIVE ABSTRACTING.

Relational Competence. The knowledge and ability to use the skills necessary for the development, maintenance, and termination of interpersonal relationships. See also COMMUNICATION COMPETENCE.

Relational Deterioration. Relational deterioration refers to the weakening of the bonds holding people together. At times the relationship may be weakened only mildly and may appear normal to outsiders; to the participants, however, it is clear that the relationship has weakened significantly. The obvious extreme of relational deterioration is the complete termination of the relationship. In between these two extremes are an infinite number of variations. Relational deterioration exists on a continuum from just a little bit less than intimate to total separation and total dissolution.

The process of deterioration may be gradual or sudden. Murray Davis, in *Intimate Relations,* uses the terms "passing away" to designate gradual deterioration and "sudden death" to designate immediate or sudden deterioration. An example of "passing away" is when one of the parties in a relationship develops close ties with a new intimate and this new relationship gradually pushes out the old intimate. An example of "sudden death" is when one or both of the parties break a rule that was essential to the relationship (for example, the rule of complete fidelity), and both realize that since the rule has been broken, the relationship cannot be sustained and, in fact, must be terminated immediately.

Causes of Relational Deterioration

When those factors that are important in establishing relationships are no longer operative or when they are changed drastically, it may be a cause of deterioration. For example, one of the major reasons why people seek relationships is to alleviate loneliness. When loneliness is no longer lessened by the relationship, when one or both individuals experience loneliness for prolonged or frequent periods, the relationship may well be on the road to decay. The same is true when the relationship no longer fulfills the needs for contact and stimulation (intellectual, physical, and emotional) and no longer maximizes pleasures and minimizes pains. In addition to those factors that in one form help to establish a relationship and in another form help to dissolve it, a number of other factors might be mentioned as causes of deterioration.

Psychological Changes

Psychological changes in one or both parties may contribute to deterioration. Prominent among psychological changes would be the development of incompatible attitudes and values, vastly different intellectual interests and abilities, major goal changes, and the discovery of previously unknown differences. To the extent that these are incompatible with those of the other individual, the relationship will be shaky.

Behavioral Changes

Behavioral change, like psychological change, is also significant. For example, the individual who once devoted much time to the other person and to the development of the relationship but who later becomes totally absorbed in business or in school and devotes all free time to business activities or studying is going to find significant repercussions from this change. The individual who becomes addicted to drugs or alcohol will likewise present the relationship with a serious problem.

Context Changes

Contextual changes may also exert considerable influence on the relationship. Some relationships cannot survive separation by long distances. This is a particularly difficult problem for people in the military. The physical separation is too important for many people, and many such relationships deteriorate, as stereotyped in the "Dear John" letters of war years. Long incarceration in prison or long hospital confinement are also context changes that may lead to severe trouble for a relationship.

Status Changes

When there are significant changes in the status relationship between two people or between one member and a third party, the relationship may undergo considerable change and possibly deterioration. In F. Scott Fitzgerald's *Tender Is the Night,* we see the same kind of situation, though here it is between a young psychiatrist, Dick Diver, and a wealthy and beautiful patient, Nicole Warren. While Nicole is mentally ill and in need of Dick's care, the relationship flourishes for both; each apparently serves the needs of the other. But as Nicole gets stronger, Dick gets weaker; the relationship changes drastically and ultimately deteriorates.

Competing Relationships

Sometimes the relationship changes because of the development of another relationship with some third party. At times this may be a romantic interest; at other times it may be a parent; frequently it is a child. When an individual's needs for affection were once supplied by the other party in the primary relationship and are now supplied by a child, the primary relationship is in for considerable alteration and sometimes termination.

Decreasing Commitment

An important factor influencing the course of deterioration is the degree of commitment the individuals have toward each other and toward the relationship itself. All our relationships are held together in part by our degree of commitment. And the strength of the relationship, including its resistance to possible deterioration, is often directly related to the degree of commitment of the individuals. When relationships show signs of deterioration and yet there is still a strong commitment to the relationship—a strong desire to keep the relationship together—the individuals may well surmount the obstacles and reverse the process. When that commitment is weak and the individuals doubt that there are good reasons for staying together, deterioration seems to come faster and stronger.

Sometimes commitment is conceived in terms of material considerations; people may feel committed because they have invested all their money together, because they have established a business together, or because they own real estate together. At other times the commitment is based on time considerations. People may feel that since they have lived together for these past 10 or 15 years, too much would be lost if the relationship were terminated. Sometimes the commitment is based on emotional investment; so much emotional energy may have been spent on the relationship that the individuals find it difficult even to consider dissolving it. Or people may feel committed because they care for each other and for the relationship and feel that for all its problems and difficulties, the relationship is more good than bad, more productive than destructive, more pleasurable than painful. And this is the kind of commitment that will function to stem and perhaps reverse deterioration. Other bases for commitment (materialism, time, emotional investment) may function to preserve the surface features of the relationship, but will probably have little influence on preserving its meaning and intimacy.

Sex

Few relationships are free of sexual problems and differences that cannot easily be resolved. Sexual problems rank among the top three problems in almost all studies of newlyweds. When these same couples are surveyed later in their relationship, the sexual problems have not gone away, they are just talked about less; apparently the individuals resign themselves to living with the problems. In one survey, for example, 80 percent of the respondents identified their marriages as either "very happy" or "happy" but some 90 percent of these said that they had sexual problems.

Although sexual frequency is not related to relational deterioration, sexual satisfaction is. Research clearly shows that it is the quality, not the quantity, of one's sexual relationship that is crucial. When the quality is poor, affairs outside the primary relationship may be sought. And, although there is much talk of sexual freedom within and outside primary relationships, the research is again clear: extra-relational affairs contribute significantly to breaking up for all couples, whether marrieds, cohabitors, gay men, or lesbians. Interestingly enough, even "open relationships"—those in which the individuals permit each other sexual freedom outside the primary relationship—create problems and are more likely to break up than the traditional closed relationship. This is true for all relationships except those of gay men who seem the only ones who can effectively separate sexual encounters from loving relationships.

Work

Unhappiness with work often leads to difficulties with relationships. Problems at and with work cannot, it seems, be separated from one's relationships. Dissatisfaction with work is often associated with relational deterioration. This is true for all types of couples. With heterosexual couples (both marrieds and cohabitors), when the man is disturbed over the woman's job—for example, she earns a great deal more than he does or she devotes a great deal of time to the job—the relationship is in for considerable trouble and this is true whether the relationship is in its early stages or is a well-established one. Often the man expects the woman to work but does not reduce his expectations concerning her household responsibilities. Here the man becomes resentful if the woman does not fulfill these expectations and the woman becomes resentful if she takes on both outside work and full household duties. It is a no-win situation and as a result the relationship suffers.

Although the stability of a relationship is not hampered by the husband doing little or no housework, stability is hampered when the husband perceives the wife doing less than he thinks she should. Another instance of inequality in heterosexual couples concerns ambition. Women want their partners to be ambitious in their work; men who are not ambitious are less appreciated by their partners and their relationship loses stability. However, men do not appreciate ambitious women; relationships with ambitious women are less stable than those with unambitious women. Further, it is found that the more ambitious, the more work-devoted partner is the one more likely to leave the relationship.

A further work-related issue (and one that is closely related to "contextual change" discussed above) that contributes to relationship dissolution is the time couples spend together. Blumstein and Schwartz observe: "Spending too much time apart is a hallmark of couples who do not stay together." If couples take separate vacations, meet with different friends, eat separately, and spend a great deal of time at work and away from home, their relationships are less likely to survive. It is likely that time away from each other is both a cause and an effect of relationship deterioration. Time away from each other seems to cause problems for a relationship but is also a reflection and an effect of a deteriorating relationship; as the relationship deteriorates we feel less desire to spend time together and look for other ways to gain satisfaction. The more time spent away, the more problems arise; the more problems arise, the more time we spend away from each other. It is a spiral that often grows larger and larger until the relationship dissolves.

Financial Difficulties

In surveys of problems among couples, financial difficulties loom large. Money is perhaps the major taboo topic for couples beginning their relationship and yet it proves to be one of the major problems faced by all couples as they settle into their relationship. Twenty-five to thirty-three percent of couples rank money as their primary problem. Almost all couples rank it as one of their major problems. Financial difficulties are perhaps most obvious when the family is large; when the children are small, expensive, and noncontributing; and when only one spouse can work. But even when both individuals work, financial problems do not cease. Rather, the conflict centers on the amount of money each brings in.

Perhaps the major reason why money is so important in relationships is because of its close connection with power. Money brings power; this is true in business and it is true in relationships. The person bringing in the most money wields the most power. This person has the final say on, for example, the purchase of expensive items as well as on decisions having nothing to do with money. The power that money brings quickly generalizes to nonfinancial issues as well.

The unequal earnings of men and women create further problems regardless of who earns more. In most heterosexual relationships, the man earns more money than the woman. Because of this men possess a disproportionate share of power. This creates, as Shulamith Firestone points out in *The Dialectic of Sex,* a situation in which the woman, because of her lack of power, will often turn to manipulative and underhanded tactics to get what she wants. This type of tactic also generalizes with the result that we have a relationship in which dishonesty and deception are the normal modes of interpersonal interaction.

When the woman earns more than the man, the problems are different. While our society has finally taught women to achieve in business and the professions, it has not taught men to accept this very well and as a result the higher-earning woman is often resented by the lower-earning man. This is true for both marrieds and for cohabitors.

Financial difficulties are not limited in their effects but often interact with other relationship dimensions to create further problems. For example, men who earn little or less than their female partners, or who worry about not being good providers often avoid sex during paydays, when their self-perceived inadequacy is particularly salient. This avoidance feeds back and causes other difficulties especially because the man may not be aware of why he is avoiding sexual intimacy. Often partners perceive this decreased drive as an indication that they are no longer interesting to their mates or that they have found someone outside the relationship. Jealousy and suspicion may quickly follow.

Money also creates problems by virtue of the fact that men and women view it differently. To men, money is power; to women it is security and independence. To men, money is accumulated to exert power and influence; to women, money is accumulated to achieve some sense of security and to make her less dependent on others. Conflicts over how the couple's money is to be spent or invested can easily result from such different perceptions.

The most general equation we could advance would be: Dissatisfaction with Money = Dissatisfaction with the Relationship. This is true for married, cohabitors, and gay men but not for lesbian couples who seem to care a great deal less about financial matters. This difference has led some researchers to postulate (though without substantial evidence) that the concern over money and its equation with power and relational satisfaction is largely a male point of view.

Communication in Relational Deterioration

Like relational development, relational deterioration involves unique and specialized communication patterns. These patterns are in part a response to the deterioration; we communicate the way we do because of the way we feel our relationship is deteriorating. These patterns are also causative, however, in the sense that our deteriorating relationship is itself influenced by our communication patterns. In fact, it would be impossible to determine which communication pattern is cause and which is effect.

Withdrawal

Perhaps the easiest communication pattern to see is that of a general withdrawal. Nonverbally, this withdrawal is seen in the greater space each person seems to require and the ease with which tempers and other signs of disturbance are aroused when that space is encroached upon. Other nonverbal signs include the failure to engage in direct eye contact, the failure to look at each other generally, and the lessening of touching behavior. All these changes seem to be a part of the desire to withdraw physically from the emotional pairing. Verbally, withdrawal is seen in a number of different ways. Where once there was a great desire to talk and to listen, there is now less desire and perhaps none. At times phatic communication (q.v.) will also be severely limited since the individuals do not want any of its regular functions served. At other times, however, phatic communication (or what would appear to be phatic communication) is engaged in as an end in itself. Whereas phatic talk is usually a preliminary to serious conversation, here phatic communication is used as an alternative or to forestall serious talk.

Self-Disclosure

Self-disclosing communications decline significantly. Self-disclosure may not be thought worth the effort if the relationship is dying. We only wish to self-disclose to people we feel close to, and when a relationship is deteriorating we feel all but close to the other person and so we naturally have no desire to self-disclose. We also limit our self-disclosures because we feel that the other person may not be accepting of our disclosures—an essential assumption if disclosures are to be made in the first place.

Supportiveness

Where once supportiveness characterized the relationship, defensiveness is now the more prevalent characteristic. In many relationships that are deteriorating one party blames the other; no one wants to assume the blame for the failure of a relationship, and it seems difficult to believe that no one really caused the breakup. Instead, it is easier to blame the other person. The primary method available for dealing with accusations of blame is defensiveness.

Deception

Deception increases as relationships break down. Sometimes this takes the form of clear-cut lies which may be used to avoid getting into added arguments over the reasons for staying out all night or for not calling or for being seen in the wrong place with the wrong person. At other times the lies may be used because of some feeling of shame; we do not want the other person to think less of us even though we fully realize that the relationship is deteriorating. At other times we may not want to appear to be the cause of the problem, and so we lie. Sometimes the deception takes the form of avoidance—the lie of omission. Whether by omission or commission, deception runs high in relationships that are deteriorating.

Evaluative Responses

One of the most obvious communication changes is the increase in negative evaluation and the decrease in positive evaluation. Where once we praised the other's behaviors or talents or ideas, we now criticize them. Often the behaviors have not changed significantly; what has changed is our way of looking at them. This negative evaluation frequently leads to outright fighting and conflict, and although conflict is not necessarily bad, it often happens that in relationships that are deteriorating the conflict is not resolved. Neither party may care enough to go through the effort of resolving the conflict, and so it either surfaces the next day or perhaps escalates into an all-out battle. Seldom does it go away.

Request Behaviors

During relational deterioration, as William Lederer points out, there is a marked change in the types of requests made. When a relationship is deteriorating there is a decrease in requests for pleasurable behaviors ("Will you fix me my favorite desert? The one with the whipped cream and nuts?" or "Hug me real tight?"). At the same time there is an increase in requests to stop unpleasant or negative behaviors ("Will you stop bragging about your ex-husband's money?" or "Will you stop monopolizing the phone every evening?").

Another instance of the change from positive to negative evaluation is seen in the sometimes gradual, sometimes sudden decrease in the social niceties that accompany requests. From (1) "Would you please make me a cup of coffee, honey; I'm exhausted" it goes to (2) "Get me some coffee, will you?" to (3) "Where the #!!**//!! is the coffee?"

Exchange of Favors

One of the main reasons that relationships are developed and maintained is that the rewards exceed the costs. When a relationship deteriorates the costs begin to exceed the rewards, until a point is reached when one or both individuals feel the costs are too high (and the rewards too low) and the relationship is terminated. During relational deterioration there is little favor exchange, compliments once exchanged frequently and sincerely are now rare, and positive stroking is at a minimum. Nonverbally, we avoid looking directly at the other, smile seldom, infrequently (if at all) touch, caress, and hold each other.

Relational Deterioration Management

A few suggestions for managing deterioration, whether that entails an attempt to save the relationship or an attempt to terminate it as quickly as possible, are offered here.

Flexibility

Perhaps flexibility, a willingness to bend and to change, is the major quality in successful relational management, whether we are talking about the development or the deterioration of a relationship. If one or both of the parties lose flexibility, the problems confronting the individuals stand little chance of being dealt with effectively. This flexibility includes a willingness to be open to the other person's feelings, to recognize one's own subjectivity in viewing the situation, and to listen openly to alternative points of view and always with a willingness to change if the situation calls for it.

Tentativeness

When positions are stated as absolutes, it is psychologically difficult for an individual to retract what has been said. "I could never love you again," "I can't bear to touch you," or "I always hated your mother" are statements that will prove at best difficult. Similarly, decisions are not necessarily absolute or final or permanent; they can be changed and should be changed if the situation seems to warrant it. To assume that decisions are permanent and unalterable prevents one from exploring other possible decisions and from recognizing that a mistake may have been made and that now a better decision might be instituted.

Openness to Communication

One of the major failures in communication is closing the channels of communication so that any attempt to resolve differences becomes impossible. There must always be a willingness to communicate because the only way relational deterioration is going to be dealt with is through communication. This is not to say that the parties should continue to communicate at all costs. At times it may be necessary, even helpful, to separate, to be with one's own thoughts and to cool off by oneself or with another person. The willingness to continue communication at a later time, however, must always be there.

Selfishness and Honesty

In all aspects of relationships, but especially in relational deterioration, we have an obligation not only to our partner but also to ourselves, as well as to perhaps various other people. A good example of this is the individual who stays in a relationship, even though it is unproductive and causes only grief, for fear of hurting the other person. But this only causes this person to hurt herself or himself instead. This is a foolish kind of deception. While the other person may be content to live with this kind of relationship, often it would be better to terminate it.

Closely related to the obligation to self is honesty. When a relationship is deteriorating we need to be honest enough with ourselves and with the other person to confront the sources of the difficulty—to look honestly at ourselves, at the other person, and at the relationship itself and to analyze what has gone wrong and what will have to be changed if the relationship is to survive. And, more importantly, we need to ask ourselves if the survival of the relationship is in the best interests of the parties involved. It may be—or it may not be. Both possibilities need to be considered. That there are tremendous difficulties in breaking up should not blind us to the very real difficulties that may be faced in staying together.

[Mark L. Knapp, *Interpersonal Communication and Human Relationships* (Boston: Allyn and Bacon, 1984); William J. Lederer, *Creating a Good Relationship* (New York: Norton, 1984); Steve Duck and Robin Gilmour, eds., *Personal Relationships. 3: Personal Relationships in Disorder* (New York: Academic Press, 1981); Steve Duck, ed., *Personal Relationships. 4: Dissolving Personal Relationships* (New York: Academic Press, 1982); Steve Duck, ed. *Personal Relationships. 5: Repairing Personal Relationships* (New York: Academic Press, 1984); Philip Blumstein and Pepper Schwartz, *American Couples: Money, Work, Sex* (New York: Morrow, 1983).]

Relationship Development. Relationships are established in stages.

The five-stage model presented in the accompanying illustration seems a suitable one for describing at least some of the significant stages in the development of relationships.

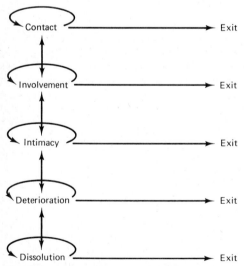

The five-stage model of relationship development.

The Five Stages

At the first stage we make *contact,* there is some kind of sense perception— we see the person, we hear the person, we smell the person. This is the stage of "Hello, my name is Joe"—the stage where we exchange basic information that is generally preliminary to any more intense involvement. According to some researchers, it is at this stage—within the first 4 minutes of initial interaction— that we decide if we want to pursue the relationship or if we want to get out. It is at this stage that physical appearance is so important because it is the physical dimensions that are most open to sensory inspection. Yet, qualities such as friendliness, warmth, openness, and dynamism are also revealed at this stage as well. If we like the individual and want to pursue the relationship we proceed to the second stage, the stage of involvement.

The *involvement* stage is the stage of acquaintances, the stage at which we commit ourselves to getting to know the other person better and also to revealing ourselves to the other person. If this is to be a romantic relationship, then we might date at this stage; if it is to be a friendship relationship, we might share our mutual interests—go to the movies or to some sports event together.

At the third stage, that of *intimacy,* we commit ourselves still further to the other person and, in fact, establish a kind of primary relationship where this individual becomes our best or our closest friend, lover, and/or companion. This commitment may take many specific forms; for example, it may be a marriage commitment, it may be a commitment to help the person or to be with him or her, or a commitment to reveal our deepest secrets. The commitment made is a special one; it is a commitment that we do not make to everyone but only to a select few. This intimacy stage is reserved for very few people—sometimes just one and sometimes two, three, or perhaps four. Rarely do we have more than four intimates, except, of course, in a family situation.

The next two stages are the other side of the progression and represent the weakening of bonds between the parties in the relationship. At the *deterioration* stage we begin to feel that this relationship may not be as important as we had previously thought. We grow further and further apart. We share less of our free time together and when we do there are awkward silences, less self-disclosures, and in general, a self-consciousness in our communication exchanges. At this stage we are not exactly sure what to call our "intimate." The person is not quite a lover or an ex-lover, not really a close friend but not an ex-friend either. This deterioration stage is that awkward in-between stage of neither here nor there. If this deterioration stage continues unaltered, we enter the stage of dissolution.

The *dissolution* stage is the cutting of the bonds tying the individuals together. If a marriage, then the dissolution is symbolized by a divorce, although the actual relational dissolution takes the form of establishing separate and different lives away from each other. This is the point of "goodbye"—the point at which we become ex-lovers, ex-friends, ex-husbands, ex-wives, and so on. At times this is a stage of relief and relaxation—finally it is over and done with. At other times this is a stage of intense anxiety and frustration—of recriminations and hostility, of resentment over the time ill-spent and now lost. In more materialistic terms, it is the stage where property is divided, where legal battles ensue over who should get the Mercedes and who should get the Rolls Royce. It is the time of child custody battles.

Movement Among the Stages

The illustrated model contains three types of arrows. The Exit arrows indicate that each stage offers the opportunity to exit the relationship. After saying "hello" we can say "goodbye" and exit. The vertical or "movement" arrows going to the next stage and back again represent the fact that we can move to another stage, either one that is more intense (as say from involvement to intimacy) or one that is less intense (say from intimacy to deterioration). We can also go back to a previously established stage. For example, you may have established an intimate relationship with someone but did not want to maintain it at that level. At the same time you were relatively pleased with the relationship and so it was not really deteriorating. Rather you just wanted it to be somewhat less intense and so you might go back to the involvement stage and reestablish the relationship at that more comfortable level. And of course we may skip stages, although instances of this are probably not as common as one might think. Often people in a relationship may appear to be skipping a stage when they are merely passing through a particular stage very quickly. The stages may last for different periods of time; there is no fixed time period that any stage must occupy. Stages may be extremely short or extremely long in duration.

The "self-reflexive" arrows—the arrows that return to the beginning of the same level or stage—signify that any relationship may become stabilized at any point. We may, for example, continue to maintain a relationship at the intimate level without the relationship deteriorating or going back to the less intense stage of involvement. Or we might remain at the "Hello, how are you" stage—the contact stage—without getting involved any further.

[Joseph A. DeVito, *The Interpersonal Communication Book,* 4th ed. (New York: Harper & Row, 1986); Steve Duck and Robin Gilmour, eds. *Personal Relationships. 2: Developing Personal Relationships* (New York: Academic Press, 1981); Mark L. Knapp, *Interpersonal Communication and Human Relationships* (Boston: Allyn and Bacon, 1984).]

Relational Dissolution. The ending or termination of a relationship. See also RELATIONAL DETERIORATION.

Relational Repair. The process or act by which one attempts to stop or reverse relational deterioration; the process of improving a deteriorating relationship.

[Steve Duck, ed., *Personal Relationships. 5: Repairing Personal Relationships* (New York: Academic Press, 1984).]

Relation, Maxim of. See CONVERSATIONAL MAXIMS.

Release Date. The date a communication may be broadcasted, printed, or otherwise made public. See also ADVANCE COPY.

Relic Area. A geographical area that has been isolated and because of this isolation has retained old dialect forms and/or has prevented the spread of its own dialect forms.

Remote Coverage. A live broadcast from the scene of the event.

Repair. See CONVERSATIONAL REPAIR.

Repetition. The restatement of a concept or proposition using the same words.

Report Message. That part of a message containing the content or substance. See also CONTENT AND RELATIONSHIP COMMUNICATION.

Repression. A defense mechanism whereby individuals block from their conscious awareness feelings that are anxiety provoking.

Reproductive Memory. A view of memory as relatively passive where the stimuli are stored and remembered without alteration or as they were processed; opposed to reconstructive memory (q.v.).

Request Behaviors. See RELATIONAL DETERIORATION.

Rescind. To revoke a previously adopted decision.

Resistance. In therapy, the unwillingness of a patient to cooperate with the therapist to understand and help solve the problem(s).

Response. Any bit of overt or covert behavior in reaction to some stimulus.

Response Latency. The length of time intervening between a stimulus and a response.

Restatement. A form of amplifying material in which an idea is repeated but in different words.

Restricted Code. The code, sublanguage, or dialect of the working classes; opposed to elaborated code (q.v.). A restricted code is "restricted" in the sense that the linguistic alternatives are limited; the speaker of a restricted code has relatively few options. Consequently, restricted codes are relatively easy to predict. Another aspect of restriction is that this speaker does not make explicit the subjective intent; intentions are seldom elaborated or explicit.
[Basil Bernstein, "Language and Social Class," *British Journal of Sociology* 11 (1960): 271–276.]

Restricted Environmental Stimulation Therapy (REST). A therapeutic approach in which stress is reduced and the motivation to change behavior is achieved through sensory isolation.

Resumé. A brief history of one's relevant background and qualifications used as part of one's application for employment.

Retention. The persistence of some learned behavior during a period of no rehearsal or practice.

Reticence. The reluctance to engage in communication; avoidance of social or public interaction. Reticence is viewed as a problem of inadequate communication skills. See also SHYNESS; UNWILLINGNESS TO COMMUNICATE; APPREHENSION.
[Gerald M. Phillips, *Help for Shy People* (New York: Spectrum, 1981).]

Rhetoric. The art of speaking effectiveness. To Aristotle (384–322 B.C.) *(Rhetoric)*, rhetoric was the art of observing in any given case all the available means of persuasion. In contemporary usage it refers to effectiveness in both written and oral communication, and is also used to refer to messages that are untruthful or exaggerated as in the expression "mere rhetoric." Here, a few of the more influential definitions of *rhetoric*:

Plato: "The sum of it I call flattery. Of this study there appears to me to be many other divisions, and one of them is that of cookery; which indeed, appears to be an art, but I maintain is not an art, but skill and practice. I also call rhetoric a division of this, and personal decoration, and sophistry, these four divisions relating to four particulars."

Francis Bacon: "The duty and office of Rhetoric is to apply Reason to Imagination for the better moving of the will."

George Campbell: "On speaking there is always some end proposed, or some effect which the speaker intends to produce on the hearer. The word *eloquence* in its greatest latitude denotes, 'That art or talent by which discourse is adapted to its end.' All the ends of speaking are reducible to four; every speech being intended to enlighten the understanding, to please the imagination, to move the passions, or to influence the will."

I. A. Richards: "Rhetoric, I shall urge, should be a study of misunderstanding and its remedies. We struggle all our days with misunderstandings, and no apology is required for any study which can prevent or remove them."

Kenneth Burke: "If I had to sum up in one word the difference between the 'old' rhetoric and a 'new' (a rhetoric reinvigorated by fresh insights which the 'new sciences' contributed to the subject), I would reduce it to this: The key term for the old rhetoric was 'persuasion' and its stress was upon deliberate design.

The key term for the 'new' rhetoric would be 'identification,' which can include a partially 'unconscious' factor in appeal."

Rhetorical Interrogative. A type of rhetorical question (q.v.) that serves as a kind of pause filler, for example, "you know?" or "okay?"
[William G. Powers, "The Rhetorical Interrogative: Anxiety or Control," *Human Communication Research* 4 (1977):44–47.]

Rhetorical Question. A question used more for effect than to elicit any answer; a statement phrased in question form for which both speaker and listener have the same answer.

Rhetorical Sensitivity. Five qualities have been identified as characterizing the rhetorically sensitive person: (1) accepts role-taking as a necessary part of the human condition; (2) avoids stylized verbal behavior or consistency for the sake of consistency; (3) adapts or changes on the basis of the communication interaction; (4) distinguishes between all available information on the one hand and information that is acceptable for communication on the other; and (5) recognizes that ideas can be expressed in different (multiform) ways.
[Roderick P. Hart and Don M. Burks, "Rhetorical Sensitivity and Social Interaction," *Communication Monographs* 39 (1972):75–91; Roderick P. Hart, Robert E. Carlson, and William F. Eadie, "Attitudes Toward Communication and the Assessment of Rhetorical Sensitivity," *Communication Monographs* 47 (1980):1–22.]

Rhetorical Situation. The entire context that gives rise to some rhetorical communication, including, for example, the speaker and audience, their relationships to each other, and the difficulties that encourage rhetoric.
[Lloyd F. Bitzer, "The Rhetorical Situation," *Philosophy and Rhetoric* 1 (1968):1–14; Richard Vatz, "The Myth of the Rhetorical Situation," *Philosophy and Rhetoric* 6 (1973): 154–161; Scott Consigny, "Rhetoric and Its Situations," *Philosophy and Rhetoric* 7 (1974): 175–186.]

Rhetoric as Epistemic. An approach to rhetoric as a way of knowing.
[Robert L. Scott, "On Viewing Rhetoric as Epistemic," *Central States Speech Journal* 18 (1967):9–17; "On Viewing Rhetoric as Epistemic: Ten Years Later," *Central States Speech Journal* 27 (1976):258–266; "Rhetoric and Epistemology" (special issue) *Central States Speech Journal* 32 (Fall, 1981).

Rhetoric of the Streets. The rhetoric of "contemporary protest groups."
[Franklyn S. Haiman, "The rhetoric of the Streets: Some Legal and Ethical Considerations," *Quarterly Journal of Speech* 53 (1967):99–114, and "Nonverbal Communication and the First Amendment: The Rhetoric of the Streets Revisited," *Quarterly Journal of Speech* 68 (1982):371–383.]

Rhinolalia. Excessive nasal resonance.

Rhythmic Movements. Bodily movements that depict or visually imitate the rhythm or pacing of an event.

Right Movers. Persons whose eye gestures move to the right when answering questions or solving problems and who therefore allegedly use their left brain more extensively. See also LEFT MOVERS.

Risky-Shift Phenomenon. Many of our everyday decisions involve some degree of risk. Given two alternatives, one usually involves more risk than the other, and the amount of risk we are willing to take will play some part in our decision-making process. An interesting phenomenon concerning risk has emerged from research on small group communication and has come to be called the *risky-shift* phenomenon. Generally, it has been found that decisions reached after discussion are riskier than decisions reached before discussion. Thus, if we have to choose between two alternatives, we would be more apt to choose the riskier alternative after discussion than before. It has also been found that decisions are more risky in group-centered rather than in leader-centered groups.

Although the procedures to investigate the risky shift have varied greatly from one researcher to another, the general procedure is to present participants with a number of cases involving a decision between a safe but relatively unattractive alternative and a risky but relatively attractive alternative. For example, M. A. Wallach, N. Kogan, and D. J. Bem used the following case: "An electrical engineer may stick with his present job at a modest but adequate salary, or may take a new job offering considerably more money but no long-term security." The subjects would then indicate their decisions individually and then discuss the case in a small group. After the discussion each subject would indicate his or her decision a second time. In terms of our example, before discussion the engineer would be advised to stick with his present job but after discussion to take the job offering the higher salary but less security.

Research has indicated that the risky-shift phenomenon seems to hold for both sexes, for all subject areas, and for both hypothetical and real situations. The inevitable question that arises is, Why does this happen?

Some possibilities are: (1) risk is highly valued in certain roles; (2) taking risks is a cultural (American?) value and people raise their status by taking risks; (3) the risky individual is the most influential member of a group and therefore succeeds in influencing other group members in the direction of greater risk taking; and (4) individual responsibility is diffused in a group, whereas when one is alone the responsibility is one's own.

[M. A. Wallach, N. Kogan, and D. J. Bem, "Group Influence on Individual Risk Taking," *Journal of Abnormal and Social Psychology* 65 (1962):75–86; Roger Brown, *Social Psychology* (New York: Free Press, 1965); Marvin Shaw, *Group Dynamics: The Psychology of Small Group Behavior,* 3d ed. (New York: McGraw-Hill, 1981).]

Ritual. A system or collection of behaviors built around a special occasion; a collection of ceremonial behaviors. In psychology, rigid behavior patterns (generally irrational ones).

Role. The part an individual plays in a group; an individual's function or expected behavior.

Role Call Vote. A method of voting in which the names of the members are called and the members indicate their vote aloud.

Role Conflict. The conflict that results from the incompatibility of the behaviors expected from the various roles one individual plays; a situation in which the behavior expected of one role conflicts with the behaviors expected of another role.

Role Model. One who exemplifies a pattern of behavior to be followed by others; one whose behaviors are imitated.

Role Playing. The process of acting out the role of another, often undertaken as a therapeutic procedure for increasing understanding and sensitivity; a problem solving technique based on creating emphatic understanding.

Role Reversal. A therapeutic procedure for increasing mutual understanding in which each of the two parties act out the roles of the other. This procedure is used in a variety of settings (for example, in organizations) where understanding for the roles of others is essential.

Roman à Clef. From the French "novel with a key," a novel in which real persons are depicted but with fictitious names. Also known as "livre à clef."

Romeo and Juliet Effect. The intensification of a relationship (especially a romantic one) as a result of parental opposition. See also REACTANCE.

[R. Driscoll, K. E. Davis, and M. E. Lipetz, "Parental Interference and Romantic Love: The Romeo and Juliet Effect," *Journal of Personality and Social Psychology* 24 (1972):1–10.]

Rootedness, Need for. The need to feel that one has a place in society.

Royalty. The monies received by an author or artist from the profits derived from the sale of the book, song, television series or other work; a percentage of the profit received by the publisher or producer.

Rubric. In a book or manuscript, some kind of title or heading that stands out from the rest of the text, for example, being printed in a different type, being underlined, or being in a different color.

Rule of Grammar. A statement of the relationships between or among linguistic units. Rules may be prescriptive or descriptive: a *prescriptive* rule states the ways in which linguistic units should occur in "proper" grammar whereas a *descriptive* rule expresses the ways in which linguistic units do in fact occur in normal everyday speech. Rules may also be explicit or implicit: an *explicit* rule is one that is stated and taught to speakers as a formal rule of grammar whereas an *implicit* rule is one which is not formally stated but which speakers nevertheless follow in their normal speech. Rules exist on all levels of language usage—on the phonological, semantic, and syntactic levels.

Rules, Communication. See COMMUNICATION RULES.

Rules Theory. An approach to communication theory that attempts to identify the communication rules that operate in the communicative act, rules that determine or influence the messages that are encoded and decoded.
[Donald P. Cushman, "The Rules Perspective as a Theoretical Basis for the Study of Human Communication," *Communication Quarterly* 25 (1977):30–45; Donald P. Cushman, Barry Velentinsen, and David Dietrich, "A Rules Theory of Interpersonal Relationships," in *Human Communication Theory,* Frank E. X. Dance, ed. (New York: Harper & Row, 1982); Susan Shimanoff, *Communication Rules: Theory and Research* (Beverly Hills, Calif.: Sage, 1980).]

Rumor. Messages based on unverified information that are easily started and spread but are often difficult to stop.
[Ralph L. Rosnow, "On Rumor," *Journal of Communication* 24 (Summer 1974):26–38.]

Sapir–Whorf Hypothesis. See LINGUISTIC RELATIVITY.

Sarcasm. A bitter personal remark; harsh personal derision.

Satire. A style of communication in which folly, vice, and other individual and social abuses are ridiculed, at times with a view to bringing about change.

Satisfaction. The degree to which one feels comfortable, pleased, or reward by some behavior or event; an internal reinforcer. The accompanying inventory provides a measure of communication satisfaction and also identifies some of the variables involved in satisfaction.

INTERPERSONAL COMMUNICATION SATISFACTION INVENTORY

Instructions for use with actual conversation:

The purpose of this questionnaire is to investigate your reactions to the conversation you just had. Please indicate the degree to which you agree or disagree that each statement describes this conversation. The 4 or middle position on the scale represents "undecided" or "neutral," then moving out from the center, "slight" agreement or disagreement, then "moderate," then "strong" agreement or disagreement.

Scheme   **271**

INTERPERSONAL COMMUNICATION SATISFACTION INVENTORY (*Continued*)

For example, if you strongly agree with the following statement you would circle 1;

The other person moved around a lot.

Agree: <u>1</u> : <u>2</u> : <u>3</u> : <u>4</u> : <u>5</u> : <u>6</u> : <u>7</u> : Disagree

1. The other person let me know that I was communicating effectively.
2. Nothing was accomplished.
3. I would like to have another conversation like this one.
4. The other person genuinely wanted to get to know me.
5. I was very *dis*satisfied with the conversation.
6. I felt that during the conversation I was able to present myself as I wanted the other person to view me.
7. I was very satisfied with the conversation.
8. The other person expressed a lot of interest in what I had to say.
9. I did *NOT* enjoy the conversation.
10. The other person did *NOT* provide support for what he/she was saying.
11. I felt I could talk about anything with the other person.
12. We each got to say what we wanted.
13. I felt that we could laugh easily together.
14. The conversation flowed smoothly.
15. The other person frequently said things which added little to the conversation.
16. We talked about something I was *NOT* interested in.

Scoring Key:

For items 1, 3, 4, 6, 7, 8, 11, 12, 13, 14: Strongly Agree = 7; Moderately Agree = 6; Slightly Agree = 5; Neutral = 4; Slightly Disagree = 3; Moderately Disagree = 2; Strongly Disagree = 1.

For Items 2, 5, 9, 10, 15, 16: Strongly Agree = 1; Moderately Agree = 2; Slightly Agree = 3; Neutral = 4; Slightly Disagree = 5; Moderately Disagree = 6; Strongly Disagree = 7.

[Michael L. Hecht, "The Conceptualization and Measurement of Interpersonal Communication Satisfaction," *Human Communication Research* 4 (Spring 1978):253–264, and "Toward a Conceptualization of Communication Satisfaction," *Quarterly Journal of Speech* 64 (February 1978):47–62.]

Saturation. The ratio of available communication receivers (for example, radios and televisions) to the number of households in any specific area. Saturation figures provide researchers with a measure of the potential audience within any given geographical area.

Scapegoating. The process of heaping blame, problems, and so forth, onto one person, the scapegoat.

Scene. In Kenneth Burke's system of rhetoric, the context, setting, or situation in which the act (q.v.) occurs; the social, cultural, and physical setting in which the act takes place; answers the question, Where was the act performed? See also PENTAD.

Schema (*pl.* Schemata). A cognitive framework into which specific parts of an event or process are fit; an organized structure of information on a particular concept. Schemata influence a variety of psychological and psycholinguistic (q.v.) processes, for example, perception, memory, comprehension, retrieval.

Scheme. Any figure of speech in which the words are arranged in a particular way so as to convey a particular meaning. In the scheme, the literal meanings of the words are retained.

Schismogenesis. Gregory Bateson introduced this term to refer to the process by which behavior patterns are intensified. In *complementary* schismogenesis, the differences between the two persons increase as when, for example, a protector-dependent relationship develops such that both protector and dependent roles become intensified. In *symmetrical* schismogenesis, a behavior stimulates a similar behavior and each grows in intensity; for example, aggressiveness stimulates aggressiveness.

[Gregory Bateson, *Naven* (Cambridge; Cambridge University Press, 1936).]

Schizophrenia. A psychosis where an individual becomes unresponsive to other people and to the environment; psychotic reaction characterized by a loss of contact with reality.

Scientific Approach to Organizations. As its name implies, this approach holds that scientific methods should be applied to organizations to increase productivity. Scientifically controlled studies will enable management to identify the ways and means for increasing productivity and ultimately profit. The scientific management approach owes much of its formulation to the theories of Frederick W. Taylor, most thoroughly presented in his *Scientific Management* published in 1911.

In his analysis of the scientific management school, John Baird notes that it is characterized by three essential concerns. First, it views the organization as departmentalized and specialized. Organizations, especially large and complex ones, are to be divided into departments and specialized according to the nature of the tasks to be accomplished. Second, the organization is to be structured into formally established hierarchies depending on the status, function, and authority of individuals within the organization. Third, the operations of the members are viewed largely, if not exclusively, in terms of their contribution toward accomplishing the goals of the organization.

In this view productivity is largely a physical and physiological problem. It is viewed in terms of the physical demands of the job and the physiological capabilities of the workers. Time and motion studies are perhaps the most characteristic type of research and are designed to enable the organization to reduce the time it takes to complete a specific task—to cut down on energy expended, to best fit the person to the task. Taylor, for example, conducted time and motion studies of coal shoveling, and analyzed and compared different sizes of shovels and the various tasks to be accomplished. As a result, he was able to reduce the number of workers needed to do the same work from 600 to 400 to 140. Under this system, workers were to be paid according to individual performance; there was a clear reward system. In this approach communication is viewed as the giving of orders, as the explaining of procedures and operations. Only the formal structure of the organization and the formal communication system are recognized.

One of the studies conducted within this general approach was a study of lighting effects at the Western Electric Company's Hawthorne works in Illinois. The study, conducted in 1924, sought to investigate the effects of lighting on performance. But the results did not fit what was expected. Whether the lighting was increased or decreased, productivity increased. Workers in both the experimental and control groups increased in productivity. Researchers from the Harvard University School of Business were brought in to help explain the results, and a series of studies was done between 1927 and 1932 to measure the various effects of differing working conditions. The major conclusion was that social factors, rather than physical and physiological factors, accounted for the differences in worker productivity.

See also HUMAN RELATIONS APPROACH TO ORGANIZATIONS; SYSTEMS APPROACH TO ORGANIZATIONS.

[John Baird, Jr., *The Dynamics of Organizational Communication* (New York: Harper & Row, 1977).]

Script. In transactional analysis (TA) (q.v.), scripts are the directions for living our lives complete with a cast of characters and roles, stage directions, dialogue, and plot. Cultural scripts are given to us by the culture and provide us with guides to proper dress, rules for sexual conduct, gender roles, and value systems; family scripts contain directions for each member of the family. See also LIFE POSITIONS.

[Eric Berne, *Games People Play* (New York: Grove Press, 1964).]

Script Analysis. The analysis of an individual's life script (q.v.) or unconscious life plan.

Second. A voiced agreement with a proposal during a meeting; a procedure designed to ensure that at least two members are in favor of the motion before an assembly spends time considering it.

Secondary Group. A group whose members have relatively weak relationships with each other and where mutual influence and attraction are also weak. See also PRIMARY GROUP.

Secondary Reinforcement. A type of reinforcement whose value is learned or acquired through its association with a primary reinforcer (q.v.). See also REINFORCEMENT.

Secondary Territory. Space used regularly but on a limited basis. See also PRIMARY TERRITORY.

[I. Altman, *The Environment and Social Behavior* (Monterey, Calif.: Brooks/Cole, 1975).]

Secret. Information intentionally concealed from others.

[Sissela Bok, *Secrets: On the Ethics of Concealment and Revelation* (New York: Vintage Books, 1983).]

Segmentals. Speech sounds (phonemes, q.v.) emitted in a linear, left-to-right sequence. See also SUPRASEGMENTALS.

Selection Deficiency. See SIMILARITY DISORDER.

Selective Exposure. The tendency to take in (or expose oneself to) information selectively, usually in ways that are consistent with one's beliefs and attitudes. See also PERSUASION, PRINCIPLES OF.

Selective Inattention. The defensive response of inattention to matters that might prove threatening to the self.

[Harry Stack Sullivan, *The Interpersonal Theory of Psychiatry* (New York: Norton, 1953).]

Selective Perception. The tendency to perceive stimuli selectively, usually in ways that are consistent with one's beliefs and attitudes and needs.

Selective Retention. The tendency to retain certain information and to forget other information based on one's needs and attitudes.

Self-Acceptance. Being psychologically comfortable with ourselves, with our virtues and vices, abilities and limitations.

Self-Actualization. To Abraham Maslow, a motive that leads one to pursue the role that one is fitted for, for example, if one sees oneself as a poet then one must write poetry; a motive concerned with actualizing one's potential, of becoming what would prove most self-fulfilling; the only real motive, according to Kurt Goldstein, that the human organism has; a universal human impulse that encompasses all of the other supposed motives such as security, sex, and curiosity.

[Abraham Maslow, *Motivation and Personality* (New York: Harper & Row, 1970); Kurt Goldstein, *The Organism* (New York: American Book, 1939).]

Self-Adaptors. Nonverbal behaviors that serve some personal need, for example, autoerotic activity. See also ADAPTORS.

Self-Alienation. A condition or state in which an individual does not know himself or herself; the state of being unaware of one's own psychological being. One who does not self-disclose (q.v.) to others is often judged to be a self-alienated person.

Self-Attribution. An attempt to understand our own behavior by understanding its causes and motivations. See also ATTRIBUTION.

Self-Awareness. Understanding and insight into oneself, one's attitudes, values, beliefs, strengths, and weaknesses. A few ways to increase self-awareness may be identified.

Ask Yourself About Yourself

There are a number of ways to do this. One way is to take a "Who Am I?" test informally. Take a piece of paper, head it "Who Am I?," and write 10 or 20 times, "I am. . . ." Then complete each sentence trying not to give only positive or socially acceptable responses; just respond with what comes to mind first. Second, take another piece of paper, divide it into two columns. Head one column "Strengths" or "Virtues" and the other column "Weaknesses" or "Vices." Fill in each column as quickly as possible. Third, using these first two "tests" as a base, take a third piece of paper and head it "Self-improvement goals" and complete the statement "I want to improve my . . ." as many times as you can in, say, 5 minutes. Whether or not these methods are used is not important; what is important is that you begin a dialogue with yourself about yourself. Further, remember that you are constantly changing; consequently, these self-perceptions and goals also change rapidly, often in drastic ways, and therefore need to be updated at regular and frequent intervals.

Listen to Others

We can learn a great deal about ourselves from seeing ourselves as others do. Conveniently, others are constantly giving us the very feedback we need to increase self-awareness. In every interpersonal interaction people comment on us in some way—on what we do, on what we say, on how we look. Sometimes these comments are explicit but most often they are only implicit. Often they are "hidden" in the way in which others look at us, in what they talk about, in their interest in what we say. We need to pay close attention to this kind of information (both verbal and nonverbal) and utilize it to increase our own self-awareness.

Actively Seek Information About the Self

Actively seek out information to reduce your blind self (q.v.). Utilize some of the situations that arise every day to gain self-information: "Do you think I was assertive enough when asking for the raise?" or "Do you think I'd be thought too forward if I invite myself to their house for dinner?" Do not, of course, seek this information constantly; your friends would then surely and quickly find others with whom to interact. Yet, you can make use of some situations—perhaps those in which you are particularly unsure of what to do or how you appear—to reduce your blind self and increase self-awareness. See also JOHARI MODEL.

See Yourself from Different Perspectives

Each of us is viewed differently by each of our friends and relatives. To each of these we are a somewhat different person. And, yet, we are really all of these.

Practice seeing yourself as do the people with whom you interact. For starters, visualize how you are seen by, for example, your mother, your father, your teachers, your best friend, the stranger you sat next to on the bus, your employer, your neighbor's child. Each of these people sees you differently. Because you are, in fact, a composite of all of these views, it is important that you can, for a moment, see yourself through the eyes of these significant others. The experience will surely give you new and valuable perspectives on yourself.

Increase the Open Self

The extent to which you reveal yourself to others—the degree to which you increase your open self (q.v.)—influences at least two dimensions of self-awareness. First, when you reveal yourself to others, you reveal yourself to yourself at the same time. At the very least you bring into consciousness or into clearer focus what you may have buried within. As you discuss yourself you may see connections that you had previously missed, and with the aid of feedback from others, you may gain still more insight. Second, by increasing the open self you increase the likelihood that a meaningful and intimate dialogue will develop, and it is through these interactions that you best get to know yourself. But, there are risks involved in revealing yourself and these need to be taken into consideration too. See also SELF-DISCLOSURE.

Be Conscious of Your Life Position (q.v.)

Recognize when you are functioning with an inappropriate and self-descriptive script. Recognize that a negative self-image (the "I'm not O.K." position) may have been internalized when you were very young and may be a totally inadequate reflection of who you are now. Further, a negative self-image will invariably impair your general effectiveness; it often makes one frightened to take risks, to see accomplishments as less important than they really are, or to see in many situations failure when it would be just as easy to see success. These scripts can be changed; the scripts can be rewritten. Substitute the productive "I'm O.K." position script for the unproductive, self-destructive "I'm not O.K." script. Similarly, realize that other people, too, are "O.K." and have a great deal to contribute to society in general and to each of us in particular. These *is* strength in unity, and we profit a great deal from learning and utilizing the insights and talents of others.

Self-Concept. An individual's evaluation of oneself; an individual's self-appraisal.

Self-Confidence as a Speaker. One of the most important qualities separating the effective from the ineffective speaker is confidence. Confidence also seems to separate the speaker who derives enjoyment from the speaker who derives nothing but pain and anxiety. Fortunately, confidence is not something magical that some people have and others do not; rather, it is a quality that we can all develop and improve. Here are a few suggestions for developing your self-confidence as a speaker.

Prepare Thoroughly

This is probably the major factor in instilling confidence in a speaker. Preparation would include everything you do from the time you begin thinking about your speech to the time you deliver it. Most important is the thorough research of the topic. This will help to eliminate any fears you may have of not being able to answer questions (should there be a question period following your speech) or of saying something that may be perceived as incorrect or naive. The more you know about your topic, the more confident you will feel and the more confidence you will project to your audience. Thorough preparation also includes learning your speech well so that you will not have to rely on your notes. Eliminating the fear of forgetting what you want to say will go a long way toward building your self-confidence.

Familiarize Yourself with the Speaking Situation

The more familiar you are with the speaking situation—the room in which you will speak, the arrangement of the chairs, the type of audience you will address, and so on—the more confident you will become. Familiarity with any situation increases one's ability to control it; the speaking situation is no exception. If you are speaking in a classroom, then you are already familiar with the situation, but it would also help if you could view the room from the point of view of the speaker. Perhaps a day or two before you are to speak, stand in front of the room, look it over, and try to imagine the entire speaking situation as it will be when you deliver your speech. Then, when you do go to the front of the room to give your speech, you will face the familiar instead of the unexpected and your confidence will probably increase.

Develop the Desire to Communicate

Too often we rehearse negative "scripts"; we tell ourselves over and over again how much we will dislike the public speaking experience and how terrible we are as speakers. If you approach the public speaking situation negatively—with a firm desire to get the experience over with as soon as possible—you will project this image to the audience and will inevitably lower your own self-confidence. Substitute positive scripts. Tell yourself that the experience can be an enjoyable one (it really can be!). With time, you will find that you are operating with a more positive and a more confident view of the entire speaking encounter.

Rehearse

Rehearsing your speech and its presentation is most essential for increasing self-confidence. Often a lack of confidence is brought on by thoughts of failure; with increased rehearsal we lessen our chances and our thoughts of failure and of course increase our general effectiveness and our general self-confidence.

One general rule to follow in rehearsal is to rehearse as a confident, fully in control speaker; rehearse with a positive attitude and perspective. Do not give yourself negative criticism during rehearsal. When you then present the actual speech, you will find that you can present the speech as you rehearsed it, with confidence. This self-confidence will be communicated to the audience in a variety of ways—by the way you walk, the way you stand, the way you maintain direct eye contact with the audience, the way you deliver your ideas, the way you handle audience questions, and so on.

Each speaking experience—like each rehearsal—should add to your self-confidence. Repeated speaking experiences will help to further develop your self-confidence.

Develop a Communicator Self-Image

By a "communicator self-image" is meant a view of yourself as a capable, proficient, and most importantly, confident communicator, a person who is effective in getting her or his message across to others. This image may be enhanced by thinking of ourselves as confident speakers and perhaps equally important, by acting as if we are confident speakers. Acting confidently will go a long way toward making us view ourselves as confident and eventually in actually making us confident. The process, it seems, occurs in three steps: (1) we act as if we are confident; (2) we come to think of ourselves as confident; and (3) we become confident. All this is not to suggest that we should fool ourselves or that we should engage in self-deception. Rather, it is to suggest that we can build positive qualities by acting as if we already possess them. This "acting as if" will help make these positive qualities a more integral part of our thinking and our behavior.

Self-Disclosure. A type of communication in which information about the self that is normally kept hidden is communicated to another person. Because self-disclosure is a type of communication, overt statements pertaining to the self as well as slips of the tongue, unconscious nonverbal movements, written confessions, and public confessions would all be classified as self-disclosing communications. Only new knowledge is useful. To tell someone something he or she already knows would not be self-disclosure; in order to be self-disclosure some new knowledge would have to be communicated. Further, to be self-disclosure, the information must be such that it is normally kept hidden. To tell someone your age, religion, or political leanings would only be self-disclosure if you normally keep these data secret or hidden from most people.

Self-disclosure involves at least one other individual. In order to self-disclose, the communication act must involve at least two persons; it cannot be an *intra*personal communication act. Nor can we, as some people attempt to, "disclose" in a manner that makes it impossible for another person to understand. This is not a disclosure at all. Nor can we write in diaries that no one reads and call this self-disclosure. To be self-disclosure, the information must be received and understood by another individual.

Gerard Egan, in *Encounter,* makes another distinction that may prove useful. He distinguishes between *history,* which he calls "the mode of noninvolvement," and *story,* which he calls "the mode of involvement." History is a manner of revealing the self that is only pseudoself-disclosure. It is an approach that details some facts of the individual's life but does not really invite involvement from listeners. Story, on the other hand, is authentic self-disclosure. In story individuals communicate their inner selves to others and look for some human response rather than just simple feedback. The speaker takes a risk, puts himself or herself on the line, and reveals something significant about who he or she is and not merely what he or she has done.

Dimensions of Self-Disclosure

Self-disclosures may differ from one another in terms of five basic dimensions or qualities. Perhaps the most obvious is the *amount* of self-disclosure that takes place. The amount of self-disclosure may be gauged by examining the frequency with which one self-discloses and the duration of the self-disclosing messages, that is, the time taken up with self-disclosing statements. A second factor is the *valence* of the self-disclosure, that is, the positiveness or negativeness of the self-disclosure. We can self-disclose favorable and flattering things about ourselves as well as unfavorable and unflattering things. A third factor is the *accuracy* and *honesty* with which one self-discloses. The accuracy of our self-disclosures will be limited by the extent to which we know ourselves. Further, our self-disclosures may vary in terms of honesty. We may be totally honest or we may exaggerate, omit crucial details, or simply lie. The fourth factor is *intention* to self-disclose; that is, the extent to which we disclose what we intend to disclose, the extent to which we are in conscious control of the self-disclosures we make. Fifth, self-disclosures may vary in terms of *intimacy*. We can disclose the most intimate details of our lives, we may disclose items that we regard as relatively peripheral or impersonal, or we may disclose items that lie anywhere in between these extremes.

Factors Influencing Self-Disclosure

Self-disclosure occurs more readily under certain circumstances than under others. A few of the more significant factors influencing self-disclosure are identified here.

The Disclosures of Others: The Dyadic Effect

Generally, self-disclosure is reciprocal. In any interaction self-disclosure is more likely to occur if the other person has previously self-disclosed. Self-disclo-
sure follows self-disclosure. This is the dyadic effect; what one person in a dyad does, the other person does as a response. This dyadic effect in self-disclosure implies that a kind of spiral effect operates here, with each person's self-disclosures serving as the stimulus for additional self-disclosures by the other person.

Audience Size

Self-disclosure is more likely to occur in small groups than in large groups. Dyads are perhaps the most common situations in which self-disclosure takes place. A dyad seems more suitable because it is easier for the self-discloser to deal with one person's reactions and responses than with the reactions of a group of three or four or five. The self-disclosure can attend to the responses quite carefully and, on the basis of the support or lack of support, monitor the disclosures, continuing if the situation is supportive and stopping if it is not supportive. With more than one listener such monitoring is impossible since the responses are sure to vary among the listeners. Another reason is that when the group is larger than two, the self-disclosure takes on aspects of exhibitionism and public exposure. It is no longer a confidential matter; now it is one about which many people know. From a more practical point of view, it is often difficult to assemble in one place at one time only those people to whom we would want to self-disclose.

Topic

The topic influences the amount and type of self-disclosure. Certain areas of the self are more likely to be self-disclosed than are others. We would more likely self-disclose information about our job or hobbies, for example, than about our sex life or financial situation. Sidney M. Jourard found that self-disclosures about money (for example, the amount of money one owes), personality (for example, the things about which one experiences guilt), and body (for example, one's feelings of sexual adequacy) were less frequent than disclosures about tastes and interests, attitudes and opinions, and work. Clearly, the first three topics are more closely related to one's self-concept, and disclosures about these are therefore potentially more threatening than are disclosures about one's tastes in clothing, one's views on religion, or one's pressures at work.

Valence

The valence (the positive or negative quality) of the self-disclosure is also significant. Positive self-disclosures are more likely to be engaged in than negative self-disclosures and may be made to nonintimates as well as to intimates. Negative self-disclosures, on the other hand, take place most often with close intimates and usually after considerable time has elapsed in a relationship. This finding is consistent with the evidence that shows that self-disclosure and trust are positively related.

Research indicates that we develop greater attraction for those who engage in positive self-disclosure than for those who engage in negative self-disclosure. This is particularly significant in the early stages of a relationship. Negative self-disclosures to a stranger or even a casual acquaintance are perceived as inappropriate, no doubt because such self-disclosures violate our culture's norms for such communications. This may suggest a warning: If your aim is to be perceived as attractive, consider curtailing negative self-disclosures at least in the early stages of your relationships.

Sex

Most research indicates that generally women disclose more than men but that both men and women make negative disclosures about equally. Men and women give different reasons for avoiding self-disclosure. The main reason for avoiding self-disclosure, however, is common to both men and women and it is: "If I disclose, I might project an image I do not want to project." In a society where one's image is so important—where one's image is often the basis for success or failure—this reason for avoiding self-disclosure is expected. Other reasons for avoiding self-disclosure, however, are unique for men and women. For men the reasons reported are: "If I self-disclose, I might give information that makes me appear inconsistent," "If I self-disclose, I might lose control over the other person," and "Self-disclosure might threaten relationships I have with people other than close acquaintances." Lawrence Rosenfeld sums up the male reasons for self-disclosure avoidance: "If I disclose to you, I might project an image I do not want to project, which could make me look bad and cause me to lose control over you. This might go so far as to affect relationships I have with people other than you." The principal objective of men is to avoid self-disclosure so that control can be maintained.

In addition to fearing the projection of an unfavorable image, women avoid self-disclosure for the following reasons: "Self-disclosure would give the other person information which he or she might use against me at some time," "Self-disclosure is a sign of some emotional disturbance," and "Self-disclosure might hurt our relationship." The general reason why women avoid self-disclosure, says Rosenfeld, is: "If I disclose to you I might project an image I do not want to project, such as my being emotionally ill, which you might use against me and which might hurt our relationship." The principal objective in avoiding self-disclosure for women is "to avoid personal hurt and problems with the relationship."

Rosenfeld summarizes the results of his investigation by observing: "The stereotyped male role—independent, competitive, and unsympathetic—and the stereotyped female role—dependent, nonaggressive, and interpersonally oriented—were evident in the reasons indicated for avoiding self-disclosure. Seeking different rewards from their interpersonal relationships, many males and females go about the business of self-disclosing, and *not* self-disclosing, differently." You might wish to test some of these findings yourself by talking with your peers about the reasons they avoid self-disclosure and about the reasons for their reasons. Why do men and women have different reasons for avoiding self-disclosure? What is there in the learning histories of the two sexes that might account for such differences?

Race, Nationality, and Age

There are racial and national differences in self-disclosure as well. Black students disclose significantly less than do white students, and students in the United States disclose more than similar groups in Puerto Rico, Germany, Great Britain, and the Middle East. There are even differences in the amount of self-disclosure in different age groups. Self-disclosure to a spouse or to an opposite-sex friend increases from the age of about 17 to about 50 and then drops off.

Receiver Relationship

The person to whom the disclosures are made also influences the frequency and the likelihood of self-disclosure. Research, however, has not been able to identify fully the specific characteristics of the person with whom self-disclosure is most likely to take place. Most studies have found that we disclose more often to those people who are close to us, for example, our spouses, our family, our close friends. Some studies claim that we disclose most to persons we like and do not disclose to persons we dislike regardless of how close they are to us. Thus, we may disclose to a well-liked teacher even though this teacher is not particularly close and yet not disclose to a brother or sister who is close but who we may not like very much.

We are more apt to disclose to people we see as accepting, understanding, warm, and supportive. Generally, of course, these are people we are close to and like. Still other studies claim that a lasting relationship between people increases the likelihood of self-disclosure, while others find that self-disclosure is heightened in temporary relationships, for example, between strangers on a train.

Male college students are more likely to disclose to a close friend than to either of their parents. But, female college students disclose about equally to their mothers and to their best friends but do not disclose very much to their fathers or to their boyfriends.

As might be expected, husbands and wives self-disclose to each other more than they do to any other person or group of persons. "This confirms the view," says Jourard in *The Transparent Self,* "that marriage is the 'closest' relationship one can enter, and it may help us the better to understand why some people avoid it like the plague. Anyone who is reluctant to be known by another person and to know another person—sexually and cognitively—will find the prospective intimacy of marriage somewhat terrifying." There is some evidence to suggest, however, that wives from the lower social classes disclose most not to their husbands but to their women friends.

Sources of Resistance to Self-Disclosure

For all its advantages and importance, self-disclosure is a form of communication that is often fiercely resisted. Some of the reasons for its resistance should be examined.

Societal Bias

Perhaps the most obvious reason for our reluctance to self-disclose, according to Gerard Egan, is that we have internalized the societal bias against it. We have been conditioned against self-disclosure by the society in which we live. The hero in folklore is strong but silent; he bears responsibilities, burdens, and problems without letting others even be aware of them. He is self-reliant and does not need the assistance of anyone. Men have internalized this folk hero. Women are a bit more fortunate in this respect. They are allowed the luxury of some self-disclosure; they are allowed to tell their troubles to someone, to pour out their feelings, to talk about themselves. Women are allowed great freedom in expressing emotions, in verbalizing love and affection; men are more restricted, they are conditioned to avoid such expressions. These, men have been taught, are signs of weakness rather than strength. This societal bias is reflected even in our evaluations of self-disclosing men and women. For example, women who disclose a great deal are generally evaluated positively but men who disclose a great deal, regardless of the subjects they disclose, are evaluated negatively.

Fear of Punishment

Many people resist self-disclosing because of a fear of punishment, generally in the form of rejection. We may picture other people laughing at us or whispering about us or condemning us if we self-disclose. These mental pictures help to convince us that self-disclosure is not the most expedient course of action.

We may also fear punishment in the form of tangible or concrete manifestations, such as the loss of a job or of friends. At times this happens. The ex-convict who self-discloses a past record may find himself or herself without a job or out of a political office. Generally, however, these fears are overblown. These fears are often excuses that allow us to rest contentedly without self-disclosing.

Fear of Self-Knowledge

Another possible reason we resist self-disclosure is what Egan calls fear of self-knowledge. We may have built up a beautiful, rationalized picture of ourselves—emphasizing the positive and eliminating or minimizing the negative. Self-disclosure often forces us to see through the rationalizations. We see the positive aspects for what they are, and we see the negative aspects that were previously hidden.

Rewards of Self-Disclosure

A number of researchers and theorists argue that self-disclosure is perhaps the most important form of communication in which anyone could engage. This is not to imply that there are no risks involved; there are dangers in self-disclosing, and we will consider some of these later. Here, however, we focus on the rewards or advantages of this form of interpersonal communication.

Knowledge of Self

We cannot know ourselves as fully as possible if we do not self-disclose to at least one other individual. By self-disclosing we gain a new perspective on ourselves, a deeper understanding of our own behavior. In therapy, for example, very often the insight does not come directly from the therapist; while the individual is self-disclosing, he or she recognizes some facet of behavior or some relationship that was not known before. Through self-disclosure, then, we may come to understand ourselves more thoroughly.

Ability to Cope

Improved ability to deal with our problems, especially our guilt, frequently comes through self-disclosure. One of the great fears that many people have is that they will not be accepted because of some deep, dark secret, because of something they have done, or because of some feeling or attitude they might have. Because we feel these things as a basis for rejection, we develop guilt. By self-disclosing such feelings and being supported rather than rejected, we are better prepared to deal with the guilt and perhaps reduce or even eliminate it. Even self-acceptance is difficult without self-disclosure. We accept ourselves largely through the eyes of others. If we feel that others will reject us, we are apt to reject ourselves as well. Through self-disclosure and subsequent support, we are in a better position to see the positive responses to us and are more likely to respond by developing a positive self-concept.

Energy Release

Keeping our secrets to ourselves and not revealing who we are to others takes a great deal of energy and leaves us with that much less energy for other things. We must be constantly on guard, for example, lest someone see in our behavior what we consider to be a deviant orientation, attitude, or behavior pattern. We might avoid certain people for fear they will tell this awful thing about us, or avoid situations or places because if we are seen there, others will know how terrible we really are. By self-disclosing we rid ourselves of the false masks that otherwise must be worn.

Communication Effectiveness

Self-disclosure is also helpful in improving communication efficiency. Since we understand the messages of others largely to the extent that we understand the other individuals, we can better understand what an individual means if we know the individual well. We can tell what certain nuances mean, when the person is serious and when he or she is joking, when the person is being sarcastic out of fear and when out of resentment, and so on. Self-disclosure is an essential condition for getting to know another individual.

Meaningfulness of Relationships

Self-disclosure is necessary if a meaningful relationship between two people is to be established. Without self-disclosure meaningful relationships seem impossible to develop. By self-disclosing we are in effect saying to other individuals that we trust them, that we respect them, that we care enough about them and about our relationship to reveal ourselves to them. This leads the other individual to self-disclose in return. This is at least the start of a meaningful relationship, a relationship that is honest and open and goes beyond surface trivialities.

Physiological Health

Recent research demonstrates that people who self-disclose are less vulnerable to illnesses. Self-disclosures seem to protect the body from the damaging stresses that accompany nondisclosure. For example, bereavement over the death of someone very close is linked to physical illness for those who bear this alone and in silence, but is unrelated to any physical problems for those who share their grief with others. Similarly, women who have suffered sexual trauma experience a variety of illnesses (for example, headaches and stomach problems). Women who kept these experiences to themselves, however, suffer these illnesses to a much greater extent than do those who talked with others about these traumas. Persons who do not self-disclose have also been found to have less effective immunization systems than those who self-disclose. The physiological effort required to keep one's burdens to oneself seems to interact with the effects of the burden or trauma to create a combined stress that can lead to a variety of diseases and illnesses.

Dangers of Self-Disclosure

Undoubtedly there are numerous advantages to be gained from self-disclosure. Yet these should not blind us to the fact that self-disclosure often involves very real risks. An investment analogy may prove useful: when the payoffs or potential gains are great, so are the risks. When the payoffs are small, so are the risks. The same seems true of self-disclosure. When the potential rewards of self-disclosure are great so are the risks. These potential rewards and risks need to be weighed carefully before engaging in significant self-disclosure. The risks may be of various types—risks to one's job, to one's professional advancement, to one's social and family life, and to just about any and every aspect of one's life. Politicians who disclose that they have been seeing a psychiatrist may later find their own political party no longer supporting their candidacy and voters unwilling to risk having someone who needed analysis in a position of power. Men and women in law enforcement agencies, such as city or state police officers or FBI agents, who disclose that they are homosexuals or lesbians may soon find themselves confined to desk jobs at some isolated precinct, prevented from further advancement, or charged with criminal behavior and fired. Teachers who disclose their former or present drug behavior or that they are living with one of their students may find themselves denied tenure, teaching the undesirable courses at the undesirable hours, and eventually being victims of "budget cuts." And the teachers or students who find a supportive atmosphere in their interpersonal communication course and who disclose about their sex lives, their financial conditions, or their self-doubts, anxieties, or fantasies may find that some of the less sympathetic listeners may later use that information to the self-discloser's detriment.

In making your choice between disclosing and not disclosing, keep in mind—in addition to the advantages and dangers already noted—the irreversible nature of communication. Regardless of how many times we may attempt to qualify something, "take it back," or deny it, once something is said, it cannot be withdrawn. We cannot erase the conclusions and inferences listeners have made on the basis of our disclosures. I am not advocating that you therefore refrain from self-disclosing, but only reminding you to consider the irreversible nature of communication as one additional factor involved in your choices.

Self-Disclosure Guidelines

Because self-disclosure involves both potential rewards and dangers, examine carefully the predicted consequences before deciding whether or not to self-disclose. Almost equally difficult is responding appropriately to the disclosures of others. Because self-disclosure is so important and so delicate a matter, guidelines are offered here for (1) deciding whether or not and how to self-disclose and (2) responding to the disclosures of others.

Guidelines in Self-Disclosing

Each person has to make her or his own decisions concerning self-disclosure; there is no universal answer that can be given. Further, your decision will be based on numerous different variables, many of which were considered in the previous discussion. The following guidelines will help you raise the right questions before making what must be *your* decision.

Consider the Motivation for the Self-Disclosure. Self-disclosure should be motivated out of a concern for the relationship, for the others involved, and for oneself. Self-disclosure should not be an exercise in exhibitionism, an opportunity to parade one's sexual fantasies, past indiscretions, or psychological problems. Self-disclosure should serve a useful and productive function for all persons involved.

Consider the Appropriateness of the Self-Disclosure. Self-disclosure should be appropriate to the context and to the relationship between speaker and listener. Ideally, self-disclosures should grow naturally out of the developing situation and relationship. Generally, the more intimate the disclosures, the closer the relationship should be. It is probably best to resist intimate disclosures with nonintimates or casual acquaintances or in the early stages of a relationship. This suggestion is especially applicable to intimate negative disclosures.

Consider the Opportunity Available for Open and Honest Responses. Self-disclosure should occur in an atmosphere where open and honest responses can be made. Don't hit and run. Avoid self-disclosure when the people involved are under pressures of time or when they are in a situation that will not allow them to respond as they might wish.

Consider the Clarity and Directness of the Self-Disclosure. The goal of self-disclosure is to inform—not to confuse—the other person. Often, however, we self-disclose only partially or self-disclose in such an oblique and roundabout way that the listener walks away more confused than before the disclosure. If you are going to self-disclose, consider the extent of the disclosure and be prepared to disclose enough to ensure the necessary understanding, or perhaps reconsider whether you should self-disclose at all.

But, the most important suggestion in this regard is to disclose gradually. Disclose in small increments. When disclosures are made too rapidly and all at once, it is impossible to monitor your listener's responses and to retreat if the responses are not positive enough. Further, you prevent the listener from responding with his or her own disclosures and thereby upset the natural balance so helpful in this kind of communication exchange.

Consider the Disclosures of the Other Person. During your disclosures give the other person a chance to reciprocate with his or her own disclosures. If such reciprocal disclosures are not made, then reassess your own self-disclosures. The lack of reciprocity may be a signal that for this person at this time and in this context, your disclosures are not welcomed or appropriate.

Consider the Possible Burdens Self-Disclosure Might Entail. Any potential self-discloser should carefully weigh the potential problems that may be incurred as a result of a disclosure. Can you afford to lose your job should you disclose your previous prison record? Are you willing to risk failing the course should you confess to having plagiarized your term paper?

Ask yourself whether you are making unreasonable demands on the listener. For example, consider the person who swears his or her mother-in-law to secrecy and then self-discloses to having an ongoing affair with a neighbor. This type of situation, it seems, places an unfair burden on the mother-in-law who is now in a bind to either break her promise of secrecy or allow her son or daughter to believe a lie.

Guidelines in Responding to Self-Disclosures

When someone discloses to you, it is usually a sign of trust and affection. In serving this most important receiver function, keep the following in mind.

Practice the Skills of Effective and Active Listening. The skills of effective listening are especially important when listening to self-disclosures: listen actively, listen for different levels of meaning, listen with empathy, and listen with an open mind. Paraphrase the speaker so that you can be sure you understand both the thoughts and the feelings communicated. Express understanding of the speaker's feelings to allow the speaker the opportunity to see these more objectively and through the eyes of another individual. Ask questions to ensure your own understanding and to signal your own interest and attention.

Support the Discloser. Express support for the person during and after the disclosures. Refrain from evaluation during the disclosures; concentrate on understanding and empathizing with the discloser. Allow the discloser to pace himself or herself; don't rush the discloser. Make your supportiveness clear to the discloser through your verbal and nonverbal responses.

Reinforce the Disclosing Behaviors. The difficulty of self-disclosure makes it important that you reinforce the disclosing behavior throughout the experience. No reinforcement or too-little reinforcement is likely to be interpreted as indifference or disapproval with the result that the self-disclosing stops short. Nod your understanding, echo the feelings and thoughts of the person, maintain appropriate eye contact, and otherwise indicate your positive attitudes toward the discloser and the act of disclosing.

Keep the Disclosures Confidential. When a person discloses to you it is because she or he wants you to know these feelings and thoughts. If the discloser wishes others to share these, then it is up to her or him to disclose them. If you reveal these disclosures to others, all sorts of negative effects are bound to occur.

Don't Use These Disclosures Against the Person. Many self-disclosures expose some kind of vulnerability, some weakness. If we later turn around and use these against the person, as we might in beltlining (q.v.), we betray the confidence and trust invested in us. Regardless of how angry we might get, we need to resist the temptation to use any self-disclosures as weapons. If we do use the disclosures against the person, the relationship is sure to suffer and may, in fact, never fully recover. Remember too: we can never uncommunicate.

[Sidney Jourard, *Disclosing Man to Himself* (New York: Van Nostrand Reinhold, 1968) and *The Transparent Self,* rev. ed. (New York: Van Nostrand Reinhold, 1971); Gerard Egan, *Encounter: Group Processes for Interpersonal Growth* (Belmont, Calif.: Brooks/Cole, 1970); W. Barnett Pearce and Stewart M. Sharp, "Self-Disclosing Communication," *Journal of Communication* 23 (December 1973):409–425; Lawrence Rosenfeld, "Self-Disclosure Avoidance: Why I Am Afraid to Tell You Who I Am," *Communication Monographs* 46 (March 1979):63–74; Steven Naifeh and Gregory White Smith, *Why Can't Men Open Up? Overcoming Men's Fear of Intimacy* (New York: Clarkson N. Potter, 1984).]

Self-Efficacy. A feeling of effectiveness and ability; the perception of oneself as capable and powerful enough to effect change and a willingness to accept the consequences of any ineffectiveness.

[Albert Bandura, "Self-Efficacy Mechanism in Human Agency," *American Psychologist* 37 (1982):122–147, and "Self-Efficacy: Toward a Unifying Theory of Behavioral Change," *Psychological Review* 84 (1977):191–215.]

Self-Esteem. The positive evaluation one attributes to one's own self-concept.

Self-Evaluative Rules. Those rules, in contingency rules theory (q.v.), that connect persuasive action to an individual's standards of behavior. See also ADAPTIVE RULES.

Self-Fulfilling Prophecy. A self-fulfilling prophecy is a phenomenon that occurs when we make a prediction or formulate a belief that comes true because we have made the prediction and acted on it as if it were true. Identifying the four basic steps in the self-fulfilling prophecy should clarify this important concept and its implications for communication.

1. We make a prediction or formulate a belief about a person or a situation. (For example, we make a prediction that Pat is awkward in interpersonal encounters.)
2. We act toward that person or situation as if that prediction or belief was in fact true. (For example, we act toward Pat as if Pat was in fact awkward.)
3. Because we act as if the belief is true, it becomes true. (For example, because of the ways in which we act toward Pat, Pat becomes tense and manifests awkwardness.)
4. We observe our effect on the person or the resulting situation and what we see strengthens our beliefs. (For example, we observe Pat's awkwardness and this reinforces our belief that Pat is in fact awkward.)

If we expect people to act a certain way or if we make a prediction about the characteristics of a situation, our predictions will frequently come true because of the self-fulfilling prophecy phenomenon.

A widely known example of the self-fulfilling prophecy is the Pygmalion effect. In one study of this effect teachers were told that certain pupils were expected to do exceptionally well—that they were late bloomers. The names of these students were actually selected at random by the experimenters; however, the results were not random. Those students whose names were given to the teachers actually did perform at a higher level than did the other students. In fact, these students even improved in I.Q. score more than did the other students.

Eric Berne, in *Games People Play,* and Thomas Harris, in *I'm O.K., You're O.K.,* both point out the same type of effect but in a somewhat different context. These transactional psychologists argue that we live by the scripts that are given to us by our parents, and that we essentially act in the way in which we are told to act. Much like the children who were expected to do well, we all, according to transactional psychology, live by the scripts given to us as children.

[Robert K. Merton, *Social Theory and Social Structure* (New York: Free Press, 1957); Paul M. Insel and Lenore F. Jacobson, eds., *What Do You Expect? An Inquiry into Self-Fulfilling Prophecies* (Menlo Park, Calif.: Cummings, 1975).]

Self-Help. That area of therapy or personal improvement techniques that the individual undertakes and effects alone.

Self-Help Group. A group of nonprofessionals who gather together to focus on and improve some problem common to all or most of the members. Alcoholics Anonymous is perhaps the most popular and well-known of the self-help groups.

Self-Monitoring. Self-monitoring may be viewed as the manipulation of the image that we present to others in our interpersonal interactions. High self-monitors, for example, will carefully adjust their behaviors on the basis of feedback from others so that they may produce the most desirable effect. Their interpersonal interactions are manipulated in an attempt to give the best and most effective interpersonal impression. Low self-monitors, on the other hand, are not concerned with the image they present to others. Rather, their interactions are characterized by an extreme openness in which they communicate their thoughts and feelings with no attempt to manipulate the impressions they create. Somewhere between the high and the low self-monitors lie most of us. You may wish, at this point, to take the accompanying brief self-monitoring test.

SELF-MONITORING TEST

These statements concern personal reactions to a number of different situations. No two statements are exactly alike, so consider each statement carefully before answering. If a statement is true, or mostly true, as applied to you, circle the T. If a statement is false, or not usually true, as applied to you, circle the F.

1. I find it hard to imitate the behavior of other people.   T   F
2. I guess I do put on a show to impress or entertain people.   T   F
3. I would probably make a good actor.   T   F
4. I sometimes appear to others to be experiencing deeper emotions than I actually am.   T   F
5. In a group of people, I am rarely the center of attention.   T   F
6. In different situations and with different people, I often act like very different persons.   T   F
7. I can only argue for ideas I already believe.   T   F
8. In order to get along and be liked, I tend to be what people expect me to be rather than who I really am.   T   F
9. I may deceive people by being friendly when I really dislike them.   T   F
10. I am not always the person I appear to be.   T   F

Scoring

Give yourself one point for each of questions 1, 5, and 7 that you answered F. Give yourself one point for each of the remaining questions that you answered T. Add up your points. If you are a good judge of yourself and scored 7 or above, you are probably a high self-monitoring individual; 3 or below, you are probably a low self-monitoring individual.

"The Many Me's of the Self-Monitor" by Mark Snyder. Adapted from "Impression Management" by Mark Snyder in the book, *Social Psychology in the Eighties,* 3d ed., by L. S. Wrightsman and K. Deaux. Copyright © 1981 by Wadsworth, Inc. Reprinted with permission of Brooks/Cole Publishing Company, Monterey, California.

When high and low self-monitors are compared, a number of interesting differences are noted. For example, high self-monitors are more apt to take charge of a situation, are more sensitive to the deceptive techniques of others, and are better able to detect self-monitoring or impression management techniques when used by others. High self-monitors prefer to interact with low self-monitors. They seem to prefer to live in a relatively stable world with people who will not be able to detect their self-monitoring techniques. By interacting with low self-monitors, the high self-monitors are more likely to be able to assume positions of influence and power. High self-monitors also seem better able to present their true selves than are low self-monitors. For example, if an innocent person is charged with a crime, to use the example cited by Mark Snyder (on whose research this discussion is based), the high self-monitor would be able to present his or her innocence more effectively than would a low self-monitor.

Self-Presentation. An explanation for the self-serving bias effect (see ATTRIBUTION) that holds that the self-serving bias is a reflection of one's need or wish to present oneself positively in public.
[G. Weary and R. M. Arkin, "Attributional Self-Presentation," in *New Directions in Attribution Research,* III, J. H. Harvey, W. J. Ickes, and R. F. Kidd, eds. (Hillsdale, N.J.: Erlbaum, 1981).]

Self-Reference Terms. Expressions that refer to the speaker, for example, first person pronouns as well as expressions such as *this speaker* or *this writer.*

Self-Reflective Abstraction. A form or type of abstracting in which the abstraction is of itself, as when, for example, we think about our thinking, love our love, or fear our fear.

Self-Reflexiveness. That quality of a system by which it can refer back to itself. Language is self-reflexive in that one can use language to talk about language. See also METALANGUAGE.

Self-Reinforcement. The process of rewarding or being supportive of oneself.

Self-Serving Bias. See ATTRIBUTION.

Self-Talk. The intrapersonal talk through which we internalize irrational and illogical assumptions that create personal and interpersonal adjustment difficulties. See also RATIONAL EMOTIVE THERAPY.
[Albert Ellis and Robert A. Harper, *A New Guide to Rational Living* (No. Hollywood, Calif.: Wilshire, 1975).]

Semantic(s). Meaning; that branch of language study concerned with meaning.

Semantic Differentiation. Perhaps the most popular of all the methods of measuring meaning is semantic differentiation. In this procedure a word is rated on selected bipolar 7-point scales. The scales are of three types or meaning dimensions. The evaluative dimension uses such scales as good-bad, sad-happy, valuable-worthless, and bitter-sweet. The potency dimension uses such scales as strong-weak and light-heavy. The activity dimension uses such scales as hot-cold, active-passive, and fast-slow. By using such scales, meanings may be indexed for (1) different concepts by the same subject, (2) the same concepts by different subjects, or (3) various concepts by the same subjects at different times (for example, before and after therapy, before and after taking a specific course, or before and after hearing a specific communication).

As an example, take the concept of "a college education" as rated by the typical college graduate. It might look something like the accompanying scale.

College Education

Good			X					Bad
Sad			X					Happy
Strong		X						Weak
Light						X		Heavy
Hot					X			Cold
Active		X						Passive
Valuable		X						Worthless
Bitter				X				Sweet
Fast							X	Slow

An example of semantic differential scales.

[Charles E. Osgood, George J. Suci, and Percy H. Tannenbaum, *The Measurement of Meaning* (Urbana, Ill.: University of Illinois Press, 1957); Donald K. Darnell, "Semantic Differentiation," in *Methods of Research in Communication,* Philip Emmert and William D. Brooks, eds. (Boston: Houghton Mifflin, 1970), pp. 181–196.]

Semantic Feature. An atom or dimension of meaning, for example, abstract, male, animate; taken together the semantic features may be said to define the meaning of a word. Semantic features are binary and each term is defined as either possessing or not possessing the feature. Semantic feature tables may be constructed for various terms to illustrate their degree of similarity and difference, for example:

	Dog	*Husband*	*Tree*
Living	+	+	+
Animate	+	+	−
Human	−	+	0
Domestic	+	0	0
Canine	+	−	0
Male	±	+	0

Semantic Generalization. The generalization of a response—originally conditioned to one stimulus—to another stimulus on the basis of similarity in meaning.

Semanticity. The feature of human language that refers to the fact that some words have specific meanings (denotations) in the objective world. All human languages possess semanticity, but not all words have denotations (for example, *of, the,* and *is* do not have objective referents in the world).

Semantic Memory. The retention of linguistic and conceptual knowledge including, for example, the meanings of words, the rules of mathematics, scientific formulas, and the like; opposed to episodic memory (q.v.).

Semantic Priming. The process of facilitating mental access to a word by presenting the subject with words of similar meaning to prime the recall of the target word.

Semantic Reaction. A total response; a response of the organism-as-a-whole; a reaction that is determined by what the whole situation means to an individual.

Semantics. That portion of grammar concerned with meaning: word meanings, the historical development and changes in word meanings, semantic features (q.v.), and the rules for the combination of words to produce meaningful utterances.

Semantic Satiation. The loss or decrease of meaning as a result of prolonged exposure or massed repetition of a word or other linguistic form.
[Samuel Fillenbaum, "Verbal Satiation and the Exploration of Meaning Relations," in *Research in Verbal Behavior and Some Neurophysiological Implications,* Kurt Salzinger and Suzanne Salzinger, eds. (New York: Academic Press, 1967), pp. 155–165.]

Semantic Space. That area—delineated by various polar terms such as good-bad, strong-weak, fast-slow—in which the connotative meaning for a concept may be located. See also SEMANTIC DIFFERENTIAL.

Semantic Theory. The theory of meaning; that part of linguistic theory concerned with meaningful elements and relevant rules.

Semantogenic. Caused by semantics or labels; used most widely in reference to a problem or disorder whose origin may be found in the labels assigned to it.

Semblance. An outward appearance, a public view of a person; presenting to the public a view of oneself that is generally restricted to the roles that are considered appropriate and good; a pseudoself-disclosure in which the real self is kept hidden; opposed to transparency (q.v.).

Sememe. The meaning of a morpheme (q.v.).

Seminar. A small group gathered together to consider specific issues and topics; a type of graduate course in which students and professor explore various theoretical issues, experimental findings, and so on.

Semiotics. The science of signs, both verbal and nonverbal. Charles Morris, for example, identifies three areas of semiotics: *syntactics,* or the study of the relationships among signs; *semantics,* or the study of signs and their meanings; and *pragmatics,* or the study of the uses and effects of signs.
[Charles Morris, *Writings on the General Theory of Signs* (The Hague: Mouton, 1971); Richard A. Fiordo, *Charles Morris and the Criticism of Discourse* (Bloomington: Indiana University Press, 1977).]

Sensitivity Group. A small group that has as its purpose the increase in sensitivity and awareness of oneself, others, and one's interpersonal problems. The focus of the small group is on the interpersonal interactions and interpersonal problems of its members.

Sensory Memory. That part of memory in which visual or auditory stimuli, for example, are retained for a brief period before pattern recognition (q.v.) occurs.

Sensory Motor Period. The first of Jean Piaget's (1896–1980) stages of child development occurring at birth and continuing to about 1½ to 2 years of age. Here the child sees himself or herself at the center of the world and also learns to distinguish self from others. During the later part of this stage, the child learns that objects continue to exist even when they are removed from his or her perceptual field, an ability known as object permanence.

Sequential Communication. Communication in which messages are passed from A to B, B to C, C to D, and so on; linear communication. See also SERIAL COMMUNICATION.

Serial Communication. Serial communication refers to messages sent along a chain of people. We see this kind of communication all around us; we hear something, tell a friend, who then tells another friend, who then tells someone else, and so on. In an organization, this is how rumors spread; generally, the system works quickly and efficiently.

In a particularly important study of rumor conducted by Gordon Allport and Leo Postman in 1945, the results showed that three distortions interfered with effective and efficient serial communication: leveling, sharpening, and assimilation. In *leveling,* the number of details is reduced, some are omitted entirely, and some lose their complexity. In leveling, we reduce the original message to a more simplified form that is more easily transmitted to the next person.

At the same time that details become omitted in leveling, other details become crystallized and heightened in a process called *sharpening.* One or two or three aspects of the message that may be particularly relevant to you become highlighted, emphasized, and perhaps embellished.

Assimilation refers to the tendency to rework messages that we receive in terms of our own attitudes, prejudices, needs, and values. Thus, for example, if we had an extremely negative attitude toward management and we received a message that was ambiguous in its evaluation of management, we might not see the ambiguity. We might assimilate this message into our own value system and see a negative evaluation. In passing this message on to others, it is the negative evaluation that is transmitted. The next person receiving the message knows nothing of the original ambiguity, but learns only the now explicit negative evaluation.
[Gordon W. Allport and Leo Postman, *The Psychology of Rumor* (New York: Holt, Rinehart and Winston, 1947); William V. Haney, "Serial Communication of Information in Organizations," in Joseph A. DeVito, ed., *Communication: Concepts and Processes,* 3d ed. (Englewood Cliffs, N.J.: Prentice-Hall, 1981), pp. 169–182.]

Serial Port. See PORT.

Serial Position. The position a stimulus occupies in a series. A serial position effect is observed in learning a series of words. Generally, terms at the beginning are learned easiest, those at the end next easiest; those in the middle are the most difficult. See also PRIMACY; RECENCY.

Serial Processing. Analysis of one item at a time, in a sequence.

Seriatim. From the Latin meaning "done after another," a method of considering a proposal in which each part is taken separately and in order.

Sexism. Negative attitudes toward members of one sex, used almost exclusively to refer to stereotypical and discriminatory attitudes toward women.

Sex Role. The role (attitudes, values, and behaviors) that is viewed as belonging to men or women by a given society solely on the basis of sex.

Sex Role Stereotype. A fixed impression of an individual based on the traditional view of male and female roles.

Sex Typing. A process by which children learn the behaviors considered appropriate for their sex.

Shadow. In Jungian psychology, the animal instincts or "side" of a person.

Shaping. A conditioning (q.v.) procedure in which the desired behavior is produced through a process of reinforcing successive approximations to the desired behavior.

Share. The percentage of television homes tuned in to a specific program at a specific time.

Sharpening. A process of message distortion in serial communication (q.v.) in which some detail that is preserved in successive versions gains in importance. See also LEVELING; ASSIMILATION; SERIAL COMMUNICATION.

Shield Law. The law that protects reporters against demands that they reveal the sources of their information.

Shift-of-Opinion Ballot. Widely used technique for quantifying the changes (shifts) of opinion that take place after hearing a speech or debate or reading some written material. Ballots are completed before and after exposure to the communication and shifts are measured.

Short-Term Memory. Temporary memory, generally lasting around 30 seconds. Short-term memory capacity seems to be limited to 7 $+$ 2 items.
[George Miller, "The Magical Number Seven, Plus or Minus Two: Some Limits on Our Capacity for Processing Information," *Psychological Review* 63 (1956):81–97.]

Shyness. The *Random House Dictionary* defines *shy* as "bashful, retiring, easily frightened away, timid, suspicious, distrustful, reluctant, wary." *Roget's Thesaurus* groups *shy* with such terms as *cowardly, fearful, spiritless, soft, fainthearted, unobtrusive, unassuming, modest, diffident, retiring, humble, sheepish,* and *blushing.*

Shyness may vary from extremely mild to extremely severe. Some people are shy only to the point of being a bit uncomfortable in certain situations or with certain people, while others are so shy that they are totally debilitated and cannot function interpersonally at all. Most shy people exist somewhere in between these extremes.

An individual might be shy with certain people, in certain situations, or with certain people in certain situations. Some people become shy when dealing with specific types or classes of people. Philip Zimbardo notes that of the students who indicated that they were shy with certain people, 70 percent specified that they were especially shy with strangers, while 64 percent said "opposite sex persons," 55 percent said "authorities by virtue of their knowledge," 40 percent said "authorities by virtue of their role," and 21 percent said "relatives."

Of the contexts that generate shyness, being the focus of attention in a large group, as in giving a speech, was noted by 73 percent of the shy students, while 68 percent noted that they were shy in large groups generally. Other contexts noted for inducing shyness were general social situations, new social situations, situations calling for assertiveness, situations in which the person is being evaluated, situations in which the individual needs help, and small task-oriented groups.

Most people experience shyness at some time in their lives; shyness seems nearly universal but varies in terms of degree. Shyness seems not to be restricted to any specific age group or to either sex, although it does appear to be somewhat more prevalent among children of school age than among adults. And so there seems to be some evidence that some people may grow out of their shyness. Contrary to some popular conceptions shyness is not necessarily more prevalent in women, although nonassertiveness is.

The symptoms of shyness vary greatly from one person to another and from one situation to another. Perhaps the most commonly experienced symptom of shyness is an increased heart rate, when one can almost hear the heart pounding. Perspiration increases, sometimes to the point at which beads of perspiration stream down the face. We may blush and when we become conscious of it, we may become even more self-conscious so that the blush deepens. When others call it to our attention, we may experience a further increase in both self-consciousness and blushing—but also a release because we no longer have to try to hide it. We may experience "knots" or "butterflies" in the stomach accompanied by rumblings and a tenseness. In extreme cases we may experience shaking and trembling—a sight that is quite common among novice public speakers. The audience gets the feeling that the speaker's legs are never going to hold out and that sooner or later he or she will collapse.

When in an interactional situation some shy people avoid direct eye contact and bodily directness, finding it difficult, for example, to stand parallel with others. Instead they stand at an angle, almost as if they will be better able to run away in that position. Shy people may experience breaks in fluency, they may stammer or stutter, make frequent word and sentence corrections and changes, and use numerous and prolonged periods of pause. Some of these pauses are filled with vocalizations such as *ur, ah,* and the like, while others are totally silent.

Shy people may also experience feelings of inadequacy because they cannot function effectively in such situations; sometimes the harder they try, the more difficult it becomes. Feelings of self-consciousness increase and make matters even worse.

See also APPREHENSION; RETICENCE; UNWILLINGNESS TO COMMUNICATE.
[Philip G. Zimbardo, *Shyness: What It Is What to Do About It* (Reading, Mass.: Addison-Wesley, 1977).]

Sidebar. A short newspaper article usually run in conjunction with a longer, major article and which presents some highlight or other aspect of the major article.

Sign. Something that stands for or signals something else and that bears a natural, nonarbitrary relationship to it, for example, dark clouds are a sign of rain. See also SYMBOL.

Signal and Noise, Relativity of. The principle of verbal interaction that holds that what is signal (meaningful) and what is noise (meaningless interference) is relative to the communication analyst, the communication participants, and the communication context.

[Robert E. Pittenger, Charles F. Hockett, and John J. Danehy, *The First Five Minutes: A Sample of Microscopic Interview Analysis* (Ithaca, N.Y.: Paul Martineau, 1960).]

Signal Detection Theory. A theory holding that the perception of a signal is influenced by the strength of the signal and the expectation or motivation of the perceiver; a theory that predicts the likelihood of one "perceiving" a signal in a noisy environment when the signal does not really occur but is expected to occur.

Signal Reaction. A conditioned response to a signal; a response to some signal that is immediate rather than delayed. See also SYMBOL REACTION.

Signal-to-Noise Ratio. The ratio of meaningful sound (signal) to meaningless sound (noise).

Significant Other. A person who is especially important to us, who influences us in a variety of ways, and whose opinions of us are particularly important.

Signified. The meaning or idea that a speaker has in mind and wishes to communicate when using a particular word or phrase. See also SIGNIFIER.

Signifier. The word or words used to express an idea or meaning. See also SIGNIFIED.

Sign Language. Gesture language that is highly codified, for example, a hitchhiker's gesture.

Sign Off. See LOG OFF.

Sign On. See LOG ON.

Sign, Reasoning From. A form of reasoning in which specific clues are used to draw some general conclusion. The clues are taken as a sign that the conclusion or general condition is also present.

Silence. Don Fabun noted that "the world of silence may be a cold and bitter one; like the deep wastes of the Arctic regions, it is fit for neither man nor beast. Holding one's tongue may be prudent, but it is an act of rejection; silence builds walls—and walls are the symbols of failure." Thomas Mann, in one of the most-often quoted observations on silence, said, "Speech is civilization itself. The word, even the most contradictory word, preserves contact; it is silence which isolates." On the other hand, the philosopher Karl Jaspers observed that "the ultimate in thinking as in communication is silence," and Max Picard noted that "silence is nothing merely negative; it is not the mere absence of speech. It is a positive, a complete world in itself."

The one thing on which all observations are clearly in agreement is that silence communicates.

Functions of Silence

One of the most frequent functions of silence is to allow the speaker time to think. In some cases, the silence allows the speaker the opportunity to integrate previous communications in order to make the necessary connections before the verbal communications may logically continue. In other instances it gives the speaker or the listener time for previous messages to sink in. At still other times the silence allows the individual to think of his or her future messages. In many instances people remain silent in order to prepare themselves for the intense communications that are to follow. It is rather like the calm before the storm. Before messages of intense conflict, as well as before messages confessing undying love, there is often silence. Again, the silence seems to prepare the receiver for the importance of the future messages.

Some people use silence to hurt others. Silence is used as a weapon, and we often speak here of giving someone "the silent treatment." After a conflict, for example, one or both individuals might remain silent as a kind of punishment. Children will often imitate their parents in this and will refuse to talk to playmates when they are angry with them. Silence to hurt others may also take the form of refusing to acknowledge the presence of another person; here silence is a dramatic demonstration of the total indifference one person feels toward the other. It is a refusal to recognize the person as a person, a refusal to treat him or her any differently than one would treat an inanimate object. Such silence is most often accompanied by blank stares into space, a preoccupation with a magazine or some manual task, or perhaps by feigning resting or sleeping. Here the nonverbal movements reinforce silence as a refusal to acknowledge the individual as a person.

Sometimes silence is used as a response to personal anxiety or shyness or threats. One might feel anxious or shy among new people and prefer to remain silent. By remaining silent the individual precludes the chance of rejection. It is only when the silence is broken and an attempt to communicate with another person is made that one risks rejection. At other times the silence may be a kind of flight or escape response made to threats by another individual or group of individuals.

Silence may be used to prevent the verbal communication of certain messages. For example, in conflict situations silence is sometimes used to prevent certain topics from surfacing and to prevent one or both parties from sticking their proverbial feet into their proverbial big mouths. In conflict situations silence often allows us time to cool off before uttering expressions of hatred, severe criticism, or personal attacks, and here it serves us to good advantage.

Like the eyes or face or hands, silence can also be used to communicate varied emotional responses. Sometimes silence communicates one's determination to be uncooperative or one's defiance; by refusing to engage in verbal communication we defy the authority or the legitimacy of the other person's position. In more pleasant situations, silence might be used to express affection or love, especially when coupled with long and longing stares into each other's eyes. In many religious ceremonies, for example, reverence is signaled by silence. Silence is often used to communicate annoyance, usually coupled with a pouting expression, arms crossed in front of the chest, and nostrils flared.

Of course, silence is often used when there is simply nothing to say, when nothing occurs to one to say, or when one does not want to say anything. James Russell Lowell expressed this best, I think: "Blessed are they who have nothing to say, and who cannot be persuaded to say it."

Cultural Relativity

The communicative functions of silence in the previous situations are not universal. The Apache, for example, regard silence very differently. Among the Apache mutual friends will not feel the need to introduce strangers who may be working in the same area or on the same project. The strangers may remain silent for several days. During this time they are looking each other over, attempting to determine if the other person is all right. Only after this period would the individuals talk. During the courting period, especially during the initial stages, Apache individuals remain silent for hours; if they do talk, they generally talk very little. It is only after a couple has been dating for several months that they will have lengthy conversations. These periods of silence by the men are generally attributed to shyness or self-consciousness. The use of silence is explicitly taught to the women, and they are especially discouraged from engaging in long discussions with their dates. Silence during courtship is to many Apache a sign of modesty. When a young woman speaks a great deal, she is thought to be betraying prior experience with men, and in some cases, it is seen as a sign of the woman's willingness to engage in sexual relations.

[Thomas J. Bruneau, "Communicative Silences: Forms and Functions," *Journal of Communication* 23 (1973):17–46; Helen M. Newman, "The Sounds of Silence in Communicative Encounters," *Communication Quarterly* 30 (1982):142–149; K. H. Basso, " 'To Give Up on Words': Silence in Western Apache Culture," in *Language and Social Context,* Pier Paolo Giglioli, ed. (Baltimore: Penguin Books, 1972).]

Silent Language. A general term denoting all nonverbal communication.

[Edward T. Hall, *The Silent Language* (New York: Doubleday, 1959).]

Similarity Disorder. A type of aphasia (q.v.), described by Roman Jakobson (1896–1982), resulting in a loss of the ability to select linguistic elements. Also referred to as "selection deficiency." See also CONTIGUITY DISORDER.

Simile. A figure of speech in which two unlike things are compared by using the words *like* or *as* as in, for example, "He takes charge like a bull" or "He's as gentle as a lamb."

Simple Sentence. A sentence with one independent clause (q.v.).

Single Access Hypothesis. The hypothesis proposing that in hearing (processing) a linguistic ambiguity, only one meaning (usually the correct one) is accessed; opposed to the multiple access hypothesis (q.v.).

Sin License. A type of disclaimer (q.v.) in which the speaker states that she or he is about to break a socially accepted rule: "I realize that this is no time to talk about money, but. . . ." See also DISCLAIMER.

Skin Hunger. As used by Ashley Montagu, a need or desire for touching, often prevented by societal taboos.

[Ashley Montague, *Touching: The Human Significance of the Skin* (New York: Harper & Row, 1971).]

Slander. Verbal defamation. See also LIBEL.

Slang. The language used by special groups that is not considered proper by the general society; language made up of the argot (q.v.), cant (q.v.), and jargon (q.v.) of various subcultures which is known by the general public.

[H.L. Mercken, *The American Language* (New York: Knopf, 1971).]

Slant. The point of view or approach of a message that gears the message to the needs and wants of a specific audience.

Sleeper Effect. Research has shown that there is a tendency to disassociate the source from the message after a period of time. For example, you might hear that the student body president thinks that required courses in college lead to a high failure rate and a totally elective system leads to a high percentage of students graduating. At some later time you may find that you remember the messages, but have forgotten the sources. Thus, you can easily recall the connection between required courses and failure rate, but you forgot where you heard that information. As this example illustrates, the initial source of the information is crucial and in one sense tells you the degree of confidence you can have in the arguments and conclusions. But because of the tendency to disassociate source and message, you lose this vital piece of information. This disassociation of source and message and the later recall of (and even agreement with) the message is often referred to as the "sleeper effect." The sequence of events might go something like this;

1. A low credibility source argues that X is Y.
2. You disbelieve the argument and even "forget it" because of your low opinion of the source.
3. At a later date, you yourself argue that X is Y, forgetting that the argument originally came from this source of such low credibility.

This, essentially, is the sleeper effect; the argument that X is Y was "sleeping." [Carl I. Hovland and Walter Weiss, "The Influence of Source Credibility on Communication Effectiveness," *Public Opinion Quarterly* 15 (1951):635–650.]

Slicks. Magazines printed on shiny ("slick") paper which are generally elaborately printed and produced.

Slips of the Tongue. See SPEECH ERRORS.

Slogan. An attention-gaining phrase, used widely by advertisers. Slogans are ideally easy to remember and often become identified with a product or person. [Robert E. Denton, Jr. "The Rhetorical Functions of Slogans: Classifications and Characteristics," *Communication Quarterly* 28 (1980):10–18.]

Slurring. Speech characterized by the omission, partial production, or production with little force of the words being conveyed.

Slush Pile. The collection of unsolicited manuscripts that accumulate in an editorial office.

Smart Terminal. A computer terminal that can perform a number of processing functions (for example, formating and recording data); opposed to a dumb terminal (q.v.).

SMCR Model of Communication. A model of communication developed by David Berlo that was particularly influential during the 1960s in defining the domain of communication. The principal function of the model was to identify those elements or variables that are important in the process of communication. In fact, Berlo labeled it "a model of the ingredients in communication." In this model there are four major components: source-message-channel-receiver (SMCR). Each of these can be looked at as containing elements or variables essential to communication. That is, each of these four components contains subcomponents which must be considered in describing the communication process. In regard to the source or speaker, one must consider such factors as communication skills (speaking and writing abilities), attitudes, knowledge, social system (for example, the roles fulfilled, the functions one is expected to perform, the prestige attached to the speaker), and cultural system (for example, the beliefs and values dominant in the speaker's culture and the various acceptable and unacceptable forms of behavior). Similarly, one needs to consider the identical factors in discussing the receiver except that in the communication skills area, the focus would be on listening and reading abilities.

There are three main factors in the message: content, treatment, and code. The *content* consists of such things as the assertions the speaker makes, the information presented, the facts and opinions advanced. The *treatment* refers to the way or style in which the content is presented; it is, in a sense, the form given to the content. When a speaker encodes a message he or she has various choices available; decisions at these choice points define his or her treatment of the content. The *code* refers to the language used and its rules, for example, English.

Each of these three components consists of elements and structure. The elements of the content are the individual ideas or facts, and the structure is the pattern of these ideas and their organization. The elements of the treatment are the individual choices the speaker makes and the structure is the pattern of these choices. The elements of the code are the phonemes, morphemes, words, and so on, and the structure is the grammar of the language.

Messages can come through any of the five senses or channels—sight, hearing, touch, smell, and taste.

[David Berlo, *The Process of Communication* (New York: Holt, Rinehart and Winston, 1960).]

Smiling. Smiling begins soon after birth. It is a kind of smiling that is indiscriminate, undifferentiated, unfocused, and apparently without communicative significance, at least in the mind of the child. It does seem to occur more often when the child has eaten and is ready to sleep and so is probably an expression of the child's satisfaction. Around the fifth week of life, this undifferentiated smiling is replaced by a focused smiling that fixes on specific objects and persons. From this point on, the smile serves numerous and varied communicative functions.

We may smile, for example, to demonstrate nonaggressive intentions as when we step on someone's foot or bump into someone on the street or in a bus. Here we offer a faint smile to indicate that we did not mean anything aggressive in our actions. Obviously, we smile to indicate pleasure and satisfaction. And we seem to do this even when alone; we seem to be telling ourselves that we are pleased and satisfied. We smile to indicate embarrassment or even acceptance of a not-so-favored alternative. A hooker will smile to communicate her intentions to a john; a mother will smile to indicate approval for her child's actions; and a poker player will smile to hide a bluff.

And, of course, the very same smile will vary in meaning from one situation to another. Take, for example, a woman smiling and then place her in such contexts as: (1) a crowded singles bar in New York while talking with her girlfriend but looking at a man at the bar; (2) in a classroom after a professor returns the term papers; (3) at a tennis match after just winning the last point; (4) sitting in a chair all alone in a state mental hospital.

Smiling behavior, of course, does not occur in isolation but rather accompanies a number of other nonverbal gestures as well. The eyes generally change, usually getting wider, the pupils dilate, and the body seems more relaxed and at ease.

A number of persons have investigated the differences in smiling behavior. For example, when approaching strangers women have a tendency to smile more frequently than do men. It has been reported that smiling is most frequent among those living in the Southeast of the United States and those who smile the least live in the Great Lakes area. There are even age differences. Benjamin Spock, for example, claims that older persons smile almost automatically at people they interact with, while the younger generation does not.

Charles Darwin argued that smiling was innate—a universal human expression of pleasure. Contemporary nonverbal researchers such as Paul Ekman have argued this same universality. In his *The Face of Man* Ekman proposes that smiling is taken as a sign of pleasure throughout the world, which would lead us to assume that smiling is an innate reaction to pleasure. Others, such as Ray Birdwhistell and Erving Goffman, for example, believe that smiling and in fact most nonverbal behavior is the result of learning and that great differences exist from one culture to another.

[Bernard Feder and Elaine Feder, "Smiles," *Human Behavior* 7 (December 1978):43–45.]

Snarl Words. Words that appear to be descriptive of reality but are actually only expressive of one's negative feelings about something or someone. See also PURR WORDS.

[S. I. Hayakawa, *Language in Thought and Action* (New York: Harcourt, Brace, Jovano-vich, 1972).]

Social Adaptation. The process by which one adjusts to the rules and customs of the social and cultural milieu.

Social Class. The status of an individual, usually based on income, education, and occupation. Generally, three classes are identified: upper, middle, and lower and each of these, in turn, may be divided into three subdivisions: high, middle, and lower, yielding a total of nine levels or classes. The social class to which one belongs is revealed most clearly in one's speech and can generally be detected by naive listeners in a matter of seconds.

Social Comparison. A process whereby one compares his or her own behavior, beliefs, or attitudes with those of others and evaluates and tests the validity of one's attitudes, opinions, values, and behaviors thereby reducing uncertainty about oneself.

Social Control Theory. A theory of language origin articulated by Grace deLaguna holding that speech sounds were necessary to control the environ-ment, for example, to signal danger or some behavior desired by other members. [Grace deLaguna, *Speech: Its Functions and Development* (1927) (Bloomington: University of Indiana Press, 1963).]

Social Dialect. A cultural variation of a language spoken by a particular social group or class of the population; opposed to regional dialect (q.v.). See also DIALECT.

Social Distance. The third proxemic (q.v.) distance, ranging from 4 to 12 feet; the distance at which business is usually conducted.

Social Exchange and Equity Theory. Social exchange theory claims that we develop relationships in which our rewards or profits will be greater than our costs. We involve ourselves in relationships that will provide us with rewards or profits—basically, those things that fulfill our needs for security, sex, social approval, financial gain, status, and so on. But rewards or profits involve some cost or "payback." For example, in order to acquire the reward of financial gain, an individual might have to give up some degree of freedom. The cost of gaining parental approval might be a loveless marriage or giving up a relationship that provided other types of rewards or gains.

Using this basic economic-oriented model, social exchange theory puts into clearer perspective our tendency to seek profit (gain or reward) while incurring the least cost (punishment or loss). If you think about your current or past relationships, you will be able to see quite clearly that the relationships you pursued and maintained have been those that provided you with greater profit and greater need fulfillment than cost. Those relationships you did not pursue or that you terminated were probably those whose costs or losses exceeded the rewards or profits; these were the relationships where there was more dissatis-faction than satisfaction, more unhappiness than happiness, more problems than pleasures.

Most of us have an expected baseline, a kind of comparison level of what we expect in a relationship. When our expectations are exceeded, we experience relationship satisfaction—as when, for example, we derive greater rewards than we had originally anticipated. When our expectations are not met or when our experiences fall short of these expectations, we experience relationship dissatis-faction.

Equity theory builds on social exchange theory and claims that not only do we seek to establish relationships in which rewards exceed costs, but that we also experience relationship satisfaction when there is an equal distribution of rewards and costs between the two persons in the relationship. That is, not only do we want our rewards to be greater than our costs, but we want our rewards to be about equal to our partner's rewards and we want our costs to be about equal to our partner's costs. The happiest couples seem to be those in which there is equality in rewards and costs, where each member derives about the same amount of reward and each pays about the same cost. The unhappiest person—as might be predicted—is the one who pays more costs than the partner and derives less reward than the partner.

We can easily find a number of practical guidelines for relationships in this approach. Here are just four.

Exchange Rewards

In any relationship, there are going to be costs—financial problems, job tension, house and apartment problems, interpersonal differences and conflicts. Offset these costs by exchanging favors or rewards. The phone call to say "I love you," the card for no reason, the flowers, the tight squeeze, the specially prepared meal, the prolonged kiss are examples of rewards that can be exchanged easily and that go a long way toward offsetting the inevitable costs incurred in any relationship.

Bear Your Share of the Costs

As equity theory makes clear, we become dissatisfied when we have to bear an unfair share of the costs. Remember that our relational partner will feel the same way. When the costs seem to weigh unfairly on your partner, share these to make the relationship more equitable.

Intensify the Exchange of Rewards in Times of Rising Costs

When a relationship experiences problems (that is, when the costs begin to exceed the rewards), many people will respond passively, waiting for the situation to change or allowing the relationship to deteriorate further. These passive approaches solve nothing and seem to ensure that the relationship will in fact deteriorate. Instead, this is the time for an active approach, for intensifying the exchange of rewards and favors. The empathic understanding, the extra attention, the increased touching and holding can often be used to counteract rising relationship costs.

Increase Rewards to Reduce the Attractiveness of Alternatives

When the costs of a relationship exceed the rewards, the attractiveness of alternatives (for example, some third party) increases. The grass next door looks especially green when ours is but weeds and mud. But when the rewards exceed the costs, the attractiveness of alternatives decreases. The moral is simple: If you want your competition (and we all have competition) to be decreased in attractiveness, structure the situation to increase the rewards and decrease the costs. [J. W. Thibaut and H. H. Kelley, *The Social Psychology of Groups* (New York: Wiley, 1959); H. H. Kelley and J. W. Thibaut, *Interpersonal Relations: A Theory of Interdependence* (New York: Wiley/Interscience, 1978); Elaine Walster, G. W. Walster, and E. Berscheid, *Equity: Theory and Research* (Boston: Allyn and Bacon, 1978).]

Social Facilitation. The facilitating effect that the presence of others has on one's behavior. In reality, the presence of others does not always serve to facilitate behavior; in some situations it may even have adverse effects.

Socialization. The process by which an individual acquires the rules and norms of society.

Social Judgment-Involvement Theory. A theory of attitude change based on a two-stage process: (1) a judgment of the new position relative to one's existing attitudes, for example, how different is this new attitude from the ones already held, and (2) attitude change or nonchange based on this discrepancy between initial and proposed attitudes. In this theory attitudes are judged as falling into one of three areas: latitude of acceptance (q.v.), latitude of rejection (q.v.), and latitude of noncommitment (q.v.).
[Carolyn W. Sherif, Muzafer Sherif, and Roger E. Nebergall, *Attitude and Attitude Change: The Social Judgment-Involvement Approach* (Philadelphia: Saunders, 1963).]

Social Kinesics. The area of kinesics (q.v.) concerned with the role and meanings of different bodily movements.

Social Learning Theory. Theoretical position developed largely by Albert Bandura which holds that behavior is a function of the interaction of inner processes and external or environmental factors.
[Albert Bandura, *Social Learning Theory* (Englewood Cliffs, N.J.: Prentice-Hall, 1977).]

Social Norms. Explicitly or implicitly stated rules concerning appropriateness of behavior.

Social Penetration. A theory of interpersonal relationships, developed by Irwin Altman and Dalmas Taylor, that describes relationships in terms of the number of topics talked about and the degree of "personalness" to which these topics are pursued. The number of topics about which the individuals communicate is referred to as *breadth;* the degree to which the inner personality—the inner core—of a person is penetrated in the interpersonal interaction is referred to as *depth.*

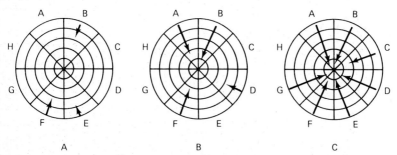

Social penetration with (A) acquaintance, (B) friend, and (C) intimate.

Let us represent an individual as a circle and divide that circle into various parts. These parts would represent the topics or areas of interpersonal communication or breadth. Further, visualize the circle and its parts as consisting of concentric inner circles. These would represent the different levels of communication or the depth. Representative examples are provided in the accompanying illustration. In order to provide specific examples, the circles are all divided into eight topic areas (identified as A through H) and five levels of intimacy (represented by the concentric circles). Note that in circle A only three of the topic areas are penetrated. Two of these are penetrated only on the first level and one of them is penetrated to the second level. In this type of interaction, three topic areas are talked about and they are discussed at rather superficial levels. This is the type of relationship that we might have with an acquaintance. Circle B represents a more intense relationship, a relationship that is broader (here four topics are discussed) and in which the topics are discussed to a deeper level of penetration. This is the type of relationship we might have with a friend. In circle C we have a still more intense relationship. Here there is considerable breadth (seven of the eight areas are penetrated) and depth (note that most of the areas are penetrated to the deepest levels). This is the type of relationship we might have with a lover, a parent, or a child.

All relationships—friendships, loves, families—may be profitably described in terms of these concepts of breadth and depth—concepts which are central to the theory of social penetration. In its initial stage a relationship would normally be characterized by narrow breadth (few topics would be discussed) and shallow depth (the topics that are discussed would be discussed only superficially). If early in a relationship topics are discussed to a depth which would normally be reserved for intimates, we would probably experience considerable discomfort. When intimate disclosures are made early in a relationship we feel something is wrong with the disclosing individual. As the relationship grows in intensity and intimacy, both the breadth and the depth increase and these increases are seen as comfortable, normal, and natural progressions.

When a relationship begins to deteriorate, the breadth and depth will, in many ways, reverse themselves—a process of *depenetration*. For example, while in the process of terminating a relationship, you might eliminate certain topics from your interpersonal interactions and at the same time discuss the topics you discuss in less depth. You would, for example, reduce the level of your self-disclosures and reveal less and less of your innermost feelings.
[Irwin Altman and D. Taylor, *Social Penetration: The Development of Interpersonal Relationships* (New York: Holt, Rinehart and Winston, 1973).]

Social Perception. The process through which we learn about others and about the society as a whole.

Social Pressure Theory. A theory of language origin advanced by philosophers John Locke and Adam Smith holding that language developed out of the primitives' needs to make their wants intelligible to others, and as a result these primitives uttered various sounds that soon came to mean the object to which they referred.

Sociobiology. The study of the innate aspects of social behavior; the study of social behavior in an evolutionary context.
[Edward O. Wilson, *Sociobiology: The New Synthesis* (Cambridge, Mass.: Harvard Univ. Press, 1975).]

Sociodrama. A therapeutic technique that uses dramatization in an effort to teach individuals interpersonal and social skills.

Sociofugal-Sociopetal Axis. A category of proxemic behavior denoting the relation of the axis of one person's shoulders to another's. Nine main divisions are identified: parallel (face-to-face), 45° angle, 90°, 135°, 180°, 135°, 90°, 45°, and parallel (back-to-back). See also PROXEMICS; PROXEMIC BEHAVIOR CATEGORIES.

Sociogram. A diagrammatic representation of interpersonal attraction in groups. The diagram is constructed from group members' ratings of their peers as friends; those who rate as friends by numerous members are called "stars"; those rating as friends by none are referred to as "isolates."

Sociolinguistics. The science of language in its social context. As a science sociolinguistics is concerned with such topics as dialects (q.v.), attitudes toward speech variations, taboo (q.v.) and euphemism, language loyalty, language relativity (q.v.), and, in general, those issues where sociology and language overlap.

[Ralph Fasold, *The Sociolinguistics of Society* (New York: Basil Blackwell, 1984).]

Sociometry. A method for measuring interpersonal attraction (and the lack of it) in groups through individual ratings. See also SOCIOGRAM.

[J. L. Moreno, ed., *The Sociometry Reader* (New York: Free Press, 1960).]

Socratic Method. A method for discovering and teaching truth through a question-and-answer format; the method demonstrated by Socrates in Plato's dialogues. See also DIALECTIC.

Soft Copy. Output displayed on a screen of the computer; opposed to hard copy (q.v.).

Software. The instructional programs prepared for computer use; the programs that "instruct" the computer.

Solecism. Derived from Soloi (an ancient city where ungrammatical Greek was spoken), a linguistic error; substandard usage.

Solidarity Semantic. Reciprocal terms of address that illustrate that the individuals are equal and have a close relationship. When two persons exchange mutual first names, the relationship is characterized by solidarity rather than power differences. See also POWER SEMANTIC.

[Roger Brown and Albert Gilman, "The Pronouns of Power and Solidarity," in *Style in Language,* Thomas A. Sebeok, ed. (Cambridge, Mass.: M.I.T. Press, 1960), pp. 253–276; Roger Brown and Margarite Ford, "Address in American English," *Journal of Abnormal and Social Psychology* 62 (1961):375–385.]

Solresol. A proposed universal language based on the musical scale.

Somatotonia. A temperament type of the mesomorphic (q.v.) personality as developed by William Sheldon; characterized by aggressiveness and the love of physical danger and risk taking.

[William Sheldon and S. S. Stevens, *The Varieties of Temperament* (New York: Harper & Row, 1942).]

Somatotype. Developed by William Sheldon, a classification of body type according to three basic dimensions: endomorphy (roundness), mesomorphy (muscularness), and ectomorphy (thinness). Body types, in Sheldon's theoretical system, were then related to personality factors. In nonverbal communication research, these body types are often used to illustrate that we develop expectations about personality on the basis of physical appearance.

[William H. Sheldon, *The Varieties of Human Physique* (New York: Harper & Row, 1940); William Sheldon and S. S. Stevens, *The Varieties of Temperament* (New York: Harper & Row, 1942).]

Sophists. In ancient Greece, traveling teachers who taught, among other things, the art of rhetoric (q.v.) for a fee; a term that has come to refer to those who engage in spurious argument. Because the Sophists charged a fee and challenged many of the socially accepted "truths," they acquired an unfavorable reputation.

Sorites. A series of syllogisms in which the conclusion of one serves as the major premise of the next one (often the conclusions are merely implied rather than explicit).

Sound Wave. Fluctuations in air that are perceived as sound.

Source. Any person or thing that creates messages. A source may be an individual speaking, writing, or gesturing or a group of persons formulating an advertising policy, or a computer solving a problem.

Sour Grapes. Devaluing a goal as a reaction to one's failure to achieve or attain it.

Space-Binders. A class of life that maintains itself by moving about in space and combining materials from various different places, for example, animals are space-binders. See also CHEMISTRY-BINDERS; TIME-BINDERS.

Spatial Movements. Bodily movements that depict or reflect spatial relations, for example, rapid hand motions to depict the passing of a speeding car.

Speaker Apprehension. See APPREHENSION.

Speaking in Tongues. See GLOSSOLALIA.

Specialization. The feature of language that refers to the characteristic of human language serving no purpose other than that of communication. Human language (unlike a dog's panting, for example) does not serve any biological function; it is a specialized system.

Spectatoring. The feeling or attitude that one is a spectator watching one's own performance and developing anxiety because it is judged unsatisfactory.
[David D. Burns, *Intimate Connections* (New York: Morrow, 1985).]

Speech, A (as literary genre). Richard Murphy has defined a speech as "a prose composition of varying length, fashioned for a specific or generic audience, usually but not necessarily spoken and listened to, written or recorded in some way on brain, paper, or tape for permanence, in which are interrelated author, reading or listening audience, theme, and occasion; it has ethical appeal and universality, moving force and fluency; its design is artistic, and its purpose is to direct the reader or listener to a conclusion selected by the composer."
[Richard Murphy, "The Speech as Literary Genre," *Quarterly Journal of Speech* 44 (1958): 117–127.]

Speech Act Theory. An approach to language that focuses on sentences as performing certain acts, for example, when the Justice of the Peace says "I now pronounce you husband and wife," this sentence constitutes the act of marrying the people. Such sentences contain verbs known as "performatives" (for example, to promise, nominate, congratulate, thank, or apologize).
[J. L. Austin, *How to Do Things with Words* (Oxford: Oxford University Press, 1962); J. R. Searle, *Speech Acts* (Cambridge: Cambridge University Press, 1969).]

Speech Community. A group of persons using the same language.

Speech Disorder. Any speech mannerism that calls attention to itself or causes the speaker psychological or physical discomfort.

Speech Error. A general term covering a wide variety of spoken errors, for example, spoonerism (q.v.), blend (q.v.), haplology (q.v.), misderivation (q.v.).
[Victoria A. Fromkin, "Slips of the Tongue," *Scientific American* 229 (December 1973): 110–116.]

Speech Pathology. The study of the causes and treatment of speech and language disorders (q.v.).

Speech Recognition. The recognition of speech by a computer.

Speech Situation. The entire context in which an oral or written message is produced.

Speech Synthesis. Production of speech by computer.

Speech Therapy. The treatment of speech disorders (q.v.).

Spin Off. A television series in which minor or secondary characters from one series become the major characters of a new series (the spin off).

Spoken and Written Lnaguage. See ORAL STYLE.

Spontaneity. The communication pattern in which one verbalizes what one is thinking without attempting to develop strategies for control; encourages supportiveness (q.v.); opposed to strategy (q.v.).

Spontaneous Recovery. The reoccurrence of conditioned behavior after prior extinction.

Spondee Words. Words that contain two syllables, each of which receive approximately equal stress, for example, "birthday." In literature, a metrical foot having two accented syllables.

Spoonerism. Named after the Reverend W. A. Spooner (1844–1930) who frequently mixed up words, a form of speech error in which initial phonemes (q.v.) or syllables are interchanged, for example, saying "the queer old dean" instead of the intended "the dear old queen."

Spread of Effect. The reward that strengthens the connection between stimulus and response that is generalized to include responses occurring before and after the rewarded response. See also EFFECT, LAW OF.

Spread Sheet. A computer program enabling one to "spread out" numerical data on the computer screen, used widely for financial planning.

S-R Theory. Stimulus-response theory; a psychological theory that asserts that learning is the result of connections made between stimuli and responses.

Stability. The principle of perception that refers to the fact that our perceptions of things and people are relatively consistent with previous conceptions.

Stage Fright. Fear of communicating, most usually used to refer to a fear of speaking in public. "Communication apprehension" (q.v.) is the more general term.

Star. See SOCIOGRAM.

Stasis. That point on which an argument turns; the major issue around which an argument revolves; generally, a static state, a state of inactivity.
[Otto Dieter, "Stasis," *Communication Monographs* 17 (1950):345–369; Ray Nadeau, "Some Aristotelian and Stoic Influences on the Theory of Stases," *Communication Monographs* 26 (1959):248–254.]

Static Evaluation. The tendency to retain evaluations without change while the reality to which they refer is constantly changing.

Often when we form an abstraction of something or someone—when we formulate a verbal statement about an event or a person—that abstraction, that statement, has a tendency to remain static and unchanging, while the object or person to whom it originally referred may have changed enormously. Alfred Korzybski used an interesting illustration in this connection. In a tank we have a large fish and many small fish that are the natural food for the large fish. Given freedom in the tank, the large fish will eat the small fish. After some time we partition the tank, the large fish on one side and the small fish on the other, divided only by a clear piece of glass. For a considerable time the large fish will attempt to eat the small fish but will fail each time; each time it will knock into the glass partition. After some time it will "learn" that attempting to eat the small fish means difficulty and will no longer go after them. Now, however, we remove the partition, and the small fish swim all around the big fish. But the big fish does not eat them and in fact will die of starvation while its natural food swims all around. The large fish has learned a pattern of behavior, and even though the actual "territory" has changed, the "map" remains static.

T. S. Eliot, in *The Cocktail Party,* said that "what we know of other people is only our memory of the moments during which we knew them. And they have changed since then . . . at every meeting we are meeting a stranger."

Status. The relative level one occupies in a hierarchy; status always involves a comparison, and thus one's status is only relative to the status of another. In

Western culture, occupation, financial position, age, and education level are significant determinants of status.

Status Conferral. See MASS COMMUNICATION FUNCTIONS.

Status Role. The role a high status individual fulfills in a group by being a member. The group gains in status by having this high status individual as one of its members.

Stereotype. Originally, a printing term that referred to the plate that printed the same image over and over again. In communication, refers to a fixed impression of a group of people through which we then perceive specific individuals. Stereotypes are most often negative (Martians are stupid, uneducated, and dirty) but may also be positive (Venusians are scientific, industrious, and helpful). In literature, a character used to represent an entire group or class of people.

Stigma. Some negative identifying characteristic that distinguishes an individual and sets that individual apart from other members of the group, for example, body deformity, extreme ugliness, stuttering, criminal record, history of mental illness. See also PAIR STIGMA.
[Erving Goffman, *Stigma: Notes on the Management of Spoiled Identify* (Englewood Cliffs, N.J.: Prentice-Hall, 1963).]

Stimulus (S). Any internal or external change in energy which activates an organism.

Stimulus Generalization. The process by which a response conditioned to a particular stimulus is generalized to a different but similar stimulus.

Stimulus-Response Models of Communication. Models of communication that assume that the process of communication is a linear one, beginning with a stimulus that then leads to a response.

Stimulus Word. A word designed to evoke some kind of response.

Stock Issue. Issues or points of contention that can be used in analyzing and debating most propositions; standard questions useful for analyzing any problem. Stock issues may focus on, for example, policy (Is there a need for change?), value (Is the proposed change beneficial or desirable?), and fact (Is the alleged fact true?).

Stoicism. A philosophy founded by Zeno of Citium (c. 335-263 B.C.) extolling the virtues of passivity and freedom from excess of both joy and grief: nothing is under human control except our view of the world so energy should not be spent on changing things but on accepting things the way they are. In rhetoric, the stoics emphasized plain language and facts and were criticized by Cicero and other rhetoricians who favored the more elaborate and ornate styles of speaking.

Stranger Anxiety. A fear in children (generally from 8 to 15 months) of strangers. High communication apprehensives often retain this anxiety into adulthood.

Strategy. The use of some plan for the control of other members in a communication interaction which guides one's own communications; encourages defensiveness (q.v.); opposed to spontaneity (q.v.).

Stress. In language, emphasis on a syllable or word in speaking or writing, for example, by increasing vocal volume or by using bold or italicized type. In psychology, a condition of psychological or physical tension.

Stress Inoculation Training. A cognitive stress preventive training in which clients are taught ways to prepare for stressful encounters, to lessen the effects of stress, and to develop more effective interpersonal coping behaviors.
[Donald Meichenbaum, *Cognitive Behavior Modification* (New York: Plenum, 1977).]

Stroking. *Stroking* is a term that has creeped into the general vocabulary, no doubt because of its central importance in transactional analysis and in human interaction generally. Stroking behavior acknowledges the existence, and in fact the importance, of the other person; it is the antithesis of indifference. When we stroke someone, whether positively or negatively, we are acknowledging her or him as a person, as a significant human being.

Stroking may be verbal, as in "I like you," "I enjoy being with you," "You're a pig," or nonverbal, such as a smile, a wink, a pat on the back, a hug, or a punch in the mouth. As these examples illustrate, stroking may be positive or negative. Positive stroking generally takes the form of compliments or rewards and consists of those behaviors we would normally look forward to, enjoy, and take pride in. They would bolster our self-image and make us feel a little bit better than we did before we received them. Negative strokes, on the other hand, are punishing; they are aversive. Sometimes, like cruel remarks, they hurt us emotionally or psychologically; sometimes, like a punch in the mouth, they hurt us physically.

Transactional analysts argue that people *need* to be stroked; otherwise, they will shrivel up and die. And, of course, it is positive stroking that most people are after. But if they cannot secure positive stroking, they will settle for negative stroking. The assumption here is that indifference is the worst fate anyone could suffer and that anything short of that is welcomed. If positive stroking cannot be had, and if the only alternatives are negative stroking or indifference, the individual will choose the negative stroking.

Many interpersonal encounters are structured by one or even both participants almost solely to get stroked. People may buy new clothes to get stroked, may compliment associates so that they stroke back, may do favors for people in order to get stroked in return, may associate with certain people because they are generous with their strokes, and so on. Marriages and other primary relationships are often entered into because they hold the promise of frequent stroking. Stroking leads to more effective interpersonal communication when it helps to reinforce productive and satisfying behavior patterns or, alternatively, when it functions to decrease unproductive and unsatisfying patterns.
[Eric Berne, *Games People Play* (New York: Grove Press, 1964).]

Structuralism. A school of psychological thought, founded by Wilhelm Wundt (1832–1920), which defines the subject matter of psychology as the contents of consciousness (structuralists formalized and used introspection extensively).

Style. The selection and arrangement of linguistic features that are open to choice. See also STYLISTICS.
[Joseph A. DeVito, "Style and Stylistics: An Attempt at Definition," *Quarterly Journal of Speech* 53 (1967):248–255.]

Stylistics. That area of language concerned with the study of style (q.v.).
[L. T. Milic, *Style and Stylistics: An Analytical Bibliography* (New York: Free Press, 1967); R. Bailey and D. Burton, *English Stylistics: A Bibliography* (Cambridge, Mass.: M.I.T. Press, 1968).

Suasoria. An elementary declamation (q.v.) exercise; opposed to controversia (q.v.). The subjects for suasoria were generally taken from history; the student speaker would provide some historical figure with advice and argue for or against a particular course of action.

Subculture. A group whose beliefs or behaviors distinguish it from the larger culture of which it is a part and with which it shares numerous similarities.

Subjectivity. The principle of perception that refers to the fact that one's perceptions are not objective but rather are influenced by one's wants and needs and by one's expectations and predictions of the perceiver.

Sublanguage. A variation from the general language that is used by a particular group or subculture existing within the broader, more general culture.

Sublanguages serve a variety of functions and come in a variety of forms.

Functions of Sublanguages

Sublanguages serve numerous different functions, depending on the particular subculture, the communication context, and a host of linguistic and nonlinguistic variables. Here we identify a few of the more pervasive functions.

To Facilitate Subcultural Communication

One of the most obvious facts about language and its relation to culture is that concepts that are important to a given culture are given a large number of terms. With sublanguages, the same principle holds. Concepts that are of special importance to a particular subculture are given a large number of terms. Thus one function of sublanguages is to provide the subculture with convenient synonyms for those concepts that are of great importance and hence are spoken about frequently. To prisoners, for example, a prison guard—clearly a significant concept and one spoken about a great deal—may be denoted by *screw, roach, hack, slave driver, shield, holligan,* and various other terms. Sublanguages provide the subculture with convenient distinctions that are important to the subculture but generally not to the culture at large.

Sublanguages serve to increase the codifiability of the general language. *Codifiability* refers to the ease with which certain concepts may be expressed in a language. Short terms are of high codifiability; long expressions are of low codifiability. All languages and sublanguages seem to move in the direction of increasing codifiability. As a concept becomes important in a culture or subculture, the term denoting it is shortened or some other simpler expression is adopted to denote it; thus *television* becomes *TV, motion picture* becomes *movie,* and *lysergic acid diethylamide* becomes *LSD* or simply *acid.*

To Serve As a Means of Identification

By using a particular sublanguage, speakers identify themselves to hearers as members of that subculture—assuming, of course, that the listeners know the language being used. Individuals belonging to various nationality-based subcultures will frequently drop a foreign word or phrase in the conversation to identify themselves to their audience. Similarly, homosexuals and ex-convicts will at times identify themselves by using the sublanguage of their subculture. When the subcultural membership is one that is normally hidden, as in the case of homosexuals and ex-convicts, these clues to self-identification are subtle. Sublanguages also function to express to others one's felt identification with that subculture as when blacks address each other as *brother* and *sister* when meeting for the first time. The use of these terms by blacks as well as the frequent use of foreign expressions by members of various national groups communicate to others that the speaker feels a strong identification with the group.

To Ensure Communication Privacy

Sublanguages enable members of the subculture to communicate with one another while in the presence of nonmembers without having their conversation completely understood. A common example of this occurs in stores that attempt to take unfair advantage of customers. Salespersons will describe arriving customers as *J.L.* (just looking), *skank* (cheap individual), *T.O.* (turn over to an experienced salesperson), or *palooka* (one who is on a buying binge).

To Impress and Confuse

One of the less noble functions of sublanguages—capitalized on by numerous professionals—is to impress and at times confuse outsiders. The two functions, I think, often go hand in hand; many people are impressed in direct proportion to their confusion. Insurance policies and legal documents are perhaps the best examples. In many instances this technical language is used to impress and confuse people. Then, when there is doubt about something, the insurance adjustor and lawyer begin with an advantage—they understand the language whereas you and I do not. Similarly, in evaluating and in signing such documents, we are unable even to ask the right questions because there is so much we do not understand.

Physicians and many academicians are also in this class. We are easily impressed by the physician's facile use of technical terms and are more apt to pay for the services of those who—like the witch doctors of primitive societies— know the language. To talk of a *singultus spasm* or *bilateral periorbital hematoma* instead of hiccups or a black eye does little to aid meaningful communication.

Kinds of Sublanguages

Argot is the specialized vocabulary of some disreputable or underworld subcultures. It is the sublanguage of pickpockets, murderers, drug dealers, and prostitutes. Expressions such as *college* (meaning prison), *stretch* (jail sentence), *to mouse* (to escape from prison), and *lifeboat* (a pardon) are examples of argot. In its true form argot is not understood by outsiders. Today, with television and movies so much a part of our lives it is difficult for any group, however specialized and "underground," to hide its specialized language.

Cant designates the specialized vocabulary of any nonprofessional (usually noncriminal) group and would include, for example, the specialized sublanguage of the taxi driver, the truck driver, the CB operator, and the soldier. As is the case with argot, these vocabularies would ideally not be understood by nonmembers were it not for television and film. Expressions such as *dog* (meaning a motor vehicle inspector), *kidney buster* (hard riding truck), and *sweatshop* (bulletproof cab with poor ventilation) are examples of cant.

Jargon is the technical language of a professional class, for example, college professors, writers, medical doctors, and lawyers. Terms such as *perceptual accentuation, inflationary spiral, behavioral objectives,* and others used throughout your college experience are examples of professional academic jargon, as are the technical terms for the proofreading and editing of a writer, for the diseases and medications of a doctor, and for the legal documents and criminal offenses of the lawyer.

Slang is the most general of the terms and designates those vocabulary terms that are derived particularly from cant and argot, that are understood by most persons, but that would not necessarily be used in "polite society" or in formal written communications. Terms such as *skirt* (meaning woman), *skiddoo* (leave fast), *goo goo eyes, hush money, booze, brass* (impudence), and *to knock off* (to quit working) are examples of slang. Slang is usually short-lived. Terms such as *skirt, skiddoo,* and *goo goo eyes* are rarely used today, and when used conjure up an image of an antiquated, out-of-touch-with-reality type of person. There are, of course, exceptions to this short life; some slang terms have been around for decades and remain classified as slang. For example, according to famed lexicographer H. L. Mencken, *booze* dates back to the fourteenth century, *brass* to 1594, and *to knock off* to 1662.

With the passage of time and increased frequency of usage, slang terms enter the general language as socially acceptable expressions. When this happens, new terms are needed and therefore coined by the subcultures. The old terms are then dropped from the sublanguage since they now serve none of the functions for which they were originally developed. This is just one of the ways in which new words enter the language and sublanguages are kept distinct from the general language.

Subliminal Advertising. Advertising whose messages are addressed to the subconscious mind and therefore presented at a level below that required for conscious awareness, for example, the messages may be presented at an extremely rapid speech or low volume in order to avoid conscious recognition.

Subliminal Perception. The perception of stimuli without conscious awareness.

Subliminal Persuasion. Persuasion occurring without conscious awareness.

Subscription TV. Television signals transmitted in such a way that special equipment is needed to unscramble and receive them, hence a fee may be charged for this special equipment. Also referred to as "pay TV" (q.v.).

Subsidy Press. A publishing company where the author pays all or part of the costs of publishing his or her book. Also referred to as "vanity press."

Subvocal Speech. Inaudible movements of the speech mechanism that are thought to accompany thinking, reading, and similar linguistic (q.v.) and psycholinguistic (q.v.) processes.

Suffix. See AFFIX.

Suggestibility. A predisposition to accept the attitudes and opinions of others; a readiness to be persuaded.

Superiority. A point of view or attitude that assumes that others are not equal to oneself; encourages defensiveness (q.v.); opposed to equality (q.v.).

Supportiveness. An attitude of an individual or the atmosphere surrounding a group that is characterized by openness, the absence of fear, and a genuine feeling of equality. Messages evidencing description (q.v.), problem orientation (q.v.), spontaneity (q.v.), empathy (q.v.), equality (q.v.), and provisionalism (q.v.) are assumed to lead to supportiveness. See also DEFENSIVENESS.
[Jack Gibb, "Defensive Communication," *Journal of Communication* 11 (1961):141–148; William F. Eadie, "Defensive Communication Revisited: A Critical Examination of Gibb's Theory," *Southern Speech Communication Journal* 47 (Winter 1982):163–177.]

Suprasegmentals. Aspects of speech that are superimposed on and that are spread over other elements, for example, stress, pitch, pause. See also SEGMENTALS.

Surface Structure. The abstract structure of a sentence that is produced by application of phrase structure (q.v.) and transformational rules (q.v.). Surface structure is converted into speech by the application of phonological rules and into written form by the application of morphographemic rules.
[Noam Chomsky, *Aspects of the Theory of Syntax* (Cambridge, Mass.: M.I.T. Press, 1965).]

Sweep. That time during which the rating services (Nielsen or Arbitron) measure the popularity of the various television markets. Sweeps usually last four weeks and currently are measured during February, May, and November.

Syllepsis. A figure of speech in which one word links together two very different items with the resultant construction being grammatically correct; a type of zeugma (q.v.) except that in zeugma the resultant construction is ungrammatical.

Syllogism. A form of reasoning and argument consisting of three statements: a major premise ("all men are mortal"), a minor premise ("Socrates is a man"), and a conclusion ("Socrates is mortal").

Symbol. A signal used to represent something but that bears no natural relationship to it, for example, purple as a symbol of mourning. Words are symbols in that they bear no natural relationship to the meaning they symbolize. See also SIGN.

Symbolism. The process whereby one thing is used to represent another; the use of symbols (q.v.).

Symbol Reaction. A reaction that is made with some delay and usually after some analysis. See also SIGNAL REACTION.

Symmetrical Relationship. In a symmetrical relationship, two individuals mirror each other's behavior, with the behavior of one serving as a stimulus for the same type of behavior in the other person. For example, if one member nags, the other member responds in kind; if one member expresses jealousy, the other member expresses jealousy; if one member is passive, the other member is passive. The relationship is one of equality with the emphasis on minimizing the differences between the two individuals. See also COMPLEMENTARY RELATIONSHIP; SYMMETRY THEORY.

Symmetry Theory. A theory of attitude change developed by Theodore Newcomb which holds that we attempt to persuade others in order to achieve symmetry or consistency.
[Theodore M. Newcomb, "An Approach to the Study of Communicative Acts," *Psychological Review* 60 (1953):393–404.]

Sympathy. Concern for another person; agreement with and consideration for the feelings of others; compassion. See also EMPATHY.

Symposium. A collection of ideas and opinions in oral or written form, often used to refer to a group of experts each of whom addresses one aspect of a topic in a relatively formal presentation (in a speech or article).

Synchronic. A branch of linguistics that deals with the description of languages at a specific time in their development. See also DIACHRONIC.

Synchronicity. In Jungian psychology, a principle stating that the occurrence of two events of similar meaning (for example, two fires) may be unrelated in terms of causality (caused by two different factors).

Synchrony. See BEHAVIORAL SYNCHRONY.

Syncopation. The process by which a sound in a word is lost during the historical development of the language.

Syndicate Method. A method for improving organizational communication. In the syndicate method, a committee is formed and charged with the investigation of a specific issue—for example, the proposed restructuring of the office space or the effectiveness of the current reward system or the problem of upward communication. The syndicate studies the issue by reviewing the relevant literature, by conducting interviews with workers, with managers, and with experts in the field, and by examining how other organizations handle the issue. The syndicate prepares a report and delivers it to others within the organization. A discussion and evaluation of the report is then conducted. As a result, suggestions may be implemented, changes made, and so on.
[Earl Planty and William Machaver, "Upward Communications: A Project in Executive Development," *Personnel* 28 (January 1952):304–318.]

Syndication. The sale of programs or articles to individual stations, newspapers, or magazines.

Synecdoche. A figure of speech in which a part is substituted for the whole, the genus for the species (or the whole) is substituted for the part, the species for the genus.

Synectics. Coined from the Greek meaning "the combining or joining of seemingly irrelevant elements," it is an approach to group problem solving that emphasizes getting away from predictable and structured approaches and utilizing approaches designed to unlock the members' creativity.
[W. J. Gordon, *Synectics* (New York: Collier Books, 1961); M. Prince, *The Practice of Creativity* (New York: Collier Books, 1970).

Synesthesia. The perception of a sense different from the one being stimulated as in, for example, perceiving sound as hot or cold or color as loud or soft.

Syntagmatic Relationship. The relationship existing between linguistic elements such that one calls forth the other because they occur together in language use, for example, *table* and *cloth* represent a syntagmatic relationship. See also PARADIGMATIC RELATIONSHIP.

Syntagmatic Response. A word association based on the response's close connection with the stimulus through frequent pairings in language usage, for example, giving *channel* or *set* as a response to *television*. See also PARADIGMATIC RESPONSE.

Synonym. A word that has the same meaning as another.

Syntality. The personality of a group; the traits (the mental structures that lead to behavioral consistency and regularity) of a group, for example, a family, a religion, or an occupation. These group traits, or syntality, influence the personality development of its members.
[Raymnond B. Cattell, *Personality and Motivation: Structure and Measurement* (New York: Harcourt, Brace, Jovanovich, 1957).]

Syntax. That part of grammar dealing with the structural aspects of language; the rules for the formation of sentences.

Syntax Error. A grammatical error caused by the incorrect application of the rules for combining words. In computer terminology, an error caused by incorrectly using the appropriate rules of the computer language.

Synthetic Criticism. See CRITICISM.

Synthetic Language. A language in which relationships are expressed by changes in word forms, for example, the grammatical function of a word is expressed in a word suffix or prefix. Latin was a synthetic language. See also ANALYTIC LANGUAGE.

System. An organized collection of interrelated elements that performs one or more functions.

Systematic Desensitization. See DESENSITIZATION.

Systems Approach to Organizations. The systems approach combines some of the best elements of the scientific and human relations approaches. Most important, however, it emphasizes the fact that an organization is a system in which all parts interact and in which each part influences every other part.

Ideally, the organization is to be viewed as an open system—open to new information, responsive to the environment, dynamic and ever-changing. A closed system, in contrast, is closed to new information, unresponsive to the environment, and static or unchanging.

The systems approach argues that both the physical and physiological factors of the scientific management approach and the social and psychological factors of the human relations approach are important, and each influences the others. All must be taken into consideration if a fully functioning organization is to be achieved.

Here too, communication is extremely important; communication is what keeps the system vital and alive. If a system is to survive and if its parts are to be coordinated and its activities synchronized, communication is essential. Communication is what relates the various parts to each other and what brings in the new ideas.

The systems approach emphasizes that the organization, the whole, is more complex than the sum of all its parts simply because the organization is the sum of its parts PLUS their interactions, as well as the effects of these interactions, and the effects of these effects, and so on.

See also HUMAN RELATIONS APPROACH TO ORGANIZATIONS; SCIENTIFIC APPROACH TO ORGANIZATIONS.

[Everett M. Rogers and Rekha Agarwala-Rogers, *Communication in Organizations* (New York: Free Press, 1976).

Table, To. To set a motion aside; a motion to remove another motion from consideration by the assembly.

Tabloid. A newspaper approximately five columns wide. Originally the term applied to newspapers publishing sensational content but now is used to refer to the size of the newspaper.

Taboo. Language taboo refers to verbal behavior that is forbidden by the society for reasons that are not always clear; generally it is for some vague and seemingly irrational reason. Language taboo is universal; all languages and all societies have language taboos built into their social structure.

Taboo Origins

Stephen Ullmann, in *Semantics,* notes that there are three general origins of language taboo. The first are taboos rooted in fear. We may fear being punished by God, for example, and so we avoid naming the dead or avoid using the name of God or of the Devil. Similarly, fear perhaps motivates our not taking the name of God in vain. The second is the taboo of delicacy. This taboo centers on an avoidance of unpleasant topics and leads us to avoid talking of topics relating to death, illness, and disease. The third is the taboo of propriety. This leads us to avoid certain sexual references, swear words, and naming certain parts and functions of the body. And although it is true that we no longer say *limbs* or *benders* instead of *legs,* there are many parts of the body for which we avoid speaking the terms we think, and instead employ some other term that is more socially acceptable.

Taboo Variations

Although taboo is a language universal, its form varies from one language to another and from one culture or subculture to another. Thus, the terms under taboo in our culture may not be under a taboo in other cultures. Even within any culture or subculture, what is and what is not taboo varies on the basis of a number of factors. Taboo varies greatly with age, for example. Young people are more restricted in their language usage than are adults. Adults are allowed to talk about topics that are forbidden to children and in language that children would be punished for using. Taboo also varies on the basis of sex. Our society and, in fact, most societies allow men greater freedom. That these different taboos still operate is seen when the speech of men and women is analyzed; male speech contains a far greater number of taboo expressions than does female speech.

Taboo also varies with the educational and intellectual level of the individual. Uneducated persons generally demonstrate greater freedom of expression—in part because they do not have alternative expressions. The educated do have these alternatives and, at least when in "polite society," will use these rather than the taboo expressions. The communication context also influences the frequency and strength of taboo expressions. Generally, as the formality of a situation increases so do the linguistic restrictions. There are, for example, greater restrictions in a classroom than there are in the cafeteria. Perhaps the most important variable influencing taboo is the speaker-listener relationship. If the speaker and listener are equals there are usually less restrictions on their speech than if they were of widely differing statuses. There is less restriction between two teachers than between either a student and a teacher or a teacher and a dean.

Taboo Alternatives: Euphemisms

In all languages there are alternative expressions that are used instead of taboo expressions and these are called *euphemisms.* These are the nice words designed to replace taboo expressions and to sweeten topics that may be unpleasant or less than desirable—and so we say *mortician* instead of *undertaker;* and instead of *toilet* we say *restroom* (though few really rest there) or *bathroom* (though we are not going to bathe) or *little boy's* or *little girl's* room (though we are grown men and women). H. L. Mencken, in his *The American Language,* identifies hundreds of such euphemistic substitutions: *collection correspondent* for *bill collector; section manager* for *floor walker; superintendent* for *janitor;* and *sanitary officer* for *garbage man.*
[H. L. Mencken, *The American Language* (New York: Knopf, 1971).]

Tact. Coined by B. F. Skinner on the basis of such words as *contact,* a verbal operant (q.v.) under the control of some nonverbal stimulus; a labeling response. By labeling, the tact makes contact with the nonverbal environment.
[B. F. Skinner, *Verbal Behavior* (New York: Appleton-Century-Crofts, 1957).]

Tactile Communication. Touch is perhaps the most primitive form of communication. In terms of sense development, it is probably the first to be utilized; even in the womb the child is stimulated by touch. Soon after birth the child is fondled, caressed, patted, and stroked by the parents and by any other relative who happens to be around. The whole world wants to touch the new infant. Touch becomes for the child a pleasant pastime, and so he or she begins to touch. Everything is picked up, thoroughly fingered, and put into the mouth in an attempt to touch it as closely as possible. The child's favorite toys seem to be tactile ones—cuddly teddy bears, teething rings, and even pieces of blankets. Much in the same way as children touch objects in the environment, they also touch themselves. As children mature and become sociable, they begin to explore others through touch, though again there are certain parts that are forbidden to touch or to have touched by others. Nonverbal researcher Lawrence Frank has observed that some of the ways in which we dress our bodies—the clothing we wear, the jewelry, and even the make-up and general cosmetics—send out invitations to others to touch us. The way we adorn our bodies indicates our readiness and our willingness to be touched, though often on a subconscious level.

Functions of Touching Behavior

Touching as a form of communication can serve any number of functions. In fact, one would be hard pressed to name a general function of communication that could not be served by tactile communication. Special note, however, should be made of a few major functions normally served by tactile communication.

Sexual Expression

Touch seems to be the primary form of sexual interaction. From fondling one's genitals as a child, to kissing, to fondling another individual, to sexual intercourse, touch plays a primary role. Men shave or grow beards, women shave their legs and underarms, and both use body oils and creams to keep their skin smooth in a conscious or subconscious awareness of the powerful role of touch as a form of communication.

Consolation and Support

We put our arms around people, hold their head in our hands, hold their hands, or hug them in an attempt to empathize with them more fully. It seems like an attempt to feel what the other person is feeling by becoming one with them—perhaps the ideal in empathic understanding.

In almost all group encounter sessions touch is used as a supportive gesture. Generally, we do not touch people we dislike (except in fighting with them), so the very act of touching says, "I like you," "I care about you," "I want to be close to you," and so on. Touching implies a commitment to the other individual; where and how we touch seems to determine the extent of that commitment. To shake someone's hand, for example, involves a very minor commitment. Our culture has, in effect, defined handshaking as a minor social affair. But to caress someone's neck or to kiss someone's mouth implies a commitment of much greater magnitude. "Touch is such a powerful signalling system," notes Desmond Morris, "and it's so closely related to emotional feelings we have for one another that in casual encounters it's kept to a minimum. When the relationship develops, the touching follows along with it."

Power and Dominance

In *Body Politics*, Nancy Henley argues that touching behavior can also be a sign of dominance. Consider, as Henley suggests, who would touch whom—say, by putting one's arm on the other person's shoulder or by putting one's hand on the other person's back—in the following dyads: teacher and student, doctor and patient, master and servant, manager and worker, minister and parishioner, police officer and accused, businessperson and secretary. Most people brought up in our culture would say that the first-named person in each dyad would be more likely to touch the second-named person than the other way around. It is the higher-status person who is permitted to touch the lower-status person; in fact, it would be a breach of etiquette for the lower-status person to touch the person of higher status.

Henley further argues that in addition to indicating relative status, touching also demonstrates the assertion of male power and dominance over women. Men may, says Henley, touch women in the course of their daily routine—in the restaurant, in the office, and in the school, for example—and thus indicate their "superior status." When women touch men, on the other hand, the interpretation that it designates a female-dominant relationship is found not acceptable (to men), and so this touching is explained and interpreted as a sexual invitation.

Who Touches Whom Where

A great deal of research has been directed at the question of who touches whom where. One of the most famous studies was that conducted by Sidney M. Jourard, a summary of whose findings is presented in the first illustration *(A)*. In the first figure, labeled "Body for mother" we have the areas and frequency with which these areas of a male college student's body were touched by his mother. The second figure records the areas and frequency with which these areas were touched by the student's father, and so on. The key within the figure indicates the percentage of students who reported being touched in these areas.

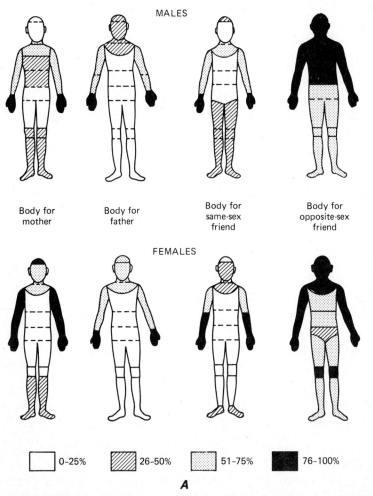

The amount of touching of the various parts of the body as reported by male and female college students. *Source:* From S. M. Jourard, "An Exploratory Study of Body-Accessibility," *British Journal of Social and Clinical Psychology* 5(1966):221–231.

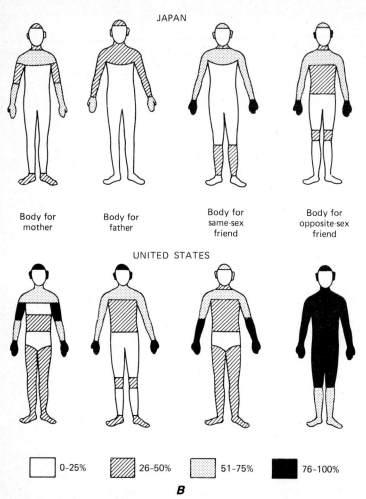

JAPAN

Body for mother

Body for father

Body for same-sex friend

Body for opposite-sex friend

UNITED STATES

0–25%   26–50%   51–75%   76–100%

B

Areas and frequency of touching as reported by Japanese and United States college students. *Source:* **From Dean C. Barnlund, "Communicative Styles in Two Cultures: Japan and the United States," in A. Kendon, R. M. Harris, and Mr. R. Key, eds.,** *Organization of Behavior in Face-to-Face Interaction* **(The Hague: Mouton, 1975).**

Jourard reports that touching and being touched differ little between men and women. Men touch and are touched as often and in the same places as women. The major exception to this is the touching behavior of mothers and fathers. Mothers touch children of both sexes and of all ages a great deal more than do fathers, who in many instances go no further than touching the hands of their children. The studies that have found differences between touching behavior in men and women seem to indicate that women touch more than men do. For example, women seem to touch their fathers more than men do. Also, it seems that female babies are touched more than male babies. In an investigation of the wish to be held versus the wish to hold it was found that women report a greater desire to be held than to hold; and whereas men also report a desire to be held, it is not as intense as that of women. This, of course, fits in quite neatly with our cultural stereotypes of men being protectors [and therefore indicating a prefer-

ence for holding] and women being protected (and therefore indicating a preference for being held).

A great deal more touching is reported among opposite-sex friends than among
same-sex friends. Both male and female college students report that they touch
and are touched more by their opposite-sex friends than by their same-sex
friends. No doubt the strong societal bias against same-sex touching accounts,
at least in part, for the greater prevalence of opposite-sex touching that most
studies report.

The Jourard study was replicated 10 years later when support was found for
all of Jourard's earlier findings, except that in the later study both males and
females were touched more by opposite-sex friends than in the earlier study. In
another similar study, college students in Japan and in the United States were
surveyed. The results are presented in the second illustration *(B)*. The results
present a particularly dramatic case for cross-cultural differences; students from
the United States reported being touched twice as much as did students from
Japan.

[Ashley Montague, Touching: *The Human Significance of the Skin* (New York: Harper &
Row, 1971; Nancy M. Henley, *Body Politics: Power, Sex, and Nonverbal Communication* (Englewood Cliffs, N.J.: Prentice-Hall, 1977).]

Tag Question. A linguistic phrase tacked on to the end of a sentence that asks
for a specific "yes" or "no" answer, for example, "You liked the dinner, didn't
you?" The tag asks for agreement with the speaker. This type of sentence structure has been found to be more frequently used by women than by men.

[Robin Lakoff, *Language and Women's Place* (New York: Harper & Row, 1975).]

Tailpiece. See COLOPHON.

Taken For Granted. That which needs no further analysis, explanation, or development; messages understood by both senders and receivers but not put into
verbal or nonverbal codes.

[Robert Hopper, "The Taken-for-Granted," *Human Communication Research* 7 (1981):
195–211.]

Talking Chimps. The human urge to communicate is seen, perhaps in its most
blatant form, in our effort to communicate with the lower animals, particularly
the chimpanzees.

W. N. and Louise Kellogg were perhaps the first to record their efforts to teach
Gua, a 7½-month-old chimp, a human language. The Kelloggs raised Gua along
with their son Donald, two months Gua's senior. Gua was treated in almost every
way like a human child and like the human child no special effort was made to
teach her language. Although there was some success, for the most part the
experiment ended in failure. Gua did learn to produce different sounds to mean
different things, but these were relatively few. She did manage to understand
numerous different sentences (approximately 70, it was reported) and even surpassed Donald in her apparent comprehension of language. But the interesting
thing was that even though Gua at one time surpassed Donald in comprehension,
she could not be made to respond appropriately to novel utterances, that is, to
sentences she had not been explicitly taught.

Improving somewhat on the procedures used with Gua, Keith and Cathy
Hayes began seeing their chimp almost immediately after birth and took her into
their house when she was only six weeks of age. The Hayeses treated their
chimp, Viki, like a retarded child and gave her specific instructions in language.
According to the Hayeses, Viki learned to say three words, though not terribly

distinctly, and responded to a number of different utterances. She is reported to have responded appropriately to novel utterances, but the extent of this ability does not seem clear.

Some researchers have reasoned that chimps have failed to learn human language not so much because they are incapable intellectually but rather that they are physiologically incapable of producing the sounds. Since the speech signals are not essential to language, recent attempts have focused on teaching chimps human language but through a means that is natural to their species. Allen and Beatrice Gardner of the University of Nevada attempted to teach Washoe sign language, the language of the deaf. Washoe learned a number of words and simple sentences, but it was not always clear if she was also learning the rules for sentence construction. She was able to respond appropriately to many novel utterances and learned to use approximately 300 two-word sentences, but Washoe soon became too difficult to handle and other smaller chimps, that were easier to handle, were substituted.

Sarah, under the direction of psychologist David Premack, is reported to have learned language with remarkable rapidity. Premack created a language for Sarah consisting of plastic pieces that adhere to a magnetic board. Each plastic piece corresponded to a word. In learning the language Sarah had to place the appropriate pieces on the magnetic board. Thus, if she was shown a banana and wanted it she had to first select the plastic piece that meant banana and place it on the board. In one report Sarah was said to have learned 8 names of people, 21 verbs, 6 colors, 21 food names, and 27 concepts—for example, key, table, shoe, dress. Sarah was also able to create and respond appropriately to sentences as complex as "Sarah, insert apple red dish, apple banana green dish." But perhaps the most remarkable feat Sarah is reported to have learned is the concept "name of." When teaching Sarah a new concept she is shown the object and the word (plastic piece) and the relationship term "name of" and apparently has been able in this way to quickly learn the terms for new concepts. The implications of this single accomplishment are vast. Conceivably—and apparently this is one of the main motives of the study—Sarah, after mastering the language fully, might well be able to teach it to her offspring who in turn might teach it to theirs, and so on. The days of *Planet of the Apes* are perhaps far away but chimps and human beings communicating might not be.

Lucy, raised at the Yerkes Laboratory, was taught to communicate by pressing buttons on a computer to indicate her wants. Each request would have to be phrased in a "sentence" complete with a period. If the "sentence" was well formed, Lucy would be granted her request for candy, banana, or open window.

Herb Terrace raised still another chimp, Nim Chimsky. Elaborate socialization procedures were instituted, and Nim apparently lived life much as a human child would. At the beginning of this experiment Nim seemed to have been functioning at a relatively high level, but Terrace has claimed that not only has Nim failed to learn language but that the other chimps have not mastered language in any meaningful sense either. Terrace, along with Noam Chomsky, now argues that language seems impossible for any animal to master and that the observed responses of animals which at first appear to be "language" are simply conditioned responses emitted without any awareness of what they are doing.

[A. J. Premack, *Why Chimps Can Read* (New York: Harper & Row, 1976); Herbert S. Terrace, *Nim: A Chimpanzee Who Learned Sign Language* (New York: Washington Square Press, 1981).]

Talk Therapy. Therapy that focuses on talking as the method through which psychological improvement will be produced; general term for all traditional psychotherapies; opposed to drug therapy which relies on the administration of chemicals to alter the mental processes.

Task Force. A group of people charged with accomplishing a specific task, after which the group is abandoned or dissolved.

Task-Oriented Group. A group whose members focus almost exclusively on the task at hand, such as solving a problem, and devote little attention to the social-psychological aspects of the group and its members.

Taste Blindness. The loss of the ability to perceive the basic taste qualities of salt, sweet, sour, and bitter.

Tautology. A circular statement; a redundant statement containing two expressions that have the same meaning, for example, "The bachelor is unmarried," or express redundancy, as in "He spoke orally and gestured nonverbally."

Taxonomy. A set of words that cover a particular domain but do not overlap, for example, *son* and *daughter* cover the same domain of "children" but do not overlap—*son* and *daughter* represent a taxonomy.

Taylor's Horizon Principle. A principle of organizational communication that holds that in business only those communications that fall within one's horizon or jurisdiction should be received; a principle designed to prevent information overload (q.v.).

Technical Time. Time that is precisely measured, for example, 30 seconds, 2 minutes; scientific time; opposed to formal time (q.v.) and informal time (q.v.). See also TEMPORAL COMMUNICATION.

Tele. Used by J. L. Moreno, a feeling that is projected by one person toward another. Positive tele and negative tele are feelings of attraction and dislike, respectively.

Telecommunication. Generally used to refer to such communication media as television, radio, telephone, and telegraph; communication at a distance; communication via computer connections.

Teleconference. A conference among people physically separated but connected to each other by means of telephone or computer hookups.
["Teleconferencing: A Status Report," *Journal of Communication* 28 (Summer 1978):119–163.]

Telegraphic Speech. The speech of a child in which function words (q.v.) are omitted leaving only the content words (q.v.) with the result that the speech resembles that of a telegram.

Teleology. A belief that goals determine behavior; the belief that behavior is directed by a force toward some predetermined goal.

Teller. A person who counts the votes at a meeting. Also referred to as a "monitor."

Temporal Communication. Significant messages are often communicated by our use of time, an area of nonverbal communication referred to as *chronemics*. Three types of time are often distinguished.

Technical or *scientific* time (q.v.) is that used when precise measurement is essential. Perhaps the most common example is the scientist's millisecond (one-thousandth of a second). The radio and television advertiser also uses technical time when talking of 15-second and 30-second commercials, in which each second may cost thousands of dollars.

A second type of time is *formal* time. Here the customary temporal units of hour, day, week, month, and so on are used.

The third type is *informal* time. Here time is measured with such general terms as *soon, right away, anytime, later, when you get ready, as soon as I can, when I finish this,* and so on. It is this area of informal time that presents the most difficulties in communication since the meanings assigned to these general temporal units vary greatly from one person to another and from one culture or subculture to another. Regardless of how time is evaluated or what type of time we refer to, time communicates just as surely and sometimes more forcefully than words and gestures.

Time is especially linked to status considerations. For example, the importance of being on time varies directly with the status of the individual. If the person is extremely important, we had better be there on time; in fact, we had better be there early just in case he or she is able to see us before schedule. As an individual's status decreases, it is less important for us to be on time. Even the time of dinner and the time from the arrival of guests to eating varies on the basis of status. Among lower-status individuals dinner is served relatively early, and if there are guests, they eat soon after they arrive. For higher-status people dinner is relatively late, and a longer period of time elapses between arrival and eating—usually the time it takes to consume two cocktails.

Promptness or lateness in responding to letters, in acknowledging gifts, and in returning invitations all communicate significant messages to other individuals. Such messages may be indexed on such scales as interest-lack of interest, organized-disorganized, considerate-inconsiderate, sociable-unsociable, and so on.
[Edward T. Hall, *The Silent Language* (New York: Doubleday, 1973).]

Tenor of a Metaphor. The implied or intended meaning of a metaphor (q.v.); the meaning of a metaphor beyond its literal meaning. See also VEHICLE.

Terminal Response. The final goal or stage in a training procedure.

Territorial Aggression. Behavior designed to expand or defend one's territory; aggressive displays or actual fighting aimed at maintaining one's ownership of territory. See also TERRITORIALITY.

Territorial Dominance. In interpersonal relationships, the dominant behavior of a person when in one's own territory, for example, in one's own territory, one is more likely to initiate interaction and to maintain control of the conversation.

Territoriality. The possessive or ownershiplike response to an area of space or to particular objects.

Signaling Ownership

Many male animals stake out particular territories and signal their ownership to all others. They allow prospective mates to enter but defend it against entrance by other males of the same species. Among deer, for example, the size of the territory signifies the power of the buck, which in turn determines how many females he will mate with. Less powerful bucks will be able to hold on to only small parcels of land and consequently will mate with only one or two females. This is a particularly adaptive measure since it ensures that the stronger members of the society will produce most of the offspring. When the "landowner" takes possession of an area—either because it is vacant or because he gains it through battle—he marks it, for example, by urinating around the boundaries.

These same general patterns are felt by many to be integral parts of human behavior. Some researchers claim that this form of behavior is innate and is a symptom of the innate aggressiveness of humans. Others claim that territoriality is learned behavior and is culturally based. Most, however, seem to agree that a great deal of human behavior can be understood and described as territoriality regardless of its possible origin or development.

If we look around at our homes we would probably find certain territories that different people have staked out and where invasions are cause for at least mildly defensive action. This is perhaps seen most clearly with siblings who each have [or "own"] a specific chair, room, radio, and so on. Father has his chair and mother has her chair. Similarly, the rooms of the house may be divided among members of the family. The kitchen, traditionally at least, has been the mother's territory. Invasions from other family members may be tolerated but are often not welcomed, and at times they are resisted. Invasions by members not of the immediate family, from a sister-in-law, mother-in-law, or neighbor, for example, are generally resented much more.

Like animals, humans also mark their territory. In a library, for example, you mark your territory with a jacket or some books when you leave the room. You expect this marker to function to keep others away from your seat and table area. Most of the time it works. When it does not work, there is cause for conflict.

Signaling Status

The territory of humans (like that of animals) communicates status in various ways. Clearly the size and location of the territory indicates something about status. Status is also signaled by the unwritten law granting the right of invasion. High-status individuals have a right (or at least more of a right) to invade the territory of others than vice versa. The boss of a large company, for example, can invade the territory of a junior executive by barging into his or her office, but the reverse would be unthinkable.

[Robert Ardrey, *The Territorial Imperative* (New York: Atheneum, 1966); I. Altman, *The Environment and Social Behavior* (Belmont, Calif.: Wadsworth, 1975), pp. 111–120.]

Testimony. A form of amplification in which the opinions, beliefs, predictions, or values of some authority or expert are presented, or in which the report of some event or situation is presented by a witness.

Testing Relationship. One of four cohabitation patterns common among students and identified by C. A. Ridley and colleagues, a relationship in which the individuals test the suitability of the relationship; opposed to Linus blanket (q.v.), convenience (q.v.), and emancipation (q.v.) relationships.

[C. A. Ridley, D. J. Peterman, and A. W. Avery, "Cohabitation: Does It Make for a Better Marriage?" *The Family Coordinator* 27 (April 1978):129–137).]

Textual Behavior. The verbal response assumed to take place while reading a written text, verbal behavior that is under the control of orthographic or print signs; verbal behavior under the control of text material.

[B. F. Skinner, *Verbal Behavior* (New York: Appleton-Century-Crofts, 1957).]

Textual Criticism. The procedure involved in establishing a definitive edition of a speech or literary text; the art of defining what the author or speaker actually wrote or said.

T-Group. Training group; a group devoted largely to the development and improvement of interpersonal skills.

Thematic Apperception Test (TAT). A projective test where persons are asked to tell a story with reference to relatively ambiguous pictures.

Thematic Structure. Those parts of a sentence that relate it to the context in which it is spoken or written.

Theoretical Criticism. That branch of criticism concerned with the development of criteria for the evaluation of literary and rhetorical discourse. See also CRITI-CISM; PRACTICAL CRITICISM.

Theory. A general statement or principle applicable to a number of related phenomena; a set of assumptions about the way in which something operates.

Theory X. The assumption that people do not want or like to work and if possible will avoid it, and as a result people need to be persuaded to engage in work and to be closely supervised; opposed to Theory Y (q.v.).
[Douglas McGregor, *The Human Side of Enterprise* (New York: McGraw-Hill, 1960).]

Theory Y. The assumption that people want to work and are interested in it, that people can exercise control over themselves and do not need to be closely supervised, and that they can establish their own objectives and will work productively to the achievement of these objectives; opposed to Theory X (q.v.).
[Douglas McGregory, *The Human Side of Enterprise* (New York: McGraw-Hill, 1960).]

Therapeutic Communication. Communication that has a healing effect either instrumentally, as when it facilitates other health-producing activities, or in a consummatory manner when, for example, the communication itself serves a therapeutic effect as in catharsis.
[Charles M. Rossiter, Jr., "Defining 'Therapeutic Communication,'" *Journal of Communication* 25 (Summer 1975):127–130.]

Thermal Code. A category for the analysis of proxemic behavior denoting the type of body heat detected. Four major categories are identified: conducted heat detected, radiant heat detected, heat probably detected, and no heat detected. See also PROXEMICS; PROXEMIC BEHAVIOR CATEGORIES.

Thesis. The central theme of a speech, essay, or any communication; the main assertion in an extended message. Also used to refer to an extended research project completed for a master's or doctoral degree.

Ticket. An utterance that initiates a conversation; an utterance that allows one to begin a conversation with another, for example, "Fine day today, isn't it?" See also DEMAND TICKET.
[Harvey Sacks, "On the Analyzability of Stories by Children," in *Directions in Sociolinguistics,* John J. Gumperz and Dell Hymes, eds. (New York: Holt, Rinehart and Winston, 1972).]

Timbre. See QUALITY.

Time-Binders. A class of life that survives by passing information on from one generation to another, thus making knowledge cumulative, for example, human beings are time-binders. See also CHEMISTRY-BINDERS; SPACE-BINDERS.
[Alfred Korzybski, *Time-Binding: The General Theory* (Lakeville, Conn.: Institute of General Semantics, 1954).]

Time-Compressed Speech. Speech that is compressed mechanically without any gross distortion of the speech signal, used extensively in developing materials for the blind.

Tinnitus. Ringing in the ear; the noises that one hears in one's head.

Tip-of-the-Tongue Phenomenon (TOT). The phenomenon that occurs when one cannot recall a particular word even though it is known and one feels it is on the tip of one's tongue. When this occurs, the individual can generally recall the number of syllables, the initial letter, and the syllable receiving primary stress. Further, the words that come to mind during the search procedure undertaken to locate the desired word are often similar in form and/or meaning.

[Roger Brown and David McNeill, "The 'Tip of the Tongue' Phenomenon," *Journal of Verbal Learning and Verbal Behavior* 5 (1966):325–337.]

Token. The total number of words used in a text. See also TYPE; TYPE-TOKEN RATIO.

Tolerance. A decrease in susceptibility to the effects of a drug when that drug is administered repeatedly.

Tongue Showing. Sticking out one's tongue, often seen when one is engaged in some difficulty or unpleasant task.

Topics. See TOPOI.

Topoi (*sing.* Topos). Lines of argument. Aristotle distinguished two main types: general topoi that are applicable to all arguments and special topoi that are specific to individual fields. For example, the general topoi of practicality, of justice, and of honor would be applicable to all subject matters; these are a part of rhetoric (q.v.), classically conceived. The specific topoi of physics, psychology, or economics are more exacting and belong to these disciplines rather than to rhetoric.

TOT. See TIP OF THE TONGUE PHENOMENON.

Total Feedback. The quality of speech that refers to one's ability to receive all the communication that one sends.

Touch Code. A category of proxemic behavior denoting the amount and the type of physical contact taking place during an interaction. Seven major categories are identified: holding and caressing, feeling and caressing, prolonged holding, holding, spot touching, accidental touching, and no contact. See also PROXEMICS; PROXEMIC BEHAVIOR CATEGORIES.

Toulmin Model. One of the most insightful ways to analyze an argument for a speech is to lay it out according to a model developed by Stephen Toulmin, a British philosopher and logician—whether it is your own that you are contemplating using or one used by someone else. In Toulmin's model there are three essential parts and an additional three parts that may be used depending on the argument and the audience. The three essential parts are claim, data, and warrant.

The *claim* is the conclusion you wish the audience to accept; it is the proposition you want the audience to believe is true or justified or right. For example: *Tuition will be increased.*

The *data* are the facts and opinions, the evidence, used to support your claim. For example: *The college has recently incurred vast additional expenses.*

The *warrant* is the connection leading from the data to the claim. The warrant is the principle or the reason why the data justify (or warrant) the claim. For example: *Tuition has been in the past and is likely to continue to be the principal means by which the college pays its expenses.*

In addition to these three elements (which are essential to all arguments), there are three other optional elements that may or may not be present depending on the type of argument advanced and the nature of the audience to be persuaded.

The *backing* is the support for the warrant—the supporting material that backs up the principle or reason expressed in the warrant. Backing is especially important if the warrant is not accepted or believed by the audience. For example: *Over the last 40 years, each time the college incurred large expenses, it raised tuition.*

The *qualifier* is the degree to which the claim is asserted; it is an attempt to modify the strength or certainty of the claim. The qualifier is used only when the claim is presented with less than total certainty. For example: *probably.*

The *reservation* (or rebuttal) specifies those situations under which the claim might not be true. For example: *unless the college manages to secure private donations from friends and alumni.*

Usually these six parts of an argument are laid out in diagrammatic form to further illustrate the important relationships. A diagram of the example follows.

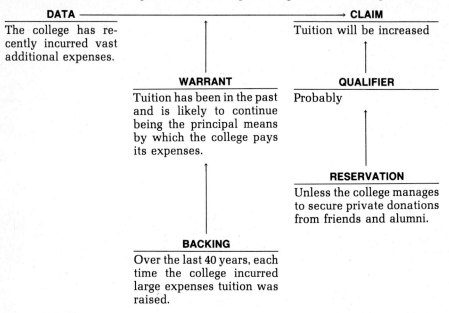

DATA ──────────────────────── → CLAIM

The college has recently incurred vast additional expenses.

Tuition will be increased

WARRANT

Tuition has been in the past and is likely to continue being the principal means by which the college pays its expenses.

QUALIFIER

Probably

RESERVATION

Unless the college manages to secure private donations from friends and alumni.

BACKING

Over the last 40 years, each time the college incurred large expenses tuition was raised.

The main value of Toulmin's system is that it provides an excellent method for analyzing arguments, which is especially appropriate to the public speaking situation. The following questions may help to further enable you to analyze the validity and possible effectiveness of your arguments:

1. Are the data sufficient to justify the claim? What additional data are needed?
2. Is the claim properly (logically) qualified? Is the claim presented with too much certainty?
3. Is the warrant adequate to justify the claim on the basis of the data? Does the audience accept the warrant or will it need backing? What other warrants might be utilized?
4. Is the backing sufficient for accepting the warrant? Will the audience accept the backing? What further support for the warrant might be used?
5. Are the essential reservations stated? What other reservations might the audience think of that should be included here?

[Stephen Toulmin, Richard Rieke, and Allan Janik, *An Introduction to Reasoning* (New York: Macmillan, 1979).]

Traditional Transmission. The feature of language that refers to the fact that human languages (at least in their outer surface form) are learned. Unlike various forms of animal language that are innate, human languages are transmitted traditionally or culturally. This feature of language does not deny the possibility that certain aspects of language may be innate.

Trait Apprehension. A fear of communication generally, regardless of the specific communication situation or context; a fear of all communication situations; opposed to state apprehension (q.v.). See also APPREHENSION.

Trait Theory. A view of personality that holds that there are certain underlying predispositions (or traits) that direct behavior.

Trait Theory of Leadership. A theory that assumes that there are certain traits (physical or psychological) that make an individual a leader and that distinguish this person from nonleaders.

Transactional. The relationship among elements in a system such that each influences and is influenced by every other element. Communication is viewed as a transactional process since no element is independent of any other element.

Transactional Analysis (TA). An approach to analyzing and improving transactions between and among people. The major insights of TA concern the life positions (q.v.) or scripts (q.v.) that people maintain and that influence their lives, the ego states (q.v.), and the types of transactions (q.v.) that exist between people.
[Eric Berne, *Games People Play* (New York: Grove Press, 1964).]

Transactions. The patterns of interaction between and among people. See also COMPLEMENTARY TRANSACTIONS; CROSS TRANSACTIONS; ULTERIOR TRANSACTIONS.

Transcendence, Need for. The need of an individual to resolve conflicts. For the person who loves himself or herself this need for transcendence will be achieved by acting creatively and thus overcoming one's passive nature; for the person who feels powerless and incapable of creativity, he or she transcends his or her environment by destroying it. Within each person is the capacity for creativity and self-destruction.

Transcription. The symbolization of speech in written form. See also PHONEMIC TRANSCRIPTION; PHONETIC TRANSCRIPTION.

Transfer. A persuasive technique in which a speaker establishes a connection between himself or herself and some highly credible source and seeks to have this high credibility transfer to himself or herself.

Transference. The process by which a patient transfers feelings about others to the therapist.

Transformation. A type of linguistic operation that changes (transforms) one linguistic structure into another by means of addition, substitution, or deletion. In logic, a rule by which inferences may be made.

Transformational Grammar. A grammar consisting of rewrite rules (q.v.) and transformational rules (q.v.)—from which the type of grammar gets its name—which attempts to describe or generate all and only the sentences of the language (i.e., none of the nonsentences) and to do so by accounting for the native speaker's intuitions about language.
[Noam Chomsky, *Aspects of the Theory of Syntax* (Cambridge, Mass.: M.I.T. Press, 1965).]

Transformational Rules. Grammatical rules that operate on deep structures (q.v.) and convert these to surface structures (q.v.). Transformational rules (T-rules) rearrange, add, subtract, or substitute elements in the deep structure.

Transparency. A condition in which one discloses oneself to others and is open to the disclosures of others; a willingness or tendency to allow others to experience and to know us, and ourselves to experience and know others.
[Sidney M. Jourard, *Self-Disclosure* (New York: Wiley-Interscience, 1971).]

Triangle of Meaning. One of the most insightful characterizations of meaning is provided by I. A. Richards in the "triangle of meaning."

Suppose that you were to ask me what I mean by a "college education." I might answer in any number of ways: (1) I might say that a college education is the accumulation of approximately 125 credits in various subjects with a concentration in one or more of these subjects over a period of approximately 4 years. (2) I might say that a college education can be the most enjoyable and most profitable experience any person could have. (3) Instead of saying anything, I might take you to a college and let you observe the process of a college education, insofar as that is possible.

In each of these instances "meaning" was interpreted differently. In the first, in which I defined a college education in terms of credits, I interpreted "meaning" to refer to the words *college education.* In the second, in which I told you my feelings about a college education, I interpreted "meaning" to refer to my own feelings about college. In the third, in which we observed the process of a college education, I interpreted "meaning" to refer to the actual thing or referent. These three aspects are illustrated in Richard's triangle of meaning, presented in the accompanying illustration.

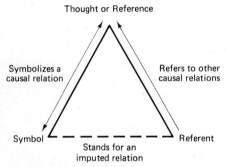

The triangle of meaning.

Focus first on the points of the triangle. On the bottom left is the Symbol, a word or phrase or sentence. In this view of meaning the symbol refers objectively to the thing it symbolizes. At the apex is the Thought or Reference. This refers to the thought that the speaker has of the concept, in this case the thoughts about a college education. At the bottom right is the Referent, the actual object or process or event talked about, in this case the process of a college education. The three answers to the question of what I mean by a college education each focused on one of these aspects of meaning. The definition focused on the symbol, the expression of feelings on the reference, and the observation on the referent.

Focus next on the relationships illustrated by the sides of the triangle. Between the symbol and the reference there is a casual relationship in both directions. Using the term *college education* causes various thoughts or references in the mind of the listener which are similar to those in the mind of the symbol user. Also, the thought or reference about a college education will cause the individual to use certain symbols or words.

Between the referent and the reference the causal relationship goes only from the referent to the reference. By observing a particular object (referent), it causes us to have certain thoughts or references about the object. But thinking about an object does not cause it to appear; hence, the arrow does not go from reference to referent.

The relationship between symbol and referent is perhaps the most important of these relationships. Note that between the symbol and the referent, there is no direct causal relationship. The relationship between the symbol and the referent must go through the thought or reference. Put differently, the symbol does not refer directly to the referent; there is nothing inherent in the symbol that will lead us to find a particular referent, nor is there anything in the referent that will lead us to find a particular symbol (assuming, of course, that we had not already learned the words for the thing).

This relationship is also important because it illustrates that meanings are in the thoughts or references that people have and not in the symbols. There is nothing four-legged about the word *horse;* there is nothing sweet in the word *sugar.*

[C. K. Ogden and I. A. Richards, *The Meaning of Meaning* (New York: Harcourt Brace Jovanovich, 1923).]

Tribute, Speech of. A speech designed to pay some kind of tribute to some person or event, for example, the eulogy (q.v.), the presentation, the commendation.

Trigger Words. As used by Virginia Satir, words that trigger images and feelings of pain and hurt from one's past and, as a result, one reacts to these triggers as if the situation or experience was repeated.

[Virginia Satir, *Making Contact* (Berkeley, Calif.: Celestial Arts, 1976).]

Trivium. The three basic subjects taught in the medieval university: logic (q.v.), grammar (q.v.), and rhetoric (q.v.). See also QUADRIVIUM.

[David L. Wagner, *The Seven Liberal Arts in the Middle Ages* (Bloomington: Indiana University Press, 1983).]

Trope. A general term denoting the figures of speech in which one word is used to mean something other than its ordinary meaning, for example, a metaphor (q.v.) is a trope.

Trust. Faith in the behavior of another person; confidence in another person that leads us to feel that whatever we risk will not be lost.

[Bobby R. Patton and Kim Giffin, *Interpersonal Communication* (New York: Harper & Row, 1974).]

Turn-Around Time. The time between the submission of a program and the completed execution of it by a computer.

Turn-Denying. Communicating nonverbally or verbally that one does not desire or intend to exchange one's role as listener for that of speaker.

Turn-Maintaining. Maintaining one's role as speaker (source) rather than exchanging it for a listening (receiver) role.

Turn-Requesting. Communicating nonverbally or verbally one's desire or intention to speak.

Turn-Taking. The conversational behavior in which interactants exchange the roles of source and receiver.

Turn-Taking Cues. Nonverbal and verbal behaviors that communicate the desire to exchange the roles of source and receiver, for example, raising an index finger, opening one's eyes wide, pursing one's lips, verbal starts such as "I . . ." or "mm-hmm."

Turn-Yielding. Giving up one's turn as source and exchanging it for the role of receiver.

Two-Sided Message. A persuasive message that presents the arguments on both sides of the issue, favoring the arguments on one side and counting the arguments on the other. This technique seems to prove effective with an audience that knows the arguments against the proposal being advocated. Speakers using this technique, as opposed to presenting only one-sided messages (q.v.), are generally accorded greater credibility.

Two-Valued Orientation. A point of view in which events are seen or issues are evaluated in terms of two values, for example, right or wrong, good or bad. Often referred to as "the fallacy of black-or-white" and "polarization" (q.v.).

Type. The total number of different words in a particular text. See also TOKEN; TYPE-TOKEN RATIO.

Type-Token Ratio. The ratio of the number of words (tokens, q.v.) to the number of different words (types, q.v.) in a text; often used as a measure of language sophistication, redundancy, and readability.

U. Upper class; refers to speech and other behaviors characteristic of the upper classes as contrasted with non-U or not upper class.

UCLA Loneliness Scale. A scale for the measurement of interpersonal loneliness.

UHF. Ultra high frequency; television channels 14–83.

Ulterior Transactions. A class of transactions, somewhat more complex than complementary (q.v.) or crossed (q.v.) transactions is that of ulterior transactions. In ulterior transactions, of which there are 6480 types, more than two ego states (q.v.) are involved at the same time. Here there is an unspoken or hidden agenda, which is generally communicated nonverbally. Consider, for example, the following dialogue:

STUDENT: (Handing the teacher a term paper while looking at the floor and speaking too softly) This is the best I could do on the topic you assigned me.

TEACHER: (Accepting the paper with an expression of annoyance) Well, I'll read it and let you know.

On the surface the student's message is Adult to Adult, but the ulterior message is Child to Parent (I've been a bad student). The teacher responds on the surface as Adult, but the ulterior and nonverbal message (the expression of annoyance) is from Parent to Child and punishes the student.

We might diagram this transaction as follows (generally, dotted lines are used to indicate ulterior transactions):

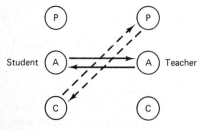

These ulterior transactions are the substance of game behavior. Although individuals play games to win, the players are not winners in the usual sense.

More often they are losers. "Games," note Muriel James and Dorothy Jongeward in *Born to Win,"* prevent honest, intimate, and open relationships between the players. Yet people play them because they fill up time, provoke attention, reinforce early opinions about self and others, and fulfill a sense of destiny."
[Eric Berne, *Games People Play* (New York: Grove Press, 1964).]

Ultimate Terms. In Richard Weaver's (1910–1963) theory of rhetoric, those terms that are accepted throughout the culture and to which the culture pays great respect. Ultimate terms are the primary means for motivating individuals and reveal the values of a culture. Weaver identifies three major types of ultimate terms: *god terms* are those that are positively valued by the culture and which possess the capacity to demand sacrifice of people—*progress* and *American* are god terms. *Devil terms,* the counterpart of god terms, are negatively valued by the culture; *Nazi* and *Fascist* would be considered devil terms. *Charismatic terms* are terms that derive their power to demand sacrifice by convention or common consent rather than from observable referents (as with god terms); often the origin of their charismatic power is obscure and at times contradictory; *freedom* and *democracy* are charismatic terms in many countries.
[Richard M. Weaver, *The Ethics of Rhetoric* (South Bend, Indiana: Regnery/Gateway, 1953); Sonja K. Foss, Karen A. Foss, and Robert Trapp, *Contemporary Perspectives on Rhetoric* (Prospect Heights, Ill.: Waveland Press, 1985), pp. 45–75.]

Ultramicrofiche. See MICROFICHE.

Uncertainty Reduction Theory. An approach to interpersonal relationships that posits that relationships progress and develop as the individuals reduce their uncertainty (gain information) about each other.
[Charles R. Berger and R. J. Calabrese, "Some Explorations in Initial Interaction and Beyond: Toward a Developmental Theory of Interpersonal Communication," *Human Communication Research* 1 (1975):99–112.]

Unconditional Positive Regard. Total and unreserved positive regard; positive regard untainted by any negative evaluations. According to Carl Rogers, the desired attitude of a counselor. Total acceptance of whatever a client has done as appropriate and normal for this person in this circumstance.
[Carl R. Rogers, "A Theory of Therapy, Personality, and Interpersonal Relationships, as Developed in the Client-Centered Framework," in *Psychology: A Study of a Science,* III, S. Koch, ed. (New York: McGraw-Hill, 1959), pp. 184–256.]

Unconditioned Response (UCR). A response that is elicited by a stimulus without any learning; a reflex. See also CONDITIONED RESPONSE.

Unconditioned Stimulus (UCS). A stimulus that elicits a response without any learning. See also UNCONDITIONED STIMULUS.

Undelayed Reaction. A reaction that is immediate; a signal response (q.v.); a reaction made without any conscious deliberation.

Understatement. A figure of speech where there is a deliberate minimizing of some quality as in, for example, after receiving an "A+" the student says "I did O.K." The effect of understatement is to emphasize that which was understated.

Unfilled Pause. A silent pause, a pause not filled with such hesitation phenomena as *ah* and *er;* silent pause of unusual length or a lengthening of certain sounds; opposed to filled pause (q.v.). See also HESITATION PHENOMENA.

Uni-Comm. Communication of values held by various groups or associations through nonelectronic means to a large audience, including, for example, bumper stickers, tattoos, graffiti, shopping bags, and postage stamps.
[Gary Gumpert, "The Rise of Uni-Comm," *Communication Quarterly* 23 (Fall 1975):34–38.]

Uniqueness Theory. A theory holding that each person has a desire and a motivation to be unique, to stand apart from the crowd; opposed to similarity. See also ATTRACTION.

[C. R. Snyder and H. L. Fromkin, *Uniqueness: The Human Pursuit of Difference* (New York: Plenum, 1980).]

Unity. The singularity of purpose that a speech or essay should evidence.

Universal of Communication. A feature of communication that is common to all communication acts, for example, a message, a source.

Universal of Language. A feature of language that is common to all known languages. See also UNIVERSAL OF COMMUNICATION.

Unknown Self. In the Johari model (q.v.), the self that is unknown to both oneself and to others but is assumed to exist from information derived from projective tests, dream analysis, slips of the tongue, and the like. See also JOHARI MODEL.

Unvoiced Sound. Sound produced without vibration of the vocal cords; opposed to voiced sound (q.v.).

Unwillingness to Communicate. A type of communication apprehension (q.v.) that refers to an individual's reluctance or unwillingness to communicate with others. See also SHYNESS; RETICENCE; APPREHENSION.

[Judee K. Burgoon, "The Unwillingness-to-Communicate Scale: Development and Validation," *Communication Monographs* 43 (1976):60–69.]

Upward Communication. Upward communication refers to messages sent from the lower levels of the hierarchy to the upper levels—for example, line worker to manager, faculty member to dean. The type of information communicated is usually concerned with (1) job-related activities—that is, what is going on on the job, what was accomplished, what remains to be done, and similar issues; (2) job-related problems and unresolved questions; (3) ideas for change, suggestions for improvements; and (4) job-related feelings about the organization, about the work, about other workers, and similar issues.

Upward communication is vital to the maintenance and growth of the organization. It gives management the necessary feedback on worker morale and possible sources of dissatisfaction. It gives subordinates a sense of belonging, of being a part of the organization. And it provides management with the opportunity to learn of new ideas, which often originate from line workers. But although extremely important to the organization, upward communication is extremely difficult to handle. One problem is that messages traveling up the ladder are often messages higher-ups want to hear. Workers are usually reluctant to send up negative messages for fear that they will be viewed as troublemakers. So workers may send only positive messages and thus prevent management from obtaining an accurate view of what is going on. Often the messages that are sent up, especially those concerning worker dissatisfaction, are not heard or responded to by management because of its preoccupation with productivity or because it does not know how to deal with such problems. When these messages are ignored, workers feel there is no point to sending such messages. Then dissatisfactions fester and become major problems.

Sometimes the messages never get through: Gatekeepers (q.v.) may be so rigid that certain types of messages are automatically rerouted. When the issues concern clarification of job assignments, many workers prefer to go to other workers rather than to management for fear that they will be thought incompetent.

Still another problem is that management, preoccupied with sending messages down the ladder, has lost some capacity for receiving messages. Managers are so used to serving as sources for messages that they become very poor listeners. Workers easily sense this and, quite logically, don't waste their time on any more upward communication. One further barrier is the purely physical one; management is frequently physically separated from the workers. Usually management offices are on other floors of the building, and not infrequently they are in other cities. It becomes difficult in such situations to go to management with a work-related problem that needs immediate attention.

Yet for all its problems, upward communication is perhaps the most important type of organizational communication. Management needs to recognize its need to receive such messages and may even have to establish formal mechanisms for it, such as the open line program (q.v.). It seems essential that management view upward communication as a positive contribution to the growth of the organization and to the maintenance of the morale and satisfaction of its workers.

[Bruce Harriman, "Up and Down the Communications Ladder," *Harvard Business Review* (September–October, 1974):143–151; Robert M. Wendlinger, "Improving Upward Communication," *Journal of Business Communication* (Summer 1973):17–23; Both of the preceding articles also appear in *Readings in Interpersonal and Organizational Communication,* 3d ed., Richard C. Huseman, Cal M. Logue, and Dwight L. Freshley, eds. (Boston: Holbrook Press, 1977).]

Usage Label. A label that is generally used with dictionary entries and that describes the general context in which the word normally occurs. Usage labels may indicate regional contexts (for example, "New Eng."), temporal contexts (for example, "archaic"), and stylistic contexts (for example, "nonstandard").

User Friendly. A computer or computer program that is easy to learn and use.

Uses and Gratification Theory. In any given situation, we may reasonably ask why an audience chooses to select a particular medium. Wilbur Schramm, in *Men, Messages, and Media,* proposes a formula:

$$\frac{\text{promise of reward}}{\text{effort required}} = \text{probability of selection}$$

Under the promise of reward Schramm includes both immediate and delayed rewards. The rewards would focus basically on the satisfaction of the needs of the audience—that is, we attend to a particular mass communication because it satisfies some need. The specific nature of these needs is covered from a somewhat different perspective in our discussion of the functions of mass communication.

The effort required for attending to mass communications may be looked at in terms of the availability of the media and the ease with which we may use the media. We must also consider such factors as the expense involved and the time investment. For example, there is less effort required—less expense, less time lost, extreme ease in using the media—in watching television than in going to a movie, and there is less effort in going to a movie than there is in going to a play. When we divide the *effort required* into the *promise of reward,* we obtain the *probability of selection* of a particular mass communication medium.

This approach to media has come to be referred to as the *uses and gratifications approach.* It assumes that the people's interaction with the media can best be understood (1) by the uses they put the media to and (2) by the gratifications they derive. This represents a distinct move away from the concentration on what the media do *to* people. Typical gratifications are escape from everyday worries, relieving of loneliness, emotional support, the acquisition of information helpful in dealing with the outside world, social contact, and numerous other benefits. The main assumption of this approach is that audience members actively and consciously link themselves to certain media for certain purposes, that is, to obtain certain gratifications. The media are seen in this approach as competing with other sources (largely interpersonal) to serve the needs of the audience.

[Alan M. Rubin, "Uses and Gratifications," in *Research in Broadcasting,* Joseph R. Dominick and James Fletcher, eds. (Boston: Allyn and Bacon, 1983).

V

Vagueness. The uncertainty over the meaning of a word or phrase, for example, *healthy* and *sick* would be considered vague since the precise limits of *healthiness* and *sickness* cannot be identified.

Valence. The psychological attractiveness of objects, people, or ideas to individuals. Positive valence refers to attractiveness whereas negative valence refers to unattractiveness.

Validation. The process or act of accepting another's thoughts or behaviors.

Validity. The quality of a test that refers to its ability to measure what it purports to measure.

Value. The relative worth of an object; a quality that makes something desirable or undesirable; an ideal or custom about which we have emotional responses, whether positive or negative.

Value Judgment. An evaluation of some work, person, or idea based on their perceived value rather than on any objective criteria.

Value System. The collected values an individual holds (consciously or subconsciously) and that influence one's attitudes and behaviors.

Vanity Press. See SUBSIDY PUBLISHING.

Variable. A quantity that can increase or decrease; something that can have different values, for example, stock market issues.

Vehicle of a Metaphor. The literal meaning of a metaphor (q.v.). See also TENOR.

Venn Diagrams. Developed by John Venn (1834–1923), English philosopher and logician, circular diagrams used to represent the logical relationships among propositions; used frequently as a visualization of the validity-invalidity of syllogisms (q.v.).

Verb-Adjective Ratio. The ratio of adjectives to verbs in one's speech, used as a measure of emotional stability. Greater instability was associated with more active (verb) constructions.

[David P. Boder, "The Adjective-Verb Quotient: A Contribution to the Psychology of Language," *Psychological Record* 3 (1940):309–344.]

Verbal Ability. The ability to comprehend and produce language, a measure of general intelligence.

Verbal Leakage. See LEAKAGE.

Verbal Learning. That area of learning concerned with linguistic symbols.

Verbal Operant. A bit of verbal behavior controlled by its consequences rather than by a previously occurring stimulus.

Verbal Suggestion. A process of influencing the thoughts or behaviors of another person without his or her awareness.

Verb Complexity Hypothesis. An hypothesis that identifies the complexity of a sentence with the complexity of its verb.

Verbigeration. See CATALOGIA.

Verbomania. See LOGORRHEA.

Verification Principle. The principle or criterion used to identify or assess the meaningfulness of a proposition in logical positivism (q.v.).

Verso. A left-hand page in a book.

VHF. Very high frequency; television channels 2–13.

Vicarious Experience. Experiencing something indirectly through observing the experiences of others rather than directly through firsthand experience.

Vicarious Learning. Learning from the experiences of others rather than from one's own experiences.

Videotex. Any electronic system by which computer-based information is communicated or made available to an audience.

Vineland Social Maturity Scale. A measure of maturity that includes an individual's communication abilities. The measure involves having people who know the subject assess the subject on selected abilities including socialization, self-help, and occupation.

Viscerotonia. A temperament type of the endomorphic personality, as developed by William Sheldon, characterized by love of comfort and the need for approval and affection.
[William H. Sheldon and S. S. Stevens, *The Varieties of Temperament* (New York: Harper & Row, 1942).]

Visible Speech. Speech that has been converted by electronic means to visible symbols that may be read by the deaf.

Visual Aids. A form of amplification (q.v.) ranging from the use of a chalkboard to films, slides, charts, and the like. See also AUDIOVISUAL AIDS.

Visual Code. A category of proxemic (q.v.) behavior denoting the amount and the type of visual contact taking place during an interaction. Four major categories are identified: sharp (focused directly on the other person's eyes); clear (focused about the other person's head and face but not eyes); peripheral (having the other person within the field of vision but not focused on the head); and no visual contact (for example, looking at the ceiling or into space). See also PROXEMICS; PROXEMIC BEHAVIOR CATEGORIES.

Visualization Step. In the motivated sequence (q.v.), this step is the fourth part of the public speech in which the speaker visualizes and illustrates the results that would accrue from putting the solution—advocated and explained in the previous step—into operation.

Vocabulary. The words of a language or dialect. Active vocabulary refers to those words an individual can use in speech whereas passive vocabulary refers to those words an individual understands or recognizes.

Vocal Characterizers. Paralanguage (q.v.) vocalizations such as laughing/crying, yelling/whispering, moaning/groaning, whining/breaking, and belching/yawning.

Vocalics. General term for vocal but nonverbal behavior that is more frequently referred to as paralanguage (q.v.).

Vocal Play Theory. A theory of language origin, articulated by Danish linguist Otto Jespersen (1860–1943), holding that language developed out of play, that is,

primitives played by making sounds which soon came to stand for names of people and things and later extended to other nouns and objects.
[Otto Jespersen, *Language: Its Nature, Development, and Origin* (New York: Macmillan, 1922).]

Vocal Qualifiers. Paralanguage (q.v.) vocalizations, variations in pitch height (overhigh to overlow), intensity (overloud to oversoft), and extent (drawl to clipped).

Vocal Segregates. Paralanguage (q.v.) vocalizations such as "uh-uh," "uh-huh," "sh," and the pause.

Vogue Words. Words that are fashionable at the present time but which usually fade quickly; trendy words. See also BUZZ WORDS.

Voiced Sound. Sound produced with vibration of the vocal cords; opposed to unvoiced sound (q.v.).

Voice Loudness. A category for the analysis of proxemic behavior denoting the intensity of the voice during an interaction. Seven major categories are identified: silent, very soft, soft, normal, normal+, loud, and very loud. See also PROXEMICS; PROXEMIC BEHAVIOR CATEGORIES.

Voice Qualities. Aspects of paralanguage (q.v.), specifically pitch range, vocal lip control, glottis control, pitch control, articulation control, rhythm control, resonance, and tempo.

Voice Stress Analyzer. A device that analyzes voice for indicators of emotional stress that would not be detectable by the unaided listener.

Volapuk. A candidate for a universal language that is pronounced exactly as it is written, developed by Johann Schleyer (1831–1912), a Bavarian priest, in 1879.

Volume. The relative intensity of the voice.

Vulgar Language. The language of the masses, the uneducated, as opposed to the formal language of the literary establishment.

Vulgate. The language of the uneducated group or common people. Also used to refer to the Bible as translated from the Hebrew by St. Jerome.

W

Warm Fuzzy. A compliment or some positive expression that makes the other person feel good; a positive stroke (q.v.).

Warrant. In Toulmin's (q.v.) model for analyzing arguments, the connection leading from the data (q.v.) to the claim (q.v.)—the principle or reason why the data justify (or warrant) the claim.

Wavelength Threshold. The level at which sound or light waves can be perceived.

Wave Theory. In linguistics, a model used to explain how related languages developed. The theory holds that linguistic changes spread like waves on water, affecting neighboring areas a great deal and having lesser effects on more remote areas.
[Holger Pederson, *Linguistic Science in the Nineteenth Century,* John Spargo, trans. (Cambridge: Cambridge University Press, 1931).]

Weltanschauung. From the German meaning "world view," the term now refers to a view of the world as seen from a particular perspective, for example, a romantic or a psychological framework.

Wernicke's Aphasia. Language loss produced by brain damage in which comprehension of speech is lost. Named after Carl Wernicke (1848–1905), the German neurologist who identified the area of the brain (called Wernicke's area, q.v.) that controls the comprehension of speech.

Wernicke's Area. An area of the brain that when damaged results in receptive aphasia (q.v.).

Whistle Blowing. The process of calling attention to some wrongdoing, usually to matters that pose a public threat.
[Alan F. Westin, *Whistle Blowing! Loyalty and Dissent in the Corporation* (New York: Pantheon Books, 1980).]

Whistled Language. A type of telephonic communication that uses whistled signals to send messages; used in La Gomera, one of the Canary Islands.
[T. Stern, "Drum and Whistle Languages: An Analysis of Speech Surrogates," *American Anthropologist* 59 (1957):487–506.]

White Noise. A continuous random noise.

Who Are You? A projective test used to analyze an individual's self-concept. In this test, the subject responds several times to the question, "Who are you?"
[J. Bugental and S. Zelen, "Investigations into the 'Self-Concept,' I. The W-A-Y Technique," *Journal of Personality* 18 (1950):483–498.]

Wireless. Communication system without wires connecting the source and receiver.

Wit. A form of humor, usually of an intellectual type.

Women's Words. Words that have been viewed as being characteristically feminine, for example, *pretty, darling,* and *lovely.*

Wooing. The process of winning someone romantically; the process by which one seeks the love or affection of another.
[David E. Outerbridge, *The Art of Wooing: A Guide to Love and Romance* (New York: Clarkson N. Potter, 1984).]

Word Association. A psychological technique in which the subject is presented with a list of words and is asked to respond with the first word that occurs to him or her. Word associates may be *free* (here the subject may respond with any word that occurs to him or her) or *controlled* (here the subject must respond with specific types of words, for example, opposites).

Word Association Test. Developed by Francis Galton (1822–1911), a projective test in which a subject responds to a word with the first word that comes to mind. See also WORD ASSOCIATION.

Word Processor. A computer software program for writing, editing, and printing. A "dedicated" word processor is an electronic system devoted exclusively to writing, editing, and printing.

Word Salad. General term for unintelligible speech usually consisting of real words and neologisms (q.v.) created by the speaker. Word salad speech is usually associated with brain damage or severe psychopathology.

Working Vocabularly. See ACTIVE VOCABULARY.

Writer's Block. Psychological inhibition preventing one from producing creative writing.

Writing. A means of communication using conventionally accepted visible markings and symbols (q.v.).

Writing Apprehension. Anxiety and inhibitions concerning writing. The Writing Apprehension Test (WAT) presented here provides a measure of the degree of one's writing apprehension. (See also APPREHENSION.)

WAT

Directions: Below are a series of statements about writing. There are no right or wrong answers to these statements. Please indicate the degree to which each statement applies to you by marking whether you (1) Strongly Agree, (2) Agree, (3) are Uncertain, (4) Disagree, or (5) Strongly Disagree with the statement. While some of these statements may seem repetitious, take your time and try to be as honest as possible.

		SA	A	UN	D	SD
1.	I avoid writing.	1	2	3	4	5
2.	I have no fear of my writing being evaluated.	1	2	3	4	5
3.	I look forward to writing down my ideas.	1	2	3	4	5
4.	My mind seems to go blank when I start to work on a composition.	1	2	3	4	5
5.	Expressing ideas through writing seems to be a waste of time.	1	2	3	4	5
6.	I would enjoy submitting my writing to magazines for evaluation and publication.	1	2	3	4	5
7.	I like to write my ideas down.	1	2	3	4	5
8.	I feel confident in my ability to clearly express my ideas in writing.	1	2	3	4	5
9.	I like to have my friends read what I have written.	1	2	3	4	5
10.	I'm nervous about writing.	1	2	3	4	5
11.	People seem to enjoy what I write.	1	2	3	4	5
12.	I enjoy writing.	1	2	3	4	5
13.	I never seem to be able to clearly write down my ideas.	1	2	3	4	5
14.	Writing is a lot of fun.	1	2	3	4	5
15.	I like seeing my thoughts on paper.	1	2	3	4	5
16.	Discussing my writing with others is an enjoyable experience.	1	2	3	4	5
17.	It's easy for me to write good compositions.	1	2	3	4	5
18.	I don't think I write as well as most other people.	1	2	3	4	5
19.	I don't like my compositions to be evaluated.	1	2	3	4	5
20.	I'm no good at writing.	1	2	3	4	5

Scoring the WAT

1. Add the scores for items 1, 4, 5, 10, 13, 18, 19, and 20.
2. Add the scores for items 2, 3, 6, 7, 8, 9, 11, 12, 14, 15, 16, and 17.
3. Complete the following formula:
   WAT Score = 48 − (total from step 1) + (total from step 2).

If your score is above 60, you have some writing apprehension. If your score is above 72, you are probably a high writing apprehensive.

[John A. Daly and M. D. Miller, "The Empirical Development of an Instrument to Measure Writing Apprehension," *Research in the Teaching of English* 9 (1975):242–249.]

Written and Spoken Language. See ORAL STYLE.

Xenophobia. An abnormal fear of strangers, especially of interacting with strangers; negative attitudes toward those who are not members of one's own groups, for example, those of different races, nationalities, and religions. See also STRANGER ANXIETY.

Yerkish. An artificial computer language taught to chimpanzees in the Yerkes Laboratories and named in honor of psychologist Robert M. Yerkes (1876–1956).

Yo-He-Ho Theory. A theory of the origin of language holding that speech began as responses to the stress of work, that is, as primitives exerted effort in lifting, for example, sounds were uttered that eventually came to denote the act of lifting or the object being lifted.

You-Messages. Messages that evaluate the person spoken to without referencing the speaker's responsibility for or ownership of the feelings; messages that blame or assign responsibility to the person spoken to; opposed to I-messages (q.v.).

Zeitgeist. The cultural spirit or feeling that influences a society (its attitudes, its philosophy, its ideas) at any given time.

Zenger Case. A famous legal case in which German-born, New York journalist John Peter Zenger (1697–1746) was arrested for libel in 1734. After serving 10 months in jail awaiting trial, the jury declared him innocent since they ruled his charges against William Cosby, New York colonial governor, were true. The ruling in this case remains one of the cornerstones of freedom of speech and of the press.

Zero. In linguistics, the absence of an element, for example, the plural morpheme for *sheep* or *fish* may be described as a zero element (0); the plural of *sheep* may then be described as *sheep* + 0 = *sheep*.

Zero Sum Game. A game in which the gains and the losses add up to zero, for example, if *A* wins 2 (+2) and *B* losses 2 (−2), the sum is zero.

Zeugma. The use of a verb to govern two objects (or two subjects) although it is only appropriate to one of them, for example, "He fought valiantly against the rebels and a bad cold." When used by a competent stylist, zeugma is used for achieving some special effect, usually a humorous one; when used by an inexperienced writer, it calls attention to its ungrammatical nature. See also SYLLEPSIS.

Zoom. A focused film shot in which one small part of the filmed scene is enlarged to fill up the entire screen; a type of lens used for long-range, close-up shots.